THE DANCE PROGRAM

A New Series of Publications in the Field of Dance and the Related Arts

Volumes in Preparation

Total Education in Ethnic Dance, by Madame La Meri

Giselle, by Violette Verdy, with Ann Sperber, *illustrated by Marcia Brown*

Dance Out the Answer, an autobiography, by Madame La Meri, *foreword by John Martin*

On Tap Dancing, by Paul Draper, *edited and compiled by Fran Avallone*

Olga Preobrazhenskaya, a biography, by Elvira Roné, *translated by Fernau Hall*

Ballerina, a biography of Violette Verdy, by Victoria Huckenpahler

The Bournonville School (in four volumes), including music and notation, by Kirsten Ralov, *introduction by Walter Terry*

I Was There, by Walter Terry, *compiled and edited by Andrew Wentink, introduction by Anna Kisselgoff*

The Bennington Years: 1934-1942, a chronology and source book, by Sali Ann Kriegsman

The Art and Practice of Ballet Accompanying (in two volumes), by Elizabeth Sawyer Brady

The Ballet Russe (in four volumes), edited by George Jackson

Imperial Dancer, a biography of Felia Doubrovska, by Victoria Huckenpahler

Antony Tudor, a biography, by Fernau Hall

Dancer's Diary, by Dennis Wayne, *introduction by Joanne Woodward*

RUTH PAGE

RUTH PAGE

AN INTIMATE BIOGRAPHY

John Martin

Foreword by Margot Fonteyn ———————————

MARCEL DEKKER, INC.   NEW YORK AND BASEL

Library of Congress Cataloging in Publication Data

Martin, John Joseph, 1893-
    Ruth Page : an intimate biography.

    Includes index.
    1. Page, Ruth. 2. Dancers--Biography. 3. Chore-
ographers--United States--Biography.
GV1785.P26M37   792.8'092'4 [B]   76-18427
ISBN 0-8247-6490-0

MARCEL DEKKER, INC.

270 Madison Avenue, New York, New York 10016

Current Printing (last digit):

10 9 8 7 6 5 4 3 2 1

PRINTED IN THE UNITED STATES OF AMERICA

Foreword

My first thoughts on Ruth Page are of a lively and amusing friend, full of wise observations on the world, art and people. Nothing escapes her attention, and her life now spans great changes in the scene of dance in Europe and America, so she is able to sum up all the important figures in dance of the last forty or fifty years, as well as pass judgment on the current stars. And her close friends are by no means limited to the ballet world; she is interested in all the arts and in the world about her.

Her life has been quite international, with a particular affection for France. She has so much to tell that it is more than time for it to be put into a book, and it is right that John Martin should be the one to describe her work as dancer and choreographer, which has a particular place in the American ballet scene. She has used important designers and brought together the theme, music, decor and choreography in a balance that followed the example of Diaghileff, and she has presented the finest dancers with her company in Chicago.

Ruth's husband, Tom Fisher, was the ideal contrast: the serious lawyer who relaxed happily amidst the disorganized crises of our mad ballet world. He encouraged and helped her through a thousand difficulties and successes with his appreciation of her talents, and his understanding of the intricacies of ballet business—as well as his great patience with the usual chatter of dancers.

Ruth has hardly changed at all since I first knew her. She still has a dance studio wherever she lives, and is the central force directing and inspiring the work in progress, so even now, there is the story of her new company and school set up under the Ruth Page Foundation to continue the tale of this great lady right into the present and the future.

Contents

Illustrations

vii

Some Conclusions
to Begin With

This is definitely not a book about dancing; what it is about is a woman who has been obsessed by dancing since the day of her birth. That pivotal event occurred on March 22, 1900, which makes Ruth Page seventy-four as these lines are written. She has amassed an enormous amount of career since she made her professional debut in the corps de ballet of Anna Pavlova's company on a tour of Latin America when she was eighteen, and there are no indications whatever but that she will go right on amassing more. She has danced or choreographed or both from Buenos Aires to Fairbanks, from Manchester to Bangkok, from Tokyo to Paris, from Moscow to Havana, from Oslo to Monte Carlo; alone, with a partner, with her own companies and with other people's; from the Ballet Russe of Diaghileff to the Federal Dance Project of the WPA, in opera companies and "show biz"; with piano, with orchestras large and small, with dialogue and to her own speaking of poetry.

She has been, indeed, one of the real pioneers of American ballet though not for chauvinistic or altruistic or any other objective motives; she was herself American—very substantially Mid-American—and she simply had to dance anywhere and everywhere, under whatever conditions she could find or, if not find, make for herself. Among our most American icons is the pioneer woman dedicatedly scanning the distant frontier in her linsey-woolseys, but it has not always occurred to us that just as devoted and courageous pioneering can be done in tutu and toe-shoes, standing on the brink of perpetual footlights, projecting the archetype of all smiles into the dim and resistant region beyond.

1

This, it goes without saying, is the most important thing about her; the next most important thing is her marriage to Tom Fisher. Though notably free in its attitude, it could scarcely have been closer or more substantial, however unconventional for its time. That it lasted with undiminished validity for forty-four years should be evidence enough.

Tom was a brilliant lawyer, as rich in bravura as any ballerina, a kind of legal personification of the daring young man on the flying trapeze. No wonder she has said that there was never a hint of dullness in their life together. Together, indeed, in the literal sense, they seldom were for any extended periods, what with her perpetual tourings and his dashings about the country for various clients in various courts, and especially the weeks and months he spent in Texas again and again on the most fantastic case of his life, which spread over a period of forty years. But they wrote to each other daily (or almost so) when they were apart, and the correspondence which survives in considerable bulk, gives off a lively glow of affection and common interest, even though much of it deals with business problems and financial crises. He was her strong right arm in the management of her career and her company—her legal, financial and tactical mentor. She is firmly convinced, in spite of substantial evidence to the contrary, that she never acted against his recommendations, which is perhaps one of the happy anomalies that make for conjugal felicity.

His death in 1969—a long, slow death surrounded, quite characteristically, by extraneous cliff-hanging suspense and drama—left her shaken, wobbly, rudderless. But she did not succumb; probably it was not so much that she pulled herself together as that her self pulled her together. She has often attributed the success of their marriage to their being apart so much, and this may well have established some trace for her to live by now. Certainly he is in her thinking and her conversation as much as ever, and with something recognizably akin to the way she used to talk of him during the accepted absences of the past. Her way of living and her professional practices remain as nearly what she knows he would recommend as she can make them—or, more accurately, as she ever did make them. Essentially she still consults him, as it were, on policy, but her dependence on him for every managerial and financial procedure was so complete that now she finds herself an innocent in a threatening wilderness of fiscal decisions. Her constant complaint is that without him she has nobody to talk to, and by this she means not only about business but also about everything else in their common life. Since they were a highly articulate pair, it is easy to understand what she means.

There can have been few dancers who have brought their non-dancing husbands so continually into their professional careers; and certainly it was the other way round as well, for as her lawyer, the manager of her affairs and her spokesman in all her projects, he was constantly identifying himself as her husband. As a result, her scrapbooks teem with references to her as "the wife of the distinguished attorney, Thomas Hart Fisher," or "who in private life is Mrs. Thomas Hart Fisher." In St. Tropez, which was their habitual summering place in late years, and especially Tom's favorite haunt, she was, and still is, virtually unknown as Ruth Page and is simply Madame Fichère. This disturbs her not at all, for it characterizes her as the lively, rounded and cultivated human being she has always enjoyed being, instead of as a nebulous public figure whom nobody knows.

Tom was as inherently social as she, and their private and public lives merged easily. There was something in their relationship that acted almost like an organic feedback mechanism; they were extremely proud of each other, eager to help each other and to bask in what they conceived of as each other's glory. Tom had no firsthand knowlege of dancing or any of the other arts as a practitioner of them, but he was a wizard at contracts, promotion, the exploitation of the values of timeliness, the procuring of "impossible" rights to "inaccessible" musical scores tied up by generations of heirs. Ruth knew less than nothing about business and law and delighted in being able to indulge her ignorance, but she could be an irresistible hostess to Tom's associates and an equally irresistible guest.

As a team they were practically unbeatable, and they knew "but everybody." A listing of their friends would have filled (and probably did) countless social registers, Almanachs de Gotha and Dunn and Bradstreets. In addition to this beau-mondainerie, and pretty generally mixed in with it by the common agency of the arts, there was more than a hint of demimondainerie, or at least of frank Rive-Gaucherie, for the Fishers knew and spoke the language of musicians and patrons of music, painters and patrons of painting, dancers and patrons of dancing—as well as actors, directors and producers; designers, couturiers and sculptors; critics, poets and publishers. They consorted easily and gleefully with Bohemians and Philistines, the naughty and the nice, without even changing their caps. Their extracurricular social program, indeed, would have been inconceivable for people who did not really enjoy other people—preferably those who practiced creativeness and good conversation, it is true, but people, whether or no.

Regardless of what the calendar has to say about Ruth today, old is the last adjective in the dictionary to apply to her. She is still a beautiful woman, restless with energy, warm, vivacious, self-aware, soignée. She is essentially a visual person and knows very well how she looks. Her hair, worn shortish with bangs, is a warm chestnut, a trifle richer than it was originally. She has a flair for clothes, with both the figure and the carriage to wear them, and she has made the round of international salons of *haute couture* with something very like creative pleasure for years.

Of course, she has grown up. If in the logic of events she may weigh a pound or two more than she did when she was dancing regularly, they have distributed themselves with admirable finesse. This is probably the result, though it is certainly not the motivation of the daily ballet class (or at the very least the daily barre) that she engages in, come storm or shine, partly as a matter of muscular habit but mainly from temperamental compulsion. Sometimes these ritual workouts take place at her own ballet school in Chicago, sometimes alone in the private studio that constitutes the most important room (far more so than the kitchen) in each of her four places of what might be called peripatetic residence.

These latter consist of, first of all, a Chicago headquarters in a spacious apartment in a fine old lakeshore building; second, a small "modern" (1933) steel house farther north on the lake at Hubbard Woods, the community where Tom was born; third, a little house in Montparnasse (which she named Les Trois Pastèques after a painting made there by Antoni Clavé of his wife with three carved watermelons), and fourth, an old transformed Provençal olive-oil mill two villas away from Brigitte Bardot at St. Tropez, where she has built herself a large studio in what was originally a stone barn with a hayloft, just across the courtyard from her living quarters.

To have four places of residence has nothing to do with pretentiousness; it is a natural consequence of her life of itinerancy, which has inevitably assigned an enormous proportion of her time to planes, trains, ships, buses, private cars and even trucks on occasion, while the rest of her time, the essential creative time, is forced to allot itself virtually to wherever she happens to be between vehicles. At each of these oases, where her stopovers are long enough to allow for the normalities of living and the awareness of regional charm, she has planted a few roots to be returned to familiarly and affectionately, including, of course, adequate studios to create in, perhaps to rehearse in, and specifically to stretch in. For of all the vehicles of transiency themselves, only the now all-but-obsolete ship provides space for the diurnal rites of the barre.

But she manages to do her stretches in a surprising number of unlikely situations. In her living room, for example, where she is chatting with intimates or associates (or possibly even with casual visitors; who knows?), off will go a shoe quite without warning and up will unwind a leg in a slow développé aimed at the ceiling, no matter where she is sitting, and she will not miss a syllable of the discourse or alter an inflection during the procedure. After you have known her for a while your learn not to notice it.

One general principle that must be stressed forthwith, if you are to have any social rapport with dancers, is the necessity to understand above all how completely they live in their musculature. Unless you are thus prepared, you may possibly find them, as a class, dull companions. They need not be, of course, but it is a risk that must be considered. It can be something of a shock to you, for example, to dine after a performance with a sparkling sylph who has just done endless turns on the tip of her toes, been levitated somehow inexplicably to her partner's strong right hand held straight-arm above his head and wafted down like an autumn leaf to within an inch of the floor before he persuades her, no doubt against her will, to return to some gravitational control, smiling the while with impish playfulness and cooler than a mint frappé, only to discover as she wolfs a two-inch-thick sirloin, medium rare, that she has no conversation whatever beyond the threatening condition of her right knee and her left heel, and the bruises her inept partner's clawlike fingers have inflicted upon her tender ribs and thighs. It might not make you any happier, either, to know that as soon as she conveniently can, she will hurry back to her hotel room and soak for a blessed hour in a warm tub, probably with Epsom salts added. But if this devastating disenchantment should come upon you, don't blame her. The fault, dear Brutus, lies altogether in ourselves, not in the stars we so brashly date, with no notion of what makes them twinkle.

Ruth is just as muscularly oriented as any of these nymphs. Her favorite soaking time happens to be between 2 and 4 a.m., and she keeps a warm tub standing for periodic immersions during these hours. She is a late reader and a sketchy sleeper, and her radio, tuned well down, dispenses soft music all night beside her bed. But soak she must and stretch she must, for when her muscle tone is off, she is completely out of sorts, physically and dispositionally. Yet quite unlike the tediously self-diagnosing sylph, she is a fascinating interlocutor on any civilized topic (omitting, of course, business, housekeeping, politics and other such quotidian stupidities) in any company, with or without sirloin.

The explanation is simply that when she drew her first breath, for causes genetic, astrological or accidental, she was already just as much a potential Madame Fichère as she was a potential balletomaniac. That she can participate in animated and cultivated conversation while practicing aerial techniques on the drawing-room sofa indicates that there is no dichotomy involved.

Until samples have been collected and analyzed of the content of the conversations during which she slips so unexpectedly into her drawing room développés, it cannot be said with authority whether this is simply an unrelated idiosyncrasy or an automatic form of therapy to maintain her social equilibrium under burgeoning provocations in the dialogue. Certainly she used these same techniques, expanded into the form of a full barre, in other social situations.

Not long ago, for example, she was one of six speakers, all career women in different fields, at a luncheon given by a North Shore women's club to which she has belonged for many years. A questionnaire consisting of half a dozen items was sent along with the invitation, apparently to provide a basis for comparing the different areas of activity of the several speakers. It arrived at Ruth's at a moment of professional tizzy—orchestrations missing, probably lost in transit; unexpected changes threatened in staff personnel; and all the customary bedlam that surrounds the glamorous world of the theatre unseen from the front—and the prospective luncheon failed to register with her at all except as a note on her calendar. There, on the very verge of the event, it came to life somewhat startlingly. But she wanted to go, even if *noblesse* had not *obligée*, and she went, albeit in a bit of a flurry.

"Well," she said, with a sophisticated assumption of bitterness, as she stood in the doorway ready to depart, "do I look like a suburban housewife?" She was wearing a dazzlingly simple polka-dot confection (Dior? St. Laurent?), white shoes, a large floppy straw hat and custom-shaped dark glasses, and the only possible answer to her purely rhetorical question was no, for what she actually looked like was an artist trying to look like a suburban housewife and succeeding.

About five o'clock that afternoon, when the household began to reassemble, the apartment was quiet, as usual, except for sounds of heavy breathing coming from the studio. There at the barre was Ruth, with her suburban-housewife paraphernalia replaced by old black practice clothes, in a healthy sweat, all but kicking the back of her head in her exertions.

"Had to relax," she panted; "never saw such beautiful, brilliant women . . . spoke marvelously . . . all of them stuck to the questionnaire . . . was never so nervous in my life . . . I was last . . . threw out the questionnaire and just talked . . . awful. . . ."

She was palpably cross, but when the barre was finished, followed no doubt by a bit of a soak, you would never have suspected anything of the sort. She emerged with the familiar poise and easy grace; there simply had never been any unpleasant episode.

To be sure, this was a minor, virtually peripheral, disturbance, but it suggests the possibility that some people may be such self-sufficiently constituted organisms, so elementarily unimpeded, that any needed therapy provides its own methods reflexively, and not only without conscious planning but even without eventual awarenes. A muscularly oriented Madame Fichère might conceivably be just such a person.

MEMORABILIA

In fact, there can be no reasonable doubt about it; the evidence is to be found in the accumulation of more or less grubby little diaries that have already covered over thirty years of her life and show no indication of being discontinued. Someday they should be made available to those who are interested in the psychology of dancers as people. But they certainly cannot be offered for public inspection until everybody in the field whose dander is raisable is already safely dead.

There has always been something too good to be true about Ruth's consistent unflappableness. She has seemed, in a way, a puzzling contradiction, half sophisticated and half naive; not naive in the sense of gaucheness, by any means, but of openness, honesty and basic humility. Of course, since she is a theatre person, she is always performing a bit, offstage as well as on, for her response to people is automatic, but there is never a trace of phoniness about it. She is, indeed, totally unphony.

What is particularly noteworthy, however, is that a performer, an artist, a public figure, surrounded by other performers, artists and public figures, can also be so totally unbitchy. She is essentially in competition with all these others, say what you will, and therefore subcutaneously critical or jealous or both in varying degrees, besides being latently on the defensive against their corresponding attitudes toward her. No amount of good breeding or innate social grace can account for that; it has to be either a colossal arrogance that does not admit the possibility of being competed with or a gross insensitiveness that is not aware of it. Manifestly it is neither. The clue is to be found in the diaries.

Why in general do people keep diaries—that is, beyond their assumedly basic function as account books, as noncommittal, nonreflective memo pads, balancing, as it were, the petty cash of routine daily activity? ("Went to see Aunt Jenny. Couldn't play tennis because of rain. Must remember to pay back the five bucks I borrowed from L. Had a slight headache this morning. Hope I am not coming down with a cold.")

But beyond this pedestrianism what common motive could have activated, say, Mme. de Sévigné and the "Gloomy Dean" of St. Paul's, or "La p'tite Margot" de Valois and Boswell, or Pepys and Kafka?

Fundamentally all diaries seem to fall into two main categories, both of them thoroughly egocentric: there are those that are designed, whether consciously or not, to be read ultimately by others, and those that are designed, on the contrary, for inviolable privacy and are kept under lock and key to make sure they never see the light of day.

The former are rooted in that natural human conceit that makes everybody think, probably rightly, that there is an engrossing book to be made of his life if only he could—or would—write. Since many diarists are convinced that they not only can but will write, sooner or later they transmute their journals into apologias, confessions and multivolumed autobiographies, which they justify by the assumption that they make conspicuous contributions to their times. And there is no doubt that many of them do; history would be balder without them.

The conceits that govern the second category are, on the other hand, repressive rather than expansive. They belong to the timid, the lonely, the introverted, saying their mea culpas in solitude or delving by the midnight candle into ever more personal and esoteric areas to the point of morbidity. Or perhaps, again, "keeping" a diary may mean progressively treasuring memories to be returned to—for reassurance or pride or rueful sentiment—with as full recall as possible.

Then, in opposition to all of these, there is Samuel Pepys, who was, in all conscience, far from being lonely or timid, rueful or morbid, yet still took such pains to keep his journals private that he couched them in a personal system of shorthand that only the most skillful code-breaking was able eventually to penetrate.

Ruth's diaries belong in both main categories and in neither of them; her deliberate intentions possibly belong to the first, her procedures to the second, but her compulsive purpose quite elsewhere. Since the diaries provide the vital substance of this biographical presentation, it is essential to pursue the subject further.

As for deliberate intentions, she does not remember when or why she started keeping a diary; she has no recollection of having kept one as a child (she was probably far too outgoing for that), and the earliest volume that has turned up dates from 1942, when she had been married for seventeen years and had had a career for even longer. Her post-hoc rationalization (which may actually be more than that) is that they were to become the basis of an auto-biography when she got around to writing one. That time actually arrived, however, toward the end of 1970 while she was touring around in the Caribbean in search of atmosphere for a new ballet, but all she wrote was a few valuable pages of childhood memories antedating the earliest diary by half a lifetime, and even this approach was soon abandoned. Eventually, with the apparent intent of salving her autobiographic urge, she began to write (and still continues to do so from time to time) a series of pungent sketches of people she has known and worked with. They make fascinating reading but are no more an autobiography than Ernest Thompson Seton's *Wild Animals I Have Known* is one.

As far as procedures are concerned, the diaries are clearly not intended to be read by anybody else—even literally speaking. Many of them are written on her knee aboard planes and buses, in ink or pencil, and Pepys' personal short-hand is no less scrutable to the searching eye. What is more, the substance seems just as indifferent to communicativeness as the penmanship. Often it omits any report at all of some major development of her life. She seems to pass over all such as so many normal results of metabolism and just as unneces-sary to mention as the fact that she was born. She is writing out from them instead of in toward them. Consequently, unless these crucial events happen to be in some measure familiar from other sources, they can only be deduced in broad outline from her reactions to them in what she writes. It is as if the heroine in the old melodrama simply told how hard it had been to get her wrists unbound and how shattered her nerves were afterward and neglected to mention that she had been tied to the railroad tracks. Ruth is not deliberately avoiding anything or trying to keep anything secret; her whole concern is focused on what goes on from there. She is not being observant but responsive, conceding the drumbeat only in terms of its reverberations.

During her many years of touring she amassed an enormous amount of data about the problems involved. Her company performed not only in what few theatres still survived but also in former movie palaces, convention halls, high school and college auditoriums and even gymnasiums, in large cities and on small campuses; and by some irresistible impulse she recorded the size, shape and texture of every stage floor (an understandable mania with dancers); the facilities, if any, for hanging scenery; the state and number of dressing rooms (again, if any); the hotels and restaurants and their comparative bearableness; and even the hosts and hostesses en route according to whether they served coffee and cookies to be partaken standing up at the inevitable after-performance parties or the real food that dancers need, to be eaten sitting down.

Her overall opinion, here consistently developed, of the architects who build school auditoriums, and the local authorities who allow them to do so, is a devastating one. She knew perfectly well that she could do nothing at all to change or avoid these monstrosities, any more than she could change the drum-beat after it had sent out its reverberations, but she went right on compiling her dismal catalogue, not as the perpetuating of data but because it dealt emotionally with the everpresent problem that had to be met.

That is the strong motivating undercurrent all through the diaries; if there was no problem involved, there was likely to be no specific mention. There was always, to be sure, the overwhelming problem of her artistic life—how to keep her ballets, which she had created with such labor, taste, care and talent, whether for provincial tours or metropolitan opera houses, from being mauled and distorted, deprived of scenery and space and lighting and all the style that she had endowed them with. She suffered many deaths for the same cause in her relations with her dancers, whom she had chosen, developed, treasured, loved and hated and forgiven and hated and loved again, day by day, for what they did and did not do. To make matters ironically worse on the tours, where mayhem was most widely prevalent, audiences loved what they saw though without really having seen it. Not that she did not want them to love it, but that she did want them to have seen it.

Obviously she can be writing only for herself, but is she even doing that? She never looks at the diaries once she has written them—not even to make practical use of all the physical data she has collected. Only recently when she was gathering together her extensive personal archives from various corners where they had been accumulating dust she read them all for the first time before turning them over for the purposes of this book. Her reactions included surprise, incredulity and occasional dismay. She pronounced them "boring" and "sick-making"; she not only did not want anybody else to read them under any conditions but did not even want to read them herself.

Yet she has kept right on writing them. And in this we have the key to the motivation and the persistence of the diaries: what she has written is in itself of the utmost unconcern; what is solely important is the writing of it. Here is the same kind of reflexive therapy as the workout at the barre, though in a less peripheral area. No wonder she is repelled by rereading the old record; to do so is inevitably to revive all the old horrors from which it has released her. Clearly, also, the writing is by nature and necessity private, for it is in substance what she is thinking aloud, completely unbuttoned, and certainly she wants no eavesdroppers. The evolution of the diary as the self-designated instrument of this therapy has something almost of Jamesian pragmatism about it; it becomes what it does.

It is not surprising, then, that in this process she does not trouble to make prime statements; her need here is not creative. Nor does she take pains to record events for their own sakes; what she records are personal reactions to events, and this not in the least for the sake of what is sometimes called "self-expression." Her whole overt career, devoted to the making of prime statements, provides amply for her "expressive" needs.

Through all the vagaries of a procedure that is not objectively defined, she is intent in the main upon arguing out the solutions of problems, either with some specific person in absentia (generally Tom, in matters of going forward, but often, and quite bitterly, with some real or fancied antagonist who seems particularly hostile or competitive at the moment) or simply with her own immediate estimate of the possibilities of the situation, the writing out of which clarifies them for her and serves her central purpose of decision making. The final decisions are rarely recorded, since they occur outside the functions of her recording. If they prove to be bad decisions, we may read about them later in the form of new problems, but if they are good ones, we can only read between the lines and make our own deductions.

When the problems involve people, they can evoke fairly unrestrained personal attacks. Underlying everything is the perhaps innate animalistic defense of her amibitions, her goals, her rights, her procedures, against all opposition. These diaries are not idle time-pleasing; they are a support of life purposes. Here it is of major importance to realize how utterly feminine Ruth is. She is certainly a "liberated" woman, in the genuine rather than the cultish sense, but fortunately she has not been liberated from what the French so aptly called *la différence,* and it is this—feminity itself—that helps to make her pervasive drive a force to be reckoned with. That feminine drives are different in character from masculine drives goes without saying, but they are not inferior in intensity. They are less rational and more intuitive, more insidious and tenacious because less mighty in raw striking power. Also, their frustrations may seek nagging petty compensations far more often, and at perhaps more vicious levels, in what is popularly termed "bitchiness"—an eloquent piece of slang that is itself pointedly female.

If this particular practice is completely alien to Ruth in her poised and normal personal behavior, the explanation is now obvious; it is simply that she disposes of it fully and satisfyingly in her diaries. Here she vents her spleen with splendid passion on all who seem even to have cast their personal shadow across the path she has chosen to travel. She attributes dishonest motives to them and accepts any scurrilous rumor that tends to discredit them; she even records one whispered secondhand tale of a colleague who is alleged to have returned home unexpectedly and found her husband in bed with another man. No wonder she was dismayed when she read the diaries over for the first time.

There is absolutely nothing of all this in her actual three-dimensional self, which is warm, cordial and open, without suspiciousness, guile or guilt. Nor does she have any trace of a hangover about the people she has thus privately maligned and demolished, or even any memory of having demolished anybody. It is as if the writing of it had also been the erasing of it.

A pertinent entry in one of the diaries of the early fifties deals with an informal dinner party for a small group of dancers in her Chicago apartment. One of the guests, a European ballerina not famous for tact or accuracy, was sounding off "bitichily," and largely fictionally, about herself and her relations with some of her glamorous associates, male and female, when a friend of Ruth's who was not a dancer happened to drop in. Of necessity she sat on the sidelines listening. She was much amused, Ruth records, by "the dreadful panning that was going on." Later, in private, she asked Ruth if all dancers felt that way about each other, and Ruth adds retrospectively: "As a matter of fact I guess they do—all except me. I seem to love all dancers. What is wrong with me?" It is a touching bit, because it is absolutely genuine and, despite all the evidence just submitted here, basically true. Not, of course, of the one-dimensional creature of the diaries, but of the whole Ruth, divested in camera of occupational venoms and viruses.

The diaries have thus been a thoroughly successful therapy, more efficacious by far, and infinitely less expensive, than many weeks on a psychiatrist's couch. It may be that a normal and sensitive "psychosoma" knows best where its therapy lies. She is instinctively right, without a doubt, about wanting its intimate records locked carefully away, if not actually destroyed. It would be a calamitous injustice if this one-dimensional image of her were to prevail. There will be occasion later on to press this point further when the diaries are quoted more fully.

There is no denying, however, that on the surface these diaries seem very like all other diaries in their concern with the daily petty cash. She too goes to see Aunt Jennie, though she probably adds that the old lady is boring. She too has to pay back the five bucks she borrowed from L., though if she happens to add that he is interesting, you may be sure that he is one of the numerous males who produce a glint in her penmanship.

"Interesting" and "boring" are her standard diaristic verdicts on people and things, indicating whether or not they have any claims upon her further consideration. She has pronounced the diaries themselves boring, and, again on the surface, she is quite right. There are all those visits to the hairdresser, the shopping, the dress fittings; all those people who are met for lunch or cocktails or dinner by chance or appointment; the dancers bumped into casually in ballet classes or looked at vainly in auditions; all the theatres, movies, operas, concerts, art galleries that simply have to be attended.

Nevertheless, even these have a certain value, especially when she has missed a few days and, now settled down on a long plane flight, is almost visibly trying to remember what in the world she did last Tuesday. When she finally gets into her swing, it becomes clear that these have been the warm-ups that have brought her to the real issues. The warm-ups themselves, however, are not unrewarding. They teem with people. Some of them are simply public figures whom she meets en passant and is content to dismiss en passant, though not always without terse comment. Others are part of her international circle of personal and professional friends, who are by no means exempted from slings and arrows. Still others are her longtime collaborators, often eccentric and difficult, but gifted and hence forgivable. Frequently, isolated details inadvertently put flesh on the bones of projects and dilemmas previously sketched in only vaguely. But everywhere evident are the workings of a lively, eager and tenacious mind, in terms of the obstacles it has had to deal with. And through the sheer mass of spontaneous words, with its inevitable aridities, its unbridgeable lacunae, and its references to episodes past that are inexplicable to you because she has seen no necessity to explain them to herself, themes develop, patterns emerge and a basic narrative somehow gets itself told.

There are also omissions that seem equally inexplicable and for the same reason. For instance, there are many references, barbed and otherwise to girls with their boy friends and to boys with theirs, but even in such a journal as this, so honest as to seem like thinking aloud, there is no mention of either casual or romantic sex encounters of her own.

Yes, actually there is one, which by its very solitariness emphasizes rather than contradicts these statistics. It came at a time of great stress, served a vitally restorative purpose, was recognized for exactly what it was and brought to a harmonious end, for it had resolved the disturbing problem it had posed.

To assume that there were no other such encounters would be altogether out of character with a marriage like hers and Tom's, which, though not at all what we classify nowadays as "open," was definitely ajar. It would almost have to have been with two such brisk and vital people who were frequently apart from each other for long periods. Again, she is not concealing anything, but since there were apparently no unresolved problems involved in her sex life as a whole—as by nature there should not be in anybody's—she found no necessity to explain anything to herself.

The potency of the diaries can perhaps be epitomized by contrasting Ruth with the famous lady in Edward Lear's limerick who, with quite unwarranted smugness, smiled as she rode on a tiger. Ruth, with diary and pen in handbag, was far from smug when she mounted the beast, but when they returned from the ride, it was the tiger who was inside, with the smile on the face of Madame Fichère.

AESTHETICA

Since Ruth herself is so eminently feminine, it follows naturally that her art is also. It is this that sets it apart and gives it its originality and its style. Not that it is sweet or coy, timid or ladylike; on the contrary, it has continually run into censorship problems, and its range is free and courageous, often tackling material that might seem to anybody else to be as intractable as it is unconventional.

Not very long ago in Chicago she urged an assembly of potential ballet sponsors to "be adventuresome, be chic," and in those four words she summed up neatly her own aesthetic approach, though with no awareness that she was doing anything of the sort, or even that she had anything so definite as an aesthetic approach. It is necessarily in large measure an outgrowth of Diaghileff's revolution but without anything of his bumptiousness. It involves a delicatization, a simplicity of stance, a gracious channeling such as he would not have tolerated. In fact, when Bronislava Nijinska, the first of the major twentieth-century women choreographers, was working on her production of *Les Noces* for him, he expressed privately certain reservations about her choreography, which he considered "a bit too feminine." But on this very reservation of his Ruth has developed her art and become probably the most basically feminine of all the women choreographers working in the tradition of the classic ballet.

The woman choreographer did not come into her own until after the first World War, though, to be sure, the most famous of them all dates back two hundred and fifty years. This was the revolutionary Marie Sallé; her fame, however, rests not upon the fact of being a woman but upon what she accomplished in the humanizing of an art that had always been of the very stuff of artifice and convention. Undeniably her revolution was womanly in substance and conviction, but that it was notably feminine in quality is open to doubt. Such a purpose as hers certainly called for great adventuresomeness, but it was much too absorbed in humanization to have any time for chic. Indeed, it was implicitly opposed to chic, since its reason for being was a return to nature, the very antithesis of chic. The subtler aspects of Sallé's revolution are impossible to assess over so long a perspective, but visually, at least, the substitution of relevant costuming for the sumptuous irrelevance of established ballet couture would seem inevitably a backward step for chic.

For Ruth chic itself is part of the adventuresomenees—a sophisticated stripping down of what is sheerly sumptuous to the requirements of a necessary core of relevance, but retaining by the pointed elegance of its selectivity the essence of the original panache. This applies to all the elements that comprise a work. She seems, indeed, to see everything together in the preliminary flash that sets her off; the bare idea is already clothed in form and style, in movement and choreography, in costume, scenery and light, in music, drama (perhaps even words) and, of course, casting—all of which fit in with a revealed perfection that she must now proceed to achieve in esse. This is the painful ordeal of "composing," which consists not just of the devising of choreography (or "creating," as she calls it) but of objectifying the total vision bit by bit—finding the specialists in each field best able to see eye to eye with her, discarding, adapting, substituting, restoring—while still keeping the original glow alive.

Perhaps in something of the same way a creative couturier sees the patron before him as already the ultimate smart lady she will be when realized. If there are lumps and bumps here and there in the "subject," they are the very stuff that provides the challenge necessary for creativity. After all, perfection does not need to be clothed and consequently does not inspire clothing; it is complete in its state of nudity and would be profaned by draping. If the figure of speech can be pushed further still, Ruth's ballet emerges as characteristically a form of symbolic *haute couture*; that is, the realization of the human comedy, with all its frumpiness and frailty, in its ultimate charm and substance. It makes for a warm and delicious aesthetic.

Besides being feminine, her approach is distinctly French—as *haute couture* is distinctly French—though it is withal profoundly Mid-American. You would never mistake her work for that of Roland Petit or Janine Charrat or Maurice Béjart, nor do the French, though they have found it definitely to their taste. Like so many Mid-American artists, she deplores the lack of artistic responsiveness in her native area, and she often wonders why she does not go to France to live. But she never does, for all that she has two homes there. The basically romantic pioneering ardor of the American plains fires her with a demand that she cannot do without, but it is the no-nonsense realism of French sophistication that enables her to see through the lumps and bumps, the frumpiness and frailty, to the projection of her adventurous vision.

Sometimes her native persuasion has turned her to outright Americana, than which more unlikely material for the traditional ballet would be hard to find. The subject matter itself, then, leads necessarily to adventuresomeness in idiom and structure, to the enrichment and the denial of the traditional vocabulary with fresh movements and syntaxes. *Frankie and Johnny, Billy Sunday, The Bells* (after Poe), *Hear Ye! Hear Ye!* (dealing with American courtroom practices) could scarcely depart more widely from both the Taglioni and the Petipa eras, and those fundamentalist balletomanes who consider *Swan Lake, Act II* as the *rites de passage* into classical puberty refuse to consider them as ballets at all. Which, of course, is strictly up to them.

But she is not one to go in for any reviving of standard classics, and particularly not of the everpresent *Swan Lakes* and *Giselles.* Somewhat to her own surprise, she has staged an annual large-scale production of *The Nutcracker* in Chicago for some years at Christmastime under the auspices of the *Chicago Tribune,* but this is primarily of civic provenance, as a project designed chiefly for the children of the city, scads of whom participate in it along with the international stars especially imported for it. There is always the hope that this may lead to something more adult, more native in substance, more proudly local.

She has never danced the Swan Queens herself and has never wanted to; her direction is from here forward, not from here back. From her early years as solo recitalist she has been consistently ahead of the procession, with new ideas, new styles and practices, new composers and designers. She is militantly against that gruesome commercial trio—nostalgia, inertia and tackiness—against bargain-basement productions for purely financial purposes (bread-and-butter programs, as they are called); against "show biz" with its catering to any section of the public that will pay.

For audiences, indeed, she has a lively respect and a generous concern. She is eager to please them, but only by showing them what she likes herself and considers forward-looking, evocative and excellent. Her greatest contribution may consist of just this—her constant touring with the attitude not of a toady but of an aesthetic evangelist. In something of this same area her first great idol, Anna Pavlova, though she was certainly no aesthetic evangelist, also made her greatest contribution, whatever her intention may have been, simply by taking the ballet to new and undeveloped fields. Not that Ruth, any more than Pavlova before her, has any "message," any personal commitments, political or ideological; she is led by her conviction that sprightly artistic "ideas" clad in sprightly artistic form will speak for themsleves. It is no wonder that in the generally wretched housing of her "school-storming" tours she has had so many heart-breaks. Without the chic, what becomes of the adventuresomeness? Here, indeed, her passion may be greater than that of her illustrious predecessor.

The fact that she does not go in for introspection and breast-beating does not mean that she is an abstractionist, dealing in "pure form," or a music "visualizer" in either the romantic Denishawn sense or the classic Balanchinian. No matter how classic the technique she may employ or how modern her view-point, she is fundamentally romantic in that she deals with people in situations, not simply with bodies in movement. Generally there is a story with individu-ally characterized dancers, or if not a literary story, a clear theme, visualizable as such. Much sound intellectual effort lies behind her results, but the works themselves are primarily sensory. Often they are touched with a nice feeling for humor that ranges even as far as broad satire.

Choreography—that is, the steps, the phrases, the technical invention—is not an end in itself for her; it is the material out of which the "idea" is inventively tailored to make it experienceable when properly worn by the dancers. Her touring programs have generally included bravura pas de deux, out of Russia or Denmark, by various American and European guest artists, but these are only stellar punctuations for her own works, which she does not base on technical tours de force. Apparently, if the general American public is to be enticed to the box office, there must be superstars, preferably European but in any case with "names" approximately ten feet tall. Only under such an umbrella can works of merit in their own right find shelter. Or so say the booking agencies, and they are in a position to know.

One of the most ingenious categories of her repertory stems neither from Americana nor from any ballet precedent but, ironically enough, from the opera. This is no doubt a form of compensation for years spent in the opera house, staging with undauntable hope and enthusiasm, those generally thankless, basically unwanted ballet interludes that so many of the old operas require. Such an activity can be an artistic purgatory to a choreographer with musical, visual and theatrical background and a sense of creative dignity—especially for one like Ruth, who dearly loves opera per se.

However, there are so few areas in which a choreographer can work with continuity that if there is an opening in an opera house, he embraces it philosophically, thinking perhaps that it is better to be treated as a rimless and spokeless wheel than to have no axle at all to attach to. If there is insufficient working space in the building, he soon discovers that it is the ballet that goes down into the furnace room to rehearse or to take class, holding on to coal bins and plumbing pipes for want of a barre and counting—and *one* and *two* and— since there is no piano. If there is a question of who is to get a rise in salary, it goes to the cleaning women, of course; if the stage is crowded with the scenic designer's complex of ramps and platforms, what little square footage remains is assigned to the chorus singers, massed where they can best stare at the conductor. This is all quite de rigueur.

But Ruth is not only adaptable and resourceful; she is also devoted and blessedly naive, and eventually she managed to make the opera serve at least as a means of keeping together a group of dancers of her own selection who could tour between opera seasons as the nucleus of a ballet company with relative permanence.

This, of course, was only an organizational arrangement; the operas themselves sparked a quite independent artistic inspiration to match it. With her family background of music she had inherited a certain happy familiarity with many of the scores, and her strong bent for the theatre had made them even more exciting as a potential medium for the evocation of specific and essentially poetic dramatic action. But stage presentations seemed unaware of these potentialities; for the most part they were the nadir of absurdity, lacking all dramatic credibility, all theatrical imagination, all visual and motor sensibility, and existing entirely as exhibitions of competitive vocalism. As a child she had gone into mirthful hysterics over them, but working in the midst of them gave them a different aspect, considerably less amusing.

It was quite obvious that the opera had either forgotten or willfully abandoned its origins as "theatre," patterned by the Renaissance after the theatre of classic Greece, embracing all the arts in one, and had given itself unreservedly into the Italianesque hands of those whose sole passion was for virtuoso singing and who were able to pay for it. In all honesty and logic, such performances should be moved out of the theatre and into the concert hall without meaningless and obstructive "productions" and mise en scène. This would allow the singers to devote themselves to what they are qualified to do—namely, to sing—without having to make spectacles of themselves. (As, for example, in the embracing of each other, presumably in the grip of uncontrol-labe passion but for anatomical reasons perforce at an angle like the poles of a tepee, meeting only at the neck.)

Since, however, such a drastic change of milieu is patently unrealistic, how about approaching the crisis from the other side? How about leaving the singers undisturbed in the sacrosanct opera house and quietly moving the operas out from under them, placing their performance in the hands of dancers and trans-porting them into the area of genuine "theatre"? To assume the presence of such unlikely Machiavellian notions in Ruth's head is unwarranted, for there is no evidence to support it; nevertheless, putting her two inspirations together, that is exactly what she did.

An obvious precedent is to be found in Fokine's original staging of Rimsky-Korsakoff's fantastic opera *Le Coq d'Or* for Diaghileff in 1914, when the requirements of the libretto (adapted from Pushkin) were so manifestly beyond the powers and the physical appearance of opera singers that Diaghileff, at the suggestion of Benois, decided at the very inception of the project to seat the singers in tiers at either side of the stage in Gontcharova's choirlike crimson robes while the entire stage action was performed by a cast of dancers. Some twenty years later, when Fokine revived the work for another company, he went even further and dispensed altogether with the singers (and with them, of course, the words). Ruth was well aware of all this, having performed in a later produc-tion of the work by Adolph Bolm, but her own procedures were quite different in orientation and in substance, as well as more general in scope.

True to her instinct that chic is inseparable from adventuresomeness (even perhaps a technique for achieving it), she stripped down the sumptuousness of "grand" opera to a core of selectively effective elegance and gave it a new life as theatre ballet. For a happy change the characters looked like what they were supposed to be, behaved like animated people in normal health and were quite aware of each other in person instead of obliquely through a common awareness of the conductor. Thus lovers comported themselves believably as such sans problems of anatomical angulation. Since verbalization takes longer than gesture, vocalization than movement, much dramatic and musical deadwood was disposed of at no cost. Even some of the complicated plots proved to be intelligible when acted out, and things began to move, both literally and figuratively.

To be sure, in her lively minification of "grandeur" Ruth eliminated an integral part of "opera," and the part that operamanes like best, but she destroyed nothing and salvaged much. Stravinsky pointed out, when he was castigated for trimming down his score of *The Firebird* on the occasion of its first LP recording, that the old score was still there and so were the old recordings for those who preferred them. At last report the opera is also still there. True, the operamanes are being called upon to make up astronomical annual deficits, but it is unlikely that Ruth's opera-ballets are responsible. As a matter of fact, she is not even doing them any longer.

Provenance and Other Facts of Life

The Centrifugal Gesture

For any rounded view of Ruth Page and her career it is not enough to focus only on what might be called her genetic endowments—charm, talent, drive—as if they were the spontaneous causes of automatic results. Beyond them in time, surrounding her in space, forever impinging on her thinking and action, actually including her, in a sense, is a particular American culture of which she is both a product and a producer and against which she is also a perpetual protestant and a rebel.

America is too young, too recently and miscellaneously peopled, covers too many degrees of both latitude and longitude, to have any wall-to-wall indigenousness of culture, and, if only because of its fixed disparities of climate, altitude, topography, it is hard to see how it ever can have. Out of these disparities, however, and the special ways of life they create and foster, regional homogeneities appear and take over through simple pragmatic logic, to become inevitably the stuff of cultures. Those who are born into these individual cultural processes are rarely aware of them, for they are too normal and inevitable to invite objectivity. But objective they definitely are to those who do not grow up in them; looked at from afar, any region's particular collection of manners and customs is likely to appear as just so many eccentricities, ranging from gaucheness to snobbery. Throughout our history we have delighted in making good-natured fun of each other's regionalisms, but far from being divisive, this is a practice that gives off strong overtones of continental awareness, and may actually presage at last an overall texture of American culture, rather along the lines of Whitman's apocalyptic vision than of uniformity.

Such a multiplicity of regional tendencies might seem to imply a hopeless fractionalism, but basically they can all be grouped into as few as two major categories, and that is all that is required to set up a national cultural rhythm, so to speak. One category belongs to the long periphery of the country, exposed to all the eight winds of the heterogeneous world, blowing in and blowing out; the other belongs to the solid interior, where there is a measure of selective self-containment and the making of a common life can be got on with. The one seeks a center, the other flees from it. The heartland's concern is with permanence, safety, roots, futures—a complete reversal of the heady American myth of Manifest Destiny, of having to get to the edges of things, to see what is beyond, and even perhaps to get to the edges of that beyond, whatever it may be. What a cartoon the heartlanders, in an especially jovial mood, could make of the peripheralists—hopping frantically into their Conestoga wagons at the very foot of Plymouth Rock and taking off for Californ-eye-ay and the Pacific; whooping it up cocksurely to cross the Great Lakes and take over Canada, where boundary was clearly no more than a political fiction; crashing through the southern border to annex Mexico on the same quite obvious grounds.

Ruth Page belongs by birth and heredity to the interior, to the region long known, with a high disregard for geography, as the Middle West. It might have been called with greater accuracy the Middle East, for the Mississippi River is its spine, its aorta, its trunkline and, together with tributaries great and small, its history as well. Now, happily, it is being referred to more frequently as Mid-America, which, beyond mere geographical reference, connotes the balance and solidity that characterize a national mean.

It has, of course, no specific boundaries and is definable chiefly in terms of its cultural homogeneities, themselves to be sensed rather than defined. Long before the railroads came, its homeseekers shipped up the river from the Gulf, stopping off on the mainstream and its branches to make the beginnings of fine cities like Memphis and St. Louis, Kansas City and Minneapolis, Cincinnati and even easterly Pittsburgh. Or perhaps they have come up the Hudson to Albany and through the "canawl" to Lake Erie and westward, or up the St. Lawrence also to the Great Lakes and onward. Those who found no helpful waterways to convey them, when there was no more tidewater land to settle on, pushed across the mountains at Cumberland Gap and chopped their way west through the wilderness.

They were French and English, Scots and Irish, Germans, Scandinavians and Poles. The only thing they had in common was a passionate desire to find a place where they could settle down and make a life for themselves, as they could not do for a multitude of different reasons in the lands of their origin.

The Page family started a line of Virginia planters well before the Revolution. Certainly by the time of President Monroe they had become not only prosperous but influential, and when in 1824 Congress invited the Marquis de Lafayette to make a state visit to the republic he had helped so substantially to create, Ruth's great-grandfather was a member of the national committee organized to see to his adequate entertainment on a tour of the country not unlike a royal progress. En route to a visit to the now aged Thomas Jefferson the Marquis stopped over at the Page estate, Rosewell, and found his host so warmly congenial that they became fast friends and continued to correspond as long as they both lived.

On the host's side the relationship was perpetuated even beyond that to the present day, and in every generation each batch of Pages has named one of its sons Lafayette. This has made for a general confusion and no amount of nicknaming, such as Lafe and Fayette, has been able to clear it up. Ruth's father came within an ace of breaking the tradition, for he was the youngest of twelve children, and if he had turned out to be a girl, that would have been that. How any loyal Page household could take such a chance remains unexplained, unless perhaps an earlier Lafayette had not survived.

By this time Ruth's grandfather had migrated westward and established a new planatation near Columbia, Kentucky, where much later Ruth as a child was to spend some happy summer vacations, riding horses and running generally wild on what was left of the once vast acreage. Her Uncle James, the oldest of the twelve children, maintained the traditions of southern hospitality there, with the help of some of the old servants, until well along in years. Fine gardens surrounded the house, which was fifteen miles from the railroad and had sturdily resisted deforming modernizations.

Young Lafayette, of literary and poetic leanings as well as strong humanitarian tendencies, knew from the start that his lifework had to be medicine, and when he had exhausted all the channels for medical education open to him in his own part of the world, where he had already gone into the practice, he set out for Germany for further study. It was there that in his early thirties he met Marian Heinley, married her in Geneva in 1896 and brought her home to Indianapolis. Actually she had lived less than a hundred miles away from him most of her life.

The new Mrs. Page's ancestry was very different from her husband's. Her mother, Genevieve Latour, belonged to a French family that had come down from Canada on the trail of Père Marquette and was among the first settlers of Indiana at Vincennes in 1702. She herself was born in the equally French town of Terre Haute. Here she married into a German family whose original name of Heinle had by this time acquired a final *y* for phonetic clarification in a non-German world. Here, also, their daughter Marian was born, though shortly afterward they moved across the state line to Danville, Illinois.

Marian was of strong musical inclination, inherited apparently from her German line, and a devoted student of the piano. When she was in her teens her mother died, and much to her distress her father took a second wife with whom she was totally out of tune. For the sake of family harmony Marian was packed off to Germany to devote herself to her musical education, a solution that was entirely to her liking. At seventeen, then, she left for Leipzig, where the Conservatorium was considered the best musical school in Europe. There she remained for six years, and it was there that she met the young Dr. Page. He too was studying at the university, whose medical school was equally celebrated. To refer again to the matter of regional homogeneities, what could be more natural than for two sensitive persons with a common cultural mystique to be drawn together in a foreign country in which they were both conspicuously alien?

At any rate, back in Indianapolis they set up a home named Rosewell, containing, of course, a grand piano. Within a year or so it also contained a son, immediately christened Lafayette, to get that family commitment safely taken care of. In celebration of his arrival James Whitcomb Riley, one of his father's most cherished friends, gave him a small silver cup inscribed:

Oh, infancy, what fitter gift from age –
A little couplet for a little page.

When Ruth came along some two years later, there came along another cup, with another inscription:

This cup though filled with wine or honey dew,
May never hold as sweet a sweet as you.

When the third child arrived a year later (another son this time, named Irvine and destined to follow in his father's profession to high distinction), there was probably another cup, but until it is unearthed from its present obscurity, another Riley gem must remain unpublished.

Ruth remembers Riley only as an old man in poor health who often drove over to their house to see her father and swap jokes with him. Actually he was fifteen years or so older than her father and still touring extensively with his always popular lectures and readings of his folk poems of the heartland he knew so well at first hand. He died the year she finished high school, and her father conceived the plan for a children's hospital that was subsequently built and named in his honor.

Through all the development of his notable career as an ear, nose and throat specialist Dr. Page never relaxed his literary and poetic enthusiams. He was a member of the Gentlemen's Literary Club, and one of the papers he wrote for it was "Science and Poetry," dealing with a relationship he found vital and inherent. These were days of rich literary and theatrical accomplishment in the

Indianapolis area, and among his friends were Booth Tarkington, George Ade, Meredith Nicholson, the actor Otis Skinner and the cartoonist John T. McCutcheon. It was also a day of habitual reading aloud en famille—Dickens, Thackeray, Scott, Hugo, Dumas père, Bulwer Lytton—all the standard nineteenth century "classics." Poetry to be sure, was also high on the list at the new Rosewell, not only read aloud but also recited from memory. Ruth has written of her father that he "hated trivial conversation, and so he insisted that if we didn't have anything worthwhile to say at the breakfast table, we should each recite a verse of poetry. My favorite to recite at this time was 'O Captain! my Captain! our fearful trip is done; The ship has weather'd every rack, the prize we sought is won.' "

Mrs. Page, besides doing most of the reading aloud, also played soft music for the children to go to sleep to—thus starting a habit that Ruth continues to this day to indulge. Music, indeed, remained the dominating passion of Marian Page's life, and since it was not in the same flourishing state as literature in Indianapolis, she was determined that it should become so. She had scarcely found her footing in her new home when she organized an annual concert series of Matinees Musicales, and once that was in being, she became the driving force in the founding of the Indianapolis Symphony Orchestra. This was during the period just before Ruth was born, and when both infants emerged at about the same time, Ruth was promptly dubbed "the symphony baby." The standards her mother demanded for Indianapolis were uncompromisingly high, and once when a prominent pianist sent an advance copy of his proposed concert program, consisting entirely of popular old war-horses, she was indignant. Ruth remembers her saying: "Well, we'll never invite him to give a concert in Indianapolis again." And they probably never did, for she was a woman of strong mind and high purpose.

Alone, of course, she could not have accomplished what she did, but she was fortunate in finding a sympathetic and equally dedicated soul in the person of the local impressario, Ona B. Talbot, and they became close friends and collaborators.

The position of the artist, or any other creative person, for that matter, in an interior culture where the gesture is centripetal, is a difficult one, for the creative person is by nature a centrifugalist, so to speak, seeking the edges of things and what lies beyond them. Not content with permanence, safety, roots, futures, he demands the pursuit of the unperceived, the unproven, the intuited; he is concerned with the discovery of irrational dimensions, immaterial substances, truer truths, no matter what dangers are involved in the process. The artist, and especially the performing artist, demands also a receiving ear, a perceiving eye, a hungry mind to which to convey his intangibles. His hope is that even the most centripetal culture will eventually achieve those foreseeable futures it has concentrated upon and will turn to the pursuit of unforeseeable ones that only the adventurous vision of the artist can identify. But the rhythm of a growing culture is in terms of centuries, and the artist born into it with a single three-score-and-ten to counter with can only beat his breast and flee. Not every artist can even do that; some roots are too deep, some too precious, to be abandoned.

Marian Page contributed vigorously to the enrichment of the musical life of her community, partly for the sake of the community, partly for the sake of her art and partly for her own necessity if she was to live there. But there was more to her urgency than that; she spent hours each day at her piano, as indeed she had done for most of her life, driven by the compulsion of a personal art that seemed determined to outface the glacial pace of the cultural rhythm.

Eventually a little studio was built away from the house so that her playing would not interfere with Dr. Page's necessary concentrations. It was also designed, to be sure, for Ruth and her ballet barres and classes, for by this time she was definitely committed with her mother's active support, to a dancing career. One wall of the little building was of glass and could be opened to make performances possible for audiences seated on the lawn.

Her mother had tried to teach her to play the piano, but her hands were too small and too weak, and her obvious drive in another direction was too large and too strong. She must have begun to dance as soon as she could walk. When Mrs. Talbot brought her various artists to have tea with Mrs. Page, Ruth begged to be allowed to dance for them (or indeed for any other guests at any other time), and sometimes her mother allowed her to do so and of course played for her.

"I can remember now," Ruth wrote years later in her autobiographical mood, "what our living room was like. It was a great big room with a piano, and at one end there was a conservatory with a lot of greenery and flowers and a little bird in a cage. And off that room was my father's office-study where I could dress. I would invent all kinds of costumes, then I would enter through the door and my mother would start to play. As soon as she started to play, the bird would start to sing, and I would start to dance and dance and dance. It was hard to make me stop. I really must have been an obnoxious child, a show-off with no inhibitions whatsoever. I had friends of my own age, of course, but I found them a silly lot, and while I played along with them, I much preferred my parents' friends. I felt no generation gap and much preferred to listen to their conversation"—and of course to join it, as it were, by performing for them. Mother was fortunately more aware of the generation gap, and though sometimes she would allow as many as two dances, depending on the immediate social climate, that was her limit of permissiveness, and as she was the indispensable musician, there could be no argument.

A few months after her eighth birthday Ruth unexpectedly made the front page of the *Indianapolis News* as a dancer. The occasion was a charity garden party on the lawn of Vice-President Fairbanks, where she and her little friend

Eleanor Shaler, together with several other pupils of the local dancing teacher, Anna Stanton, performed lyrically "dressed in trailing chiffon and nothing at all on our feet." The next day on the front page was a large photograph of them with a caption saying how shocking they were. It seems that some political enemies of the Vice-President were responsible for this scandal. "My mother and father were furious, as they considered it very unladylike to have one's picture in the paper, even fully clothed."

Some three years later she and Eleanor had a new passion and begged and pleaded with Miss Stanton to let them dance on their toes, for Anna Pavlova had made her first appearance in Indianapolis. Though they had not seen her, Mrs. Page had and joined in the general acclamation. Naturally there was much conversation and many detailed descriptions were demanded. Seeing the genuine eagerness of the two children, Miss Stanton sent away for some "toe clips" for them, which they slipped into their dancing shoes "and away we soared."

When Pavlova next danced in Indianapolis two years later, Ruth herself saw her and was transported. "I was walking on air for days and days," she wrote. "I could hardly return to earth at all. I went out on my balcony at night and danced in the moonlight. I danced with the rising of the sun, and every time my mother would play the piano, which was most of the day, I would try to dance like Pavlova. I made up a new dance every day."

But Miss Stanton's was not a professional school, which would have been an anomaly in such a residential city as Indianapolis, and Ruth and Eleanor were perfectly content to go along with the barefoot "interpretive" dancing that was chiefly taught, according to the custom of the day. After all, dancing was dancing. Nevertheless, it was at this moment that Ruth really began to "train," from her point of view, "professionally."

It was an ideal period in the history of dancing for a child with such a bent for it, for a genuine renaissance was in the making. In 1909 Diaghileff had taken a Russian ballet to western Europe for the first time and created an explosion that was heard even in the cities of the American midland, which had only the faintest idea of what a ballet really was. Late in the year before, Isadora Duncan, a rebel against the ballet, who had won Europe with her eloquent and revolutionary dancing to great symphonies in Greek tunics and bare feet, had come back to win her own country as well, and succeeded in doing a tour with Walter Damrosch and the New York Symphony Orchestra that lit fires in all kinds of fields, from the educational world to the Broadway musical. In the latter, indeed, it even bred a popular song called "Every Little Movement Has a Meaning All Its Own." Shortly afterward, Ruth St. Denis, another American quasi-expatriate who had captivated Europe, returned home for a similar conquest, which was eventually to lead to the burgeoning of the whole American modern dance movement.

The next year Anna Pavlova and Mikhail Mordkin defected from the Diaghileff company and its insurgencies, which were not congenial to them, and came over with a Russian company of their own on a tour that lasted an entire season, took them from coast to coast and rekindled the long-dormant embers of the ballet in this country. In another three years the first World War was to add fuel to these fires, for with Europe closed to them, many dancers, including Pavlova, would remain on this side of the Atlantic for the duration and, in some cases, permanently. Later, even the Diaghileff company, or what remained of it after the disorganizations of the war, would finally get to America in 1916, bringing Vaslav Nijinsky with it out of Hungary, where he had been interned as an enemy alien, and would leave still other fine dancers and able teachers behind when it departed.

Ruth's career would be nourished by all these influences and would be brought to realization by some of them.

"X" BEHIND HER BACK

More specifically to the present point, Pavlova was back in Indianapolis in the autumn of 1914 with a largely new company perforce. Her association with Mordkin had ended after their one hectic American tour (when Mrs. Page had seen them), during which they had quarreled continually and publicly, and ultimately she had slapped his face in the middle of a performance—a slap that was heard around the world, for they were what is known as "hot news." After their explosive separation they had continued to tour with companies of their own, here and abroad.

When war was declared in the summer of 1914, Pavlova was caught in Berlin, and only by hook and by crook did she manage to get back to London, which had become by now her permanent home instead of St. Petersburg. She set about at once gathering together scattered remnants of her company and making replacements as well as she could. Then, with Alexandre Volinine as her partner, and several talented English girls (some of them with Russianized names) added to the troupe, she crossed the Atlantic and embarked on what proved to be five years of touring in the Western Hemisphere.

When they reached Indianapolis, Mrs. Talbot arranged for Ruth not only to meet Pavlova but also to dance for her. The circumstances seem propitious, since Pavlova was naturally on the alert for new talent for her now rootless company. When Ruth was ushered into the dressing room after the matinee performance, there sat Pavlova, in Ruth's words, "stark naked and picking her teeth." Such a twofold breach of the mores of Mid-America could not have failed to make an indelible impression.

Mrs. Page played for the audition on the, by now, stripped stage, and Ruth, as she always did when her mother played, "made up a dance." It was an ordeal for the child, for the whole company was sitting around watching. However, when she had finished, Pavlova's first response was auspicious; she untied the bow of ribbon on top of the schoolgirl head, combed out the schoolgirl pompadour and recombed the hair in the "romantic ballerina" style (Taglioni's and her own), parted in the middle and pulled back softly over the ears. "This is for dancer," she said. (It would be years before Ruth changed it.)

Her second response was more practical. She invited Ruth to go to Chicago for the coming summer to study there with her company. She had accepted an engagement to appear in the season of summer concerts at Midway Gardens, that beautiful indoor-and-outdoor cafe, concert hall, theatre, designed by Frank Lloyd Wright on the site of the old side-show area, known as the Midway, at the 1893 World's Fair. The engagement was a strategic one for Pavlova, for at the same time she was making a motion picture for Universal, which had not abandoned its Chicago studios in the general Hollywood emigration. Accordingly most of the outdoor scenes could be shot in lake-shore areas. The film was of feature length and was called *The Dumb Girl of Portici,* based on Auber's opera *La Muette de Portici,* which romanticized around the story of Masaniello. It was not in any sense a ballet film (there was no sound at that time, of course), but was designed to exploit Pavlova's celebrated gifts for mime and drama.

The Midway Garden season opened July 4, 1915, and though Ruth was enchanted, she was not nearly far enough along technically to join the company class, taught by Ivan Clustine, the new ballet master of the company. Pavlova accordingly turned her teaching over to a young Polish dancer named Jan Zalewski and later arranged for him to go to Indianapolis during the company's vacation to teach Ruth in her own studio. It was a rich experience, however, just to see what a ballet company was like in operation. They were not doing a full repertory, it is true; they performed only one ballet each night on a mixed concert program—*The Fairy Doll, The Magic Flute* (Drigo, not Mozart), *Flora's Awakening* and other typically conventional Pavlova repertory pieces.

The first contact with the professional world intensified Ruth's impatience to say good-bye to the humdrum life of Indianapolis and get on with her career. But there was still one more year of high school to be endured—not too painfully, as it proved. Her final year at Tudor Hall (daughters of "good families" in Indianapolis did not go to public schools) found her the object of envy and admiration because of the romantic calling she had apparently been tapped for. Some of her classmates' mothers may have raised an eyebrow or two, considering the general reputation of dancing girls, but she was elected class president notwithstanding. Daughters of good families in that day also did not as a rule go to college, since what they were being prepared for was a good marriage, but they frequently did go to finishing schools in the East. For an entirely different set of reasons, that was the plan agreed upon by Ruth and her parents; she was to spend two years at Miss Williams's and Miss McLellan's French School for Girls in New York. It had to be New York, of course, where things happened, and she had to be fluent in French if she was to function adequately in the ballet world. But that was a whole year off.

Meanwhile she made her first public—though not professional—appearance. It was in a James Whitcomb Riley Fesitval at the Murat Theatre on October 7, 1916, designed to honor the memory of the laureate of the area (he had died earlier in the year) on the anniversay of his birth. Since the Russian ballet was now in such high vogue, the program was staged by two "Russian" dancers who had been members of Pavlova's company for two years. What with the state of Europe they had determined to settle down in this country, and just before the beginning of the Midway Garden season they had been engaged by the Chicago Grand Opera Company—one of them, whose stage name was Serge Oukrainsky, as director and premier danseur, and the other, Andreas Pavley, as guest artist. With this festival they joined forces for the first time in what was to become a long professional partnership with a ballet company of their own. The dancers they worked with here consisted chiefly of students. Ruth's mother had made her a green taffeta dress and bought her a white wig, and all their friends, according to Mrs. Page, "thought she was marvelous."

At this moment Ruth was a student only of dancing, for she had graduated from Tudor Hall in June but, because of this festival, she had not yet left for New York and the French School. Miss Williams and Miss McLellan, indeed, were to prove very lenient schoolmistresses, for they were to allow her not only to go to ballet classes outside the school but also to take time out frequently for professional engagements; in one case, at least, quite a long one.

When at last she did get to New York, she was completely surrounded by Russian ballet. Before she got there, the Diaghileff Company had already played its first season in this country, from January through April; now in October it began its second (and calamitous) one, this time under the direction of Nijinsky instead of Diaghileff.

Pavlova had opened a long engagement at the New York Hippodrome, of all unlikely places, in a huge and equally unlikely production called *The Big Show,* which was to play 426 performances until halfway through 1917. The Hippodrome was New York's greatest theatrical tourist attraction since Jenny Lind and Castle Garden, and its productions combined everything from tightrope walkers to opera divas. For Pavlova, Clustine had put together a capsule version of *The Sleeping Beauty* with elaborate scenery by Léon Bakst, who had burst into international fame with Diaghileff, and Volinine was her partner. Among the other performers on the same bill were Powers' Elephants, Milton Mooney's Horses, Toto the clown, Charlotte the ice skater, the Elm City Four plus countless singers, comics, acrobats, and a large body of chorus girls who had to swim as well as dance, sing and cavort and eventually disappear completely into a big pool from which they were never seen to emerge. The production also came up with an unexpected candidate for top honors in competition with Pavlova in the person of a pretty little Japanese prima donna named Haru Onuki. She had been provided with a special song, with words by John Golden and music by Raymond Hubbell, to point up her romantic Japaneseness. It was called "Poor Butterfly" (meaning, of course, Puccini's already immortal Cio-Cio-San) and became an instantaneous all-time "pop" classic. Onuki has long since been forgotten, but the song will probably live to challenge even *The Sleeping Beauty* for longevity.

As for the local presence of the Diaghileff ballet, its most important feature for Ruth was Adolph Bolm, who was largely to shape her career. He had often danced with Pavlova as her partner in the Imperial Ballet in St. Petersburg (he was, indeed, her lover in that period) and had even taken her on a summer-vacation tour of Scandinavia, which marked her first appearance outside Russia.

In the company's present visit to America he was the key figure, for the war had scattered not only the dancers but also many of the directorial staff, and it had fallen to him to hire replacements where he could find them, pull an adequate company into shape, rehearse the entire repertoire and of course dance himself as well. The New York opening the previous January had found him so ill, with such a high temperature and so many drugs to check it, that the next morning he could not remember whether the performance had actually taken place or not.

On the company's second visit, which started in October and included a tour to the West Coast and back, he had an accident midway through the season and was compelled to leave the company and return to New York. Then, because of the revolutionary situation in Russia and the war in Europe, he and his wife and stepdaughter decided to remain in this country permanently. Naturally he and Pavlova renewed their old friendship while they were both in New York, and it was Pavlova who introduced Ruth to him. She urged her strongly to study at his school as soon as he opened it, and of course she did.

She found his teaching inspiring, except for his barre work, which she considered downright bad and which obviously did not interest him at all. Although he was a staunch admirer of Cecchetti, he was also in tune with the new spirit that had come into the ballet with Fokine, in which technique for its own sake was no longer the object. Where she felt he functioned best as a teacher was in his inventions and experimentations, and the creative aspects of learning to dance. He never proved to be an outstanding choreographer on his own, but he was excellent at reproducing Fokine's and other people's ballets.

That he found Ruth highly talented was evidenced by his beginning almost at once to use her in his public presentations of one sort or another. She was an instinctive performer, loved to perform (even loved to have pictures taken!) and was possessed of both physical beauty and outgoing charm.

With all the glamour of Russian ballet (now virtually spelled as one word), his services were in considerable demand, and by November he had already put Ruth into her first Broadway musical. It was a revue called *Miss 1917* at the Century Theatre and it was almost as elaborate as Pavlova's Hippodrome show. Its cast included Lew Fields, Irene Castle, George White, Marion Davies, Ann Pennington, Bessie McCoy Davis, Van and Schenck, Savoy and Brennan, Cecil Lean, Cleo Mayfield, Elizabeth Brice, Charles King, Vivienne Segal, Tortola Valencia and scores of others. (The rehearsal pianist was a nineteen-year-old boy names George Gershwin, whose salary was $35 a week.)

Bolm staged a ballet for it called *Falling Leaves,* described on the program as a "poem-choreographic," with music by Victor Herbert, and a lush and much admired series of tableaux on a revolving stage designed by Josef Urban. The soloists were Bolm himself as The Spirit of the Wood and Flore Revalles as The Golden Birch. (Though not a Russian dancer, she had been hastily recruited in Paris for the Diaghileff ballet tour.) For the rest, the cast consisted of various dryads, fauns and nymphs, of whom Ruth was one. Possibly because of its overstuffed opulence, the show was a disastrous failure and limped along for a bare six weeks. But for Ruth it had its compensations. Victor Herbert, then aged fifty-eight, cast sheep's eyes at her and suggested that if she could sing as well as she could dance, he would like to write a song for her—in this show or any other one. Nothing ever came of it, but at least it did nothing to break her confidence.

Even if the show had been a great success, however, she would not have stayed with it, for about this time Pavlova invited her to join her company for a long tour of South America, beginning in January. For that she would have forgone anything; the invitation was clearly based on Bolm's recommendation, for Pavlova still listened to his advice with confidence. Later, indeed, she was to refer to Ruth affectionately as her "gift from Bolm."

Mrs. Page, like many another ballet mother, felt uneasy about letting her young and inexperienced daughter undertake so long and unpredictable a tour unchaperoned, so she decided to go along. This was eminently practicable, since Dr. Page and her older son, Lafayette, were in France with the Army, where her husband was doing research and experimentation in the treatment of gas burns, and her younger son, Irvine, who was only seventeen, was away at school. It worked out well within the company, too. Mrs. Page and Pavlova became great friends and Pavlova frequently invited them both to have tea with her.

For a beginner, and especially one with such a rapturous case of idolatry, it made no difference that the company was strictly a one-woman show. It was in general a day of stars rather than of ensembles, and both Pavlova and her husband-manager, Victor Dandré, were completely of that mind. Her repertoire was conventional and her music old-fashioned; her settings and costumes were commonplace and her company served the exclusive purpose of supporting her. Under the circumstances this was quite enough, for she was a superb dancer with a magic effect on an audience. Certainly she did not startle them with technical virtuosity; indeed, she never mastered the rabble-rousing series of thirty-two *fouettés en tournant.* Her power lay in the exquisite movement of a beautiful body, always informed by dramatic feeling and poetic impulsion. Creative she was not; persuasive she was. In her many years of almost continuous traveling she convinced mutitudes of people of the inherent powers of the ballet in terms they did not have to understand but could not help responding to.

Ruth reported that Dandré was "charming and efficient" and without him "the great tours and complicated organization would have been difficult to handle. He took care of X, as we called her behind her back, as though she were a little child—in fact he treated the whole company as though they were children, and we all adored him."

On this tour the two leading male dancers were Volinine and the American Hubert Stowitts; and on the distaff side Hilda Butsova (née Boot), an excellent dancer, was her understudy, general standby and ranking soloist. Other English girls were Muriel Stuart and Enid Brunova, and another American girl was Lisa Gardiner. There were also several other American boys. Clustine was the ballet master (as he had been for both the Bolshoi Ballet and the Paris Opéra) and also "arranged" most of the old ballets, such as *Giselle, Coppelia, The Enchanted Forest, The Magic Flute, Puppenfee, Walpurgisnacht* and *Sleeping Beauty.* Besides these, he choreographed many of the divertissements, including the *Pavlova Gavotte,* set to Paul Linke's popular tune "The Glowworm." She had intended this to be a protest against the vulgarity of the current social dances, such as the Turkey Trot and the Bunny Hug, but though audiences seemed to like it, there is no record of any damage done to either vulgarity or the ragtime dances.

The standard form of the program consisted of either a two-act ballet or two one-act ones, followed invariably by a series of eight or ten divertissements. These included a solo by Pavlova and a pas de deux with either one of her partners, numbers by other principals in varying groups, and ensembles by the corps de ballet.

The first solo Ruth was cast for was the Japanese doll in *Coppelia,* "who has nothing to do but just sit there," which made her utterly miserable. Then there was a lyrical free-style Brahms waltz danced by nine girls, three in the front row and six in the back. Ruth was in the back line, but she thought she was "just marvelous" in it. When one of the girls in the front row got sick, she was certain they would move her up as a replacement, but they did nothing of the sort, and she was heartbroken. "However," she says, "I didn't do too badly. All the people ahead of me seemed to drop out one by one, so I got to the top [*sic*] quite fast."

The only ballet ever choreographed by Pavlova herself had its première in Rio de Janeiro on this tour. It was called *Autumn Leaves* and was danced by

Pavlova, Volinine and Stowitts with a corps de ballet of autumn leaves, of whom Ruth may or may not have been one.

Throughout Latin America, she has recorded, the girls in the company were called Pavlocitas, and wherever they went they were "followed and stared at. Some man in Lima, Peru, sent me white roses every day. When we left, he sent me a box of candy to the boat. I opened it a week later and in it was a diamond and sapphire necklace. My mother made me send it right back. I never met this man!"

"Almost everyone in the company was attractive" she wrote home to a friend, "and most of them danced well. But Pavlova did not seem particularly interested in the company, and the only company class she ever gave was in one of the cities on the west coast when many of the dancers and most of the staff were ill with influenza." Apparently it was such a memorable occasion that the influenza seemed a small price to pay.

As the end of the first year was approaching, Mrs. Page wrote a letter from Havana to Eleanor Shaler on the occasion of her mother's death. As to their own plans she added: "I do not know how much longer Ruth will stay. She has gotten about as high as she can get, but rather wants to stay until they make a tour of Europe.... Unless Dr. Page should cable that he and Lafayette are coming home, Ruth and I will stay for the season here (five weeks) and then go to Mexico. The tour should end by the end of February.... The company expects now to go back to Buenos Aires in April for three months and then to England."

Much as Ruth would have liked to go to England with them, Buenos Aires was too far. And that was that. When she left the company, Pavlova gave her a handsome Spanish shawl which she still treasures.

In retrospect, Ruth has written of Pavlova: "That she was an inspiration is putting it mildly. In the 'Faust' ballet I was one of her slaves, and when I had the good luck to dance with her all alone across the entire stage I nearly fainted at the touch of her hand. I can feel her electric touch even now. Underneath her delicate, fragile-looking body and her air of total ethereality, lurked such muscles of steel and such sensuous passion that no other dancer has ever rivaled her, before or since. Her poetry and the deep melancholy of her Russian soul brought her audience invariably to tears. I weep myself even now at the thought of her."

Bolm, Beaux and Broadway

With her father home from France, her brother Lafayette back at Princeton and the family tradition of a summer vacation at their shore house on Cape Cod at Hyannisport resumed after the wartime break, Ruth set off again to her adored

New York, both to complete her scheduled two years at the French School (surely the longest and most fragmented two years in educational history) and to resume her work with Bolm.

She found the Bolm establishment increasingly lively. Streams of distinguished artists from various parts of the world flowed through the studio and the Bolms' apartment which adjoined it—Sergei Prokofieff, Carlos Salzedo, George Barrère, John Alden Carpenter, Robert Edmond Jones, Michio Ito, Roshanara, Ratan Devi . . .

Bolm himself now had three major lines of activity, all of which would involve Ruth sooner or later. For one thing, he had established a little touring company called Ballet Intime, of which she was his leading ballerina most of the time.

A second outlet for his creative energies was provided by the new form of "movie palace" that was developing over these years, in which, besides the mere showing of films, there were stage "presentations" involving orchestras, singers and dancers. Probably because of the prevailing magic of the term "Russian Ballet," Bolm was the first to stage ballets on such programs. Ruth was in many of them, though you would never have guessed it from the billing, for she was listed as Natasha Stepanova. The grandeur of Russianness had to be maintained perhaps even more for these "pop" audiences than for those of Pavlova and Diaghileff, and she welcomed the alias, for with her ideals this was slumming, though financially helpful.

The third field for Bolm was that of guest artist and choreographer in opera houses here and abroad. By the time Ruth returned from the South American tour he had already restaged Fokine's *Coq d'Or* for the Metropolitan. (When Ruth saw it, she told him she would "go to the ends of the earth to dance the role of the Queen of Shemakhan.") At the present moment he had accepted an offer to create a new ballet for the Chicago Grand Opera Company, and Ruth had fortunately got back in time to participate.

The work was primarily a project of the composer and patron of music John Alden Carpenter, who had written a score to Oscar Wilde's *The Birthday of the Infanta*. The scenery and costumes were to be designed by Robert Edmond Jones, whose only previous work in the ballet field had been Nijinsky's ill-fated *Till Eulenspiegel* three years before. Ruth was to have the title role and Bolm that of the sentimentally tragic Dwarf. Fortunately for Miss Williams and Miss McLellan it was scheduled for the Christmas holidays.

Bolm had scant respect for Serge Oukrainsky, who was the director of the resident ballet at the opera, and his colleague, Andreas Pavley. He considered them "incompetent upstarts," possibly because one of them was a Ukrainian (*vide* his stage name) and the other a Java-born Dutchman, and neither of them had had any closer contact with the Imperial Russian Ballet than their two years in Pavlova's touring company. His opinion may also have been colored somewhat by the fact that he would have liked the job of director himself. Nevertheless, it was this resident ballet company that he had to work with, and the results were highly satisfactory. A young Italian boy named Vincenzo Celli played the Bull in *The Infanta*. Another member of the cast was the also young dancer-poet-painter Mark Turbyfill, who was to become Ruth's lifelong friend and admirer. As for Ruth's own performance, it was greeted by the press with unanimous praise, and Percy Hammond, the usually acidulous drama critic on the *Chicago Tribune* went so far as to call her "perfect as the Infanta."

The following spring (*pace* Miss Williams and Miss McLellan) Bolm took his Ballet Intime to London for a season at the Coliseum. The critic on the *Daily Mail* referred to "the nineteen-year-old Ruth Page" (actually she had just turned twenty) as "the wonderful dancer at the London Coliseum"; but far more important to Ruth was the fact that Enrico Cecchetti, the favorite master of both Pavlova and Bolm, now had a school of his own in London, and on Bolm's strong recommendation she went there for daily classes.

They were large classes and included many prominent artists, for Cecchetti had become the technical lodestar of the ballet world. Among the students was a good-looking girl with exceptionally fine feet who was a successful dancer in revues and pantomimes and had recently been première danseuse of the Royal Opera, Covent Garden. She was two years older than Ruth and her name, or at least the name she used in the theatre, was Ninette de Valois.

Ruth's mother joined her in London shortly before the opening of the Coliseum engagement and kept house for her in a small flat.

There were to be other tours of the Ballet Intime on the home side of the Atlantic. One of them the next year had as its conductor George Barrère, the longtime flutist of the New York Symphony Orchestra whom Isadora Duncan remembered always for his exquisite playing of the "Happy Spirit" music from Gluck's *Orfeo* when she danced to it on her memorable tour with that orchestra in 1908. In 1922 the Ballet Intime appeared in Indianapolis under the auspices of the Matinees Musicales, of which Marian Page was still president, and the students of Tudor Hall turned out en masse to greet Ruth in her home-town debut.

THE WORLD AS OYSTER

Meanwhile, in the natural course of events, her enrollment at the French School came to an end, and when she went to Indianapolis this time, its status as home-town also ended, for she was never to live there again. Her parents' overall plan for bringing up their children was to provide them with the best education possible, after which they were on their own. Accordingly when Ruth left for New York this time, they gave her a hundred dollars and kissed her good-bye. It was the last money she ever had to take from them, even though she "faced the world" at this ceremonial emancipation as something of a spoiled brat by both upbringing and natural endowments.

As for her upbringing, it always infuriated her when her colleagues said, "Oh, well, Ruth has always had money." Her parents were, as she maintained, definitely not rich; her father was a practicing physician and surgeon and, like all physicians and surgeons with an ideal of human service, did a great part of his work without pay. They were nevertheless just as unquestionably what is known as "well off." They consorted with the "best people" both in Indianapolis, where they lived in an outlying section of the city by no means inhabited by peasants, and in Hyannisport, where their neighbors ranged from affluent to wealthy. Their own summer house was anything but pretentious, but it included a studio with a grand piano for Mrs. Page on the second floor and bedrooms for the children on the third. In Indianapolis they had the necessary contingent of household servants, so that Mrs. Page could spend considerable time not only at her piano but also in public cultural "good works"—as well as in concentrating on her daughter.

Her attitude toward Ruth was not one of maudlin pampering, which was altogether contrary to her nature; nor did it have the voguish psuedo-psychological overtones of seeking vicarious satisfaction. She had, indeed, given up the single-minded drive necessary for a performing career quite deliberately for the sake of her home and family, but there was nothing vicarious about her pursuit of music in a truly professional sense to the end of her days. Ruth was, however, her ewe lamb; she played for her, sewed for her and was generally at her beck and call. But it is possible to believe that this was in a very large measure because she recognized and embraced the evidence of an artistic urgency as deeply motivated as her own and found a kind of enriching fellowship in serving it.

So much for upbringing; as for natural endowments, Mother Nature was no less cooperative than Mother Page. She had given Ruth beauty, charm, intelligence and talent, certainly sufficient to make nonsense of the old story of young artists having to live in garrets, selling their virtue to lecherous producers, walking in and out of agents' offices with the proverbial don't-call-us-we'll-call-you ringing in their ears. Never in her life was she turned down for a job as a dancer; actually, she was quite pick-and-choosey about the jobs she consented to take. She supported herself from the start, and when she got to the point of going to bed with people, it was strictly from personal and not professional choice. What saved her from being obnoxious with all this was that she accepted the situation with complete naivety and, like poor little Oliver Twist at the other end of the scale of spoiledness, kept asking for more, and with just as compuslive a need as Oliver's.

When she boarded the train with that hundred dollars in her purse, it was probably with genuine trepidation, for she had never before had to look out for herself, but in her bones and marrow, she knew that she would never starve.

On the train with her was Mary Brandon, a niece of Booth Tarkington's, who was on a similar journey into independence, with the theatre as her particular field of preoccupation. Together they rented a tiny room in an apartment in the building where the Bolms lived and had their studio, at 15 East 59th Street. It was in a partly professional rather than a purely residential neighborhood, but one that had no overtones whatever of starving artists' garrets. Fifty paces from the front door was Fifth Avenue, the entrance to Central Park and the Grand Army Plaza with the St. Gaudens *General Sherman* on his gallant steed, complete with guardian angel bearing laurel branch. Nevertheless, the room was sufficiently ill-equipped and uncomfortable to qualify for the garret designation and all the more so since they had to share with the landlandy and her daughter an equally tiny bathroom that did double duty as a kitchen.

Mary's parents had been divorced and were now living with their respective new spouses in New York apartments, a situation that provided two places for the girls to scrounge dinners in their anticipated struggles with poverty. Mary passes out of the story at this point. She got a job in the theatre almost at once and shortly afterward became the wife of Robert E. Sherwood, who was on the verge of becoming one of the most successful playwrights of the era.

Ruth also got along pretty well, thank you. Aside from the three tours with the Ballet Intime, the local appearances of Natasha Stepanova and other Bolm enterprises, she was the subject of a ballerina statuette by a rising young sculptor, Gleb Derujinsky, and her foot was photographed for advertising purposes by a shoe manufacturer who pronounced it in print the most beautiful foot in the world. With Chester Hale, a fellow student of Cecchetti's who had toured America with the Diaghileff ballet, she danced in one of the annual Actors' Equity benefit performances. After the successful actors' strike in 1919 this had become an event of enormous prestige, and since she was born photogenic, she was always the one to emerge with her picture in the papers.

She was equally successful before the movie camera and in 1922 appeared with Bolm in the first dance film to be synchronized with recorded music—in this case the *Danse Macabre* of Saint-Saëns. It was a tale of plague-ridden medieval Spain with two lovers in the grip of Death, personified by Olin Howland. (Bolm had sent her to study Spanish dancing with Aurora Ariazza, who was living in New York; unlike many ballet masters he was always sending her to study with somebody else.) The director was Dudley Murphy, the lighting was by the distinguished photographer Francis Bruguiere and the scenery and costumes were by Nat Eastman. It was shown at the Rialto Theatre in New York in March (along with a German Paramount feature called *The Mysteries of India,* and in an unsigned review in the *New York Times* the next day the critic wrote: "Miss Page in close-ups, vivified the story with several striking expressions. Has she done anything else on the screen? Unless her work in 'Danse Macabre' is misleading, she could do something worth seeing in a dramatic role as well as a dancing one. And the Metropolitan doesn't keep her busy all the time." So far, indeed, the Metropolitan had not had the pleasure of keeping her busy at all.

Bolm enterprises were themselves not to keep her busy in New York much longer, either, for Bolm had been invited at last to take charge of the ballet of the opera company in Chicago and packed up his family and his chattels and bade farewell to New York. Cleofante Campanini, the presiding genius of the quite wonderful old Chicago Opera Company, had died a year before, and for one hilarious year Mary Garden had taken over in his place. What she came up with, not only in Chicago but also on tour, including New York, was one of the most exciting and expensive seasons in opera history. ("If it cost a million dollars," she said when she resigned perforce, "I'm sure it was worth it.") When the collapse came, which was immediately, Samuel Insull, a financial wizard with a prima donna of his own as a protégée, had picked up the pieces and put them together in the form of a company called the Chicago Civic Opera. Almost certainly through the influence of John Alden Carpenter, Bolm was appointed ballet master.

That Ruth was also to abandon New York, the center of her universe, for that same Chicago in that same Mid-America she had so happily left behind forever, she had as yet no inkling and, even if she had, would never have believed it.

New York was not altogether a matter of work; she was too much of a social animal not to have acquired a horde of congenial friends and quite a few "beaux," as she called them. Some of them derived from the well-to-do eastern families who had summer homes at Hyannisport; others she had met in the normal course of both social and professional life in New York; and there were in addition all the wartime Russian emigrés who moved in the orbit of the Bolms.

From this last category came what was certainly the most serious of her suitors; this was Sviatoslav Roerich, whose father was Nicholas Roerich, the painter. At this time and for a number of years afterward there was a small museum bearing the latter's name and devoted exclusively to his paintings on the main floor of a tall building on Riverside Drive, sponsored by a somewhat mystical-universalist-cultural-artistic organization called The Master Institute of United Arts. The paintings were large, dark, portentous, containing cryptic messages and prehistoric allusions, all of them strongly Lamaist in substance. Indeed, he had made more than one pilgrimage to Tibet and the mountain fastnesses of China and India. What more natural then that it should have been he who was chosen to design the settings and costumes for Michel Fokine's Polovetsian dances from *Prince Igor* in 1909? The Polovetsi were a Slavic people so ancient and obscure of origin that not even such a fanatic in matters of authenticity as Fokine could find anything in libraries or museums to guide him in creating his choreography. Similarly, who could have been more logically chosen than Roerich four years later to design the production of the Stravinsky-Nijinsky *Sacre du Printemps,* which was a primordial mystic ritual with even less of an authentic background?

Ruth found "Svetia" a fascinating companion; what drew her to him was mainly his heritage of exoticism, which was in such sharp contrast to the chronic endoticism, as it might be termed with etymological consistency, that characterized Mid-America. He himself was soon to undertake a long tour into the mystic East, and he wrote to her en route, from such eminently worldly stopovers as Vichy and Monte Carlo, to caution her in guru fashion against her tendency toward frivolousness and to urge her to get down to the serious business of making something of herself.

Much as she liked him, she had no intention whatever of marrying him, which, when she finally had to tell him so, came as a shock. When she told him further that she was marrying somebody called Tom Fisher, he pronounced the appallingly commonplace name in cavernous tones of disbelief, against the unspoken rolling syllables of Sviatoslav Nikolaevitch Roerich.

At the opposite end of the spectrum from Svetia was John Crane, a Harvard man destined for an international diplomatic career. They had much in common and thoroughly enjoyed each other's company. Though she was not really in love with him, she might well have married him if things had fallen out a bit differently. But there appeared on the scene a handsome young lawyer from the Southwest called Tex, who had come to New York to work his way up from the bottom of an important Wall Street law firm. Besides his strong physical appeal, he had all the social graces of the South, including a talent for house-partying, yachting, country clubbing. He was romantically irresistible to her and became her first lover in fact as well as fancy. Consistent with her mores, this naturally meant that they would be married, and she went so far as to accept an engagement ring from him. But since he had not yet "spoken" to her father, she did not wear it, and eventually she returned it to him, thus, as Ruth puts it today, freeing him to make "a far better marriage to a far more brilliant woman."

As an ironic dénouement for John Crane, it was through him that she met his friend and Harvard classmate Tom Fisher, who superseded both him and Tex. But his attachment for her was to endure with overtones of tenderness throughout their lives and marriages.

CAPITULATION TO "SHOW BIZ"—AND VICE VERSA

All this, of course, was merely the background to her perpetual concern with getting ahead with her dancing. And there was the incidental matter of earning a living, which involved making the rounds of producers' offices, going to auditions, following leads from professional colleagues. It may have been from Chester Hale, then dancing in Irving Berlin's first *Music Box Revue,* that she learned that a second *Music Box Revue* was already being planned. At any rate, when the time came, she went to the audition and got the job. But when she found out when rehearsals were to begin, she turned it down without a second thought, since she was going to Europe to study and would not be back in time. She looked down her nose at "show business" as quite incompatible with the artistic goals she had in mind. When most unexpectedly she did get back in time, she was flattered to discover that they had held the job for her.

Just why they took the long chance on her is nowhere recorded, but Hassard Short, the director of the production, had certainly seen her dance (in the Equity benefit, if nowhere else, but probably in other places too, since he saw everything that was going on) and had already formed a high opinion of both her dancing and her theatrical personality. These were opinions that lasted throughout his lifetime, and they were to work together more than once and become fast friends. Even after she had moved to Chicago to live, he assured her that if only she would move back again to the Broadway stomping ground he would use her in all his shows, which were a great many.

The second *Music Box Revue* proved to be as great a success as the first one. Two of Berlin's songs, "Lady of the Evening" (sung by John Steel) and "Crinoline Days" (sung by Grace LaRue), were to rank among his classics. The cast also included Clark and McCullough (in their first great Broadway success), Charlotte Greenwood, William Gaxton, the Fairbanks Twins, Olivette, Hal Sherman, the McCarthy Sisters, Amelia Allen, Robinson Newbold, the Rath Brothers, William Seabury (who also staged the "show-business" routines) and Stowitts of the Pavlova company, who had dropped his first name by now.

The two production numbers in which Ruth appeared, conceived by Hassard Short, consisted of a "white" ballet called *Under the Chandelier* (full of "toe hops," which always got a hand, of course, but which Ruth really liked only because they strengthened her *pointes*) and a kind of Chinoiserie called *Porcelain Maid,* danced in pseudo-Chinese costumes made of oilcloth by a new young designer named Gilbert Adrian (who was soon to drop his first name also and achieve fame in Hollywood simply as Adrian). The dancing was accompanied by two singers dressed as porcelain dolls standing on teakwood stands. This was exoticism with a capital X, and Ruth was in her element. Even with all the competition from big names and comedians she was well reviewed by the critics, though theatrical critics are notoriously indifferent to dancing. *Under the Chandelier,* however, received no mention at all in the reviews, for the simple reason that it was not in the show when it opened. After the dress rehearsal Berlin and his business partner, Sam Harris, decided that they wanted nothing "classic" and threw it out. This was a decision definitely not shared by their director. Gathering his wits together, Short offered the number as it stood to the annual Equity benefit, which was in the immediate offing, and its success there was so complete that it was put back into the show at once.

"Most of the other principals danced, too," Ruth reminisces. "Charlotte Greenwood kicked higher than anyone else, and Bobbie Clark's pantomime would have rivaled the commedia dell'arte. Olivette did acrobatic comedy to 'I want to Go Upon a Dancing Honeymoon,' and Amelia Allen tied herself up in impossible knots to the music of 'Song of India' (jazzed). The Rath Brothers, two beautiful figures in white tights, did acrobatic adagio in statuesque poses reminiscent of Michelangelo; William Seabury hoofed; and there was a 'Hell' finale that out-shimmied Gilda Gray. Hal Sherman stopped the show every night in an eccentric dance, while we classicists looked on with our noses up in our own world of cloudy tutus, without realizing what a debt some of us now owe choreographically to this truly American dancer."

The show ran for 273 performances in New York, closing in late May, and after a summer break the company was reassembled (with a few cast changes) in early September for a second season on tour. The Chicago engagement opened at the Colonial Theatre in October, and immediately afterward Ruth sent home clippings and the like to Indianapolis and told about the hotel she and two other girls had moved into, way out on Lake Shore Drive. It was the Drake. Her letters were frequent and frank, though perhaps not completely so, for there are some things older generations are not capable of understanding.

She may have left Indianapolis forever, officially, but she still maintained diplomatic relations with it and a great inertia of both affection and dependence. If she was no longer tied to her mother's apron strings, at least she kept a tag end of one of them in reach, just in case. Two things, indeed, she sent home regularly; one of them was a substantial part of her salary for her family to "invest" for her, since she "didn't understand much about it"; the other was her laundry when she was on tour, for this was before the drip-dry days.

Frequently her letters got into more intimate matters, as in the following instance, in which she is obviously following up something from previous letters:

> Don't worry about my getting married. Tex and Bill and John all say I would go on dancing. Bill is out of the question. I only like him as a friend, so it's probably between Tex and John. Tex doesn't know a thing about dancing but he's sympathetic. Of course I don't think either of them would like me to be in a revue and I must say I don't blame them, but I don't know what else there is to do. I can't decide which one I like best. I like John for some things and Tex for others, so there you are. I like my dancing better than either of them.

She was dancing with a different partner now, for Stowitts had gone off to Paris, but her success was still unqualified. In a little publication called "This Week in Chicago," the reviewer, writing of "the remarkable Ruth Page," said: "This Page gal stampeded me. She is exquisite. And what is more, she dares to be feminine. For a while our best dancers were like adolescent boys rather than lovely women. Ruth has the figure of a woman, and acts like a woman, which is a great relief." After more about the show, *Under the Chandelier* is considered: "The beautiful Page again erases all former dancers from my memory. She is too lovely to be true." Curiously enough, all this was written under the by-line of "Fleurette." Just who—or rather what—was Fleurette?

Bolm was by now well established in Chicago, and she was happy to resume her classes with him during the run of the show. Already in the planning stage was an organization, again under the aegis of John Alden Carpenter, to be called Chicago Allied Arts, Inc., which was to begin operations in 1924 with Bolm as artistic director and choreographer, Eric DeLamarter as musical director and Nicolas Remisoff as designer. Ruth was invited by them to return to Chicago when her tour was over to be première danseuse. By one of those apparently fatalistic coincidences, the executive secretary of the organization was Thomas Hart Fisher. Though he had never been actively associated with the arts, he was interested in them, and Carpenter wanted a non-artist in that capacity. At this point Ruth had never heard of him.

The show closed its Chicago engagement the Saturday before Christmas, and she wrote to her mother, chiefly about plans for a New Year's Eve party at their home, when they would be playing in Indianapolis on their return tour eastward. Then came a paragraph on another topic:

> I had tea yesterday with a Mr. Fisher, a most attractive friend of John Crane's. Mr. Crane was in town yesterday and asked me to lunch but I didn't get the invitation till too late. I was sorry to miss him. I'm so sorry I didn't meet Mr. Fisher sooner. I seem to take to lawyers lately.

Mr. Fisher had undoubtedly expected to be part of Mr. Crane's luncheon party and may even have been its particular motivation. When it failed to materialize, because of the late delivery of the invitation, John, rejected but still adoring, had nobly given Tom the letter of introduction, since he himself was unable to remain in town any longer. After the matinee the two of them accordingly had gone to the Blackstone Hotel for tea. It was a case of reciprocal double-barreled sweeping-off-the-feet.

As her tour worked its way back east, Tom suddenly had to make an unconscionable number of business trips out of his father's law office, where he was employed, to New York, Boston and way stations, and each time he wrote a note from the train on the way back. In one of them he suggested that this was the hard way to do it, and maybe it would be a good idea if they thought about getting married. Though Ruth's reply is not on record, from her behavior it is fair to assume that she was unwilling to commit herself. Much as she was in love with him, it was always her career that came first, and it would be far preferable to have her cake and eat it.

Of course the family knew nothing about all the transcontinental trysting. As far as they knew, Tex was the chosen suitor, and all that remained to be done was to go through the formal procedures.

On March 11 Ruth wrote one of her characteristically chatty letters to her mother from Boston, where the show was playing. In it she reported that she had "bought a very pretty nightgown at a sale the other day," and as it was slightly soiled, she was sending it along with her laundry to be washed.

> It cost only $14. I think it is marvelous value. You can save it for the trousseau, too. Now don't think I am going to be married right away, because I haven't the vaguest idea when I will be married but it is more sensible to get things when you see them than just to go out and get them all at once, and if I marry a poor man, I believe in getting a nice trousseau. However, nothing is decided, so don't get excited. . . . I would sort of like to go to Europe either very early in the summer or else very late. I want to go to Spain and Italy and also London to study.

On April 26 another letter, this time from New York, with the tour finally at an end:

> I don't think I'll get married. Tex bores me a little at times and it's so much nicer just to dance. Tex is getting to be quite a connoisseur of dancing. . . . I don't want Tex to write to Father till I feel more sure. It is foolish to get married when I feel so indefinite.

In May she was in Indianapolis for a visit, and on the day of the Kentucky Derby in Louisville, Tom dropped in on his way back from there to Chicago. Some thirty years later he was to write to her during one of his many periods in Texas: "Today is Louisville Derby Day, which I always remember affectionately because I used a trip there to pay a call on you and your father and mother for the first time." The impression had been favorable all around, but it would have been crude and brash to "ask for her hand" at first meeting.

She did not get to Europe—to Spain and Italy and London—either early or late that summer, but it was still fixed on her agenda for the first possible opportunity. In the autumn she was back in Chicago to rehearse with Bolm for the first program of the Allied Arts, which was scheduled for the Eighth Street Theatre in late November. Naturally Tom occupied most of her non-rehearsing life.

As première danseuse she may have been slightly displeased to learn that this first program was to have as its guest star none other than Tamara Karsavina, who had not been able to come to America with the Diaghileff company because she was pregnant and was now in this country on her first (and only, as it turned out) concert tour, with Pierre Vladimiroff as her partner. It was Bolm, however, instead of Vladimiroff, who would dance with her on this program, in works they had danced together in their Russian days. In keeping with the overall purpose of the Allied Arts there would also be musical works and musical soloists, and the ballet sections would include both new and old works created by Bolm himself. For this initial program he had created two new pieces, one called *The Elopement*, to music of Mozart, and the other, *Foyer de la Danse*, after the Degas painting, to music by Chabrier. This was scarcely the most auspicious way to introduce the new resident première danseuse of a new company, who was accustomed herself to being Bolm's partner.

Late in November Ruth wrote to her mother:

> I haven't done anything of particular interest lately. Tom is away for a couple of days, so I have a little more time, which helps.

Then she got around to the real issue of the moment. She had seen the printed announcements of the forthcoming production, which were being mailed out to a list of patrons and the presumably interested public. Her name was listed virtually among the also-rans, as it appeared to her, and she had complained indignantly to the management.

> My recognition and standing as an artist are worth fighting for, but I get so sick of it. I'd like to dance for a while and not worry about all those stupid things. Of course I wouldn't expect to be billed the same as Karsavina, but I do think they should have put my name alone and said a little something about me. It really made me awfully mad and I told them so. If course I won't have [the announcements] sent to any of my friends. However, I was extremely lucky to get the star part in the Degas. That will be something anyway. [She adored the "little pink costume with the tiny blue forget-me-nots!"]

> I don't think I will stay after this first series because Maria Montero and Amata Grassi and Herbert Lee are coming out for the second series and the Spanish ballet will be featured. I ought to make some money anyway. I'll just have to go to New York and start going around to managers. My, how I hate that!

> Tom hasn't seen the announcement yet, but he doesn't seem to be at all interested in the advertising. He seems very anxious to marry me, and maybe it wouldn't be such a bad idea, although I don't think he makes any more money than Tex, if as much. However, I hope, I hope I can make more money soon.

The Allied Arts activities could never constitute a major part of anyone's performing career, since they consisted of only three "series" a year of three performances each, but they continued to have brilliant guest stars, including Vera Mirova, who in spite of her Russian name specialized in dances of the

East, and Ronny Johansson, the Swedish dancer, who was the first of the European modern dancers to make an American tour.

They continued also to be ahead of their time in Chicago and were generally pronounced "too arty." At the Goodman Theatre at a performance of Henry Eichheim's *The Rivals*, dealing with warriors in ancient Chinese style, somebody in the audience was overheard to remark, "This seems to be a collection of stamps." A nice mot but scarcely responsive; Chicago's wit was clearly sharper than its palate. The truth was, however, that though Bolm himself produced some unconventional things, sponsored some unusual artists and used a great deal of modern music, he was far from being avant-garde; if he was even "modern," it was in the well-established "standard" sense of Fokine with the Imperial Ballet rather than in the radical kick-over-the-traces style of the contemporary Diaghileff. That difference was to be made very pointed within another two or three years, as we shall see.

Meanwhile, Ruth did not go to New York to look for a job at the end of the Allied Arts' first series but stayed through the whole three years of its existence, because she had decided to marry the executive secretary of the organization.

Tom and Texas

The wedding took place on Sunday, February 8, 1925, at Rosewell. The ceremony was performed by the Very Reverend Joseph M. Francis, the aging Episcopal Bishop of Indianapolis. As far as religious affiliations were concerned, Ruth, possibly because of her father's Scotch-Irish heritage, had gone to a Presbyterian Sunday School (where she won a medal for attendance), and her mother was a Unitarian.

Be that as it may, Tom now steps conspicuously into the forefront of the story. His father was a prominent attorney in Chicago who had helped Jane Addams and Ellen Gates Starr get Hull House started in 1889 and had been appointed to succeed Richard A. Ballinger as Secretary of the Interior, after the Ballinger-Pinchot uproar in the middle of the Taft administration. Mrs. Fisher was a Boston Brahmin who ran the household with unequivocal authority.

Tom was one of eight children, of whom one brother was his twin. He was born in September 1896 in a section of the village of Winnetka then known as Lakeside but now called Hubbard Woods, north of Chicago on Lake Michigan. He was educated at the local grade school, the Chicago Latin School and for two years at the Friends' School in Washington when his family moved there in 1911. In 1915 he entered Harvard College, and after graduating three years later, he enlisted in the Navy. He had not yet finished his training as a naval flyer at the Massachusetts Institute of Technology when the war ended, whereupon he entered Harvard Law School and graduated in 1921. His Harvard activities included rowing on the varsity crew (participating twice in the Royal Henley Regatta) and, surprisingly enough, enrollment in George Pierce Baker's famous "47 Workshop" in playwriting. He never wrote any plays and had no intention of going into the theatre, but there is no doubt that he put his training to specific use in the courtroom as a trial lawyer.

It would be ironic, if it were not so elementally logical, that in spite of an animadversion to everything Mid-American Ruth rejected all her eastern and "far eastern" suitors and accepted one who, under his rich veneer of sophisticated cosmopolitanism, was even more basically Mid-American than she. This very regional kinship was in all likelihood what gave him the final advantage over far wealthier and far handsomer men than he. Actually he was neither wealthy nor handsome at all, though he was always inexplicably attractive to women. But beyond that, he and Ruth spoke the same language, were automatically companionable and "belonged" together, as it were.

What she wanted, however, and perhaps confidently expected was to take this congeniality out of the environment she found so stultifying and into fresher air. For the first ten years of their marriage she begged him to move to New York; at one time he had an excellent offer to join the law firm of Paul Cravath there, but he would have none of it. He had joined his father's firm as soon as he had won his law degree, and five years later had become a partner. When his father died in 1935, Tom opened an office of his own, and Ruth knew then that her last hope for "emigration" was gone. She has said that this was the only thing she never forgave him for.

For him the air was freer where he was. Deep inside him was a trace of cowboys-and-Indians; he had somehow inherited a feeling for the "lone prairie-e-e" situation where you could devise your own strategy and fight things out on your own terms. This was perhaps the very kernel of his character and his career. His breeding, his intellectual brilliance and his knowledge of the law translated this primitive "lonerism" into a pattern of procedure that Machiavelli himself might have admired.

One of his colleagues who had known him as an adversary in the court-room referred to him after his death as "a trial lawyer of the first magnitude [whose] work was both scholarly and carefully detailed. . . . Although," he continued, "he was a formidable and tenacious opponent, he practiced law with a charming sense of humor. He also had a deep interest in people. His cases were always very personal to him since he was fighting for the rights of his clients, many times against overwhelming odds."

This analysis is not to be questioned as far as it goes, but for complete accuracy it needs to be amended to exclude the implication of any pervasive gospel of humanism. His cases (and his out-of-court causes as well) were indeed personal to him in high degree; certainly he was fighting for the rights of his clients and was determined that they must win, but he was fighting also because he himself must win. Their rights were his weapons. Overwhelming odds were what he deliberately sought out, for the greater the odds, the greater the victory, and in a very high percentage of instances he won through sheer virtuosity. With a kind of David-Goliath obsession he looked for ever larger and more dangerous heads to aim at with his slingshot. For example, when the Ford Foundation made its epochal multimillion-dollar grants in the professional ballet field in 1963 and did not include Ruth (among others), he was all set to start sensational proceedings against them. Wiser counsels, however, prevailed, and Ruth was happily spared some gratuitous humiliation.

Inevitably there was a price to pay. By always hitting as high as he could reach he antagonized many sections of the influential public—bankers, judges, politicians, the press. Up to a point this only stimulated him further, for it provided a fresh challenge, but ultimately it was his undoing as far as his reputation was concerned. During the last few years of his life and even on his deathbed, where he was fighting to the end against a backlash from the most important case of his career, his public image was so blackened that to the man in the street he seemed an out-and-out crook.

That he actually was a crook would be hard to believe. For one thing, he was too smart to need to be; for another, he was so in love with the whole field of litigation that it would have been the height of frustration for him to win without exercising his technical mastery of the limitations of prescribed procedure. He was more than familiar with every byway and roadblock and just how far it was possible to make use of them to get off the highway and back without trespass. One of his great ambitions was to write a book on the need for a sweeping reform of the law, based of necessity on his having poked into every area of its manipulability. Far more than Ruth he was essentially a prima ballerina assoluta. In personal and normally extra-litigious territory, where his conduct was not restricted by an imposed discipline, where there was no opposing counsel to object and no judge to sustain objections, the only restraints he faced were those that he chose to impose on himself, and they were few.

Ruth has said that people either loved or detested him; what she did not add was that frequently they were the same people at different times. For his part, much as he loved "people," his relations with "individuals" were highly variable; though he was habitually generous with friends, he sometimes dunned them, completely without malice, for sums he had lent them cordially in times of emergency; he spent dollars to collect pennies of suspected imbalance from local booking agents of Ruth's touring company, whom he had in a sense "two-timed" himself by playing them against each other in matters of overlapping territory. On occasion he put his ingenious mind to the fabrication of hilariously elaborate fictions—exceeded in intricacy only by the late Rube Goldberg's mechanical fantasies—which he circulated where they could be best calculated to plant suspicion about the motives of the most innocent and unsuspecting "villains," themselves scarcely even aware of his existence. He was a master of extrapolation, constantly flexing his muscles in what amounted to a form of Yankee intellectual "machismo."

With all this, however, he remained a fascinating man to be with, socially gracious, well read, knowledgeable, witty, endlessly entertaining with his devious tales. His duality was neatly pinpointed by Paul DuPont in accepting an invitation to visit him and Ruth at their Hubbard Woods home. Paul, high-strung and vulnerable, had been a dancer in the Allied Arts productions, had since become a talented stage designer and costumer, and in all these capacities had worked with Ruth. It was an old, if frequently contentious, "family" friendship, and at this moment he had only partially recovered from a wrathful protest (not altogether without justification, be it said) against Tom's cavalier treatment of him. In his not exactly unctuous note of acceptance he wrote: ". . . I don't mean that it won't be nice to be with you. On the contrary . . . I happen to like you, despite I think you are sometimes too shrewd for your own good, high-handed and a few other unsavory things . . . but yet, you are the best raconteur I know and a real charmer when you are so disposed . . . together you and Ruth are wonderful hosts . . . so I look forward to seeing you." This was the very essence of Tom's built-in automatic method of balancing his behavioral budget.

There can be no doubt that his shenanigans were frequently harmful to Ruth. In one or two well-documented instances they actually cut her off from the very channels she wanted to establish. But it would be idle to speculate on what direction her career might have taken or how much more or less she might have accomplished without him. The particular career she did make and the freedom she enjoyed in the making of it could not have been achieved but for his prodigious labors in her behalf. To be sure, she had already started a successful career before she met him and at the time of their marriage was earning more money than he was, but no professional concert or theatrical manager could have approximated his offices.

Hundreds of letters in the files, written by him and his staff, make it incredible that he could have been engaged in a brilliant career of his own at the same time. There were what might be called upper-level dealings, in both Europe and America, about performing rights to music and librettos and matters of royalties, some of which took months of litigation and went to the highest courts of the countries involved; about the commissioning of composers, scenic designers and builders, costume designers and makers; with theatres and opera houses in London, Paris, Monte Carlo; with ballet companies other than her own, both here and abroad, for the presentation of her works; about the engagement of the necessary guest stars, both European and American, as well as the regular members of her company, and who was to be starred over whom; with little local concert managers and such large national ones as Columbia Artists Management about contracts and the inevitable "next season's" repertory, stars and financing.

There were complicated and persistent dealings with stagehands' and musicians' unions about not only contracts but also local provisions as to how many unneeded stagehands and baggage unloaders and the like were demanded in each town; about the buying or leasing of buses for the company, trucks for the scenery and lights, cars for the traveling stage crew, etc.

On still another level there were arrangements (often difficult) with local managers for payments to be made in cash to Ruth at the close of a performance so that the company could depart for the next town before the banks were open in the morning; requests for hotel reservations for company and crew (and especially for Ruth with her midnight soaking requirements), made in identical copies and sent to five or six hotels in each community to insure that at least one of them would come through in time for the rest to be canceled; the printing and distribution of posters with the local sponsors' names on them; emergency personnel replacements for managerial or crew dropouts or for dancers who were out with injuries or suddenly found to be pregnant.

With few exceptions all the parties to these arrangements were technical specialists as well organized in their own fields as Tom was in his. Small wonder that there were frequent agitations and battles royal. Many of them occurred outside Ruth's area of awareness, for she was absorbed in the artistic problems of creating, performing and producing, and to be able to turn everything else over to Tom and forget it was worth whatever the price might be. In these other areas, indeed, she was inclined to be the victim of an overwhelming disinclination. Though she could come through nobly in a crisis, it was much as if Tom were suddenly called on to perform *petits tours en manège.*

CAUSE CELEBRE

Besides these labors Tom was involved with others even more prodigious, and in 1928 the Fisher household became a *ménage à trois.* What Tom brought into it at that time was not a person but certainly a living presence and a demanding one for both of them for forty-one of the forty-four years of their life together. Its name, or rather its sobriquet, was the King Ranch Case, and it makes Charles Dickens's record-holding Chancery case of *Jarndyce* v. *Jarndyce* in *Bleak House* seem like a five-o'clock tea party. The second of

Tom's literary ambitions was to write the history of this case, and since he did not live to do so (the brilliant and absorbing brief he wrote for the trial is as near as he came to it), it is doubtful if the lay mind will ever be able to fathom the complicated and incredible tale. However, if the thumbnail synopsis that follows suggests a forty-one-year-long television soap-horse-opera written by Horatio Alger, superstarring Batman and introducing the pixilated ladies from *Mr. Smith Goes to Washington*, Zane Grey, Torquemada, *The Outcasts of Poker Flat*, Rasputin and Teapot Dome, that will probably be near enough.

In 1928, then, Alice Atwood, aged forty-eight, and her brother Edwin, four years younger, came into the law office of Fisher, Boyden, Bell, Boyd and Marshall, of which Tom had been a partner for the past two years. They had a potential interest in the estate of their grandmother, whose husband, Capt. Richard B. King, had put together a vast ranch consisting of nearly a million acres sprawling over seven counties in Texas along the Gulf Coast and the Mexican border. At the death of Mrs. King at an advanced age her estate was put into the hands of trustees appointed by the County Court of Kleberg County, Texas, who were to partition it among the heirs at the end of a ten-year period.

There were two other Atwoods also among the heirs; one was a married sister, Elizabeth, who remains a distant figure throughout the story, and the other was a brother, Richard, who was to spend most of his last years in a "convalescent home" as a mental case, or, according to the legal designation, "distracted." Distraction, indeed, may well have been latent in the blood. As for Edwin, he was something of an attorney, though his career remains vague in the record. It was Alice who was the dominating personality, unpredictable but with a mind of her own.

She and Edwin had come to the office on this occasion because the Texas situation had been disturbing them more and more through the three years since their grandmother's death, and they had begun to suspect that the trustees were either vacuous or venal. As far back as 1920 they had read in the newspapers of the discovery of gas somewhere in the area and had continued to read of similar developments. What they wanted to do first, then, was to demand from the trustees an accounting of their stewardship. Though they were without any substantial financial resources, they thought that through scrimping they might pay the costs of such a suit. But beyond that, they felt sure there would be more legal activity involved in the securing and the handling of their inheritance, and all they could offer an attorney by way of compensation was some sort of contingency arrangement by which he would share in whatever he won, but if he did not win, he would get no fee at all. Their present attorney was an old friend, but they doubted the extent of his aggressiveness and consequently had now come to Fisher, Boyden, Bell,

Boyd and Marshall as one of the most distinguished firms in Chicago. What they could not possibly have known was that the juniorest partner in that firm was an avatar of Jack the Giant Killer and that no matter what the situation might look like to them at the moment, they were to all intents and purposes already "in business."

But Tom was not one to commit himself on mere derring-do; he demanded first enough time to study the whole situation on the spot in Texas, including not only the contingency proposition but also the legal aspects of the preliminary accounting action. It took him five years to gather the necessary material for the latter before filing suit, with Edwin Atwood, according to his own statement, nipping at his heels the while. What he studied was, in general, the land within the approximately 350,000-acre portion out of which the Atwoods' share would eventually be partitioned, and specifically, as he put it, "to determine its physical condition for cattle and land operations, as well as the minerals which might be under the surface, and very particularly its political location." This was important because the Kleberg family (first cousins of the Atwoods) were definitely a political power in the county that bore their name.

According to Tom's description of the land some years later, it was "desert covered with cactus, which carried one cow to fifteen acres and which had no known mineral value, and therefore was worth much less than the King Estate debt" on it, amounting to some $3,000,000. The ranch had been operated at a loss for twenty years before Mrs. King's death. He also reported that the government, after five years' investigation, in making a tax settlement with him had valued the entire inheritance as worthless in both 1930 and 1937. As for the contingency business, it seemed likely that the attorney would receive little compensation, if any, if the $3,000,000 debt should be foreclosed or the trustees, in their partitioning of the property, should somehow foist off on the Atwoods inferior land. On the other hand, if the risks were great, the stakes seemed high.

In 1930, before Tom had taken any legal action, the Atwoods received, through their old attorney, an offer of approximately $200,000 each for their share of the land, whatever it might turn out to be, and he had recommended that the offer be accepted. The advice seems not unreasonable, for the Atwoods were a pair of innocents who would never be able to develop such land (or indeed any other land) themselves. They rejected the offer, however, for their new attorney had done a marvelous job of homework on the subject, in addition to a great deal of away-from-home work on the land itself, and now was ready to come forth with a specific plan for a contingency arrangement such as they had suggested earlier.

On October 1, 1930, it was signed by all parties concerned and became known as the "1930 conveyance." It involved, first of all, "an action at law or in chancery" against the trustees, to be followed by the setting up of a joint-venture development and operation of the property as a ranch by the Atwoods and Tom's law firm. This specific "action at law or in chancery" was filed in 1933 and ended fourteen years later in the Supreme Court of the United States with a victory for Tom, which he had earned not only by his sheer legal talent but also by his ingenuity, persistence and hard labor. It was the longest private litigation up to that time in the history of the United States courts.

Meanwhile a second legal action was undertaken in 1937 to deal with new legal questions that had arisen out of the unacceptable way in which the trustees had partitioned the land at the expiration of the ten-year trust in 1935. This action also went to the Supreme Court, where, as a hopeful omen of final success, Tom was victorious eight years later in 1945.

During this passage of time many things had changed. Tom had withdrawn from the firm of Fisher, Boyden, Ball, Boyd and Marshall after his father's death in 1935 and had set up for himself. The joint-venture project accordingly now involved not the original set of joint venturers but Tom and Ruth with the two Atwoods and ultimately the conveyance by the Atwoods to the Fishers of "an undivided interest in certain lands, minerals, cattle and ranching equipment" on the basis of 55 percent to the Atwoods and 45 percent to the Fishers.

In the meantime, also, Alice had been appointed by the court as Conservatrix of the estate of Richard Atwood, Distracted, and had put his legal affairs into Tom's hands as attorney. In November 1945, after his first major Supreme Court victory, Tom wrote two letters to Ruth on consecutive days from Houston (after twenty years they still corresponded virtually daily). In the first one he said: ". . . In court both yesterday and today—finally today I recovered $137,000 for Richard Atwood *in cash*, and this afternoon the judge entered the final decree giving him that amount. *So* at last his interests are finished forever in the Texas cases—now to close Edwin's and Alice's cases, and I will be through. . . . Well, the oil wells on the Atwood land keep coming in—the last was number 46. . . ."

In the second letter, as an amusing interlude, he wrote: ". . . The strangest thing yet happened about the ranch. An emissary from the President of the Republic of Nicaragua came to see me and bought me lunch. Wants (1) to hide away some of his wealth in the USA and (2) to have a place near the Border where he can go easily back and forth to Nicaragua! I refer to President Samosa (if I spell it rightly). [He didn't.] . . . There are now eleven wells being drilled *at once* in the Sauz Ranch (Atwood-Fisher). So things are looking up all right. . . ."

But looking up or not, there was still the final and all-conclusive court settlement to be made, and nobody was getting any money. The two

Atwoods were really on their uppers, and by 1937, when the second conveyance was drawn up, they had almost nothing to live on. So Tom made them a personal loan without interest to take care of their considerable legal costs and even their day-to-day living. In gratitude Alice added a codicil to her will. A year earlier she and Edwin had both made wills in Tom's office, bequeathing everything to each other. Now she added that if Edwin should predecease her, everything should go to Tom.

By 1947 the total amount of the loan came to over $125,000, of which $48,000 was in periodic sums for actual food and rent. The drain on Tom and Ruth was considerable. In 1947, however, with the second Supreme Court decision, the financial stringencies were over all around, even though the trustees did not make the final delivery of all the property until April 1950. Immediately upon the 1947 decision the four joint venturers mortgaged part of the land in order to establish some working funds and opened four-party joint accounts in several banks in Chicago and Texas, to which all of them had equal access. There were also sale-of-oil contracts amounting to a million and a half and checks from the trustees themselves amounting to several hundred thousand. Spirits were high all around.

In 1948, with everything over but the shouting, Alice made an altogether new will, this time in her own handwriting, excluding Edwin and leaving her entire estate to Tom, "out of grateful recognition of the many years during which he has been my friend, counselor and attorney." She took it to her bank in Chicago, where three bank employees witnessed it and certified to her being of "Sound Mind" (her own capitalization). Five days later Edwin followed her example; in his also handwritten will he expressed his "deep sense of gratitude and appreciation" for Tom's "services, counsel and advice" and full approval "of all his actions as my attorney and adviser to the date of this will." The will, he added, had been made "after consultation with my sister, Alice, and has her approval."

Things had been well prepared for the formal activation of the ambitious joint venture with Tom, of absolute necessity, as its manager. Chores of this sort were by nature far from onerous to him, as is indicated by other enterprises he had engaged in from time to time. They included a cattle ranch owned and operated by him and his twin brother in Florida, another ranch in Nebraska, wildcat drilling for oil, gold mining in Colorado and nickel mining on Yacobi Island off Alaska. The financial success of these projects seems to have been mixed, but his records of the development of the cattle industry were requested and welcomed by the director of the Western History Research of the University of Wyoming in Laramie, who considered that they were "not only valuable for the legal and economic history, but also, over the years, will give a pretty good insight into the mores, the culture, and sometimes the clashes of cultures between two regions of our country."

Though his salary as manager was something more than $40,000 a year, his duties were so enormous that Ruth was in despair that after having been settled against her will in Chicago, she would now have to go to Texas to live. Which, of course, she did not; but Tom almost literally did, until he quit the active management of the enterprise perforce as of the end of 1964. His resignation was necessitated by the development of his fatal illness, which the doctors had still not been able to diagnose as anything more than serious overwork. Assuredly he had long been overworking.

Then on December 2 Alice Atwood, no doubt traumatically hurt by Tom's "desertion" of her after nearly forty years of faith and devotion, turned, in complete privacy, once more to holographic will making. She now left her entire estate to a young Chicago policeman who had been kind to her over a long period (helping her across the street and the like) and whom she described as her "dearly beloved friend." This time when she deposited her will in the bank, it had already been witnessed by a second policeman who was a friend of the beneficiary's and another friend who operated a filling-station. The following August she was declared mentally incompetent at eighty-five, and put under the guardianship of her brother Edwin. Four months later, on December 11, she was dead.

When the will came up for probate the following spring, the fat was in the fire. The *Chicago Tribune* had revealed that the estate had been willed to the young policeman and that, according to "an informed source," it might amount to as much as ten million dollars. In May Ruth and Tom were summoned to testify in probate court on a citation to discover exactly what the assets of the estate were, since the attorney for the bank that was the executor of the estate said he had been unable to obtain this information from Tom thus far. The citation had instructed Tom, therefore, to bring with him the records of his transactions as manager of the four-party joint venture. This, however, he had not done, since he said that, having looked up the law, he believed that property in Texas was not within the jurisdiction of this court. But the magistrate ruled that the mere fact of his disagreeing on a point of law did not exempt him from answering the attorney's questions. His replies, however, when they came, were too indefinite to satisfy his questioner. The magistrate accordingly ordered him to produce a long list of documents demanded by the attorney and asked him how long it would take him to assemble them. Tom replied that it would probably take him ten or twelve weeks, since they were not in Chicago. He also said that he was very ill and on the verge of nervous exhaustion from overwork. Which, of course, nobody believed.

Earlier Ruth had testified that she knew absolutely nothing about Tom's dealings with the Atwoods. "I simply sign things my husband presents to me. I don't even read them. . . . I know it sounds awfully dumb. . . . I'm busy

with my ballet world. My husband's affairs are in a different world." If anybody in the courtroom had known Ruth, he would have known she was
telling the truth.

At any rate, the magistrate set a hearing for August 8 and told Tom to
have the records in court at that time. When on August 8 he did not produce
the records, he was held in contempt. Before the sentence could be imposed,
however, he had left Chicago, and his attorney reported that he was
undergoing medical treatment outside the court's jurisdiction. Which again
was certainly the truth. Again nobody believed it.

After the probate-court action the bank, as executor of Alice's estate,
together with Edwin filed suit as plaintiffs in the Chancery Division of the
County Court of Cook County, Illinois, against the two Fishers, alleging
breaches of trust, withholding of information from the Atwoods, undue
influence over Alice (including possibly the writing of her 1948 will in Tom's
favor, even though she misspelled his middle name as Heart instead of Hart),
fraud, professional malingering, manipulation of the joint bank accounts,
exorbitant salary charges and almost everything else except arson and mayhem
and demanding that both the 1930 and 1937 conveyances be canceled as
being against "public policy" and all money and property reconveyed
accordingly.

Early in the action it came to light that Edwin had bought out the
entire interest of the young policeman in Alice's estate for $100,000 in cash,
an action that, according to Tom, was clear proof that somebody had doubts
about the validity of the holograph will and the old lady's competence when
she wrote it.

Tom could not come into Illinois without being jailed under the
contempt sentence. He tried, however, to get into court simply as Ruth's
counsel, which he argued, would exempt him from arrest, but he was not
successful. If he had been allowed to participate in any way in the court
proceedings, it is dollars to doughnuts that he would have won the case by
the greatest virtuoso performance of his career. If he had been granted a jury
trial, which he was also refused, the result would have been even more certain,
for he was a great one for persuading people face to face.

The dreary business dragged on for nearly four years, during which his
health continued to worsen with increasing rapidity. The apartment building
where he and Ruth lived was kept under constant surveillance, and the
elevator operators were offered bribes (which all but one of them refused to
accept) to report his possible return. But he never went near the place.

Much of the time he lived at the Harvard Club in New York and worked
out of his New York office. Here Ruth frequently joined him. In summer
they continued to be together in Europe, especially at the little house in
St. Tropez, which he particularly liked. At other times he stayed in a motel

in Hammond, Indiana, where he could keep in close touch with the situation, and he met Ruth for clandestine dinners from time to time in the railroad station and other obscure restaurants. Sometimes he would make roundabout trips to his sister's home in Winnetka—to her considerable unease. At last, when his physical condition, which involved a gradual deterioration of the musculature, was no longer endurable, he managed to slip into a hospital in Chicago, where his ailment was finally diagnosed as amyotrophic lateral sclerosis, of which neither cause nor cure was known. It is the same ailment that had previously caused the death of Lew Gehrig.

When it was plain that he would not survive, a settlement of the agonizing suit was made out of court in April 1969, by which he and Ruth were required to return something like five million dollars (the *Tribune* reported it as "more than five" and the *Daily News* as "between three and five") and to reduce their share in the ranch project from 45 to 25 percent.

Even then the district attorney discovered that this settlement had not resolved the contempt issue, and accordingly placed two policemen outside Tom's door at the hospital, though he was quite unable to move.

When all is said and done, the layman, who is probably more pragmatic than the legal expert, may wonder what all the hullabaloo was about. Whatever technical rights and wrongs may have been argued (and there was much talk about "public policy"), everybody involved in the forty-year enterprise emerged with wealth without any other person's having been injured in the process. Could it be possible that at times "public policy" itself might warrant a little looking into?

Honeymoon of a Sort

When Ruth wrote her mother in 1924 that she rated her dancing above any of her "beaux," she really meant it, and she was including even those she had not yet met. Tom himself, much as she loved him, fell into that category as a matter of course, nor did he fall out of it when he ceased to be a beau and became a husband. His accession to a new status had not altered her direction at all; he had been expected as a matter of course simply to join her in following it. When they set out on their honeymoon, she was taking him as her ideal companion on the trip she had planned for herself a year or more ago—Spain and Italy and London. The London part was now dropped in favor of Monte Carlo, for Cecchetti no longer had a London studio but had rejoined the Diaghileff* forces at their Monte Carlo headquarters for what

---

*This, incidentally, is the spelling of his name that Ruth knew and that prevailed throughout the English-speaking world during his entire career and for some years after his death. The later trend in phonetic transliteration of Russian names, replacing the final *ff* with *v*,

proved to be his last season with them. And that, in turn, opened up a new urgency—to dance for Diaghileff. At this point, Tom was either too enraptured, too unprepared or too meek to resist.

They had time for only about a week in Paris enroute, where Ruth was concerned with how badly out of practice she was. She had wired Cecchetti from there and he was expecting her in class, but she did not want him to see her in such poor shape, and certainly she would not dance for Diaghileff "till I get well into practice again." They went to the Folies-Bergère, not to see the show but to have a talk with Stowitts, who was appearing in it. He recommended that she go to Leo Staats for classes, as his was "the best school in Paris"; but when she went, it was too late in the day and the class was over, so she rented a studio for an hour and worked by herself.

"I went to a costumer today," she wrote in what was to be almost a logbook to her mother, "to see if I could get a costume for the Degas [Bolm's *Foyer de la Danse*] made in a hurry, but they couldn't even start it till next week. However, they make the costumes for the Opéra and they make them all out of tulle and tarleton, so I thought I would just order one to see what it would be like, so she is making me one of pink tulle. I haven't the remotest idea what it will be like—I'm leaving it entirely to her. It is terribly expensive—750 francs—but I want to see how they make them over here—she is the best costumer in Paris."

It was Carnival Week along the Riviera, so she didn't have the faintest idea where they would stay in Monte Carlo, but they wound up at the Hotel d'Albion et du Littoral, and she wrote that "as far as I am concerned this is the most ideal spot on earth." As soon as they got themselves settled in, they went in search of Cecchetti. "He seemed in very good health and awfully glad to see me. He wanted to know all about you and sent his love. He is such a dear old thing. . . . I had a lesson with Cecchetti the next morning. The Diaghileff company has their class every morning at 9 and they are all obliged to come. They have a lovely big room to work in down in the basement of the opera house and as far as I can make out, they work all day. I have my lesson at 10:30 in a small room off the big room. Of course it isn't nice like the big room, but it's not bad. The first day I had to have my lesson with another outside pupil of Cecchetti who isn't very advanced, but it was all right for the first day. Now she has her lesson at 2, so 10:30 of course is a wonderful hour for me.

"I watched the Diaghileff class for a little while—they have a lot of wonderful new young dancers—really a lot of very talented ones. Ninette de Valois, that English girl who was in the Cecchetti class in London with me, is in the company. She has quite a few nice little parts and has only been in the company eighteen months. She is crazy about the work, but says she can't do another thing because they keep them working all the time. They were here for seven months last year. The Prince of Monaco supports the company although the girls all get paid very little. They have lovely dressing rooms and everything is awfully nice for them. They work in the opera and then give two ballet performances a week. Unfortunately their big season does not come until April, so they are giving none of their new ballets—only the old ones that I have seen [on previous trips to Europe].

". . . We went to the orchestra concert with Artur Rubinstein as soloist in the afternoon. It was a very delightful concert. . . . Dukelsky, that Russian boy who used to go around with Svetia and Margaret Roberts and me, was sitting right next to me, wasn't that a coincidence? Diaghileff is doing a big ballet of his in April—it is all rehearsed and finished. Massine came down from London to do it. Dukelsky said they had sixty-eight rehearsals, can you imagine! I think it must be very difficult. . . ."

The "big ballet" was *Zéphyre et Flore* to Boris Kochno's scenerio, with scenery and costumes by Georges Braque, the first of a number of ballets composed by Vladimir Dukelsky, who was also to write successful Broadway and Hollywood scores, such as *Cabin in the Sky* and *Goldwyn Follies*, under the name of Vernon Duke.

". . . An Italian boy named Celli is taking lessons with me every morning. He is the boy that took the part of the bull in the Infanta. He has been in Europe ever since and has been working all last summer in Turino with Cecchetti—he isn't bad. He said that Cecchetti was terribly disappointed that I didn't come last summer to study with him. It certainly is great to study with him again. I have so many faults and I really need him very badly. I haven't asked about the price of my lessons yet, but I hope they won't be very much because I've spent a good part of my $500. I'm sorry I ordered that ballet dress in Paris. . . ."

A few days later we find that she has been on a binge of dress buying, so the financial crisis cannot have been too acute. Or perhaps the binge did not fall within the scope of "my $500," a clarification of which never comes to light. She and Tom managed to enjoy diversions together from time to time, including a Chinese opera, a drive across the Italian border to see a performance of *Ciboulette*, with a few near-calamitous driving experiences to liven things up.

Then: "This afternoon we went to the Russian ballet. It was not in the regular theatre but a smaller, very intimate one. It seemed so funny seeing them in such a tiny little place—it was almost like the Ballet Intime [the Salle Ganne in the Casino, a chamber-music hall used by Diaghileff for

dance recitals and for experiments with the young dancers in roles danced
regularly by the older ones]. They gave Pulcinella, L'Après-midi d'un Faune,
Spectre de la Rose, and Contes de Fees (Tchaikovsky) [divertissements from
Diaghileff's sumptuous production years earlier of *The Sleeping Princess*, as he
called it]. I had seen all of them but the last although it was fun seeing the
old ones with new people.

"There is a new Irish boy named Doline [*sic*] who is *very* good. He
danced Spectre de la Rose with a girl named Nemchinova who is also
excellent, a lovely figure and a really beautiful dancer. The last ballet was
just a series of ballet divertissements and gave everybody something to do—
mostly classical—the girls all did very well—they certainly show their Cecchetti
training, although none of them seemed particularly inspired. . . .

"Afterwards Dukelsky took me around to meet Diaghileff—he was very
nice and said he would be very glad to see me dance and would come to see
my lesson some morning and then see my dances later. I told Cecchetti this
morning that I wanted to dance for him and he said yes that he wanted me to
but he would rather I would wait for a while yet and not think about my
dances at all yet, just try to get rid of some of my faults and get a little
stronger. He also said he wanted to help me with my dances and would
come some Sunday to do it. Isn't that sweet of him? He seems really
interested in me, although I certainly seem to have gotten into a lot of bad
habits and he says I need more strength in my legs, which of course I do.

"Diaghileff wanted to know how long I could stay here and of course I
couldn't tell him but I said we wanted to go to Spain for a while and he
immediately said that it would be much more valuable for me to stay here
and work with Cecchetti. I of course would prefer to do that but I am afraid
Tom will get bored—there isn't really much for him to do here. It isn't really
warm enough for swimming although he could play tennis and do things like
that if he had someone to do them with. I feel as though I never wanted to
leave here, I like it so much. . . . I couldn't be having a better time unless I
were dancing in Diaghileff's company. . . ."

Tom was probably not too bored as yet, and eventually he managed to
find "things like that" to do and people to do them with by rowing with a
Monegasque crew. Ruth was a bit more impatient than he, and since she was
afraid Diaghlieff might forget his specific arrangement to see her dance (they
had by this time made a definite appointment), she wrote him a note to
remind him, and enclosed some photographs. But all went as scheduled—or
approximately so.

"Things have been quite exciting here lately," she wrote to her mother
on March 14. "I danced for Diaghileff yesterday and it certainly was a job.
In the first place, there is only one pianist for the whole troupe and there is
only one place in all Monte Carlo where one can practice, so to get the pianist

and the room at the same time was really a stroke of genius. You absolutely never can tell when the place will be free and of course, being outsiders, we didn't like to impose on any of them. However, we finally secured the hall for two rehearsals. Cecchetti was sweet enough to come help me with my toe solo. Curiously enough, he made very few corrections and seemed very pleased with it. I did the Tchaikovsky solo, then the Bolm Chopin waltz with Chester [Hale, who was around again]. Cecchetti seemed to like them both a great deal.

"He certainly has been wonderful to me. I think I told you that he told Celli (the Italian boy who studies with Chester and me) that if I had stayed in London two years longer with him I would be Pavlova's only rival. Can you imagine that! One of the wardrobe women made me quite a nice little pink tarleton to dance in. [Whatever happened to the expensive Paris dress?] It was quite a job fixing up my wardrobe.

"Diaghileff is a very funny person. He was supposed to come yesterday to see me at 5:30. We were all ready to dance promptly and he didn't come and he didn't come and we got so tired waiting. Cecchetti and Mme. Cecchetti were nice enough to come over. Cecchetti reminded Diaghileff in the morning about it and so did Dukelsky. He finally arrived at 6:30—or later I think it was. I was quite tired from waiting around and it was so cold. However, I danced better than I expected to although not as well as when I danced for Cecchetti alone. I danced first the Tchaikovsky solo, then the waltz with Chester, then the group Chopin waltz, then the Brahms, the Martinique dance, and last the Siamese. He liked the classical dances the best although he thought the nigger [the "Martinique" she danced to a set of creole "Bayou Ballads" in the character of a little black boy] very interesting. I think he was really quite impressed because he said he wanted to talk to me and that he wanted to come see me again in class. They have never had an American girl in the company, and it seems that there is great jealousy between the different nationalities, and that Diaghileff always favors the Russians, which I suppose is natural. I am so awfully sorry that Diaghileff didn't arrive on time, because if he had I think I would have danced better. However, he couldn't have been nicer and asked me all kinds of questions. He said he wanted me very much to go on with Cecchetti.

"It seems Diaghileff has taken a sudden fancy to becoming *very* classical again. You should see the things they have been doing in the divertissements— more classical and old-fashioned even than Pavlova. They have one girl who is really a marvelous technician—Nemchinova—she is the biggest star they have now. She did 64 fouettés on her toe the other night. I've never seen anything like it. She has a lovely figure, but her face isn't so good. They haven't anybody who is as beautiful or as great an artist as Karsavina used to be. The corps de ballet are all excellent. There is one little English girl only

14 years old who makes quite a hit here. She dances very well, but she is the most hideous little thing you've really ever seen. That doesn't seem to make any difference over here as long as you dance well.

"Well, I'm glad I've danced for Diaghileff anyway—that was really a job. Chester doesn't think he will give me anything to do because I am an American—however, we'll see. Dukelsky said he was very much impressed. I think I have more charm and real talent than anybody he has now, but of course I haven't the training. They expect you to be so perfect here. . . . We couldn't have a class today because the Princess of Monaco came to watch the company class. They usually have it at 9, but on her account they postponed it till 11, so we missed our class. I can't bear to miss a day.

"Chester is a fine partner. I do hope we'll be able to get something to do while we are both here. Of course I would rather go with Diaghileff than anybody, but it does take so long to get anywhere with him—as he said yesterday, all his best stars start in the corps de ballet, and he said he thought I was probably very spoiled. . . .

"Tom and I haven't decided many definite plans as yet. We may go to Spain on Sunday for about a week, then up to Paris and London. Tom thinks I ought to have more lessons with Cecchetti, too, but I don't know whether we can arrange it or not. . . . If I stay over after Tom goes back, I wish you could come over. It would do you good and it isn't so very expensive living here in France [*sic*]. The lessons (almost private) with Cecchetti are only 500 francs a month. Think of the difference in American prices for dancing lessons! . . . You should see how the ballet works here. They are practically there from 9 in the morning till 12 at night. I think it is terrible, and almost no pay. The pianist who rehearses all day and plays for the performances at night only gets 1500 francs a night and only the very best dancers get that much. It is really awful. And they all seem to just love it and they are all so ambitious and work so hard. . . ."

It is no wonder that she hated to miss a class, because it consisted of only four people—Chester Hale, Vincenzo Celli, the little fourteen-year-old English ugly duckling, whose name happened to be Alicia Markova, and Ruth herself. All this and Cecchetti too.

As for Tom, he was not as doubtful as Chester seems to have been about Diaghileff's offering Ruth a job and cooked up a little scheme of his own to dissuade her subtly, just in case. They did not go to Spain on Sunday; they went instead to England to spend a weekend with a former Harvard roommate of Tom's, Sir "Jack" Herbert, a member of an old county family with a magnificent estate and the means to keep it up in the legendary manner of the British peerage. The visit was designed to expose Ruth to a style of life so patently superior to that of the ballet's toe-hopping slavery that she would suddenly see the light and go home with him posthaste. But it did not work out quite that way. Most of the weekend was spent in ferreting—not stately fox hunting with hound and horn but rabbit-rousing with ignominious little rodents. "That," said Ruth in retrospect, "was really something new for me, and when we got back to Monte Carlo I joined the Diaghileff ballet as fast as I could."

And Tom went home alone. His hunch, at least, was right, for Diaghileff did offer her a job and she took it, for all that it paid next to nothing, that she had to work from dawn to midnight and that she was in the corps de ballet. Little bits fell to her here and there, and Ninette de Valois coached her in them on the side, but it looked like a long road ahead, as she had sensed from the start.

She was not the only newcomer in the company this season. There was also, for one, a young boy of twenty-one from the Caucasus named Georgi Melitonovitch Balanchivadze, who had managed to slip out of the Soviet Union a year before and now, in addition to his dancing, was working on the choreography of *Barabau*, his first ballet for Diaghileff, under his newly gallicized name of Georges Balanchine. Along with him had come two other refugees from Leningrad, Alexandra Danilova and Tamara Gevergeyeva, who was to discard most of her name and emerge as Tamara Geva. Years later Balanchine and Ruth were to discuss working together on a number of projects, but the nearest they ever came to doing so was during this very spring, when he made a little dance for her, *Polka Melancolique,* quite outside the repertoire, of course. She still has it, carefully written out, in one of her notebooks.

Once she had won the coveted place in the most renowned company of its time, the rest was inevitably anticlimactic. After all, she had "done" her year in the corps de ballet seven years ago with Pavlova and had even come to the point, if only in the Allied Arts, where she resented being billed too far below Karsavina. Of course she was busy learning the repertoire, but only from the back lines, as it were, and there was still Cecchetti, but taking the company class was quite different from being one of a class of four soloists. Diaghileff had told her straightway that she was spoiled, and he was most unlikely to be influenced by her feminine beauty or to give her, as an American, anything like "most favored nation" treatment. She knew as well as anybody that she was not able, or ever would be, to do "64 fouettés on her toe." But she was accustomed as a matter of course to being "out-standing," and what with her drive, her ambition, her absorption in her career as a dancer, it is quite natural that after a few weeks she should have asked herself what she was doing there.

The solution came out of the blue in the form of a cable from Bolm, who had just signed up for another of his guest-choreographer assignments, this time at the Teatro Colón in Buenos Aires. He was staging, among other things, *Coq d'Or*, and he wanted her to dance the Queen of Shemakhan. She had told him once that she would go to the ends of the world to dance the role, and she wired him immediately that she was ready to do just that. When she broke the news to Diaghileff he was completely incredulous. Would anybody leave him to go to Bolm? It was much the same reaction as Svetia's had been when she told him she was going to marry somebody named Tom Fisher. She never regretted her decision, she has said, because with all the odds against her advancement in the company she would not have got very far before his death in 1929; but true as that may have been, she probably knew in her bones that this was not her milieu. As for Diaghileff, he never again engaged an American dancer; she had confirmed his long-held opinion of the nation.

She sailed at once to join the Bolms in Chicago and resumed her honeymooning for twenty-four hours, which had to include shopping, unpacking and repacking before embarking with the Bolms for Buenos Aires.

There she found that the South American attitude toward the ballet had not changed much in the seven years since she had last experienced it. Nice girls still did not go into it; dancing was considered to be not the oldest art but the oldest profession. Bolm was having his troubles engaging dancers, for gentlemen of fashion put their mistresses into the company and the ballet master was supposed to favor them whether they could dance or not. It was very much the old tradition of the Paris Opéra. Thus, when Bolm insisted on auditioning the dancers and choosing them for their talent only, he ran into heavy opposition from fairly influential quarters. Rehearsals were held in a place called the rotunda, which had a railing around the top where the men of the town were allowed to watch the girls work. Bolm ordered a tarpaulin put over the opening at once and again found himself in hot water.

But the biggest disappointment for him was that at the greatest gala of the season he was not to be represented at all. The dashing young Prince of Wales, later to be Edward VIII and the Duke of Windsor, was on one of his famous international good-will tours and would grace the opera house with his royal presence on August 23, when the scheduled opera would be *Loreley* (Catalani). As soon as he learned of it, Bolm used all his powers of persuasion to get one of his ballets on the program, preferably *Coq d'Or*. That, however, was ruled out at once. Though it was technically an opera, it offered nothing for singers to get their teeth—or rather their tonsils—into. Opera houses and their patrons over the world, by and large, are not primarily interested in music or even in singing, but only in singers, and none of the present virtuosi would have anything to do with it, especially since they would have to sit on the sidelines while the dancers took over the stage. Certainly not on such an occasion as this. When Bolm shifted his plea to *Petrouchka*, he was no more successful. Apparently this was to be an opera performance, and in addition to everything else *Loreley* was musically more fitting, since Rimsky-Korsakov and Stravinsky were still considered pretty "far out."

But both *Coq d'Or* and *Petrouchka* were successful enough on their own. " 'Petrouchka' I think is more popular here than 'Coq d'Or'," wrote Ruth. "Not that it is done any better but that it is more understood. Diaghileff gave it here quite a lot so it is not new to them, and they don't like to see Bolm here as the old man [the bearded and doddering King Dodon in *Coq d'Or*]. They are really very stupid artistically—they just don't know anything."

What is important about the whole gala, however, is that Ruth was chosen to dance in *Loreley*. It was to be her first contact with opera ballet, the field to which she was to devote so large and fruitful a part of her career. The occasion, accordingly, in spite of the backward-lookingness of this particular opera and the hectic circumstances of her participation in it, was of greater moment to her than her adored Queen of Shemakhan who had lured her to the ends of the earth only to desert her there and never again to be part of her life. No one would have been more incredulous than Ruth that any such thing would ever come to pass.

To her mother she wrote from her dressing room on August 20: "Am just waiting for an orchestra rehearsal for Loreley. I do two numbers—one little peasant waltz with [Giuseppe] Bonfiglio [long a leading dancer with the Metropolitan Opera where he was Rosina Galli's partner and had danced with her in Bolm's productions of *Coq d'Or* and *Petrouchka*], which is very cute but unfortunately has no ending—the other is the Ondine part that Pavlova did. I do it on my toes, with a solo and then a little bit with the corps de ballet—Bonfiglio arranged my part. I haven't the remotest idea what it will look like. I am wearing my fille aux cheveux de lin wig [made for the Debussy piece to which, like everybody else of the era, she had danced a solo] and a costume that the maid here and I rigged up made out of that silver stuff I bought in Chicago. I haven't the remotest idea what that will look like either. I know it was a terrible trouble to get it fixed right—finally Mrs. Bolm came to my aid and helped me to drape it. . . .

"The opera company has a peasant costume which I am using. I don't like it much but it will have to do as I have nothing else. The costume they wanted me to wear in the Ondine was a riot. I wouldn't have been caught dead in it. I wish they would hurry up, my feet are getting cold. . . .

"I'll be dancing Loreley Tuesday night for the Prince of Wales—wasn't I lucky? Just a piece of pure luck. They are ringing now, so I must go. Will try to write more later."

It was several days later that she reported on the performance itself: "I had rather a disastrous time with the Loreley performance. This Kyasht that

they have here simply can't manage anything, so Bonfiglio arranged my part—
we did quite a cute little waltz together, but unfortunately it has no
ending—we just wander off the stage—and also our costumes are hideous—
German peasant dresses—they could have been so cute. So that didn't amount
to much.

"The corps de ballet in the Ondine was simply terrible, so conventional
and so dull. My toe solo was fairly nice, very quiet, sort of on the style of
Pavlova's swan. I do it very well but I think my costume spoiled that too.
Mr. Bolm saw the dress rehearsal and said that I *must* change my costume,
that it looked like nothing at all. It was just a piece of silver with a few
delicate flowers on it and he said on that big stage it looked like nothing. So
I went over to the theatre the morning of the performance and went to the
wardrobe room and tried to get them to help me. They were so disagreeable
and made me so mad that I walked out and slammed the door and decided to
do it myself. So I took a taxi and went to almost every store in town before
I could find any blue or green material. I finally got some that looked fairly
correct and went back to the theatre to sew. I was quite well started when
Mr. Bolm came over and I think I looked so pathetic that he took me over to
Madame Bo's, a niece of Cecchetti who is a costumer, and asked her to fix my
costume for me. So the costume arrived about 7 o'clock. I was just scared
to death it wouldn't come. Mr. Bolm thought it looked all right but I thought
it looked like a Xmas tree. However, there was nothing to do then but wear
it. I was just sick not to have something good to dance and not to look nice.

"The performance was supposed to start at 9 and didn't start till 10:30!
And I didn't do my toe dance till 12:30, can you imagine that? I got quite a
good 'hand' in spite of the fact that the ending is very, very feeble. However,
I know I didn't look nice. I only saw one person who was out front and she
said my costume looked just like a flag and very heavy, but she thought I
danced beautifully, so that's something anyway. Really, dancing is so
terrible—unless you have a beautiful costume and a good arrangement, you
can be the best dancer on earth and it will be terrible. Dancing so seldom, I
am awfully sorry not to have done something better.

"This opera dancing requires a tremendous amount of experience, to
know what you should and shouldn't dance in and also what you should
wear. Bonfiglio has been with the Metropolitan fourteen years, so of course
he knows all the repertoire—music and all—and it takes a long time to learn it.
The Ondine part of Loreley is really no place for a soloist because the spotlight is all the time on the Loreley [Claudia Muzio]. However, live and learn!
Of course [Anna] Ludmila has the advantage of having been in opera six or
seven years. . . .

"Just sent a Prince of Wales program and a couple of criticisms—nobody
was mentioned much in the criticism, it was all about the prince. Scotto and

Serafin both congratulated me after my dance—it makes me sick every time I think of it that I didn't have the right costume, because I could really have been very good."

The ballet company, however, in spite of all the problems, proved to be a great success. So much so that though the season closed on August 30, Bolm was asked to stay over to give three all-ballet performances on September 10, 12 and 13. Meanwhile Tom had written that his office had offered him a vacation and "from his letters I see that he is crazy to come down here—as much to see South America" for the first time as to see her, since after all it would only allow them "to see each other two weeks sooner"—which apparently was a lot sooner to him than it was to her. The moment she was sure the added performances were definite, she would wire him to meet her "in Rio, if he can get away. I really think he has his heart set on doing it and of course it will be wonderful for me to have him to come home with." If she didn't stay, "then Ludmila will do Petrouchka and Sylphide. I hate to stay away any longer, but I think to do Petrouchka is worth it, particularly as they all think I can't do it and I want to show them that I can. They were all so surprised when I danced Loreley on my toes—having made my debut in Coq d'Or, they think I'm not a toe dancer. Ludmila was very good in Petrouchka, I thought, although her performance could have been more finished. . . ."

On September 1 she wrote: "Have decided to come home on the Van Dyke sailing the 14th with the Bolms. If I don't take that boat I would have to come home on the 10th with just Bonfiglio, so I think it is wiser to come home with the Bolms." (And that, of course, would make it foolish not to dance in those extra performances, which unfortunately the opera couldn't arrange any sooner.)

"We will give Petrouchka each time and probably Chinese [Eichheim's *The Rivals*], and then either the Puck of Debussy or the Chopin waltz which Bolm and I do together. One girl will have White Peacock and then the Greek group and then end with Snegourotchka or Prince Igor. Coming on the 14th will only be about ten days later and considering that long journey alone and then doing Petrouchka here, I think it is wise to stick it out. I haven't started to rehearse it but I hope to soon. . . . I am just sick that Tom can't come, but I really think it's much better for him not to. It's such a long trip and it isn't worthwhile for such a short time."

Then six days later: ". . . I danced Petrouchka last Saturday afternoon very unexpectedly, because they didn't intend to do it till the tenth. I had only rehearsed it five days and I had to go on without an orchestra rehearsal. . . . However, I got through it fine—only made two mistakes and those not very noticeable. The music is so difficult that I was scared about that. Unfortunately Bonfiglio is leaving on the tenth so Troy is learning the

Moor's part—he is very difficult to dance with because he has never worked with a girl before, so it is rather hard on me. However, I suppose we'll manage somehow. I will dance on the 10th and 12th Petrouchka, Chinese, and the Chopin waltz with Bolm (in Degas costume) and on the 13th will dance Petrouchka, Chinese, Puck with Bolm and Prince Igor."

She arrived back in Chicago on or about October 1, thus bringing to an end a unique honeymoon, during the last five months of which (minus that one-day interlude) the bridegroom was absent.

Home: A Permanent Point of Departure

Ruth and the Bolms got back from Buenos Aires just in time to begin preparing for the 1925-26 season of the Chicago Allied Arts.

But with the formalities of marriage and honeymoon duly accomplished, the next formality was the inescapable one of a home in Chicago. This involved the taking of some formidable hurdles. Ruth was utterly undomestic, had no interest in housekeeping and had never even learned to cook. (In fact, to this day she has not actually learned, though in a crisis, with divine intervention, she manages to come up with a superb piece of gustatory improvisation.) An adequate household staff was out of the question, for Tom was working in his father's office on a salary and was only now on the verge of becoming a partner in the firm. To be sure, Ruth expected to earn money from her career as she had always done, and when that materialized, it would both demand and justify her abstention from housewifely duties; but at the moment it could not be budgeted.

For another thing, the idea of settling down in Mid-America, while the world of glamorous activity revolved practically everywhere else, was the nightmare from which she was determined to awake. Indeed, the concept of settling down anywhere was basically inconceivable to her. Though she did not have visible wings on her ankles like Hermes, she had even more potent ones on the ankles of her mind, and, to mix metaphors and mythologies even further, putting a girdle round the earth in forty minutes was as native to her as to Puck.

She dearly loved Tom and would do anything possible to be with him; but to allow anything, even Tom, to come between her and her career was as impossible as to allow it or him to come between her and her eyesight or her digestive processes, for it was just as much an operative part of her as they.

"I really tried so hard to be a good wife," she wrote of this period. She and Tom joined the Indian Hill Club in Winnetka, which was the Fishers' family seat, and once she played nine holes of golf with him; but that was it. She never went back to the golf links. But she did go, smiling cooperatively, to all the Bachelors and Benedicts balls and suffered all the joke-book house-keeping misadventures of the inexperienced bride.

Almost at once she and Tom moved temporarily into the elder Fishers' town house in North State Street, where the Hotel Ambassador East now stands. Tom's mother had gone back to New England for a year to make a home for the younger of her two daughters, who was just entering college, and she did not want to leave her husband alone. It proved to be a pleasant interlude all around. According to Ruth, "the fantastic Mabel [Mrs. Fisher] knew everything about good housekeeping and therefore quarreled with her servants all the time and made life very hard for everyone around her. So maybe Walter Fisher found my 'laisser faire' attitude easier to live with. Anyway, he was an inspiration to me—his logical clear thinking, his humor, his 'pro bono publico' attitude towards life. What a valuable man to his community and how agreeable to live with; and he was so very nice to my artist friends, I adored him. We had a Swedish couple—she did all the work but he was agreeable and at least waited on the table. I was always grateful to Tom's father because he *said* he loved living with us." He was entirely amenable even when Ruth cleared out one of the large rooms and set it up as her always essential studio.

When Mrs. Fisher returned from the East, Tom and Ruth moved to a new studio apartment of their own devising, and though it was the very reverse of town-house distinction, it provided them with their first taste of quasi-permanence. They were to maintain it for a number of years as their Chicago anchorage. It was a loft, never meant to be lived in, on the top floor of a new building (now no longer standing) called Diana Court on North Michigan Boulevard, which they transformed into one very large all-purpose room plus a small kitchen and bath. If it was not aristocratic and mellow, it was supremely smart and handsome, for its décor was done by Nicolas Remisoff, who had become Ruth's friend early in their association in the Allied Arts productions and was to be her artistic collaborator in most of her own productions for years to come.

Remisoff and his family had left Russia after the revolution and settled in Paris, where he and Sergei Soudeikine worked as designers for Nikita Balieff's little revue called *Chauve-Souris*. This was an outgrowth of Moscow's "cabbage nights," in which once a week leading performers, composers, designers from the Moscow Art Theatre and other highbrow institutions let off artistic steam after hours in light and informal theatrical terms. When Balieff brought the *Chauve-Souris* to this country in the early twenties, the Remisoffs came along and decided to stay. But for all his "cabbage night" wit and verve, he was by no means a night-club designer; he was a graduate of the Imperial Academy of Art, a recognized portraitist, a muralist of stature, editor and chief designer of an important publication called *Satiricon* and a consummate theatre man. In the natural course of events he found himself in the Chicago Allied Arts with Bolm.

At this particular moment he had also been engaged to paint murals for the entrance of the Diana Court Building, so he took the elevator to the roof and did the same for his friends, the Fishers. "We had special rugs made to go with the murals," Ruth wrote. "The colors were yellow, brick red and cobalt blue, and the room was very beautiful. The tables collapsed and the rugs rolled up [presumably the bed was equally accommodating], my Steinway grand occupied one corner and I was 'creating' an adagio with Joe Kaminsky [one of the Allied Arts dancers], who was an expert in the culinary arts, so while we were working on the adagio we cooked a chicken at the same time. Both the adagio and the chicken were failures." The rent was $40, and when it was raised to $50, the Fishers "were furious."

The second year of the Allied Arts was as exciting to work in as the first one had been, but important though it was, Allied Arts could not even pretend to support its artists with its three brief "seasons" a year. In the spring, accordingly, Ruth was contemplating a renewal of her old "Natasha Stepanova" career on a twelve-week summer tour of the Balaban and Katz circuit of movie palaces such as were now flourishing everywhere. Though "it would be very difficult," she wrote her mother, "to dance four or five times a day in the middle of summer in such places as St. Louis and Kansas City," it would pay well.

Thanks to Bolm and some other roundabout developments, less remunerative but more creative projects made this unnecessary. Bolm also had to make some money, for his school had begun to run at a loss, and he was planning to go to Europe to see what he could set in motion there. One project he was discussing with the concert manager Daniel Mayer, was a possible tour of the Orient with Ruth and a company in the autumn of 1928 in association with A. Strok, the Russian manager who specialized in booking Oriental tours. One such was at this very moment successfully in action with Ruth St. Denis and Ted Shawn and the Denishawn company. Mayer was reluctant, however, because Ruth did not have a foreign name and was not well enough known internationally under her own. In no case, even under pressure, would he consider the proposed company until it had at least made a New York appearance to give it status.

So Bolm set out to build up a "name" for Ruth. He went at once to see Louis Eckstein, a wealthy, philanthropic music lover, who was about to institute a summer opera and orchestra season at Ravinia, on the lake shore not far from Winnetka. Always Ruth's champion, Bolm warmly recommended her as both première danseuse and choreographer for the impending season. Eckstein was enthusiastic about her as a dancer but was dubious about her being able to stage the ballets, since she had had no experience in that area.

Besides, he had already just about decided to turn the entire dance problem over to Andreas Pavley, not only because of his connection with the Chicago Opera but also because he had his own company, his own studio and his own accompanist and could take the entire organizational responsibility off Eckstein's shoulders at minimal cost.

"I haven't been to see him yet," Ruth wrote her mother, "or talked price to him or anything." But when she did go to see him, she emerged with the job. "Of course I know there is no money in it at present," she wrote, "but Mr. Bolm thinks it will help my 'name.' I really would have made some money with the movie-house tour but I really think at present the other is more important, particularly as we are definitely not going to the Orient next year. So I guess we can manage along on Tom's salary. If I don't get more than $500 that will just about pay for toe-shoes and costumes and incidental expenses. I do hope you will be able to help me with costumes as that is so important in opera and the 'première' very rarely uses the costumes handed out as they are usually impossible. Do you think you could make some for me?"

In spite of the old adage, lightning apparently does strike twice in the same place from time to time. Preparations for the Ravinia season had not even started when there came another bolt from the operatic heavens. In the middle of May Ruth wrote: "I got the most extraordinary letter yesterday— guess who it was from—Rosina Galli! I wouldn't have been more surprised if I had heard from the Queen of England. She wants me to come to New York to talk to her. She said she thought that an interview would be more satisfactory to both of us than a letter, so heaven only knows what it is all about. As I haven't got $100 to go trailing down there immediately I wrote her a letter today so I ought to hear from her again Monday. Tom thinks I ought to spend the money and go down to see her." Which she did.

Galli, who was both première danseuse and director of the ballet at the Metropolitan Opera, was planning to take the next two seasons off from dancing for reasons of health and wanted Ruth to replace her as principal dancer. If Ruth had been disinclined for any reason, which she was not, she would have changed her mind with alacrity when she learned that one of her roles would be the Queen of Shemakhan in a revival of *Coq d'Or*. As things worked out, however, she did not dance the role, for by the time it came along she had done so well with both press and public in the more conventional opera ballets, beginning with her debut in *The Bartered Bride*, that Galli's health suddenly improved and she assumed the role herself. It was one of her favorite roles also, and she had danced it with great success in the first American production of the opera by Bolm eight years earlier.

Nor was it only the press and the public that capitulated to Ruth, for Paul Cravath, chairman of the board of directors of the opera, who may not have been the world's greatest balletomane but had a keen eye for the ladies, offered her husband an enticing job in his New York law firm. Though that was politely declined, he remained a good friend to both Ruth and Tom and opened various doors for her from time to time.

Her surprise at having been invited to the Met seems quite reasonable. Galli obviously was not familiar with her work or she would probably not have put herself in the position of having to recover her health so precipitately. Certainly Bolm had nothing to do with it or Ruth would have been told about it, particularly at this period of "name" building. The most likely assumption is that it was Bonfiglio, Galli's partner, who instigated it on the strength of the Buenos Aires season. In any case, Ruth became the first American dancer to appear as première at the Met. That it helped her "name" is unquestionable.

TRADE SCHOOL ON THE LAKE

Ravinia, however, was far more important to her career. It was a prestigious engagement, with leading singers of the day in the operas and Eric DeLamarter, and later Isaac van Grove, as musical director and conductor of the Chicago Symphony Orchestra. But beyond that, "it was here," she has said, "that I learned my 'trade.' " Her experience with large-scale ensemble choreography was minimal—indeed, virtually nonexistent—and Eckstein's initial misgivings were amply justified, since opera choreography is the toughest assignment in the field. It is actually an interruption in the continuity of the singing, which is what the audience has come specifically to enjoy. Nevertheless, Ruth was able in short order to erase any lingering doubts from Epstein's mind and remained in the job for seven summers, until the great depression and Epstein's death put an end to the project. And besides learning the "trade" of opera choreography at Ravinia, she made her first independent ballets there.

Much of the time during those summers she and Tom stayed with his family in Hubbard Woods. It was a large family with many friends, and people were constantly coming and going. Ruth found it rather "like living in a country club." This did not make her work any easier, especially since, besides dancing and choreographing, she had also to organize the whole dance activity of the new enterprise. Suddenly one day she received notice that because of the illness of one of the singers, the week's program had been changed, and *Madame Butterfly*, which has no ballet, would be replaced by *Samson and Delilah*, which is not only full of dancing but also requires more dancers than could be provided by the regular corps, recruited from the Bolm company and studio. The result was that she spent the entire day on the telephone, calling "practically every dancer in Chicago." During this harrowing process one of the family's many visitors, who chanced to be passing through the room, coyly asked one of Tom's small nieces if she would like to be a "glamorous dancer like Aunt Ruth." To which the child replied, "I should say not! Too much telephoning." It was an apt reply, for from that day on, Aunt Ruth learned that the director of a ballet company, when she is not dancing, rehearsing or traveling, is likely to be on the telephone.

Besides the operas she was also involved in a series of free matinees for children. The programs consisted in equal parts of an orchestral concert by the full Chicago Symphony and a dance recital, made up of as many as twelve dances, with ice cream for all, on the house, in the interval. On one of these programs in her second summer, 1927, her assisting soloists were Jorg Fasting and Marcia Preble (both out of the Bolm forces) and a young dancer from California named Agnes de Mille, who had not yet made her New York concert debut, in three dances of her own.

"I learned a great deal," Ruth has written, "from performing for these children. I remember a group of dances called 'Moonlight Sailing,' for which Remisoff had made us some enchanting costumes that made us all look like little sailboats. I was carried away with the dreamy quality of this ballet, but practically the whole audience came backstage after the performance and said: 'Miss Page, what is the matter with you? You had all the sailboats going backwards.' After that I was more careful when creating for critical children."

The independent "adult" ballets that she produced at Ravinia were all a bit off the beaten track. The Ravel *Bolero* was the most important one. The music was then new, having been composed only a year earlier, in 1928. Mark Turbyfill sensed with his characteristic combination of perspicacity and poetry, exactly what Ruth had in mind in her approach in the choreography. As he pointed out, the three trombones in the score had awakened in her an awareness of the kinship between the passionate incantations of the Spanish gypsy and those of the African jungle. In choosing the cuadro flamenco for the basic form of the work, then, she was also subtly evoking the form of the Negro minstrels.

It is well to note that this was the only one of her several versions of the *Bolero* that was performed with a full symphony orchestra. The work remained in her repertoire for a number of seasons, but when it was presented in concert in a two-piano arrangement, it had to be done, for contractual reasons, under a different title. This, at the suggestion of Louis Horst, was *Iberian Monotone*, and an accurate title it was, for without the brilliance of the orchestration that was all that remained of the score. Audiences, however, continued to love the ballet.

When a year later she choreographed Ravel's *La Valse* (which he had likewise composed a year after the *Bolero*), she treated it as a fanciful struggle between "the aristocracy" (who danced on point) and "the proletariat" (who danced barefoot); thus making it one of the earliest of the social-content works that were to blossom profusely in the dance world in the years of the depression.

In 1931 she commissioned her first original score from the twenty-three-year-old Marcel Delannoy, whom Henry Prunières, the distinguished French critic, had recommended. It turned out to be *Cinderella*, in the style of the nineteenth-century fairy-tale ballet—winsome, young in spirit and in marked contrast to both the Ravel ballets that had preceded it.

Here, at the very beginning of her career as a creator of ballets Edward Moore, then music critic of the *Chicago Tribune*, wrote of her: "She starts as a dancer by being a musician. She uses better music than anyone else in her profession, and she treats it with respect, neither distorting it nor making awkward cuts. Upon it she puts the pattern of her dance, sometimes in the old ballet form, like the pretty little 'Cinderella' by Marcel Delannoy, sometimes fantastic like Ravel's Watlz, sometimes stylized, but always effective and exciting."

Ravinia, of course, occupied only her summers, and in the spring of 1927 her winter activities were diminished by the demise of the Chicago Allied Arts after a three-year struggle for survival. Bolm now turned his attention with full force to the promotion of the projected tour of the Orient the following year. It was still one of the requirements of Daniel Mayer and Strok that the now-named Adolph Bolm Ballet give a performance in New York, where it had never been seen. Mayer, excellent manager that he was, arranged to present it there under the auspices of the League of Composers, as part of their spring program. The other part consisted of chamber music conducted by Tullio Serafin of the Metropolitan Opera, and Greta Torpadie was guest soprano in the première of Richard Hammond's setting of Amy Lowell's poem "Voyage to the East" (a propitious symbol perhaps for Bolm). Ruth, who was just finishing the second of her two seasonal commitments to the Metropolitan, stepped into her customary roles along with other members of the Allied Arts "alumni." Bolm presented three of his tried and true ballets: *The Tragedy of the Cello* (Tansman), *Visual Mysticism*, a "dance poem" to music of Scriabin and Eichheim's *The Rivals*.

To his intense disappointment there was no response from either Mayer or Strok.

THE TWO APOLLOS

Almost exactly a year later, without any awareness that he was doing so, Bolm participated in the dramatizing of one of the climaxes of the modern ballet. This was the virtually simultaneous production in Europe and America of the new Stravinsky ballet that we now know as *Apollo* in two vastly different versions. The score had been commissioned for the annual chamber-music festival sponsored by Elizabeth Sprague Coolidge at the Library of

Congress in Washington. Here, naturally, its world première took place, and it was Bolm who staged it. Stravinsky, however, had already conceived the work for Diaghileff.

For the Washington première the French title, *Apollon Musagète*, was translated, not into English, for perhaps *Apollo, Leader of the Muses* seemed long and awkward, but into a kind of Anglicized Greek as *Apollo Musagetes.* Bolm chose to treat it as a romantic view of ancient classicism (Renaissance style) in decay. Though the tiny stage could accommodate no scenery as such, Remisoff's décor managed to evoke a feeling of Piranesi's engravings of Roman ruins, and what Bolm wore as Apollo was essentially the *tonnelet* and plumed headdress of the age of the *grand monarque.* The opening episode of Leto's labor and delivery of the infant Apollo was considered too obstetrical to be staged at all, and its music was simply played as an overture before the rise of the curtain. Ruth was the Terpsichore, Berenice Holmes the Polyhymnia and Elise Reiman the Calliope. Hans Kindler conducted an orchestra of strings and it was all stately, stylish and musical within its chosen approach.

On the program with it were Ravel's *Pavane pour une Infante Défunte,* staged as a duodrama called *The Vision of Don Gonzalez; Arlecchinata,* a commedia-dell'arte piece with masks, set to an eighteenth-century score of Mondonville; and *Alt Wien,* a *Fasching* episode for five dancers to music of Beethoven. The evening had thus great variety within the altogether consistent unity of Fokine's once-innovative "period romanticism."

This was on April 27. On June 12 in Paris Diaghileff presented the première of *Apollon Musagète,* in which Balanchine and Stravinsky, working in complete unity of conviction, opened the era of neoclassicism in the ballet with a flash as of lightning.

The full classic value of the work was still somewhat clouded, it is true, by the décor of a naive painter, gold wigs and costumes *à la grecque* and the air of willful *méchanceté* that characterized so much of the young Balanchine's work as well as that of Diaghileff. Not until roughly a quarter of a century later did it actually achieve its inherent purity, when under the financial stringency of the New York City Ballet at the City Center it had to dispense with painted scenery and all but the simplest "working" costumes, and all the roles were danced by young Americans in what can only be characterized as artistic innocence. The casting of Jacques d'Amboise as Apollo was perhaps what stripped the work finally to its essence.

Nevertheless the Paris première was revolutionary, whereas the Washington one was merely the respectable, professional fulfillment of an impressive assignment, containing within itself no seed of growth whatever.

Ruth seems not to have sensed that this startling dramatization of a change of epoch, in which she was a participant, might have had something to do with the fact that the Washington *Apollo* was to be her last association with Bolm, either in the flesh or in the spirit. The occasion of her impending break with him seemed so obviously to be also its cause that subtler influences were lost to view. Those influences, however, are not to be ignored. What happened specifically was that after the long silence, the Oriental tour suddenly materialized and in a most unexpected guise. By an ironic turn in the management's reticence about Ruth she was now in and Bolm was out. The new plan was to send a small, simple, young company to Japan to participate in the coronation celebrations of the new emperor, Hirohito, who had inherited the throne in 1926. For this Bolm was too Russian, too "grand" and too expensive, but he was nevertheless deeply hurt when Ruth accepted it without him.

She was, of course, still eagerly self-centered, but she could not help being conscious of the extent of his injury. It may, indeed, have given her a traumatic sense of guilt, which she has borne ever since. Only in later years did she realize how completely she had accepted his unstinted guidance, confidence and affection as a matter of course. There was nothing whatever amorous about the relationship; she was simply taken into his family and treated exactly as his step-daughter, Valitchka, who was her close friend and companion. Her respect for him was great (to the end of his days she addressed him as "Mr. Bolm"), but it was predominantly filial, which naturally implies taking things for granted. "I should have refused to go [on the Oriental tour]," she says, "but at that time I was so anxious to go off on my own! I don't think this was fair to Bolm. Anyway, that is what I did."

She could not have done otherwise; it was, however subcutaneously, a choice in direction between the two *Apollos*. As an honest Mid-American between two opposing Russianisms, she could not accept either of them as her own. The Fokine-Pavlova-Bolm direction she knew from immediate experience could only lead backward; the Diaghileff-Balanchine one, she had begun to sense, would just as clearly lead forward; but her own road in that direction she would have to clear for herself.

She and Bolm were to remain friends, of course. He was shortly to set out for California, where he had always wanted to live, to stage ballets for Hollywood and later to found a ballet company in San Francisco with the opera there. Normally he would have taken her along as a matter of course, and she might well have gone, at least for the opera seasons, but now it was the last thing in the world she wanted.

About halfway through her Allied Arts association she had created two little satirical dances that were by no means world-shaking masterpieces, but were indicative, and in their own small way revolutionary, for her. One of them was *The Flapper and the Quarterback*, a duet (nobody in America had ever heard of a pas de deux in those days) danced with Paul DuPont, and the other was an ensemble piece called *Oak Street Beach*. The music for both was by a fellow Indianapolitan, Clarence Loomis. It is doubtful that they constituted any conscious rebellion against the elaborate ethnic romanticism that prevailed in the ballet under Fokine's influence, but they were by obvious intent contemporary, American and immediate, and she was well aware that they were original. The first was a choreographic setting of John Held Jr.'s perceptive caricatures of the teen-agers of the twenties, and the second pictured in action what was essentially Chicago's summertime approximation of the Lido.

Two more or less consecutive professional experiences certainly contributed to the creation of these pieces. One was her long run in the despised revue, which, beneath its lush and lamé surface, gave her a sense of popular approach and popular timing; the other was her more recent contact, brief but first-hand, with Diaghileff, whose aesthetic took a positive delight in making impudence smart. The juxtaposition of these two operational environments, against the background of her basic Americanness, led her, if not deliberately at least logically, to the ultimate translation of Americana, including both its manner and its preoccupations, into the stuff of ballet. And this from one who adored all things exotic and never ceased to pursue them.

YON AND YONDER

The company specified for Japan was to consist of four dancers and a pianist and was to give twenty concerts between October 1 and 25 in the Imperial Theatre in Tokyo. Ruth immediately wired Ninette de Valois, her British colleague from Cecchetti and Diaghileff days, and invited her to join the company and to bring Anton Dolin along. The idea appealed strongly to Ninette and she set about trying to cancel the lease she had just signed for a new school she was preparing to open in London, but she was unable to do so. (Years later she said that if she had succeeded in canceling that lease, there probably would have been no Royal Ballet.)

In the company as finally engaged were Edwin Strawbridge, as Ruth's partner; two Chicago girls, Irene Isham and Etta Moore; and a pianist, Leonid Koshansky. The repertory demands were of formidable dimensions for a young dancer, for there were to be five entirely different programs consisting of ten dances each. With ingenuity and a bit of scrounging all fifty numbers were somehow assembled, programmed and rehearsed, and the season went very well indeed.

Besides the performing company (four of whom returned to America at the conclusion of the Japanese engagement), a nonperforming contingent also went along, consisting of Tom and Dr. and Mrs. Page. For Ruth and her parents the tour continued for some seven months longer; Tom went only as far as Peking and then home by way of Siberia. Dr. Page wanted to study the hospitals of Southeast Asia and Ruth was eager to study its dancing.

In Peking they visited a "fascinating" ex-Chicagoan named Mrs. Calhoun, who was a friend of the great actor Mei Lan-fang. She had remodeled a Chinese temple into a home for herself, and there Ruth's exotic soul reveled in being photographed in many of the magnificent costumes Mei had presented to Mrs. Calhoun.

The three Pages went on to Bali, to Burma, to Cambodia, to what were then Cochin China and Siam. Ruth took lessons wherever she could find somebody to teach her and sat eagerly through performances often of unendurable length for her companions. At an entrancing session in Burma, somewhere around daybreak her martyred father asked her pleadingly if she really had not had enough; but she hadn't.

In Pnom-Penh she "had a beautiful experience. I went to the museum and I heard some lovely music, so I opened the door and here were all these exquisite little Cambodian dancers rehearsing. I couldn't really believe my eyes. They looked like statues coming to life." She browsed around the temple of Angkor-Vat for hours; she went to Saigon; she had a letter (from heaven knows whom) to the uncle of the King of Siam, Prince Dam Rong (a name that looks less Gilbert-and-Sullivanish than it sounds), and he gave a great party for her at the Varidis Palace in Bangkok.

"I danced some of my dances for them, and when I finished the whole Siamese ballet danced for me. That was the most extraordinary night. Prince Dam Rong had three young daughters, the Princesses Poon, Pi Lai, and Chong Chitter, each of whom was learning a profession (according to what the Prince seemed to believe was the common American practice for rich young ladies). One learned to sew, one learned to paint, and one learned to cook. The table linen was made by the one who sewed. The one who learned to cook thought she would please me by making some American food for the party. She made some wonderful cakes—real works of art—but with them were frankfurters and fruit salad and some sort of concoction like an American ice-cream soda. I had to drink it, but it didn't taste much like an American ice-cream soda. Anyway, I remember that night as being something very glamorous in my life."

When she got back to Paris, the French curator she had met in the museum in Pnom-Penh was there and asked her to illustrate a lecture he was giving on Cambodian dancing. He had a costume made for her in Paris after the pattern worn by the dancers in the Angkor-Vat temple, and she danced in it for the Gouvernement Général de l'Indochine, and the Governor General sent her roses. "This was really a fascinating experience for me because here

I was—a little American nobody—performing these Cambodian dances for these very highbrow French art curators."

Characteristically, she got back to Chicago just in time to start rehearsals for Ravinia.

In 1930 she was off again on a foreign engagement, this time to Moscow. It was the period of Lenin's New Economic Policy, when contact with the outside world was being more or less cultivated, and she had been invited by the Sophil Society to give programs of "American dances" for workers' groups. She had taken the trouble to learn a bit of Russian, which vastly pleased her audiences. This was a much more modest venture than the Japanese season. No supporting company was involved, since the programs consisted entirely of solos. Two girls were needed, however, as assistants, one to play the piano and the other to take care of costume changes and general offstage matters.

Ruth's mother came along again, for her own sake as well as Ruth's. Dr. Page had died in the summer of 1929, and she was not only free to go but also in need of some such recuperative activity. Unfortunately she caught a bad cold in Russia, and rather than stay there and bluff it through, she left for Germany, where she knew the language and where her son, Irvine, following in his father's footsteps, had completed his medical education and was now director of a clinic.

Ruth joined her there on the way home, and they were led by Irvine on what amounted to a personally guided tour of the country he knew so well. Among the stopovers was the Second International Dance Congress at Munich, where Mary Wigman was scheduled to stage a large work called *Totenmal*, honoring the dead of World War I. Whether this stop was Ruth's idea or Irvine's is open to question, for, again following his father's precedent, he had fallen in love with a young American artist, not a pianist this time but a dancer, Beatrice Allen, from the Denishawn company, who was appearing in a program by foreign dancers at the congress, and it was a good opportunity to introduce her to the family.

They did not stay over for the *Totenmal*, for Ruth was anxious to get to Salzburg, where Harald Kreutzberg was making his annual appearances in Max Reinhardt's productions, including *Jedermann* on the steps of the cathedral, as part of the festival. Kreutzberg was artistically much on her mind at the moment.

DER MODERNE TANZ

The most important aspect of the whole Russian expedition proved to be not Russia itself but the journey to it, for on shipboard out of New York she had found Kreutzberg. She has said that Pavlova and he were the two great influences of her life (*pace* Mr. Bolm), and though she had seen him dance in

America, this may have been the long, leisurely, communicative occasion when that influence began to operate seriously.

He had come to New York for the first time late in 1927 as a member of Reinhardt's Vienna theatre company and had danced, among other assignments, in Reinhardt's famous production of *A Midsummer Night's Dream.* Here he had won especial acclaim, dancing opposite the charming little Viennese dancer Tilly Losch, who was the First Fairy and had also created the choreography for the production. At the very end of the company's season in January the two of them had given a dance recital of their own. It was a genuine triumph with literally hundreds of people turned away at the box office, and would certainly have been repeated except that arrangements had been made for their departure for Europe at once.

His was the first real sample of the modern German dance that New York had seen (Tilly was basically classical, though by no means rigidly so), and its success insured his return at the earliest opportunity. Accordingly, in 1929 and 1930 he had made concert tours of America, now with Yvonne Georgi, a Mary Wigman product like himself, as his costar and his lifelong friend and artistic collaborator, Friedrich Wilckens, as accompanist. It was from this 1930 tour that he was now returning to Germany—or rather, to Austria, where he lived.

In the long, free days at sea he and Ruth—and "Fritz" Wilckens as well—found themselves not only thoroughly compatible personally but also in remarkable accord in their ideas about the dance. In retrospect it is easy to see why. Though their backgrounds were totally unlike—he had come out of Wigman's *moderne Tanz* and she out of the "old-fashioned" ballet—they were both essentially free in style, urbane rather than profound, given to originality and invention instead of tradition and soul-searching, primarily visual though soundly musical, predominantly dramatic instead of abstract, and leaning in the direction of humor rather than solemnity.

Certainly a seed was planted in her mind, for this was a dance approach that hit her where she lived. By the summer of 1932 the seed had germinated to the point where she went especially to Salzburg again, worked with him at the Mozarteum, where he conducted an annual summer school, and at his invitation arranged to tour with him in joint recitals the following year in both this country and the Orient.

The logic of this development is clear. She was too innately prescient not to have felt in her bones what the dance was already going through back in the late twenties. Her parting from Bolm in 1928 had grown out of these very stirrings. Diaghileff died in the summer of 1929, Pavlova at the beginning of 1931, and the Russian ballet in the western world was in disarray. In America something called modern dance, not yet in any sense definable, had begun to emerge. Martha Graham made her New York debut in 1926, Tamiris in 1927 and Doris Humphrey in 1928. But what Graham and Humphrey were doing at this early stage of the game was not very different from what they had done with the Denishawn company. Tamiris, the youngest of the three and a non-Denishawn product, was the most "advanced"—musically, visually and in subject matter, and on the strength of this modernity she had been invited in 1928 to dance at the Salzburg Festival as the first examplar of the American avant-garde. But her career was just beginning, and it is more than likely that Ruth had not seen her. Louis Horst, Denishawn's longtime musical director, now on his own, served as accompanist for all of them through this period.

Horst also served in the same capacity for Ruth in her New York and other eastern concerts. As a matter of fact, in December 1927, while Kreutzberg was making his first appearances in this country with the Reinhart company at the Century Theatre, Horst played for Ruth in a concert at Hampden's Theatre one block away. She had brought with her Jorg Fasting, Berenice Holmes and Marcia Preble of the Bolm Ballet and of her own Ravinia company for a New York performance, and as an additional dancer she had engaged Evelyn Sabin, who until just at this time had been a member of Graham's supporting trio. Graham had dissolved the trio with the intention of concentrating, with Horst's close collaboration, on more deeply personal adventures as a soloist.

Kreutzberg, however, did not have to achieve personal outlines out of any such fog as prevailed here in the burgeoning modern dance. He came from an altogether alien, markedly German, background and had already attained what proved to be his full growth in his own style. From this new perspective modern dance had struck Ruth, as the dancing of Pavlova had struck her fifteen years earlier, as part of her own natural communicative equipment. Pavlova's dancing, for all its technical intricacies, was not bravura in intent but "expressive." It was in essence no different from Ruth's own "made-up" dances in bare feet, with waving scarves or what you will; it was only more shaped, more integrated, more deliberately communicative and of course more mature. She had not had the same personal kindling from anybody else, bur now Kreutzberg set her to creating in a new way. She had found herself irresistibly aroused by him to find fresh forms for that same old urge—pre- and post-Pavlova—to "make up" dances for herself. These were not dances that you "arranged," they had to be "made up."

By the time she actually danced with Kreutzberg on their tour in 1933 she had already made up several of them, all quite different in outward form from anything she had done before but just as completely her own in substance. She was up to her ears in a modern period.

Expanding Universe

It was not, however, quite as direct and uncomplicated as this. Human experience is far too much of a gestalt to make possible the isolation of a line of pure descent from any of its individual engrossments. Kreutzberg may have been the catalyst that touched into action a creative procedure for which, indeed, Ruth was already prepared, but there were at the same time other areas of her closely integrated personal-artistic life that required other influences to add the necessary spark.

Kreutzberg was not essentially interested in women; Isamu Noguchi, sculptor, artist at large, aesthetic iconoclast, definitely was. She met him for the first time at a concert at the Arts Club in Chicago. He was sitting directly in front of her, and he was "the most beautiful thing you have ever seen. He had a sort of lost, faraway look that was irresistible; very penetrating eyes that looked right into your soul."

He was the son of Yone Noguchi, who had come to this country from Japan in the early nineties and made a name for himself as both an imagist poet and a general interpreter of the cultures of the two countries to each other. It was in California in 1904 that Isamu was born to an American mother, Leonie Gilmour, scholarly, artistic, freethinking and courageous. The three of them returned to Japan while he was still an infant, and eventually he was sent to school in Yokohama. In 1917 his mother brought him back to this country to see that he got an American education and put him into a forward-looking school in northern Indiana. There, under the guidance of a man who became a kind of foster father, he finished high school and headed for Columbia University to study medicine.

His predestined career, however, was not to be thus sidestepped. With his finding of himself as a sculptor at just about the time of his coming of age, as he recounts in his autobiography (*A Sculptor's World*, Harper and Row, 1968) he suddenly became acutely aware both of his Japanese heritage and of his father's mission of making the two countries culturally responsive to each other. Accordingly, in spite of his mother's hitherto successful efforts to Americanize him, he dropped the name of Gilmour, under which he had grown up, and became Isamu Noguchi.

At the age of twenty-three he was off to Paris for two years on a Guggenheim Fellowship, but the Orient was in the back of his mind as his ultimate field of study. Before he left New York on that particular quest some two years later, he had not only found himself as a sculptor but had also proved himself publicly as such with two well-received one-man shows and enough money to finance his Oriental travels. Furthermore, among the people whose heads he had made he had founded two lifelong friendships—with Martha Graham and Buckminster Fuller.

It was immediately after his return to this country in 1932 that he first "looked right into [Ruth's] soul."

Ruth is convinced that her marriage to Tom never underwent a moment of genuine danger, in spite of flirtations of various intensities by both of them. But this was a more serious love affair, made especially so by their common absorption in the arts. It was the only instance in which the subject of divorce and marriage had ever been broached. By the very nature of her situation she could never have taken so final a step, as is attested, perhaps, by the fact that she did not ultimately do so. But that in no sense invalidates the depth of her attachment.

That it had a direct bearing on her new creative directions cannot be questioned; they were both working artists, in fields that overlapped in part, and their personal relationship was perhaps an aspect of their creative one. This was a time midway in that ebullient period between the two world wars when an entire generation of visionary young people was creatively at work to remake the world.

At the very start she sat to him for a sculpture—not a portrait, by any means, but the highly abstracted projection of a woman symbol to which Buckminster Fuller was to give the name of "Expanding Universe." In his autobiography Noguchi refers to it as "Miss Expanding Universe," but in his correspondence with Ruth it was simply "Expanding Universe" (or sometimes simply "Ex Uni"). In either form, however, it was an inspired title, and not alone for the sculpture, for it applied as well to their whole period of activity and described Ruth's participation in it with particular aptness. So delighted was she with the work that she asked Noguchi to have a cast made for her, which he gladly undertook to do. This was not at all the case of a vain ballerina acquiring a flattering portrait for her drawing room; it was, indeed, neither flattering nor in any sense a portrait. It was for her a symbol of the new place she was discovering for herself in the aesthetic universe that was expanding around her; a kind of icon, personal, if you will, but also of cosmic reference.

In its more specific application it became the inspiration for new dances, one of which eventually bore its title. For it Noguchi designed a costume in the form of a large "sack" made from a square of blue jersey sewed together so as to enclose her completely except for a single opening at the top for her head, and he provided sketches showing just how the cloth should be cut and sewn to allow for her manipulation of it. He made sketches also for another kind of "sack" with openings for hands and feet as well as head, and he described how she could disappear, as it were, into each opening at will to create the masses and movements she might want to achieve in her compositions. Many of these basic possibilities he had worked out experimentally with the collaboration of his young sister, Ailes Gilmour, who was a pupil of

Martha Graham and a member of her present company. Some two years later he was to design an epoch-making stage setting for Martha Graham's *Frontier*, the first of many that were to follow. It is not impossible to believe that these "sacks" may have marked his first approach to the theatre, where he was to function so brilliantly.

As for "Buckie" Fuller, he and Noguchi found early on that they shared a wide range of radical convictions about the arts, the unsuspected resources of the natural world, and the practicable potentialities they offered to a receptive society. Their friendship was a mutually stimulating one, and they helped each other along from the very beginning in whatever ways they could. At one time, for example, Noguchi spent most of the night in his studio working on models for a radically new type of car that Buckie was planning to exhibit at the forthcoming automobile show. There was actually a photograph taken of it later with Noguchi as one of its passengers, but the car itself was never put into commercial production.

This was the summer when Ruth went to Salzburg to work with Kreutzberg on dances they were to do together later on tours both here and in the Orient. It was not Noguchi, of course, who had awakened her love of the Far East; it was rather the Far East that had awakened her love for him. Her lifelong urge to flee from the constrictions of Mid-America's centering instincts had found its first satisfaction in that ecstatic eight-month tour of the Orient that had begun in Tokyo at the emperor's coronation. There can be little doubt that Noguchi's Japaneseness constituted a significant part of her attraction to him. That he was half American and had grown up a few miles away in La Porte, Indiana, could only have increased her vulnerability through the added sense of kinship.

Such an idyll could not be expected to go on forever in a world not constituted for idylls, and it was Tom, apparently with a tactfulness that left no scars on either of them, who was the agent of its dissolution. Perhaps, in any case, it had run its course; certainly it had made its contribution.

A third contributor to her new creativeness, though in a less spectacular way than either Kreutzberg or Noguchi, was Louis Horst, who was virtually the midwife of the entire American modern dance. He was, in general, such a tower of strength that dancers sought him out in spite of the causticness of the belittling they were likely to receive. His criticism indeed, could be so cold that in his composition classes over the years student after student burst into tears at his diagnoses, rushed from the studio and was discovered leaning against the corridor wall sobbing her heart out. But he was a fine musician with a perhaps unique gift for both the composing and the playing of music for dancers. In spite of his apparent indifference, his cynicism and his consistent assertion that he hated dancing, he loved it deeply and exclusively.

Ruth found him wonderful to work with. When she was struggling with some creative problem in the studio, she was delighted that instead of trying to solve it for her, he simply took up his newspaper and started to read. She knew that when she was ready to go on, he would pick up, with complete rapport, exactly where they had left off. If asked to criticize, he would be glad to accommodate, but it was at the asker's peril, for he was no flatterer. Since he and Ruth were both interested in modern music, he occasionally recommended something unfamiliar to her, especially in the German field, and they got along together perfectly. He was hard-boiled, soft-hearted and eminently professional.

Three more varied influences could scarcely have been assembled; she chose them well, by sheer instinct, to serve in the several departments of her need, but she was, as always, the mistress of her creative directions. What she came forth with—good, bad or indifferent—was likely to be authentic, dyed-in-the-wool Ruth Page. At this period she was asked by an interviewer to compare dancing on point and in bare feet, and she replied, "I like to dance on my toes—that's easy; the difficulty is to create something new on them." She was not interested in specializing, but always in expanding; her gesture was innately outward.

In January 1933 she brought three of her new works to New York in a recital at the John Golden Theatre. Though they constituted only a small proportion of her program, they announced unequivocally that she had entered a new field, and a theatreful of dancers and aficionados took note of it accordingly.

The first of them was *Variations on Euclid* to music of Mompou. Its costume was designed by the Russian painter Pavel Tchelitchev, who, in a manner of speaking, provided here still another influence. He was far more interested in painting than in theatre designing, but had designed one ballet for Diaghileff in 1928. It was the quite revolutionary *Ode*, in which he used cinematic projections, luminous paint, neon light and extremely intricate technical devices. Ruth had met him in Paris through a talented Chicago pianist, Alan Tanner, who lived with him in Paris but with whom she had worked frequently at home. Since she could not afford even to think about commissioning a ballet, she asked him simply to design a solo costume for her. Mark Turbyfill recalls having been deputized by Ruth, on his departure for a European holiday, to "give $50 to 'Pavlik' Tchelitchev in Paris" for the design.

(Later, when he came to New York, she was eager to persuade Paul Cravath to commission him to do something for the Metropolitan Opera, and she and Tom managed to get the two of them together. "He talked a blue streak," Ruth says, "and brilliantly. Tom and I were fascinated, but Mr. Cravath fell asleep.")

The costume he designed for her was really more than a costume, for it was built around two long sticks, which became at times extensions of the arms, at other times in effect another pair of limbs and again a frame to alter the relation of the body to space. In a program note she wrote that they "serve as metronomic indicators of the rhythmic mood of the geometric universe"; also they were to be used "almost as a compass in geometry, drawing fantastic patterns on the floor and forming angular projections in the air. The body is used not as a separate entity but as a part of the geometric whole, making of the dance an abstract arithmetic problem totally devoid of human emotionalism."

Two other new dances, both with music by a Chicago composer, Robert Wolf, were designed likewise without relation to the body as such but only in terms of architectural abstraction. The first was *Expanding Universe* in the large blue sack Noguchi had designed to enclose everything but the head. Again a program note: "To those who are plastically minded the dance will seem to be a series of startling poses—new inventions in design and ever remindful of twentieth century sculpture in its most abstract and fourth dimensional imagery. To those who are philosophically minded the dance will seem to be the continuous struggle of mankind through calmness and strife to expand into new ideas and new forms, ending in the complete mystery which is the universe. But for this dance, each must make his own interpretation." The second dance was called *Night Singing Through Space* and the sack this time was equipped with manipulatable elastic tapes instead of sticks and restored the feet to visibility.

In her performances with Kreutzberg later these two numbers were programmed together as *Two Songs of Space: Expanding; Swinging.* She was always renaming them. *Expanding Universe* was often called *Figure in Space.* Later she added two other dances to the *Variations on Euclid* without separate subtitles; one of them was also with music by Mompou and the other to that of Toch, and the costumes for both were by Remisoff.

At the John Golden Theatre concert, these avant-garde numbers comprised considerably less than half the program. The others consisted of old favorites: the always popular *Tropic* (Cyril Scott), dealing with equatorial decadence, with Remisoff's Polynesianlike mask and costume of tie-dyed scarves; *Possessed*, another tropical ritual, this time of religious frenzy and release, to music of Villa-Lobos; *Humoresques*, five little "musical jokes" to music of Casella (three of them with masks by Remisoff), including a particularly hilarious one of a Spanish dancer in caricature; and finally *Iberian Monotone*, with Blake Scott and a group of eight girls also in the cast.

Though Kreutzberg was not yet even on the scene, her Kreutzberg "era" had come into being with memorable effect and clearly opened new dimensions to her. When he actually came upon the scene, they toured Japan and North China and also managed to cover cities, large and small, in the United States.

There is no doubt that their programs caused consternation here and there in the less sophisticated centers, what with Ruth's "sacks" and sticks, Kreutzberg's shaven head and his psychotic *Three Mad Figures* and their dual numbers sometimes with tapes wound about their faces. Kreutzberg was to remember with delight a review of their performance in Boise City, Idaho. After a long front-page article describing each dance ecstatically, the writer summed up by saying, "They are certainly great artists, but I hope they never come again."

Progress is as Progress Does

Since apparently nothing in nature grows in a straight line, Ruth had scarcely got back from her avant-garde adventures in the Orient when the voice of the opera called her back to the paths of propriety. She was invited, indeed, by the Chicago Grand Opera Company at the Civic Opera House to join its ballet, not only as principal dancer but also as director, beginning with the season of 1934. The institution had long been undergoing changes of corporate name, of sponsorship and of artistic direction, and only the previous year had dropped the "Civic" from its title and substituted (for the time being, at least) the more traditionally respectable "Grand."

Ruth had never before been tapped for the ballet directorship of any opera, except of course the summer one at Ravinia, and she had not even danced with the Chicago opera, under any of its names, since her debut as the Infanta at the old Auditorium fifteen years ago. But it was clear that she would be very much at home, for she would be surrounded by familiar figures. Isaac van Grove was not only a conductor but also a stage director; Remisoff was one of the designers; and what with the dancers who had worked with her before, including Blake Scott and other soloists, it promised to be almost like Ravinia redivivus downtown. One notable exception was the premier danseur in the regime of her immediate predecessor, Laurent Novikoff, who was a total artistic stranger to her, though he would not remain so for long. His name was Bentley Stone.

Meanwhile she and Tom had acquired a little house of their own on the lake shore at Hubbard Woods, thanks directly to Tom's younger brother, Howard. He was an architect of strong social awareness and, especially in these depression years, was deeply concerned with providing practical and tasteful housing at a price within the range of low-income families. He had recently organized a company called General Houses, Inc., in order to experiment with the idea of manufacturing prefabricated steel dwellings, of which this one was a model. The rooms were small, but there were two bed-rooms, and the total cost was $2,000. Remisoff had stepped in at once and with his color, his décors, his choice of materials and his composition had made the rooms seem twice their size. Needless to say, Ruth would sooner or later have to add a studio.

It was also through Howard Fisher that at this same time Ruth and Tom first met Lincoln Kirstein, a former classmate of Howard's at Harvard. Kirstein had come out to Chicago primarily to write a critical report on Chicago's just-opened Century of Progress Exposition for *Hound and Horn*, the journal of literature and the arts that he had founded while he was at Harvard and still edited. As a matter of course he went to Hubbard Woods to see his friend's experimental house, and they all had dinner together.

He and Tom hit it off immediately, and since they were both quick-witted, widely knowledgeable and distinctly gossipy raconteurs, they virtually took over the evening. Tom regaled him especially with a firsthand tale about Diaghileff and John Alden Carpenter. Diaghileff had commissioned Carpenter to write the ballet *Skyscrapers*, had made many suggestions about its form and approach and straightway forgotten it. After two years of growing indignation Carpenter made a journey to Paris (with Tom along) and with considerable dudgeon withdrew the score. As soon as he got back to New York, he virtually forced it upon the notoriously ballet-hating Gatti-Casazza, director of the Metropolitan Opera, for immediate production there, with the highbrow designer Robert Edmond Jones, and the Broadway dance director Sammy Lee, as his collaborators. (Its success was of the sort known as "d'estime.")

With all the focus on Tom and tattle, however, Kirstein had plenty of occasion to be impressed by Ruth—her beauty, her intelligence, her enthusiasm, her dancer's body, the range of her dance education. He was himself on the point of becoming the American opposite number of Diaghileff (though that is not exactly the way he would have put it), and he felt that she was somebody he could work with.

As far as the 1933 World's Fair itself was concerned, its celebration of "Progress" certainly did not include the dance. The only examples it sponsored were standard hangovers of "Little Egypt" and the honky-tonk sideshows. To make up for this and other similar cultural lapses, some of Chicago's disgruntled patrons of the arts organized various compensatory events outside the fair grounds. Among them was a series of musical programs at the old Auditorium under the auspices of the League of Composers (of which John Alden Carpenter was the guiding spirit), in collaboration with the Chicago Symphony Orchestra with Frederick Stock conducting. One of these programs was given over entirely to the dance, and for it Ruth created a brand-new ballet called *La Guiablesse*.

Hall of the Mountain King (ca. 1908)

Entomologically dubious
aerial creature *sur les points.* (ca. 1910)

Falling Leaves ballet in the revue *Miss 1917*. Scenery and costumes by Joseph Urban. (*White*)

In *Les Présages* (Fokine-Liszt);
with the Pavlova Company (1918).
(*M. Ortiz, Mexico*)

With Adolph Bolm in *The Birthday of the Infanta,* Chicago, 1919.
Scenery and costumes by Robert Edmond Jones. (*Daguerre Studio*)

Scene from the film *Danse Macabre,*
with Adolph Bolm, 1922.
(*Francis Bruguiere*)

Porcelain Maid in the *Music Box Revue,* 1922.
(*G. Maillard Kesslere*)

The Queen of Shemakhan
in *Le Coq d'Or,* Buenos Aires, 1925.
(*B. de Irigoyent*)

The Flapper and the Quarterback
with Paul du Pont, 1925.
(*Eugene Hutchinson*)

Tropic (Cyril Scott).
Mask and costume by Nicolas Remisoff.
(*Edith Zistig, Münich*)

Cinderella at Ravinia, 1931.

With Harald Kreutzberg
in one of their "modern" numbers.
(*Maurice Seymour*)

With Kreutzberg in a lighter vein.
(*Maurice Seymour*)

It had been planned originally by Bolm for the Allied Arts, but by the time of the demise of that organization it had not got beyond the point of planning. The story was based on a legend of Martinique, which Bolm had found in Lafcadio Hearn's *Two Years in the French West Indies*. The book had been given to him in South America, and he read it with such excitement on the voyage home that he had tried to persuade the ship's captain to drop him off at the island for a firsthand experience of its atmosphere. Back in New York, he sought out the rising young Negro musician William Grant Still, as the only composer who could possibly recapture such subtle magic. At first Still dug into native West Indian sources for his basic materials, but he decided at last to rely rather on his own invention and imagination. When Ruth revived this project some six years later, she naturally had further conferences with him about it. At Bolm's request she had written the original scenario. Except for herself the entire cast was black, which was a revolutionary idea at that time.

From its earliest stages as a possible Allied Arts project, nobody had been more enthusiastic about it than Mark Turbyfill, whose name seems to run like a thread through the tapestry of Chicago dancing. One of his most cherished dreams was the forming of a classical Negro ballet company himself, and he had actually started classes to that end. Early on, he had cast a secret eye on a beautiful young dancer named Katherine Dunham, whom he envisioned as the first Negro ballerina. Actually, even if she had started classical training young enough for that, she was not essentially of classical temperament, but at least he knew a talented artist when he saw one and recommended her at once to Ruth. By 1933 Katherine was an anthropology major at the University of Chicago and already launched on a promising career as a dancer, with a special style of her own, theatrical in purpose though anthropological in essence.

La Guiablesse, of course, was not remotely related to the classical ballet but was couched in a free technical style with strong anthropological orientation, and Dunham was ideally qualified to be in it. Most of the supporting company was recruited from a Negro Folk-Play Group on the South Side (the young Talley Beatty was among them) directed by Bertha Mosley Lewis, and there, in a gymnasium, rehearsals were held with a company that was basically nonprofessional.

The central character, La Guiablesse (a dialectic corruption of *diablesse*), was a she-devil (Ruth), who after luring a young lover away from his adored one (Katherine), pushed him over a cliff and disappeared in a puff of smoke. The plot itself was less important than the jungle rituals and mating dances it gave rise to.

The work had a great success, and a year later, when the 1934 opera season was in preparation, it came into the picture again. Novikoff, in his four years as ballet director, had presented regularly scheduled full evenings of ballet, made up of such works as *Swan Lake (Act 2), Prince Igor,* the *Raymonda Pas de Dix* and *El Amor Brujo.* It was definitely Ruth's plan both to create new independent ballets and to continue the full evenings of ballet, though certainly without any of the old war-horses. To her surprise, however, the management invited her forthwith to revive *La Guiablesse.* She was still hopelessly involved in creating and rehearsing the incidental ballets in all the standard operas with a brand-new company, so she turned in despair to Katherine to organize and rehearse it, and to take over the title role as well. Katherine, happy to oblige, remembered it to the last detail and brought it through to everybody's complete satisfaction, assisted, according to the program, by "Her Own Corps-De-Ballet and Pupils of Her School."

The first performance was on an all-ballet program in November. The second one found itself billed, along with *Iberian Monotone,* to supplement the opera's presentation of *Salome* with Jeritza in the title role. (To add to the excitement, Gertrude Stein was present in a box.)

The work, with its all-black cast, was not practicable as part of the opera's regular repertoire, but it was excellent for Katherine's own touring company, where it was a feature of her programs for several seasons. It was the first of Ruth's ballets to be taken over by another company.

It was odd that Ruth had never seen Bentley Stone dance, for he had been with the opera since 1930 and premier danseur during the season that had just closed. Most probably it was because the opera season came along when she was away on her various tours. In this summer of 1934, however, he was engaged to direct and dance in a program of ballet divertissements for the second edition of the "Century of Progress" fair. It was inside the fairgrounds this year, in the little pavilion called the English Village, where English folk-dancers gave exhibitions throughout the day and at night were replaced by two presentations of an hour-long ballet program. Ruth Pryor, the ballerina of the opera, whom Ruth was about to replace, was the featured artist, and seven other members of the opera ballet assisted. Though they had to dance, on toe as well as off, on a floor consisting of foot-square green tiles with wide spaces between them, they managed to do it nicely. Bentley had choreographed a little Strauss waltz which came off well in spite of the uncooperative stage. This was where Ruth saw him for the first time, and she was so pleased by both his dancing and his partnering that she decided at once to keep him on as premier danseur in the company she was now engaged in forming from scratch for the opera.

He also was a Mid-American (from South Dakota), but he had come to Chicago by way of New York. He had danced there and on tour in several Broadway musicals, was a leading dancer with Agnes de Mille in Christopher Morley's famous Hoboken revival of *The Black Crook* and had been Margaret Severn's partner in a series of New York recitals.

The collaboration with Ruth worked so well throughout the opera season that when summer came along, they made a joint tour of the New England summer theatres. It was a perfectly good summer tour, but its most significant aspect was something that did not even show from the front; this was the fact that it was the first project to be sponsored by a new organization called the Chicago Ballet Company. Tom had set it up in November as, idealistically, a kind of continuation of the structure of the old Chicago Allied Arts, for the purpose of producing ballets (Ruth's ballets primarily, of course) with Chicago as its home base. Practically, until that ultimate goal could be reached, it would serve as an impersonal legal entity, virtually a holding company, for all Ruth's enterprises for whatever producing organization and under whatever name. It was duly chartered by the state of Illinois with Ruth as its president, though as far as aptitude or desire was concerned, she might as well have been chartered as Empress of Russia. It was Tom, of course, who ran it.

The first major step was taken toward the consumnation of its prime purpose immediately after the close of the 1935 opera season, when Ruth launched a ballet company of her own for the first time. Under the name of Ruth Page Ballets it gave a performance in February 1936 at the Studebaker Theatre in Chicago; substantially this was a preparatory warm-up for a New York debut under the auspices of S. Hurok at the Adelphi Theatre on March 1 and 2. The company consisted of thirty members of the opera ballet, with Bentley Stone and Blake Scott featured along with herself. The other soloists were Walter Camryn, Mark Turbyfill, Virginia Nugent, Sandra Davis, Margot Koche, Paul DuPont, Evelyn Chapman and Bettina Rosay.

The program was made up of four ballets, three of which had already been presented at one time or another during the opera seasons and elsewhere. The single new one was called *Love Song* and was set to some orchestrated songs of Schubert. All four of them were designed by Remisoff, and all but one were conducted by Van Grove.

That one was conducted by its composer, Aaron Copland, and was the first of his scores for dancing to be produced. Ruth had heard his *Music for the Theatre* at the Elizabeth Sprague Coolidge Festival of Chamber Music at the Library of Congress in 1933 and was so impressed by the theatrical gift that underlay his already familiar musical gift that she asked him to write a ballet for her. "I paid him $150," she says, "which was very hard for me to find, and he seemed delighted to get it." Its title was *Hear Ye! Hear Ye!*, and its scenario, by Ruth and Remisoff, treated wittily of a nightclub-murder trial in which all three eyewitnesses told different stories. It had its première the following year in her first season at the opera.

Of the two other works, one was a farcical bit, of which Remisoff was again coscenarist, called *Gold Standard,* set to music of Jacques Ibert; and the other one was the tried and true *Iberian Monotone.*

At the bottom of the printed program in New York was a hopeful
addendum: "For engagements write Chicago Grand Opera Company."
Hurok, much pleased, had told her that if only she had a foreign name, he
could book her everywhere. But she did not have a foreign name, the program note drew no response and nothing happened. Nevertheless, she had a
company of her own, and she knew that eventually something would happen,
because it had to happen. All that was needed was patience, perseverance and
money. Her store of patience was even lower than her store of money, but
her perseverance was doughty and indomitable.

The summer of 1936 she spent, as usual, dancing and choreographing
whatever bookings had been provided. She was director and star dancer for
the Louisville Civic Ballet, with Bentley as her partner and assistant; and an
interesting novelty was achieved at Cincinnati's famous Zoo Opera in Eden
Park, where Blake Scott was now well established in the summer as ballet
director. What she produced there was a ballet version of Gershwin's *An
American in Paris* with Paul Draper as its star.

In the spring of 1937 she was off on another solo tour, this time in
Scandinavia. (Bentley was not available as her partner, since he had joined
London's Ballet Rambert as guest soloist and choreographer for a tour of the
Continent.) In program this was no different from her other summer tours,
but in other respects there were substantial differences, for this was new
territory for her and she was the first American "concert" dancer to appear
there. Paul Cravath, however, had given her a letter of introduction to a
member of the Norwegian Chamber of Deputies; Harald Kreutzberg and Fritz
Wilckens were touring Scandinavia at the same time; Ronny Johansson, who
had been, inversely, the first of the European modern dancers to appear in
America in the days of the Chicago Allied Arts, was a tower of strength to
her, both socially and professionaly, in Stockholm, and she was by no means
in a personal wilderness.

The character of her program is clearly exemplified by the one she gave
in Helsingfors: *Chinoiserie (1 and 2)* (Mozart), *Valse Mondaine* (Castelnuovo-
Tedesco), *Possessed* (Villa-Lobos), *Figures in Space* (R. Wolf), *Love Song*
(Schubert), *Humoresques: Berceuse, Giddy Girl, Señorita* (Casella), *Variations
on Euclid* (Mompou), *Morning in Spring* (Vaughan Williams), *My Sorrow Is My
Song* (Milhaud), *Promenade* (Poulenc), *Tropic* (Cyril Scott), *Gypsy* (De Falla).

Though some of it was on point, it was nevertheless in tune with the
modern influences of the time, and a critic in Helsingfors wrote in regard to
her always popular *Tropic* that "the dancer's plastic art (feet and toes) was
phenomenal and has never been seen before." The reviews were generally
excellent.

The curtain had scarcely fallen on the final performance when she set
out on another tour, this time not as a performer but as a spectator. With

Harald and Fritz she went to Germany to see what was going on there; then with hardly time to catch her breath she was off to London. There she learned that the Markova-Dolin Ballet was presenting some Nijinska works that she had not seen in Nottingham, whereupon she broke a luncheon engagement with her old friend Bruguiere and hopped aboard the train. Here she dashed off a letter to Tom in which she wrote: "I have no nightgown or toothbrush but my little toe-shoes are in my pocketbook so I can do my barre."

As if her schedule had not been sufficiently demanding, she wrote letters about the dance in Europe to critics on the *Chicago Tribune*, the *New York Times*, the *Christian Science Monitor*, the *Dance Observer*; all of whom printed them gratefully, for they were spontaneous, informative and characteristically engaging. Far from being carbon copies of each other, each of them began where the other left off. This natural practice of friendly, even if semiofficial, correspondence made her always her own best press agent.

The opera's budget during these depression years was getting skimpier and skimpier. At the end of the 1937 season, however, she showed her mettle by somehow managing to save enough money out of her budget to stage a new work called *An American Pattern*. Its music was Jerome Moross's first ballet score, and Bentley was her cochoreographer. It must have taken some tight squeezing, since her budget for the entire season amounted to only $7,000 (plus about $500 for a rehearsal pianist), and out of this had to come dancers' salaries and many of their costumes.

Warfare—Local, Marital, Global

In January 1938, on the very heels of having squeezed *An American Pattern* out of her meager budget, Ruth was, to all intents and purposes, fired for the only time in her life. Strictly speaking, she was simply not reengaged, because the opera, which had now gone through another of its reorganizations and become the Chicago City Opera Company, had found a way to have a ballet without any financial outlay. In its official announcement to the press it did not mention Ruth at all but merely stated that Catherine Littlefield's Philadelphia Ballet, with its sixty-five dancers, would be in residence for the next season, would dance in all the opera ballets and present an all-ballet program every Tuesday evening during the seven-week season.

When the news was reported in the *Chicago Tribune* in late April, the fat was in the fire. Chicago, always jealous of its individuality, and especially tetchy about that region known as "The East," rose behind Ruth with a vigor that must have been balsam to her wounds. In the field of the arts Chicago had every right to be proud, for in its few generations as a community it had built itself a notable culture, as far as it went, with independence and self-awareness. In painting, sculpture and art education; in music, poetry and theatre; in architecture outstandingly, it had made its own way with high distinction, and in many instances had a definite edge on New York.

To make matters worse, these were the depression years, and Chicago workers were now being thrown onto relief by outsiders. There were indignant letters to the press and a great deal of talk about money—claims of cost-cutting on one hand and accusations of undercutting on the other. But whatever the financial arrangements with the incoming company may have been, it was the opera's miserly sponsors who threw the local dancers out of work, and Miss Littlefield received considerably less than justice in the fracas.

The middle thirties saw the spontaneous outcropping of a number of American ballets. In the season of 1935-36 alone Ruth's company, Catherine Littlefield's and Lincoln Kirstein's all made their debuts in their several home cities. Ruth's and Catherine's differed alike from Kirstein's in that they were both the subjective emanation, so to speak, of practicing dancers, while his was based more objectively on a long-range historico-aesthetic theory. Nevertheless, the two differed widely from each other as well.

Catherine's professional outlook and background were rooted in the traditional academic dance. She was trained first in her mother's studio, and after her studies in Europe and some bread-and-butter engagements on Broadway she took over the school herself and made it one of the best in the East. This gave her an enormous advantage when she started her own company, for except for a trio of experienced male dancers (and sometimes her dancing sister and brother) it consisted entirely of young dancers she had trained from the beginning. By the time she came to Chicago, she had already staged the first full-length production in America of Petipa's *Sleeping Beauty*, had presented her company in Europe as the first American ballet company to appear there and was very much on her toes. Eight years younger than Ruth, she was an excellent dancer, a lovely-looking girl, and for all her traditional heritage, she was the antithesis of "stuffy."

Ruth's strength, on the other hand, lay in the very absence of this "substantiality." She moved and thought in all sorts of free styles, turned her back on the established repertoire, and ventured into fresh fields that made her almost as "modern" as she was "classic," in spite of her fidelity to basic Cecchetti. She was witty, stylish, musical and intensely visual. At this point she was less "dependable" than Catherine but more "interesting." They were both now turning their attention to American subject matter, with no similarities whatever in manner or texture.

Catherine managed to survive in Chicago for three seasons, when, in spite of the reputed savings of funds, the opera found itself once again in the familiar financial morass.

WPA = WORK PROGRESSING ADMIRABLY

Ruth had immediately packed up her "doll rags," and her "dolls" as well, and taken them (or many of them) forthwith into the WPA Federal Theatre's dance project, to which she offered her services as ballet director, with Bentley at her side. She received only $150 a month (the corps members got $94), but it was probably the most productive move she ever made. She found the best working conditions she had ever experienced, she served the cause of keeping her incipient ballet company together and appearing before broader audiences, and she put together out of the general collaborativeness of the situation the ballet that, more than any other, spread her name far and wide. This was *Frankie and Johnny*, which really started her on her "adult" career.

It was one of three works that opened at the Great Northern Theatre in mid-June and ran for six weeks. The other two were *An American Pattern*, moved over from the opera house with some new dancers added from the relief rolls, and a modern dance work, created by Grace and Kurt Graff, called *Behind This Mask*. The same supporting company appeared in all three pieces, and it was by all odds the longest run that any local dance company had ever had in Chicago.

An American Pattern had a scenario by Ruth and Remisoff, and costumes by Remisoff in his best manner. It dealt with a woman—any woman—trying to escape from "the standardization of organized society," including a "typical" businessman for a husband. She seeks "conventional escapes" through a gigolo, a tycoon, a mystic and a political "agitator," but none of them works, and she ends as just another "Matron" like the three figures who have been stalking her after the manner of the Fates.

From this to *Frankie and Johnny* was a far cry. Some two years earlier in Hollywood Jerome Moross had started to write the music and sought the collaboration of the young playwright Michael Blankfort, on the scenario, but it had not been completed until Ruth commissioned it "via the WPA." Paul DuPont designed the costumes and claimed until the day he died that he had also designed the set instead of Clive Rickabaugh, the head of the local scenic union, who was officially credited with it. He claimed besides to have suggested the use of three Salvation Army lasses ("Saving Susies" on the program) as a chorus to justify the onstage singing of the ribald verses. Ruth and Bentley were indisputably the choreographers, however, and played the title roles, along with Ann Devine as Nellie and Sean Marino as the Bartender.

But whoever did what, the work could only have come to life as it did in a collaborative atmosphere, for it reeked with the hilarious raunchiness of nose-thumbing adolescence that so strongly characterized the Great Depression's revolutionary protest. That it was a controversial episode, especially since it was produced with public funds, goes without saying. Carl Sandburg had called the ballad itself "America's classical gutter song"; now one critic denounced it as bawdy, and another called it "one of the best things Mr. Roosevelt has done."

The piece was divided, rather like a suite, into seven "dances": "Bawdy House Stomp," "Frankie and Johnny Blues," "Beer Parlor Rag," "Bartender's Rag," "Frankie Tune," "Fox-Trot Murder" and "Funeral Party One-Step." Which gives an idea of the irreverent gusto that prevailed.

A second Federal Theatre dance program was presented at the Blackstone Theatre the first of March, this time without the participation of the Graffs, and ran for four weeks. Though it came forth with nothing so pungent as *Frankie and Johnny*, it did include an outstanding new work choreographed by Ruth and Bentley under the title of *Guns and Castanets*. It was a one-act version of *Carmen* and was Ruth's first adventure in making ballets out of operas, though a quite atypical one. Moross had made a very free arrangement of the Bizet score on a scenario devised by Ruth. It was very much in the tendentious tone so characteristic of the depression-born Federal Theatre, which in normal times was not in the least native to Ruth. The Spanish civil war was its milieu, with José as a loyalist soldier, Escamillo as a fascist aviator who fell out of the sky (onto the stage) in an air raid and Carmen as a café girl who did not know which side was which and did not care. From time to time a single male voice in the orchestra pit spoke lines from García Lorca's "Lament for Ignacio Sanchez Mejias."

The other numbers on this second Federal Theatre program were a revival of her *Love Song* and a group of divertissements under the title of *Scrapbook*.

It is unfortunate that Ruth did not come into the dance project sooner, for at this very moment an obstreperous Congress abolished the whole Federal Theatre, and the dance world was again on its uppers.

For Ruth and Bentley, whether with or without the rest of the company, there was still that fairly invisible organization known as the Chicago Ballet Company, which with Tom's eternal diligence had been getting them bookings through regional and national managements between opera seasons. Now they carried right on, for as long as they could, more or less on the Federal Theatre pattern, under the new name of the Page-Stone Ballet—or, in full, the Page-Stone Chicago Opera Ballet, which gave them more identity in those areas known in show-biz parlance as "the sticks."

In their first season they played forty performances with a company of thirty on a tour that covered more than four thousand miles, which was very good indeed. Also very good was the fact that in 1940 they were the first ballet from the United States to appear in South America, on a tour that took them to Havana and Curaçao and finally to Caracas for a whole month with the Municipal Opera Company. For 1941 a more extensive South

American tour was in process of being booked, but things were getting difficult because of the war in Europe; the British censor was stopping all mail at Trinidad, and it was increasingly hard to get communications through.

What was Ruth's delight, then, to receive a letter from Lincoln Kirstein telling her that he also had a tour of South America in the offing and asking her to stage *Frankie and Johnny* for his company. He had been commissioned by the U.S. Office of Commercial and Cultural Relations Between the American Republics, of which Nelson Rockefeller was head, to organize a ballet company for a goodwill tour of Latin America. Though the government's financial responsibility consisted only of getting such a company to South America and back, the idea was very much to Kirstein's liking. As a basis he planned to use the small company he had formed under the name of Ballet Caravan in 1936. Balanchine and the American Ballet as a whole had become by then part of the Metropolitan Opera setup, and Kirstein had chosen the small group from the parent company to make summer tours with the special purpose of developing American choreographers, composers and designers and, without being chauvinistic about it, using American subject matter where possible. By now, however, in 1941, the parent company had long since ended its opera association and was largely inactive; accordingly Balanchine was free to become artistic director for the South American tour of a somewhat larger organization, the name of which was now changed to the American Ballet Caravan.

Because of Kirstein's innate idealism and his wish not to use a government project for the exploitation of his own company, he invited not only Ruth but the Littlefield company and the two more recently organized American ballets—Willam Christensen's San Francisco Ballet and Richard Pleasant's Ballet Theatre in New York—to contribute to the repertory as well. Ruth was already too concerned with her own problem to worry about abstract idealism, but she, or rather Tom, saw as a possible solution to both problems the idea of combining with Kirstein to make it a joint venture. In the end Kirstein's more complicated plan could not be realized, and his own company made the tour alone.

As for Ruth's tour, it was postponed bit by bit because of the war and finally had to be abandoned. She was fretting more and more at not having done any continuous dancing since the end of the 1940 tour; this was for her a form of acute suffering. To add to the general instability of the situation, on May 8 Tom, now spending most of his time in Texas, received the following telegram: "Bentley A-1 in draft. May be called next week. Has until Friday write objections. Telephone me tonight. Will read his letter to you then. Peter."

PETER AND THE WOLF

"Peter," of course, was Ruth. This was Tom's longtime name for her, ever since the early Bolm days when she had done a dance called *Peter Pan*. There is, we are told, nothing in a name, yet one of the many inexplicable emanations of a marriage built on genuine affection is the nicknames that prevail, for when they have emerged from their intimate origins they carry over implications that make them an eloquent means of communication, and even in the presence of others their use becomes a gesture of especial closeness to the company present.

In the telegram Ruth was concerned only with the obvious professional crisis of Bentley; she was quite unaware that a second and more formidable crisis was developing in the sacrosanct area out of which "Peter" had evolved. In their long established pattern of life she was generally making extended tours and Tom was virtually commuting to Texas, and they managed to be together only on those fortuitous crossings of their individual circuits that brought them both for brief periods into Chicago. At this particular period, as it happened, Tom was having a romance on the side. Almost everybody in their circle of friends knew about it and none of them took it seriously; nor, for that matter, did the romancers themselves, but it was serving its purpose excellently. They met not only in Chicago but also on occasion in New York or wherever else their paths happened to cross, and even in the little house in Hubbard Woods. Meanwhile Ruth was so busy with the jobs Tom managed to provide for her that Peter had no inkling what was going on.

In the autumn, with the help of a New York booker she accepted an engagement to appear with Bentley for a period of weeks in the Rainbow Room in New York on the sixty-fifth floor of one of the buildings in Rockefeller Center. She had never danced in a nightclub before, and had an uncomfortable feeling that it was beneath her, but she was desperate for an opportunity to perform. Besides, since the King Ranch was not only bringing in nothing but actually draining the exchequer, the fairly plush way of life to which she and Tom were accustomed was being threatened, and it was necessary to make a little money. Bentley's call-up had been temporarily deferred, so the two of them packed up and set out for New York, with Ruth's beloved maid, Effie, who was cook, chatelaine, keeper of the wardrobe, friend and confidante, going along, as she often did.

It was on the eve of departure that Ruth stumbled upon the evidence of Tom's amorous escapade. He protested quite reasonably that though he was not in the least in love with the woman, he had not yet made any plans to renounce the call of the flesh, nor had the call of the flesh made any effort to renounce him. Under the circumstances, a bird under the bushes seemed preferable to even the most desirable of nests without a bird. Since Ruth, for all her outward poise, was patently distressed, he agreed to abandon the whole affair. To this day Ruth declares she was not jealous, and it may be true in a measure; what may have upset her was being so blatantly cuckolded—to use the expression in a disturbing reversal of its usual application.

Her letters, however, seem to indicate a femininely complex admixture of both responses. She had hardly got on the train before she started to write them:

> Dearest—I am going to bed in a few minutes and I wish I could go to bed with you. Incidentally, don't you think it would be a good idea for you to do a little mild exercise this winter other than fornicating? . . . Impossible to write on this train but I am thinking plenty. . . . I am, believe me, not at all happy to leave Chicago, although maybe it will be good for you to be alone (that is, if you will let yourself be alone) to contemplate the respective virtues and vices of your wives No. 1 and 2. I was wrong to think I could have a career and marriage too and I probably have neglected you and I'll make up for it. I am not for one second interested even remotely in my job at the Rainbow. Dancing has become to me a degraded thing and something to be ashamed of—maybe we are just acrobats who are chasing beautiful dreams. You will be my beautiful dream now. I desire you. Peter.

And the next morning, still on the train as it chugged down the shore of the Hudson:

> Beloved—The river is beautiful this morning and I hope it will erase my night thoughts which are still with me (because I haven't had breakfast)—my thoughts of the lake and our little house which was always such heaven for me. I wish it would burn down so that I could never be reminded of the two of you in our bedroom together. Forgive me but I think I will be haunted by that forever and it is so stupid to be so sentimental about a place. . . . Well, I will look for new friends but I just can't look for a new husband because you are the only husband for me. So forgive me for mentioning the past—I will think and think and think of the river and try to forget the lake. . . . One shouldn't have night thoughts that last till breakfast. Well—here comes my coffee. . . . I do so want you to be happy, my little pet. And if you *ever* want a divorce, you know there will be no scandals—no alimony and nothing to worry about. I'd rather have anything than have our marriage be humdrum. Don't read this letter. . . . Don't worry, everything is fine and I adore you. This is my punishment which I deserve.

It is perhaps not altogether irrelevant that the letter arrived air mail special delivery with six cents postage due.

Again, Sunday, Nov. 16, 10 a.m.:

> . . . How are you today, baby? Do you miss me and the cats? And Ef and our Sunday a.m. coffee? I am just about to order coffee and read the Times—you know I love that Sunday a.m. It is so warm here—like summer. I am ashamed to write so many letters. . . . I don't want to

seem to be chasing you and yet I want you to know how I feel. I just
don't feel natural with you anymore and don't know quite how to act.
I don't like to use the word "love" because you used that with her and
it doesn't seem to have any meaning. . . . I can stand *anything* but
deceit. A long kiss. Peter.

At the end of another fortnight:

. . . I love dancing every night and I *love* having Sunday off. It agrees
with my tummy. . . . Just finished our first show. We were *really* good
tonite. It's amazing how long it has taken me to get back into practice.
Believe me, a year and a half is a long time not to dance in a *dancer's*
career. And if you can understand it, you see one reason this business
hit me so hard was because I felt the dancing left me the same time you
did. . . . So all in all, forgive me if I say foolish things and act foolish.
I just have to get myself adjusted. I feel so conscience-stricken about
you. I feel I should do something for you, and if I dance I can't really.
And you know if I don't dance, I need so much more love from you
and from my friends. You have so many what I call "amitiés
amoureuses" with your girl friends . . . so I should have some. All my
girl friends have been such a flop. . . .

And so on and so on and so on.

It is easy to see that Peter was no gentleman. As for Tom, on the other
hand, there is no indication that the name of Isamu was ever whispered. With
the passing of time the tension necessarily relaxed, but in neither case were
the deeply seated antagonisms of jealousy uprooted, and they were to arise
repeatedly, if only to make a moue or two and subside.

As for the Rainbow Room engagement itself, it was a new experience
altogether for Ruth, since she had never before danced with the spectators all
around her and at such close quarters. "It is a strange and new feeling," she
wrote shortly afterward in one of those articles she was always writing, "to
look up suddenly and perhaps find someone more interested in eating a piece
of beefsteak than watching your *port de bras*. It is perhaps a little discon-
certing, too, and you will find yourself doing all kinds of things to command
his attention. When you succeed you feel at least a partial satisfaction." And
with people on all sides of her she found herself "suddenly uncomfortably
conscious of [her] 'rear.' "

She was also upset by the necessity, at such close range, for the
"natural" and the "real." "In the theatre," she wrote, "you can daub the
greasepaint on heavily and freely, enlarging your features into something
strange and interesting, but in a nightclub it seems you must look 'natural.'
You also have to wear real lace, real satins and embroideries, and your
costumes must at least appear to be expensive. You can't just pin things on
effectively with safety pins, and you can't have darns in your tights. In other
words, you have to be so careful and so 'soignée' that you can't have as much

freedom putting your costumes together as you can on the stage. Making up 'à la Helena Rubinstein' was a great bore to me."

Selecting a nightclub program from a concert repertory was another problem, for the director, John Roy, seemed to be looking for either the "very beautiful" or the "very funny." She was much surprised that he chose her *Tropic*, since "the lazy, fierce mood of the hot countries is felt in this impression of the creeping jungle of the tropics," and eventually he changed his mind and took it out. It was the first time this always successful number had found itself ineffectual. She was also surprised that he wanted the number she and Bentley danced to Liszt's piano arrangement of Wagner's "Liebestod," for it seemed both too serious and too long for a nightclub. But she was wrong. "It was not exactly what Variety calls a 'socko' number, but the audience always sat quiet and attentive, even on Saturday nights and even on 'debutante' nights, which latter were by far our most difficult audiences." As Effie pointed out, "even if they didn't understand it, they paid attention to you." Perhaps the hit of the show was their caricature of old-fashioned ballet "inanities and rivalries," called *Zephyr and Flora*, which Variety called both "socko" and "clicko."

In the midst of their engagement came that fateful December 7, and we were suddenly in the war. At first nobody came to the performances, since they thought the high building was too good a target for enemy planes, but after a few days the situation changed. The windows were all painted black, the entire staff was trained for emergencies and practice "blackouts" were announced, during which patrons were requested "to continue dancing or to remain seated."

"So let's continue dancing," writes Ruth by way of conclusion. "Shut your eyes. Hold your breath. Let the world below you stop one tiny instant. Singe your wings with stardust, black out the vulgarities you know to be there, and with 'New Horizons' ('the perfume that carries you on and on') tucked discreetly behind your ears, and your lips outlined with 'Fighting Red' ('that new brave lipstick'), build up your morale to wartime hysteria. Mr. Rockefeller, Mr. Roy and the Rainbow Room will fly you high in their steady kite, anchored so far from reality. Remain seated? No, thank you—let's dance!"

THE DESERT IN BLOOM

Not stardust, not New Horizons, not Fighting Red could ever have lulled Ruth into remaining seated throughout the war, for the only reality for her was to continue dancing—which of course she did. Bentley was in the air force for the duration; the company had disintegrated over the long dry spell, and many of them had gone to New York in search of jobs. New procedures were required, but she had two built-in resources that sparked each other into action, come hell or high water. The first was herself as a performer, and the second was a powerhouse of ideas about how to bring the first into objective being. Worrying and fretting were part of the process, but eventually something inevitably emerged. In this case two things did so and both were of major importance to her career. One was a revival of her longtime love of dancing to poetry, and the other was her first isolation of the germ of opera-as-ballet.

But there was still some pinch-hitting to be done before either of them took shape. Not even the war could alter the consistent unpredictability of Chicago's opera. After having skipped the 1941 season, it suddenly came to life in 1942 (under the name of the Chicago Opera Company) with Fortune Gallo as director. According to Cecil Smith in the *Tribune*, the contract had been signed at the last minute, and Ruth came in as ballet director even a minute later than that. Gallo had long directed a popular-priced opera company in New York and on tour, and Smith found him "insensitive." There was of course no ballet company at hand to invite in, and even the Littlefield one had just gone out of existence, partly because of the wartime shortage of men. Except for Patricia Bowman, whom Gallo had brought along from New York to be première danseuse, the company had to be put together from scratch. The ballet was now unionized for the first time, and rehearsal time had been cut accordingly (which seems to have shown from the front). But Ruth, for whom opera ballet, even in emergency conditions, had an inordinate attraction, did what she could. Walter Camryn, Stanley Herbertt and David Ahdar were among the old familiars from the pre-Littlefield days who had not yet been called up, and with Vera Mirova, Patricia Bowman, Bettina Rosay and herself in the cast she managed for the opening night what seems to have been an effective ballet in *Lakmé*, for which she used additional music from the composer's ballet *La Source*. In another instance she put together a group of four dances as an emergency prelude to *Rigoletto*, because the Gilda of the evening, Josephine Antoine, had a radio broadcast already booked for the early evening. And the season somehow ran its course.

When July came around Ruth staged the dances for "spectacular" productions of *Aida* and *Carmen* in the huge Soldiers Field, under the joint sponsorship of Gallo and the chief local impresario, Harry Zelzer. The productions were so great a financial success that Gallo, on his own, presented outdoor repetitions of them, with Ruth's collaboration again, in Cleveland and Pittsburgh. The dance unit consisted of only ten girls and two men, which is scarcely of spectacular dimensions, but after all, work is work, opera is opera, a salary is a salary, and Ruth is Ruth. She was sitting nothing out.

Her intervening springtime activities were altogether on the creative side. It was her lack of a dancing partner that led her to the idea of a solo recital based on her love for dancing to her own speaking of poetry. She had drifted naturally into this in the inspiring days of the Allied Arts, back in 1925, under the spell of Mark Turbyfill's poems. She felt in them something of the rhythms of dancing, which he as a dancer had undoubtedly put into them, however unconsciously. Now she approached it more practically and more professionally, and as soon as she had put together a program that pleased her, she flew out to Hollywood to discuss it with Remisoff, who was now permanently located there, designing for the movies. She worked with him on all her numbers and was delighted with the results. "The costumes," she found "change the movement, and really *make* the dances in a real sense." In the early spring she was in New York, and on April 13 she showed her program for the first time in a private performance, somewhat to her own surprise.

The idea had originated with Winthrop Palmer, whose particular passions among the arts were poetry and dancing. A poet of distinction herself, she had also formed a dance company called Dance Players with Eugene Loring as its central figure and had taken it out to a house of its own in Bucks County, Pennsylvania, to live and work while preparing a first program for presentation in New York. The project had perished in its infancy after this country's entry into the war, but her enthusiasms were still alive. A descendant of the Winthrops of Massachusetts and the Bushnells (she was herself born Bushnell) of Connecticut, she was as visionary and as courageous as her early American ancestors, in fields they had not dreamed of.

Ruth's new venture struck a responsive chord at once, and since she was not one to have enthusiasms without doing something about them, she engaged the little Humphrey-Weidman Studio Theatre (well off Broadway, long before there was such a formal area as Off-Broadway) and invited a hand-picked audience of her friends to demonstrate to them the potentialities of such an unorthodox medium. Whether this elite preview made any practical contribution or not to Ruth's plans, she soon had a contract with the National Concerts and Artists Corp. (Management Pop Division—such being the mysterious ramifications of commercial tour directors), and for the next several years she was to present her "Dances with Words and Music" between opera seasons and other temporarily stationary employments.

Thanks to her father, the autocrat of the breakfast table who had demanded verse instead of twaddle at the morning meal, her choice of poets was eclectic. She danced not only to Turbyfill but also to Edna Millay, Li Po, Carl Sandburg, Ogden Nash, e.e. cummings, Dorothy Parker, García Lorca, Amy Lowell, Archibald MacLeish, Beaudelaire, Eugene Field, Hilaire Belloc and various anonymous writers of limericks. It seems almost like filial disloyalty that James Whitcomb Riley was not among them.

During her first year of touring, in 1943, Tom, never shy about promotion, asked George Dillon, then editor of *Poetry* magazine, if he would care to comment on her work, and Dillon definitely did. Said he: "I have seen others dance (intransitive verb) to poetry, but Ruth Page is the only one I have seen who *dances the poems*. It is a new art experience."

She tells an amusing anecdote about herself and Alexandra Danilova, prima ballerina of the Ballet Russe de Monte Carlo: "Once I bragged to Danilova that I could speak and do pirouettes at the same time, and she said to me, 'And Root, about what do you speak when you do pirouettes?' "

The most difficult aspect of building such a program had been finding suitable music. Always a task when the idea of the dance comes first, it becomes even more so when the music must also suit specific words. In this department, the war, which had in a sense created the problem, also solved it by sending exactly the proper composer to her rescue. He was Lehman Engel, who was stationed virtually at her doorstep at the Great Lakes Naval Training Station as conductor of its concert band. He had composed scores for Martha Graham, Doris Humphrey, Charles Weidman and other modern dancers and had created and conducted a notable company of Madrigal Singers for the WPA music project, which he had continued on his own after the project had been discontinued. Of course he and Ruth knew each other (as well as every other VIP or IP or even P), partly because of a common instinct for career-making and partly out of sheer gregariousness. Beyond this, they were both lively, witty and sophisticated.

At thirty-two he was plump and cherubic, with a smile that all but cut his face in half; so, early on, when he had put on his gob's uniform in his training period, he had tried to anticipate the dignity of his officer's commission by assuming a perpetual big black cigar as part of his wardrobe to offset his genial air of juvenility. His musicianship, his artistic discipline and his authoritative conducting, however, did it better for him. He was the obvious choice to write music for Ogden Nash's "The Seven Spiritual Ages of Mrs. Marmaduke Moore" and the set of freewheeling limericks, but he was also perfectly in tune with Archibald MacLeish's lyrical "Nocturne," and the García Lorca "Lament for the Death of a Spanish Bullfighter" (as it was here titled) with its recurrent doom-ridden "five o'clock in the afternoon."

Besides this, in an area quite apart from that of the danced poems, Lehman made an even more important contribution to her art by indirectly and backhandedly kindling the spark that led to her translating operas into ballets. They had many musical enthusiasms in common, but they also had a kindred sense of abusive humor about what they did not like that sometimes led to uproarious artistic slander. One of its manifestations was a strongly negative enthusiasm for the absurdity of nineteenth-century Italian operas, with their unintelligible librettos and their general wallowing in musical bathos. *Il Trovatore* was the one that inspired their most mischievous delight, and in less time than you can bat an eye they had decided to collaborate on a ballet version of it that would shake the walls of the opera house with iconoclastic laughter. That it did not turn out at all like this is not to deny the creative vitality of the inspiration.

Naturally the two of them saw less and less of each other as their individual activities increased, and Ruth soon became so involved in an unexpected cycle of productivity that she was perpetually out of artistic breath. But she was never one to abandon a project that had caught her fancy. This one she held on to for eight years through all sorts of adventures, frustrating and triumphant, and at longer or shorter intervals it would emerge momentarily through some flash of remembered amusement. But when it finally came to fruition, it had taken a form that was the very reverse of its bantering origin and that set her on a path she was to follow for nearly twenty years.

Americana à la Russe
de Monte Carlo

This Story Ain't Got No Moral—Or Is It?

War or no war, King Ranch or no King Ranch, Tom never lost the momentum of his activities in Ruth's behalf. He was now approaching not only concert managers but also ballet impresarios. Topmost on his list of works to be pushed were *Frankie and Johnny* and *Love Song*; the latter was one of Ruth's favorites, possibly because it was classic and poetic and much nearer the norm of what she wanted to do.

The raffish *Frankie*, however, was of far greater importance not only for the progress of her art in the direction it had hinted at with *The Flapper and the Quarterback*, but also for its bold enrichment of the burgeoning American genre ballet in general. Its forthright impudence called forth gasps and even protests, but it was a work of great originality and sound craftsmanship and, though it lost some of the battles, it could not fail to win the war. It was, indeed, one of the most significant ballets of its day.

For some reason 1944 was the year when the *Frankie and Johnny* saga suggested itself simultaneously to producers in various areas of theatrical activity. In June the report got around that Katherine Dunham was planning to do her own version of it with her all-Negro company under the auspices of S. Hurok and the European impresario Leon Greanin. It was not her intention, of course, to use the version Ruth had used; she planned, indeed, to go back to the original black St. Louis milieu out of which the ballad had evolved. Tom nevertheless protested at once and often, though with no legal ground to stand on other than possibly that of "unfair competition."

105

Competition it would undoubtedly have been, for Ruth had no intention of abandoning her own production. A lively correspondence ensued, until finally the Hurok office wrote: "I think you are setting up straw men and attacking them furiously. Relax. When and if we have something to talk about, I have no doubt we shall get together." That time never came, for the Dunham production faded quietly out of the picture.

At the same time an even more threatening possibility arose when it was announced in the press that Metro-Goldwyn-Mayer would sponsor a stage musical on the *Frankie and Johnny* theme to be directed by Robert Milton, with book by John Huston (based on a play he had written and published as long ago as 1930) and music by Duke Ellington. This was a formidable combination, and no less so when a little later Jerome Kern was named as the likely composer (however unlikely he would seem to have been by nature).

The show was expected to reach New York in January or February. If this should materialize, the production of Ruth's ballet, which had never been seen outside Chicago's Federal Theatre project, would be seriously jeopardized, and she must get it on first or she would probably never get it on at all.

Then in mid-July official announcement was made of the creation of a new ballet company by George de Cuevas, eighth Marquis de Piedrablanca de Guana, Chilean born of a Spanish father and a Danish mother, and a naturalized American citizen since 1940. His wife was the granddaughter of John D. Rockefeller Sr., and there was accordingly plenty of money behind the venture. The company was called Ballet International, and a small theatre on Columbus Circle, then called the Park Theatre, was bought, elegantly remodeled and renamed the International.

The managing director of the company was Blanche Witherspoon. She had been executive secretary of the American Guild of Musical Artists (AGMA), the union to which all the dancers belonged, since its formation four years earlier; before that she had been on the board of governors of the Metropolitan Opera Guild and she was familiar with the field from all angles. In 1935 her husband, Herbert Witherspoon, the celebrated Wagnerian basso, had become director of the Metropolitan Opera upon the retirement of Giulio Gatti-Casazza. Before he could do much more than start planning, however, he died and was himself succeeded by Edward Johnson. One of the plans Witherspoon had been considering (quite possibly at the suggestion of Paul Cravath) was to turn the direction of the ballet over to Ruth, but no official appointment had been made, and Johnson instead took on Balanchine and the recently formed, but shortly afterward inactivated, American Ballet.

Now, nine years later, Mrs. Witherspoon wrote Ruth and asked her to make a new production of *Frankie and Johnny* for Ballet International. It was to go into the repertory in the fifth week of the season, that of November 26, and to have a total of ten performances with Ruth appearing as guest artist in the first one. Financially the offer was a good one, with a sizable advance against future royalties.

Ruth and Tom, according to their now established practice, acted again through their chartered Chicago Ballet Company. It owned the rights to all their material, and itself directed the execution of the scenery and costumes, more or less after the pattern of a "package" deal. Such an arrangement, however, was not acceptable to de Cuevas, who considered himself a connoisseur in these areas, and there was extensive correspondence on the issue. Regardless of firm resistance on Mrs. Witherspoon's part, however, the physical production was put into the works in Chicago under the direction of Clive Rickabaugh. On September 22 Mrs. Witherspoon, no longer in the mood to argue, wired: "Regret must withdraw offer to do Frankie. One of conditions was that scenery and costumes be manufactured in New York for which there was ample time. Returning two piano copies." Again, five days later, after further messages from Tom: "De Cuevas insists we reaffirm position taken in telegrams Sept. 22 and 26. It is most unsatisfactory to have new costumes made in Chicago. Would require refitting on arrival in New York. Furthermore all scenery and costumes are supervised by George de Cuevas himself as artistic director." To which Tom replied instantly and eagerly: "Delighted de Cuevas wishes supervise costumes. Suggest he come Chicago one trip. Will pay his expenses . . . Costumes easily adjustable. . . ." This time Mrs. Witherspoon took her time; on October 3 she wired: "Sorry but Ballet International is not interested in including Frankie and Johnny in repertoire except on conditions my telegrams of Sept. 22 and 26."

During this drawn-out argument, with no signs of yielding by Mrs. Witherspoon and with that MGM musical still looming as a threat for January, Ruth and Tom let no grass grow under their feet. They showed the film of the Federal Theatre production (Ruth always had her works filmed) to Sergei Denham, director of the Ballet Russe de Monte Carlo, and he seemed to like it. Two days after Mrs. Witherspoon's brushoff Tom sent him "two drafts of contracts relative to the ballet" for his "comments and suggestions," and another two days after that, copies of the newspaper reviews of the 1938 production, with a note suggesting that the ballet was needed in his repertoire to set off the "coolness" of Balanchine. The latter was now restaging some of his old works and creating new ones for the Ballet Russe, of which he was acting virtually as artistic director, for during these war years Kirstein was serving in the army overseas and had no plans for resuming his production activities. The entire Balanchine repertory had been offered by him to Ballet Theatre, but the company's manager had declined, much to the advantage of the Ballet Russe.

After several weeks of further negotiations the contract was finally signed between the Ballet Russe and the Chicago Ballet Company. The financial arrangement did not even approach that of the de Cuevas offer, but under the circumstances any terms were better than none.

On October 20 Tom wrote to Rickabaugh that Ruth (who was still on the road with her solo program of "Words and Music") would join the touring Ballet Russe in San Francisco in early December for a week to rehearse *Frankie*, and for the following two weeks in Los Angeles, where it would go into the repertoire for the first time, and she wanted Rickabaugh there to get the set on in correct shape. Moross, who was now in Hollywood again, would conduct the Los Angeles première. Bentley had already got leave to go to Chicago for preliminary rehearsals in early November, and he and she would both step into later performances on the road from time to time if they were not too remote from the scene. The title roles were to be danced regularly by Ruthanna Boris and Frederick Franklin, except for the New York opening on February 28 and the second performance two nights later, when Ruth and Bentley were to appear.

After all the haste and hassling to beat the musical into New York that project disappeared into the same limbo that had swallowed up Katherine Dunham's.

In mid-January Ruth wrote to Denham that their "sneak preview" of the ballet in Kansas City had gone well, but she urged that Boris and Franklin be given as many performances as possible before New York, since there was no guarantee that Bentley would be able to get away from his Topeka post. There were many problems about the physical production; the management found that the set was much too heavy and complicated for touring, particularly under wartime conditions, and would require "alterations and modifications."

Paul DuPont, already unhappy about not being credited with the design of the set, was now so upset about the changes that had been made in the costumes he had designed that he was crying on the other side of his face and demanding that his name be taken off the program. He was about to leave for the war zone in the ambulance corps and knew he would not be on hand for the New York opening, which no doubt made him especially sensitive. When Tom later sent him the reviews of the opening, along with other data about it, he replied from Germany with a blistering letter.

> Interesting . . . your having complimented Rickabaugh [in an enclosed interview] for the job he did . . . I thought it was rather cruel of you to compliment him so and then send me the carbon. Unless that was some very subtle way of turning the knife after the blow was given. *His work indeed!* But you asked *me* to send you the drawing of the set "which you painted after the Federal Theatre showing." What does that infer? That I just happen to paint a pretty picture after someone's work? Do you happen to remember what a time I had trying to sell you the idea of a realistic production . . . and a modern, that is, contemporary one, when Ruth wanted it gay-ninety? . . ."

CONFLICT OF INTEREST

Frankie and Johnny may not have been such star-crossed lovers as Shakespeare wrote about, but their somewhat more sordid tragedy was having almost as many troubles getting itself consummated. And before it was over, even Friar Laurence's potion and the tomb of the Capulets would have been fairly well approximated.

The production opened at the New York City Center exactly on schedule on Wednesday evening, February 28, and the Orestean Furies themselves could not have devised a more disastrous punctuality. The background of the catastrophe had begun building itself up in November with the altogether unrelated presentation in Philadelphia of a play called *Trio,* dealing with lesbianism, and from there had proceeded step by step with the superb economy of Greek tragedy to the predestined crisis.

In these "liberated" years of the 1970's it is difficult to grasp the horror aroused in the officially conformist attitude of the 1940's by any public mention of sexual "deviation." Naturally the New York reports of the Philadelphia opening leaned heavily on the shocking side of the occasion and, pruriency being what it is, before long private pressures were being brought to bear by religious groups, including the regular moral policing force of the Roman Catholic diocese, upon all the sundry officials around City Hall to prohibit the importation of this nefarious play into sinless New York. Less private protests by indignant letter writers were likewise being made through the columns of the newspapers, and these in turn evoked sharp replies from many important figures in the theatre as well as from the press itself, inveighing against the very concept of arbitrary censorship.

In due course, however, the play came into the Belasco Theatre shortly after Christmas and, no doubt with the help of the advance publicity, continued its mildly successful run for some five weeks. Then on Sunday, February 18, the pastor of the prestigious Fifth Avenue Presbyterian Church preached a sermon, duly reported in the papers, blasting the play and demanding that if it did not voluntarily depart forthwith, the city's Commissioner of Licenses revoke the license of the Belasco Theatre. Whatever may or may not have gone on at City Hall, that is exactly what Commissioner Moss did, and *Trio* closed perforce on Saturday night, February 24. No doubt a slogan like the familiar "banned in Boston," which has helped so many shows to survive, might have brought business to the box office, but with the threat of license revocation no other theatre's owner dared offer such a box office.

Four days later *Frankie and Johnny* was scheduled to open at the New York City Center, which was a theatre in quite a different category from that of the Belasco; it was, indeed, owned by the city itself. It had been built some years before as headquarters for a fraternal organization and contained, besides offices and the like, a sizable auditorium with a platform stage and two large balconies, all designed and decorated flamboyantly in quasi-Arabian style, and it was called Mecca Temple. During the depression years the fraternal organization found itself increasingly unable to pay its taxes, and the building was reluctantly taken over by the city as a white elephant in 1941. Since it was serving no purpose and eating its head off, the idea occurred to the then president of the City Council, Newbold Morris, and his fellow councilman Morton Baum—both deeply interested in music and the theatre— that it would be artistically and socially contributory to the city's cultural life if the building could be somehow transformed into a center for musical and theatrical performances at a price within the reach of the ordinary citizen. Accordingly they drew up a plan whereby a nonprofit membership corpora- tion, called the New York City Center of Music and Drama, would lease the building from the city for the amount it would ordinarily receive from taxes and presented it to Mayor La Guardia. He, quite aside from his political stamina and basic humanism, happened to be the son of a onetime military bandmaster, and the deal was made.

The project opened hopefully, if somewhat drearily, with a ceremonial olla podrida including Walter Damrosch and the Philharmonic Symphony Orchestra and other respected figures, and then got down to business with notable dispatch. The Ballet Russe got around to playing its first engagement there the following season and was at this moment in the opening days of its second one.

The City of New York, of course, was not involved in any way with the membership corporation that handled the bookings and producing, but several members of the city administration, in the role of private citizens, were members of the corporation. The program masthead, indeed, listed the mayor as president of the New York City Center of Music and Drama (as subsequent mayors continued to be), and Councilmen Morris and Baum were listed in other official capacities. There was also a large board of directors, including notable workers in the various musical and theatrical fields and equally distinguished patrons of the same fields, and Commissioner Moss was its chairman.

In the light of the whole censorship agitation, now capped by the actual ouster of *Trio*, the imminent debut of *Frankie and Johnny* became a delicate matter. As Tom understated the danger of the situation later in a letter: "Its subject matter can be described in such a manner as to indicate that it deals with low-down characters and situations. The fact that it is America's most loved folk song and is known to every child of five years or over, does not change the fact that anyone can accuse the song of being indecent in the same way in which practically all of the stories in the Bible or of Shakespeare can also be similarly described."

There were, indeed, indications of disapproval even within the ballet organization itself, and the Russian rehearsal pianist was, like Queen Victoria, not amused when she had to play the "revolting" score. At one rehearsal she actually refused to repeat it one more time, and the situation was saved only when Balanchine, who found the whole thing intriguing, stepped in and played it for her.

On Sunday, then, the day after the *Trio* debacle, Denham, with understandable alarm, discussed the matter with Ruth and Tom and asked that certain changes be made. Ruth agreed to make some of them, provided that she be given sufficient rehearsal time to smooth the transitions over the gaps thus made. But this could not be arranged on such short notice, since there were other ballets in the repertoire that were on the rehearsal schedule.

On Monday, February 26 (the first business day after the closing of *Trio*), Elmer Rice, the celebrated playwright, resigned from the board of directors of the City Center, declining to work in any capacity under Commissioner Moss, whose exercise of official censorship he could not condone. On Tuesday, February 27, Margaret Webster, the director of most of the Shakespearean productions of the day, acted similarly and for the same reason. Both of them made their actions known to the newspapers in strong statements. Though they were not concerned with the particular fate of *Trio* as such, they felt that the matter of arbitrary censorship was an issue that the New York theatre must face squarely. On Wednesday, February 28, *Frankie and Johnny* made its bow at Commissioner Moss's own theatre, so to speak, and the situation exploded. Just before the rise of the curtain Denham had made another plea to Ruth to make some last-minute changes, and in the light of the emergency she had agreed against her better judgment, knowing perfectly well that without the necessary adjustments the performance would be in trouble. Tom later reported euphemistically to a friend that the unrehearsed modifications "were inevitably damaging, on the whole." But they were considerably more damaging than that, for besides the trepidations and confusions they gave rise to among the dancers, the ballet itself lost its line and much of its meaning because of the minor choreographic and dramatic nonsequiturs that kept cropping up.

The result was that "on the whole" the next day's reviews were anything but enthusiastic. And while the music critic of the *World-Telegram* gave it a "rave" review back on the amusement page, the front page carried an editorial attack on Commissioner Moss.

A second performance was scheduled for two days later, and Ruth and Bentley were to have been featured again, but at the last minute they refused to go on, and Boris and Franklin replaced them. The tabloid *PM* reported the story, in part, as follows:

> Miss Page's husband told PM that "ten minutes before 'Frankie and Johnny' was given its first performance at the City Center last Wednesday, Miss Page was asked to make changes that robbed the work of 35% of its effectiveness." These changes, he charged, were

responsible for the unfriendly reception by the New York press. In preparation for the Friday performance, "they came on bended knees" and asked for still further changes, whereupon Miss Page and her dancing partner, Bentley Stone, withdrew from the company. Asked who "they" were, Mr. Fisher said "the thing was done very subtly, handled so that no one would be responsible." PM learned, however, that Commissioner Moss, assistant to the president of the City Center, had refused permission to Life Magazine to take pictures of the ballet. Orders have also been issued to the Ballet Russe, sponsors of "Frankie and Johnny," to send no pictures of the ballet to the press. Observers close to the City Center attributed the "bowdlerizing" of "Frankie and Johnny" to a hurry-up move by Moss to escape people-who-live-in-glass-houses criticism. Reviewers of "Frankie and Johnny" were quick to point out that while Moss closed "Trio" because of alleged immorality, there were "bawds, a pimp and two lesbians" in the ballet.

Some papers and news services wanted to take action pictures of this second performance, but police were stationed throughout the house (to the considerable bewilderment of the audience) to prevent them. Tom said he had insisted that Ruth refuse to appear in the performance because he did not want her to be photographed thus "scandalously." The cuts demanded by Denham in this second performance were duly made by Boris and Franklin, and though they were generally inane and indefensible, they were by no means fatal to the work. Indeed, this performance (whatever may have happened in the meantime in the way of smoothing over transitions) did greater justice to the piece than the first one had done. Naturally the newspaper reviewers were on hand again, and while some of them with delicate tastes maintained to the end that it was vulgar and unworthy, others with either stronger stomachs or cruder sensibilities found it original and funny. One of them, reviewing the dance season as a whole sometime later, chose it as the best ballet of the year.

Because it was "hot" at the box office, the management slipped it in for extra matinee performances, but as so many mothers proceeded to bring their children (after all, what are ballet matinees for?), only to demand their money back indignantly, the scheme had to be canceled. When the company went on tour, *Frankie* was banned not only in Boston but all over Canada for what Ruthanna Boris reported were "religious reasons." A year later it actually made the grade in Boston, what with a few near riots and a bit of censorship. (The Saving Susies now sang "Oh boy [instead of "Oh, Lord"] and how they could love," there was no beer at Johnny's coffin, the bartender's explicit testimony about lovemaking was toned down and the always irrelevant lesbians were deleted from the ensemble.) But the newspapers advertised it as "by public demand." It was a full year, also, before it was shown again in New York; the company had a fall season there in the meantime, but that was too near election day for the city fathers to allow *Frankie* to be exhumed.

Several years later Ruth asked Effie which one of her ballets she liked best, and Effie replied, "I like all of them except *Frankie and Johnny*." Why? "Because I can understand that one." There is no denying, however, that its hectic New York production marked the beginning of a new epoch in Ruth's career, for she had not only "crashed" the "big-time" ballet circuit but crashed it big.

OUSTED FROM EDEN

In spite of the intensity of the whole New York imbroglio it could occupy no more time than was allotted to it in the schedules of its two choreographer-guest-stars. Ruth departed immediately to resume her interrupted touring with her "Words and Music" program, and Sgt. Stone returned to his air-force barracks. Touring in wartime, even with her solo program, was arduous, for transportation was unreliable and uncomfortable, and hotels were overflowing and generally undermanned.

When she arrived in Tallahassee on April 23 for a performance at the Florida State College for Women, a telegram awaited her saying that her mother had died, altogether unexpectedly, the day before. Disciplined trouper that she was, she told her accompanist to say nothing about it, and at the conclusion of the program she attended the party in her honor that was implicit in the engagement and left at midnight for Indianapolis. The remainder of the tour was canceled.

In Chicago, when she got back there at last, she would have had quite enough to do even if things had been peaceful. She was already creatively involved in two more pieces of Americana, one about Billy Sunday and the other a theatrical projection of Poe's "The Bells." But things were not peaceful by any means; she and Tom were about to be thrown out of their Diana Court "penthouse" at 540 N. Michigan Avenue, where they had lived for fifteen years, and it was now Tom's turn to do a virtuoso act.

The building had been sold on January 30 to the Time and Life corporation which planned to use the top floor as a subscription office. Notice of eviction had been sent to Tom the following day, but his lease did not expire until November, and he had every intention of renewing it, as he had done twice since the expiration of the original ten-year lease in 1940. Accordingly, since the wartime regulations of the Office of Price Administration forbade the cancellation of residential leases, he continued to pay the monthly rent of $50 and went to law about it. Time-Life contended that it had rented the space to him for business purposes; Tom countered with details of how, long before Time-Life was the owner, he had spent $10,000 transforming a bare loft into living quarters with sound walls, picture windows and a fireplace in the expectation of living there for twenty years. Its use as a studio, he pointed out, was only incidental and certainly not commercial. He also declared that "Harry" Luce, the Time-Life publisher, whom he had known for years and whom Ruth had met at a Yale prom with Tex in the *Music Box Revue* days, had often dined with them there and "knows how I have fixed the place up."

At the end of the ninety-day grace period granted by the eviction procedure, his checks began to be returned regularly. Then on a Saturday night in August, while he and Ruth were weekending in Hubbard Woods, a truck was backed up to the building and all their personal belongings, including their clothes, were carted away to a warehouse. When Tom testified to this in court, he proclaimed that he was then wearing, of necessity, his brother's clothes. Whereupon the defendants' attorney graciously granted him the privilege of getting his own out of the warehouse, if he chose to do so; which presumably he did.

In September he gave one of his best performances when, in Circuit Court, he doubled as attorney and witness. In one role he asked all the right questions and in the other he gave all the right answers. Under cross-examination he bounded out of the witness stand from time to time to object as attorney to questions being put to him as client, until the judge in self-defense reminded him that it was hard to separate him into his respective roles of counsel and witness. He might almost have been trying to compete with the courtroom shenanigans of Erle Stanley Gardner's Perry Mason. If so, he proved himself to be just as skillful as that master of legal finesse, for the judge decided that the apartment was a home and not just a studio, since it had all the accessories of a home.

When Time-Life appealed the case, however, the Appellate Court stayed that part of the injunction that required the immediate restoration of possession to the Fishers. Tom then went to the apartment "to list his property and check on some jewelry," and once inside, he refused to leave. Though perhaps he was literally in possession of the four walls, the locks had all been changed, the water had been turned off and he was not permitted to retrieve his possessions from the Edler warehouse where they had been stored.

Ruth added succinct reports now and again in her diary:

> . . . A million troubles with 540 and we can't move in. . . . Tom got two "sitters" to meet him at 540 and they are to sit there for thirty-six hours. He pulled down the doors so they couldn't be locked and now we'll see what happens next. The Time-Fortune crowd will stop at nothing, it seems, and after all their low-down tricks we are more than ever determined to move in. . . . We went to 540. Went up to our studio which is stripped to nothing. Tom's custodian, a really tough looking hombre, was there. We went downstairs and Edler's had a truckload of our things to move in. However, Time Magazine had sent some policemen and a squad car to keep us from entering the building.

So they took a room for the night at the fairly nearby Bismarck Hotel, since their only other place of residence was in Hubbard Woods.

Tom went back to court at once, and the judge who had made the ruling in his favor ordered Henry Luce and thirteen other persons, including the manager of the building and the owner of the warehouse, to show cause why they should not be held in contempt of court.

This was in October, and it was not until the following May—a year and a half after the original notice of eviction—that the case was settled in Tom's favor. Ruth notes on May 22: "Representatives of Time Magazine showed Tom places where we might move instead of 540. They are willing to pay our rent and fix anything up that we want." What she does not note, however, is that when the case was finally settled, Time-Life, willing or not, would have to pay not just their rent but also all their interim living expenses, including entertaining.

Back in October the Fishers had moved into the Racquet Club to live. This most excellent club had been organized several years before by Tom and some of his friends who were devoted to squash racquets (in which Tom was something of a star performer) and had decided that they needed a place to indulge their hobby in easy, elegant and comfortable surroundings. It was by no means inexpensive; besides which the Fishers were the most gregarious of people and the most hospitable of hosts, and on one occasion during their residence their dinner party numbered some forty guests.

Variation II (Turbidissimo Sostenuto)

The idea of a ballet about Billy Sunday had been in Ruth's mind for more than a year, but it was *The Bells* that she was now immediately concerned with. It was less typically American—that is, Americana-ish—than Billy and belonged rather in her "Words and Music" category perhaps, as an ensemble application of the same principle. She may even have intended it for the Page-Stone company, since she conceived it first as a fifteen-minute work for a smallish ensemble.

A suitable composer was, as always, a major problem, and she could not proceed until she had one. Nicholas Nabokov found the idea interesting and suggested that the work be treated as a "ballet-cantata," but he was unable to undertake it at this time because of his army assignments. Virgil Thomson was also unavailable. But by the first of June she found that John Cage was both interested and available. He suggested that the score be written for two muted pianos, but he was not in favor of using spoken words.

That she was willing even to consider the omission of the words indicates that her concept had undergone a change during these months, and she was now thinking in larger dimensions, less suitable for the Page-Stone brief and essentially lyrical treatment than for the more theatrical style of the

Ballet Russe. Cage, however, was not willing to make an orchestration of his two-piano version, as she suggested, but agreed somewhat reluctantly to write an altogether new orchestral version. Eventually he began to doubt that what he really wanted to do (and what she wanted him to do) could be done practically in the musical situation of a regulation touring ballet company and bowed out altogether.

Before you could say "tintinnabulation," another letter had gone out, this time to Darius Milhaud, who, as a refugee from the war, was teaching at Mills College in California, and he had accepted at once. Not only accepted, but got to work. No doubt Ruth sighed with relief that at last she had a composer; she had forgotten that part about the regulation touring company and its limitations. In September she recorded in her diary that the piano score had arrived, but "the notes are so small that I can't read it al all." When she found a pianist who could read it, she found it "very virile, very fascinating in parts, but not enough quiet parts—too strenuous all the time." On further acquaintance she found it "hard to learn and difficult sometimes to count," but "Tom seems to like it."

Earlier in the summer she had gone to a party in New York at the apartment of Lucia Chase, director of Ballet Theatre, and one of the guests was Isamu Noguchi. She told him her plans for *The Bells* and as a sudden inspiration, invited him to design the production. He was much interested, but he was so busy with Martha Graham that he was afraid he would not be free in time, and suggested Marc Chagall instead.

Nevertheless, toward the end of August, Martha Graham had had to postpone her work in progress and he found himself free and ready to talk with Tom about sketches, costs and fees. It was apparent at once from Tom's letters that he had forgotten nothing and forgiven nothing. One he wrote in September was so hostile in tone that Ruth asked him not to send it, but send it he did; and two weeks later another, full of complaints about money, the "incompleteness" of the costume sketches, and other matters equally disagreeable. Then toward the end of September there was another letter so .much more equable in tone and more like a business letter it was obvious that Ruth had prevailed. On November 11 (Armistice Day?) Noguchi wrote to them both (taking note, incidentally, of Tom's change of tone). A complication had arisen in his schedule, for Martha Graham had asked him to get back to work at once on her new Carlos Chavez piece, *Dark Meadow*, which was now scheduled for performance in January. Not until that had finally taken place did he definitely commit himself.

Tom wrote to Denham on January 23 (in a letter dealing primarily with *Billy Sunday*, which was in painful labor at this same time) that "Ruth's new 'American' ballet about Edgar Allen Poe's 'The Bells' with music by Darius Milhaud and scenery and costumes by Isamu Noguchi is in final rehearsal."

The work was really only about to begin rehearsal, but the finality taken for granted so wishfully may have referred to Isamu's signature on the contract. Even that was fairly meaningless, since Isamu had not yet been admitted into the very closed-shop scenic designers' union. Tom wrote him, however, that "the Acme Scenic Studio [in Chicago] have time and men ready for you next Monday morning," and the union problem was providentially solved at the eleventh hour.

Denham, however, according to Ruth's diary sometime in March, "likes the 'Billy Sunday' idea. But not 'Bells'—not American, too abstract." They were still living at the Racquet Club, and she had been rehearsing the "Golden Bells" section of *The Bells* and having an awful time finding suitable dancers. "Last night Tom came home with all kinds of ideas about moving to New York, which got me so excited I couldn't sleep much. . . . I hope to God that I never will be fool enough to try to do another ballet in Chicago. The situation is impossible and always has been." Dancers were late to rehearsals, forgot to come, had other jobs on the side and so on and so forth.

Nevertheless, things moved along very promisingly, all things considered; so well, indeed, that on April 21 the production was in sufficiently good shape to take over a suddenly unfilled spot (of which much more later) in the Composers' Concerts series at Mandel Hall on the University of Chicago campus.

The night before the performance, which was a first tryout, Berenice Holmes, who had the leading role of the Bride, hurt her foot and there was nobody to replace her but Ruth. "Well," said Effie, "the audience certainly will be disappointed." But that is not the way it worked out. "The audience applauded like mad." Tom said she was better than Berenice because she had more dramatic sense. There were "two wonderful reviews the next day. Cassidy really thrilled me because she said I danced brilliantly, and I was so afraid I would ruin my own ballet."

The Chicago dancers were not as impossible as she had thought them, for Jerome Andrews and Robert Josias danced the other leading roles, and Claudia Cassidy called the work "vivid, sustained drama." Nikolai Malko conducted members of the Chicago Symphony Orchestra, and since the performance was part of the composers' series, the program also contained Milhaud's opera, *Orfée*.

REPRIEVE

On the strength of all this Denham changed his mind and decided he wanted the ballet for his September season after all. But there is an old theatrical superstition that a good dress rehearsal presages a bad opening night, and the New York première at the City Center on that unfortunate night in September proved that the curse had lost none of its force, even after a four-month interval. That extra time simply gave Old Man Jinx a better opportunity to get a grip on things.

Musically there was a built-in problem, as Ruth had sensed in her first readings of the score. Malko and the symphony orchestra had conquered its difficulties with three full orchestra rehearsals, but the Ballet Russe orchestra had never enjoyed the luxury of sufficient rehearsals and was besides inevitably inferior to a symphony orchestra in quality. Its then principal conductor, Emmanuel Balaban, understood the situation and had it well in hand, but before the opening of the season he left the organization to become the permanent conductor of a symphony orchestra. The young Daniel Saidenberg, of the orchestra staff, eas eager to take over and was qualified to do so, but he was not next in line and protocol prevented. So the orchestra pit remained a major hazard. As a matter of fact, the score itself demanded not only a great deal of playing but also a great deal of listening—far more than is to be expected from a ballet audience, which is not concentrating on its ears.

Besides this Denham was financially on unusually thin ice even for him, and there was never enough money for a complete dress rehearsal with orchestra, lighting and full company. Even the regular rehearsals were cut from three weeks to two, and a work like this, conceived with dramatic imagination and subtle in atmosphere, would not automatically perform itself.

In an effort to remedy the shaky situation as well as possible Ruth arranged with Ted Shawn to let the company give two last-minute performances, with piano accompaniment, by way of extra rehearsal, at Jacob's Pillow, his summer dance festival and school in the Berkshires. But the hex was still holding its own. In the second of these performances Alexandra Danilova, who danced the role of the Bride, followed the precedent of Berenice Holmes and pulled a tendon in her leg. Again Ruth had to step in at the première, this time much less well prepared than before, without a single rehearsal with the company and before the almightiness of a New York audience. It was a harrowing occasion.

The next day Tom wired Milhaud in California, listing the casualties in order of appearance and concluding: "Result New York premiere completely failed produce vivid sustained drama to quote Cassidy's Chicago criticism. In fact New York performance about 50% as well done musically and theatrically as Chicago premiere. Under existing conditions impossible open any new ballet with interesting score except on tour where first few performances will substitute for inadequate New York preparations. Ruth deeply disappointed over critical reception but hopes road performances will bring Bells to at least perfection of Chicago premiere."

Tom was reporting here only what concerned the composer; the other departments were equally damaged. Noguchi's set consisted of a skeleton church with a cross on top, which in the beginning was very low in stature and grew taller with each succeeding section until at the end, in the dance of the ghouls, it completely collapsed. A marvelous conception, which worked well enough mechanically but in an under-rehearsed and inchoate performance had really no point beyond its mechanics. His costumes were eccentric and unflattering to the human body; they had, of course, not been "edited" in action.

The audience reaction was very mixed; there were instances of tittering throughout, and at the final curtain there was some booing amid the conventional first-night bravos and oceans of pre-sent flowers. To all intents and purposes the piece was a disaster. And to omit no possible point of attack, the self-appointed protectors of religious rigidity protested against the implication that the established church could ever collapse.

But Ruth was simply not equipped to quit under pressure. The second performance a week later already showed signs of work; some costumes had been changed, a well-lit blue cyclorama had been added to the set, Ruthanna Boris had learned the role of the Bride and by sheer force made her something of a central figure, and signs of rehearsing were evident. The cast, however, was too concerned with the changes to create any atmosphere, and atmosphere was what the piece was built around.

During the tour that followed, though it is difficult to rehearse new material under traveling conditions, a revised version was developed and when it was presented in Chicago, the knowledgeable Ann Barzel, newly appointed dance critic of the *Chicago Times*, reported favorably on the revisions.

When the company returned to New York for its spring season, *The Bells* dauntlessly reappeared and covered itself with a reasonable approximation of glory under the circumstances. Ruth had pulled it into focus by strengthening its central figures. The spectator was now immediately won by the young lovers and watched with concern the collapse of their union under the attack of social decadence. (It was a prescient theme, which would have even more relevance now.) Poe's form, to be sure, grew out of no such specific scheme as this, but it was reinforced in its own terms by translation into equally valid theatrical terms. Boris had already attained the essential stature of the Bride; now Franklin joined her in a comparable realization of the Bridegroom, which was probably the first outstanding dramatic performance in his generally lyric career.

That there was still much to be done nobody understood better than Ruth. She had worked wonders in her own departments of staging, but the music remained intransigent. "To tell you the truth," she wrote after this second New York première, "I was all flapped out. . . . When you dance yourself there is a kind of physical relief, but when you sit out front and just watch you simply suffer from the contrast between what a ballet *could be* and what it is. . . . Milhaud says he will write a new 'finale,' which we hope will be simple enough for the orchestra to be able to play. I hate to change this part, but the new conductor Paul Straus (who seems to be excellent) says that even with a top orchestra the present 'finale' needs three rehearsals (which we had with the Chicago Symphony, but which are impossible with the Ballet Russe). So now we have to wait and see how long it will take! Fortunately they are taking 'The Bells' on tour to Canada, Boston and Mexico City."

Eventually the changes were made; Milhaud is reported to have said that if he ever composed another ballet, it would consist entirely of whole notes for one finger on the piano.

Variation III, with Intermezzi, Contretemps, Cadenzas and Coda

It was music also that brought *Billy Sunday* to his, or its, knees. Billy himself, with his hymn writer, Rodeheaver, as his ally, had brought thousands of sinners to their knees, and Ruth had planned to make them do the same thing to balletomanes. Her fatal mistake was to yield to the temptation of ditching the hymn-slinging Rodeheaver for more sophisticated hemidemisemi-quavers.

The idea of turning Billy into a ballet had already resulted in a finished scenario, based on his *Love Stories from the Bible*, before *The Bells* was anywhere in the picture. On the strength of her enthusiasm for the score of *Frankie*, Ruth had turned naturally to Jerome Moross as the composer of *Billy*, since it was that same raucously humorous perspective she was looking for. He actually started work on it (though he would have none of Rodeheaver!) but before he had done more than sketch it in a bit, he departed for New York to collaborate on a series of ballets with vocal scores for a Broadway producer.

As a consequence, no composer had been chosen when Remi Gassmann, then head of the Composers' Concerts series as well as a member of the university's music department, told her he would like to write a ballet for her sometime. She gave him a choice among several of her projects, and he chose *Billy*. In spite of his musical capabilities, it was a calamitous choice. For one reason, *Billy* had to be done at once, and besides his university activities, he was head of the music department at nearby Elmhurst College and also music critic of the *Chicago Times*. He was accordingly short on leisure. For another reason, he proved to be extremely coy about signing contracts.

The date for the Mandel Hall tryout of *Billy* was already set for May 24, 1945, but week after week went by and there was no sign of music from Gassmann. She was increasingly disturbed as she traveled about on her

"Words and Music" tour; and so, indeed, was Cecil Smith, the university's administrator of the Mandel Hall projects, who found himself holding the bag. Gassmann, in spite of his assurances to Smith, simply did not complete the score, and the May 24 date had to be canceled. This was the first time in her life that Ruth had failed to give an announced performance, and she was not exactly meek about it. Neither was Tom, who had been vainly trying for three months to get a contract signed.

Late in June after the college terms were over, Gassmann wrote that at last he was "working very well" in the first period of concentration he had had. In August Ruth noted in her diary that she was busy with *Billy Sunday* at Hubbard Woods and that the music, of which he had sent her the piano score of the first two episodes, seemed difficult. In mid-October, however, the score was still not finished, nor had any contract been signed.

By this time Denham, with a season to plan, was getting impatient. He had indicated early on that he wanted the work to follow up *Frankie and Johnny*, leasing it as a "package" according to the Chicago Ballet Company's practice, but until the Chicago Ballet Company had an approved score and a satisfactory designer under contract, there would be nothing to lease. In violation of all accepted procedures, then, he took the bull by the horns and got in touch with Gassmann himself in an effort to speed him up. But Gassmann, shy of making business arrangements, referred him to his publisher. Denham, as a last resort, phoned Ruth and suggested that maybe she should get a new composer. It was about time for somebody to have such a flash of inspiration, and on the strength of it Ruth wrote to Moross in New York to suggest the possibility of his finishing the score he had started even though he was busy on something else at the same time. To this he agreed, at least in principle.

Gassmann, however, was not the only elusive collaborator in this offbeat venture; there were troubles also with Alexander Calder, whom she had chosen because of his creative nonconformity to design the setting and costumes. What he planned, according to his models and sketches, consisted of a front curtain, a grand drapery, a blue "cyc," four eighteen-foot wings with "flippers," three "odd-shaped floating pieces" and a portable ramp. Surprisingly enough, all of it seemed inadequate, and Ruth offered to go either to New York or to his place in Roxbury to discuss the changes she considered necessary. But she could not pin him down to an appointment anywhere, and after the date of the Mandel Hall performance had come and gone, she wrote him in protest:

> I find collaborating with people I can't talk to very difficult. I under-
> stand how you feel about your mobiles—they are your "trademark,"
> therefore you want to use them for your first ballet. [Actually he had
> used mobiles in a setting for Martha Graham's *Horizons* in 1936.] I

don't think they are at all suitable for Billy's idea, although for something else they would be wonderful. If we could get them made cheaply I would even like to try them for our Chicago performance. . . . I have always been against scenery that you can't *use* choreographically and be part of. To make the four Bible episodes interesting, they should all be different, and with the same backdrop for all I think it will be dull. . . . It seems to me each story needs a small and amusing set that Billy can whisk on and off or that he can pull up and down by ropes or that he can fly down from the wings, or as much movement as you like in the scenery. . . .

If the letter produced any reply, that is all it produced.

Then in mid-November the situation with Gassmann took a sudden turn for the better, creatively if not contractually. Acting on a rumor from New York, Ruth wired Denham eagerly: "Understand you have complete piano score. Anxious to see it as I have only two episodes." At the moment she had three weeks free from touring engagements and wanted to use them to get the choreography started. But, she added in the wire, with Tom's presence obviously hovering over the scene, "must have music definitely approved and contract signed before starting. Please wire collect Racquet Club. Afectuosamente."

On the basis of that rumor of good news a date was set optimistically for a Mandel Hall tryout on April 24, and in mid-December she wired Gassmann that for that occasion she needed a score "for piano and not more than four, five or six incidental instruments."

In February Tom wrote Denham that he had followed through on the latter's "bootleg" approach to Gassmann, and now, "believe it or not," he had two royalty contracts between Gassmann and the Ballet Russe (not the Chicago Ballet Company), signed by Gassmann, which he was sending herewith to Denham for his signature. But Denham had no intention of dealing with Gassmann; the only contracts he would sign were with the Chicago Ballet Company for the "package" as a whole.

That "package," of course, included not only the music but the production as well, and no progress whatever had been made there. Denham did not much like Calder's designs but he still had him on the string as designer, even though he was not yet a member of the New York Scenic Designers' Union. The disturbing news that now leaked out was that he had no intention whatever of trying to qualify for membership. Ruth got quietly to work; she sounded out the ever-reliable Remisoff, Oliver Smith, Lemuel Ayres, all to no avail. For a whole month she had a new artist working sub rosa on the project, just in case. The only possible compromise would be to use Calder's costumes, though not his scenery, on April 24 at Mandel Hall simply to try them out. But when April 24 came around, *Billy* was still only a distant hope, and by the grace of God *The Bells* was ready to go on as a replacement to spare her the embarrassment of another cancellation. *Billy* was now being booked (with fingers crossed) for December 13, and with *The Bells* triumphantly off her mind, Ruth got busy with Moross again.

Six months later, no contracts for *Billy* had been signed with either a composer or a designer, and on November 6 Denham, fed up with the whole business, threw in the sponge. He returned unsigned all the contracts with both Gassmann and the Chicago Ballet Company and added: "Fight it out, boys, and let me know. . . . Understand you are planning to produce 'Billy Sunday' in Chicago. . . . I would love to see it. . . ." Now, with intensified pressuring, Tom actually got Gassmann to sign a royalty contract with the Chicago Ballet Company and duly notified Denham—who could not have cared less. By some kind of hocus-pocus Ruth was able to record in her diary that *Billy* had gone on according to schedule as a free lecture-demonstration, using the piano score, in the Renaissance Society's series managed by Roger Englander. "Great success. 150 turned away." Whether Denham was impressed by these developments or not, he had officially taken himself out of the picture.

The Chicago Ballet Company, however, had already spread its exploratory tentacles over other potential areas of production. The war had just ended and Europe was opening up. Emerson Kailey, musician, conductor and friend of both Gassmann's and the Fishers', had already departed for Paris to conduct radio broadcasts, chiefly of American music, and Tom had urged him to see what he could arrange in the way of performances for *Billy* and *The Bells*. He was so quick to establish contacts that even before the December 13 tryout Boris Kochno, artistic director of the Ballets des Champs-Elysées, had fallen in with the suggestion of a possible all-American evening, under the auspices of UNESCO or some other international organization, at the Theâtre des Champs-Elysées, in which Ruth's pieces would be re-created by her for his company.

In mid-December Gassmann also went to Paris as his first stop on an indefinite series of musical missions in Europe and promised to make his orchestration there and send it back posthaste. He was sufficiently in favor again (after *Billy* had turned away 150 people from a free performance at Mandel Hall?) for Tom to make an agreement with him to negotiate a Paris season for 1947. And he managed to come up with a number of possibilities.

KIRSTEIN CHANGES CAMPAIGNS

Nearer home there was a more substantial artistic sponsorship—or potential sponsorship—appearing above the horizon, for Lincoln Kirstein was back from the war and active again in the ballet field. Upon his release from the army he had decided to approach the producing of ballets and lyric theatre works from a different direction and had formed an organization called Ballet

Society. It would operate entirely on a membership basis and would offer four productions a year quite outside the limitations and proscriptions of the commercial theatre. There would be no general publicity and the press would not even be invited. It would be a financially risky enterprise and he was not sure he could bring it off, but at least he would try.

As soon as the announcement was made, Tom began working both sides of the street. To Denham he wrote: ". . . What do you make of the 'Ballet Society'? And is it true that Lincoln Kirstein expects to inherit $1,500,000 from his father's estate in the next fifteen months, whereupon he is to 'blossom forth' with a complete commercial company designed to 'shake the world'?" At the same time he wrote cordially to Kirstein, sent his and Ruth's blessings on his undertaking and asked that they be put on the list of associate members, though probably they would not be able to attend the productions.

Kirstein replied at once in his own and Balanchine's names to thank him for his good wishes, and gave him some quite confidential details about the financing of the project, taking it for granted that since Tom had done so much in that field himself, he would be interested. He reported also that both Hurok and Denham wanted to book the ballets sight unseen, but he had no intention of leasing them out if it could be avoided. He added that the society intended to do works by various choreographers besides Balanchine (who was for the time being in Paris working with the Opéra ballet), and he wanted very much to talk to Ruth on the subject. Naturally, he soon found himself specifically involved with Ruth and Tom and *Billy*.

He had always had a high regard for Ruth's American approach to the classic ballet, and he had got along well with Tom since the beginning of their acquaintance. Though he was as idealistic and outspoken as Tom was pragmatic and devious, he could scarcely fail to be attracted by Tom's cleverness and seeming knowledge of everything that was going on behind the scenes in the sophisticated world.

Though he had not yet heard the score of *Billy*, Balaban had told him he liked it, and Alvin Colt had hit on a comic-strip approach to the setting and costumes that he thought was a good one, though Gassmann was said to dislike it. Since Colt was too busy with Broadway shows to undertake it anyhow, that was for the nonce a dead issue.

In any case, he told Ruth, whether he did this ballet or not, he wanted to do something of hers. She had offered him, along with *Billy*, her latest enthusiasm, which was a ballet based on W. H. Hudson's *Green Mansions*. In spite of all her overlapping activities she had compulsively taken on another one. The Hudson-based work she envisioned with Frederick Franklin in the central role, speaking and singing, and all the other figures silent. Tom had already approached Villa-Lobos for the music and Miguel Covarrubias for the designing, but to no avail. At the moment it was Milhaud (Yes, Milhaud; no doubt with his one-finger whole-note plan) and Noguchi whom she had in mind. To this project, however, Kirstein was negative, for he felt, as he told her, that her strong point was the use of "the American idiom in some way."

He was "most interested" in *Billy Sunday*, but with many frank misgivings from the start. As for the work itself, he was, for one thing, basically opposed to the idea of dancers speaking. As for the Chicago Ballet Company's system of supplying the entire production on a rental basis, he was uncomfortable, as most producers were not, about an underlying moral responsibility to help recover somebody else's initial investment. Also, he wanted not only to own the works he sponsored but also to participate actively in their creation from the start.

The ballet, as she had conceived it, was "a danced sermon in four episodes," based on Billy's sermon on "Temptation." The episodes concerned David and Bathsheba, Joseph and "Mrs. Potiphar," the Wise and Foolish Virgins, and Samson and Delilah. Billy stepped into the roles of the men he was preaching about and stepped out of them again to make comment to the "congregation," eventually "swinging the bat for righteousness" and "knocking the devil out of the box" in each case.

Not surprisingly, Kirstein's misgivings about the ballet were ultimately unresolvable, and after a bull session with Ruth and Tom he decided not to proceed with the production. In a letter to Ruth, which was a brief recapitulation of their discussion, he wrote: "I now find I really don't believe in it—either the form or the subject. Put it down to a lack of a sense of humor. I don't think it's funny, and I don't think sex is a temptation, and I think the ballet has a weak book. I don't think four episodes based on more or less the same idea is essentially interesting. Also, I do not like the idea of talking. I realize that the whole thing is a sermon, but the idea of a dancer talking is offensive to me; it breaks up the whole texture of the dance."

When Tom wrote to Gassmann in Paris about the break, he dealt more explicitly with the discussion. "Strange as it may sound," he wrote in part, "Lincoln does not think sex is a temptation. He argues that it is a biological urge and that the true temptations are avarice, pride, liquor, sloth, etc. These matters he regards as definitely open to an individual's choice, whereas he regards sex as merely a biological urge which should have no connection with morals at all." In keeping with this idea of the individual's choice, each episode should end with a different specific retribution, which would prevent their being all alike. In *Frankie and Johnny*, for instance, Johnny had to be shot, not for sex but because "he was her man and he done her wrong." Ruth agreed with all this in principle, Tom reported, but what she had in mind was to project Billy's beliefs, not her own, as an example of American folklore, so to speak. It was to be Billy's sermon, not hers, though, to be sure, the responsibility for making it theatrically interesting was her own.

To Kirstein Tom wrote that though Ruth was "terribly disappointed" by his decision, she was "very much impressed by his criticism that the four episodes should have the retribution factor more strongly stressed." In fact she was "grateful to him for this most constructive suggestion," and she felt that if they should work together on other projects, his "criticism would be wonderfully helpful."

CONFUSION WORSE CONFOUNDED

Before the end of the month Denham phoned that he wanted to do *Billy* after all. He had been hovering in the background right along, gossiping and back-biting according to standard ballet-producing tactics, afraid of the built-in problems of *Billy* but not wanting Kirstein to have it. To Ruth's great surprise he also wanted *Love Song*, which she had long been trying to sell him, and he wanted it for the autumn season.

Meanwhile, however, what was immediately on her mind was a practicable repertoire for her first postwar tour with the Page-Stone company, since this time they could have only twelve dancers.

Then on April 2 she had a phone call from Hassard Short in New York that completely broke her line of thinking. He was planning to do a musical show in the autumn about Tchaikovsky, to be called *Music in My Heart*, using adaptations of his music as a score, and he wanted her to do the choreography, of which there would be a great deal. She had never choreographed a musical, and the idea intrigued her, especially as a possible escape from the harrowing ordeals of the ballet world. But she recorded in her diary the next day that she hated "the idea of the Tchaikovsky show—just another 'Song of Norway'." Also, Tom had urged her not to do it. Nevertheless, she had an idea for the *Beauty and the Beast* ballet that was indicated in the script, and there was also a kind of fascinating first-act ballet, called *Unrequited Love, or The Storm*, to be done to music of Rossini, in the pre-Petipa style of Tchaikovsky's youth, and she signed the contract.

The opening was scheduled for Philadelphia on September 15 and rehearsals would begin in New York on August 16. As it happened, this was the very day that had been set for *Billy* to go into rehearsal, which did not ingratiate her with Denham.

In the interim she dashed off a performance of Stravinsky's *L'Histoire de Soldat* for the League of Composers in New York in July and another for the Society of Contemporary Music in Chicago. . . . Paul DuPont produced a model for the setting of *Billy* that was excellent. At last! . . . Denham decided he did not want *Love Song*, which distressed her because "I think 'Billy' will be such a flop that I will need 'Love Song' to save my reputation." . . . In New York Lehman Engel bobbed up with his first installment of a score (which she "hated") for their still-extant plan for a comic *Trovatore* ballet. . . . Denham decided he did want *Love Song*. . . .

AWAY FROM IT ALL

When August 16 arrived, she started on what she summed up later as "two of the hardest months of my life."

She enjoyed everything about the show up to the Philadelphia opening, when after "rave notices . . . they started cutting and changing, and practically every night we did something new." The *Beauty and the Beast* ballet was the only thing that did not have to be remodeled, for it was in a sense a climactic number (perhaps intended as an equivalent of *The Sleeping Beauty*, which had established Tchaikovsky as a ballet composer) and had accordingly been cut and trimmed and polished into its final shape during the New York rehearsals. The other ballet fared less well, for it virtually opened the show and was a tongue-in-cheek period piece with girls dancing the male roles. It was asking too much of an average musical-comedy audience to walk in on it cold and grasp its style and purport, so it was cut in half, and then cut in half again.

The New York opening took place on October 2, and Ruth sent a note to the company:

> Ballet Girls, "Music in My Heart," Stage Door, Adelphi Theatre. Scramble your gargouillades, sit on your tutus, take weasel instead of mink, but remember the czar will be there every night expecting you to be pale, dramatic and "brilliant," as I know you will be. With appreciation and love to every one of you.

It was after this performance that the worst blow of the cutting knife fell, and it had nothing to do with conventional show-business tinkering. The *Danse Arabe*, which Ruth considered "marvelous" and the best number in the show, performed by a beautiful girl from the Ballet Russe named Pauline Godard, was not only cut but cut out, and at the demand of the same forces that had wielded the ax on *Frankie and Johnny*.

As Tom wrote the story to the Remisoffs, it awakens echoes of the intrigues of the Renaissance. The original prima donna of the show, he testified, was replaced in Philadelphia, apparently for cause, three days before the New York opening. "The moment she was out of the show, as many as eight or ten Catholic priests showed up in the audience in Philadelphia for each performance." Then at the opening performance in New York "two Catholic priests left the theatre" immediately following Ruth's *Danse Arabe* while the lights were still up, pointedly "making a disturbance" thereby. "The next morning the Catholic headquarters threatened to put the entire show on the 'index' and blacklist it for Catholics if the 'Danse Arabe' were not eliminated. Similar objection was made to some of the lyrics in the second part of the show, which followed long after the two priests had left the theatre, thus showing that the whole business was planned in advance. Actually the whole show is amazingly clean, including Ruth's dance—in fact it is so clean as to be close to the dull side without a little pepping up.

Nevertheless the management . . . acceded to the Catholic 'censoring' and eliminated the parts to which exception had been taken."

The incomprehensibility of such interference was clarified, according to Tom, when the fact became known that the dismissed prima donna was married into a wealthy Hollywood film dynasty who happened to be active Roman Catholics and who were determined to avenge her. "We were reliably told," said Tom, that her husband had "thrown a party at the Stork Club three days before the New York opening, to which he had invited all the New York critics. One of them, Ward Morehouse, on the New York Sun, told Mr. Short about 5 p.m. on the afternoon of the first performance that the show would not receive good criticisms from the New York critics." And Morehouse's prophecy proved sound, for the show received a unanimously bad press.

"This," Tom went on, "in marked contrast to the excellent notice which the show had received in the Hollywood Daily Variety the morning after the Philadelphia première"; thus proving to him that the dynasty was "able to get instantaneous and favorable notice in Hollywood when they wanted it while their in-law was in the cast." And if they could then change their orders and secure bad reviews in New York, when their in-law had been replaced, they must really have been a dynasty to reckon with.

And perhaps they were. In this instance, however, though the New York reviews were bad, it was not because of skullduggery but because the show unquestionably deserved them. The only thing that did not get a bad press was Ruth's dances, including the *Danse Arabe*, which, of course, had not yet been highhandedly excised. Incidentally, the management attempted to explain this excision, when it came, by saying that it "interfered with the action"; to which the response of somebody who had seen the show was: "What action?" Anyhow, dynasty or no dynasty, the censorship was undeniable whether its motive was revenge or authoritarianism, and Tom had a ball with one of his confidential Sherlock-Holmesian post-mortems.

Ruth's less fanciful response in her diary was: "No more shows for me!" A resolution that she almost, but not quite, kept.

BACK TO CONFOUNDED CONFUSION

These may have been two of the hardest months in her life up to that time, but the ones that followed outdid them in scope, tension and complexity. Accustomed though she was to doing several things at the same time, she would have had to be inter-computerized triplets to handle the situation.

Her tour with the revamped Page-Stone company was due to open November 10; the new group of twelve was "terrible" and there was no time even to think about new works. In October she went to Milwaukee, where the Ballet Russe was playing, to start getting *Love Song* into shape while the company was on tour, and besides that to see what she could do toward readying *Billy* for next season.

Gassman, of course, had been notified that *Billy* was definitely in the works, and the whole musical agony started again. Now it was the orchestration instead of the score that was its crux. Almost at once he "radioed" from Europe about unavoidable delays having to do with the copyist; there would be other delays and other explanations as time went on.

Toward the end of November, Ruth flew to San Francisco between her own performing dates, to rehearse briefly with the ballet company only to find that Denham had decided again not to do *Love Song* but, *horribile dictu*, to put Billy in its place in the spring season in New York. Its debut, indeed, was already set for March 2.

"I was in hysterics!" Her ultimatum was that she would not undertake to get Billy ready now unless he guaranteed her twelve out-of-town performances. Tom followed up with a letter of his own, demanding the restoration of *Love Song* to the schedule for the sake of Ruth's reputation, since *The Bells* had been an experimental "flop." "She feels that its success is assured," he wrote, and that therefore she could take the risk of doing *Billy* in the spring season, if she had the requisite numbers of performances beforehand.

In reply Denham reminded her that in accordance with a longstanding agreement with the Chicago Ballet Company he had committed himself to present the ballet during the forthcoming New York season. "We were ready," he wrote, "to proceed with the rehearsals, as provided in the agreement, in August and to continue them on tour. Unfortunately, all our schedules of rehearsals were upset by your greedy flight into a Broadway venture and by your own tour." It was physically impossible to guarantee any definite number of performances before New York. "Thus, I cannot accept your ultimative demand, not provided in our agreement, and thrown at me in the last moment by the gentle hand of an unpredictable choreographer." And he added with ominous overtones: "I do not know what your arrangement with Gassmann is but I suggest that you cable him at once to assure the timely delivery of the orchestral material." (Which, of course, she did, only to learn this time that the work was being retarded by strikes.)

As to the restoration of *Love Song* there was no word.

In the midst of the turmoil she had to fly to Texas to go on with the final engagements of her own tour, which had been characterized from the start by squabbles with local managers. Effie had gone with her, and if hotel rooms were hard to get under any circumstances, they became virtually impossible for Effie in the South. As a consequence she had to sleep in Ruth's room; but she snored, and this was no time for anybody to snore!

When she returned to Chicago briefly in January, the *Billy Sunday* situation had not changed. The score, she wrote in a letter, is a pain in the neck; Gassmann is in Paris and has sent no orchestrations; he is stubbornly ignorant of the tone of the show, the costumes, the designs, which he has seen from the beginning, since it is all the same as at the tryout at Mandel Hall.

Yet somehow, for all the aberrances and animadversions, a performance of sorts managed to get onstage at York, Pennsylvania, on January 29, still with only the piano score. Tom wired Gassmann's wife in Chicago: "Audience very enthusiastic over Billy Sunday and scenery and costumes look stunning. Good notice York paper." Which was all very well for York, but certainly had nothing to do with New York.

Accordingly Tom came up with a fresh proposal to Denham; this was to replace *Billy* with *Love Song* throughout the coming spring season at the City Center and save the New York première of *Billy* for the much more important autumn season, which was set for the Metropolitan Opera House as a twenty-fifth anniversary celebration for the Ballet Russe. Then there would be a far greater need for a "new and daring dramatic number." *Love Song*, he pointed out, was the kind of ballet that could be easily prepared between now and March 2.

To which Denham replied that to replace *Billy* was out of the question; however, three episodes of the orchestration had now arrived, and "while the music sounds very Hindemithish, I must admit the orchestration is very interesting. . . . Just calm yourself and you will see that everything will be all right."

Happily, in the midst of all this hurly-burly, there was an occasional intrusion of lightheartedness. In February, when Ruth was still traveling with the company but continually flitting in and out, Michael Mindlin Jr., the company's smart young press agent, was trying to locate her for interviews and broadcasts and sent a wire to Tom: "Important I know immediately when Miss Paige [*sic*] will be in New York and for how long. Please wire. Regards." Tom wired back at once: "Ruth arriving Monday and leaving with company for Providence on Wednesday. Please spell Page without letter 'i.' Regards." Mike's return note read: "Thanks for the speedy reply. I'll forward your spelling to the Western Union people. I know Ruth spells her last name with a 'y.' "

The final episode of the orchestration arrived at last, and by some minor miracle, on March 2, toward the end of the City Center season, *Billy* staggered into the repertoire; it would have been a major miracle if it had been a success. Though it had its brilliant moments, much of it was so sketchy as to be scarcely more than a glint in its choreographer's eye. The music was thin, self-centered and polite instead of broad, brassy and contributory. Franklin knocked himself out as Billy, talking as hard as he danced and capturing Billy's point of view with a genuine comic awareness. But the surprise of the evening was Danilova, who up to this point had always been either a Swan Queen or a flouncing soubrette, now giving a thoroughly low-comedy portrait of Mrs. Potiphar, complete with marcelled blond wig, feather boa and lorgnette, emoting over the sanctimonious Joseph with a broad Russian accent.

With a lively and pertinent score and plenty of time to develop Ruth's ideas, there might even yet have been hope for the piece, especially with a spring tour ahead for reworking. With the present score the future looked dark.

On this subject Denham addressed himself to the Chicago Ballet Company (the observance of protocol was by now quite overwhelming): "It is evident from the reports in the press that the ballet 'Billy Sunday' suffers considerably from a weak musical score and a particularly colorless orchestration. We feel that the ballet would be much improved if Mr. Gassmann would undertake to vitalize the orchestration and make it more suitable to the choreography of Miss Ruth Page. Since we have no direct relationship with Mr. Gassmann, we will ask you kindly to do the necessary work. We also take the opportunity to remind you that Mr. Gassmann has not yet prepared the orchestration for our road orchestra of twenty men. It is obvious that the music, which sounds rather anemic with forty musicians, will suffer leukemia when played by half that number."

Gassmann refused either to rewrite or to reorchestrate the score, maintaining that the trouble lay with the orchestra, which could not play it; and to a certain extent he was no doubt right.

To crown the chaos Ruth's by now well-established opposition, the Church, struck again for the fourth time. Among other demands it insisted that the Wise and Foolish Virgins be renamed Wise and Foolish Maidens in order to remove the sexual connotations from the parable and also that in the scene in which Delilah betrayed Samson to the Ku Klux Klan the crosses be removed from the Klansmen's costumes.

(It was at this unfortunate moment that the ebullient Lehman Engel emerged again for a conference about *Trovatore*. "It really should be awfully funny," Ruth wrote in her diary, "but the idea of another comedy frightens me to death." And that was probably the moment when the comic *Trovatore* died.)

She had previously accepted an invitation from the Pen and Brush Club in New York to be one of several guests at an afternoon symposium, and she welcomed the prospect as an escape from her troubles, but as it turned out, it only served to add insult to injury. Other guests included Florence Reed, the actress; Greta Stueckgold, the singer; and Anatole Chujoy, editor of *Dance News*. Her subject was to be "The American Choreographer," and she had

carefully prepared what she was to say on the basis of a twenty-minute speech.
At the last minute she discovered that both the subject and the twenty
minutes were to be shared with Chujoy, which necessitated a hastily extempo-
rized curtailment.

> If I had just told a couple of jokes [she wrote] and said two serious
> lines it would have been enough. I only discussed six choreographers—
> Balanchine, Graham, Tudor, Loring, de Mille and Dunham—and I
> carefully said *nothing* about myself. But it was too long. Then Chujoy
> got up and said that the American choreographers had practically killed
> the ballet and there hadn't been a good ballet created in the last five
> years. Then he picked three of the worst as examples: de Mille's
> "Tally-Ho," which he thinks is awful; Robbins' "Fancy Free," which he
> considers only a vaudeville skit; and "Billy Sunday," which never should
> have been started. It is no subject for a ballet, he said, and the idea of
> words with dancing is impossible. I answered him back and said the
> words were 100% successful even if one didn't like the ballet. Well,
> anyway, I was furious. I thought it showed very bad taste on his part.
> Afterwards we kissed and I said, "This is the kiss of death, Anatole."
> Florence Reed put on a personality act and did a scene from "Shanghai
> Gesture," and then we all had tea. I went home on the bus and cooled
> off and then practiced an hour and a half at the Dance Players [studio].
> I felt better after that.

The next day she gradually ceased feeling better, for she had a long talk
with Gassmann which lasted from one o'clock to ten, and "after all this
discussion I triumphed by getting exactly one 'and'-count in the finale."
Whereupon she packed up in despair and took the train to Chicago. "At
dinner I found Mr. Denham on the train, so I had two brandies with him and
he told me all about his mother in good old Russia."

Eventually Gassmann indicated a willingness to reorchestrate his music,
but she knew by then that what she wanted was a completely new score,
whether by him or another composer. "What do you think of this, Sergei?"
she wrote to Denham. Apparently Sergei did not think much of it, and what
she had to settle for was a new orchestration, to be finished by July 1, in
time for the fall season at the Met.

Predictably, the new orchestration did not appear by the date of its
deadline, and Denham phoned in mid-July to say it was now too late to
announce *Billy* for the big anniversary season or, as far as he was concerned,
for any other season until either Gassmann or somebody else produced an
entirely new score. Which was exactly the proposal he had turned down three
months before. He also reported that Danilova refused to play Mrs. Potiphar
anymore—if, indeed, there was to be any more. She had been subjected to
shocked criticism from the balletomanes, including Chujoy, for betraying the
classic ballet.

What he now wanted from Ruth for the Met season was *Frankie and
Johnny* definitely, and *Love Song* provided that certain revisions were made in

it. These she had adamantly resisted thus far, had fought with him about and still refused to make.

In a spirit of final rebellion she had Tom write a letter withdrawing all her ballets from the repertoire. Denham wired back immediately that he had already announced both *Love Song* and *Frankie* for the Met season and had all plans made to put *Billy* into rehearsal for the tour that was to follow. He demanded an answer about *Frankie* and *Love Song* by two o'clock that afternoon. The answer he got was no.

As usual at this time of year she and Bentley were playing a number of summer engagements, and when they got to Jacob's Pillow, Denham and Danilova made a point of going up to see her. In anticipation of some such confrontation Tom had just made her resign as president of the Chicago Ballet Company to prevent her saying something to Denham that he might treat as official—a maneuver that Denham had been frankly informed of. Nevertheless, he started at once to talk of her withdrawal of her works.

"Have you answered Tom's letter?" she asked. No, he had not; he could not do business with Tom and would do it only with her. "So I said nothing doing, and that I would not do my own business, and that we had just better sever relations completely. So I said good-bye, and I really hope I never have to see that man again. I hope that is the end of me and the Ballet Russe de Monte Carlo." She was off to Chicago. "Thank God—alone at last."

With the Ballet Russe thus disposed of, she got down to work at once on other things; she finished the scenario for a ballet about the unicorn called *The Triumph of Chastity* (which did not come to production until ten years later); she worked on a ballet with words, based on the famous Mrs. Jack Gardner of Boston, for which Antal Dorati was writing the score (which never came to production at all); and for immediate practical use she created a quite successful twenty-minute pas de deux (also with words) called *Harlequinade* to use on her tour with Bentley, which as usual was to begin in November. She was gloriously free and busy.

She also went, as a matter of course, to see the Chicago performances of the Paris Opéra Ballet, under the direction of Serge Lifar, which was making its first American tour. Her reaction was: "Awful but I am afraid the American public will like it because it is Paris Opera." She saw it again, also as a matter of course, shortly afterward in New York with the same reaction; but she could not have had the remotest inkling that the international scandal caused there at this time would one day have disastrous consequences for, of all disinterested persons, her.

It was probably inevitable that, in spite of the angry finalities of the summer, when the Ballet Russe got to Chicago on its tour after the Metropolitan Opera House anniversary season, she and Denham "made up," and as soon as her own tour with Bentley was finished in December, she joined the company in Los Angeles for ten days of rehearsals of *Love Song*.

She found Danilova and others altering their costumes to suit themselves, much to the displeasure of the excellent wardrobe mistress, Sophie Pourmel, and everything in the same inharmonious state as of old. As to the ballet itself, she and Denham were no more in agreement than before the great reconciliation. The one number for which he felt an obsessive distaste was a hussars' ensemble (the leading male role was that of a hussar), danced, naturally, only by men, whose costumes, just as naturally, included tights as part of the uniform. It seemed curious that this conventional ballet situation offended him, but offend him it did. He was now demanding that not only the tights be dispensed with but the men who wore them as well.

Denham and the dancers, Ruth wrote, persisted in treating the ballet "as if it were a Russian classic," instead of an American work in classic style. That, in a nutshell, was what the ruckus was all about, and had been from the start. The three American genre ballets she had done for them were clearly outside their sacrosanct Russian métier, but with this "classical" work she had stepped right into it, and of course they considered their judgment superior to hers in their own tradition.

In Houston it became clear just which Russian classic they were treating it as. Denham cajoled or bullied her into giving one performance there with the male ensemble eliminated, leaving the single male soloist alone in the work with a swarm of girls; how could you improve on Fokine's precedent of the lone man in *Les Sylphides*? She totally disagreed with the result and demanded the reinstatement of the hussars. This was not, she protested, "a kind of Sylphides-Schubertiana." Denham conformed but he did not give up. A little later he wrote her, with implied warning, that the work promised to be a success "if given in the form I saw it in Houston."

At last on March 1 it opened in New York at the City Center—and in the form Denham wanted. For all its promise of success on those terms, it got indifferent reviews. "Everybody seems to think it is too sad," Ruth meditated. "Of course love to me is sad and poetic and melancholy, but in Ballet Russe everything has to be gay all the time." What many people thought, however, had nothing to do with love's sadness but only with the fact that, for no discernible reason, she had departed from that American genre where, Kirstein had told her, her talents were exhibited at their best.

Though she did not realize it, her hope for "the end of me and the Ballet Russe de Monte Carlo" had been fulfilled, for she was never to do another ballet for them. That other hope, that she would never see that man again, had already been violated. Actually her position on both hopes was a bit ambivalent. In a letter to an English friend she wrote: ". . . [Tom] does not actually say this to me but I know that he doesn't want me to do any more ballets with Denham. He thinks Denham tears me to pieces too much, as, of course, he does everyone. However, in a funny kind of way I have gotten used to Denham and really don't feel like leaving. It is a very hard problem for me to solve. Tom inclines to having me work on my own company now. In a way I like this, but on the other hand, my ideas all use lots of people and I found even the Ballet Russe did not have nearly as many people as I want."

Whatever the turbulences, the sharp dealings, the stubborn, inborn and unreasonable oppositions, men and women who work together creatively, even though they tear each other to pieces, are likely to generate a relationship of unsuspected strength, the very negation of romance, existing quite outside the area of sex but nevertheless well within that of gender.

As for Denham, he never gave up. Almost the last act of his life, when his own company had been dormant for several years, was to phone her from New York after Tom's death, suggesting that they collaborate on the establishment of something like a big Ballet Russe de Chicago. Within the hour he had stepped off the sidewalk on Madison Avenue and been struck fatally by an automobile.

La Ville et Propriétaire
Seule de Lumière

Nothing Succeeds Like Failure

The year 1950 was when the tide turned. The war had so disrupted the dance activities of Europe that every dancer and company that could manage it had headed for the Americas, and New York had become the dance capital of the world. Now, after the war's end, all the American dancers, with or without government sponsorship, decided to return the visits of their recent guests. Hospitality was in no way involved; it was simply a matter of reciprocal invasion.

Martha Graham and her company, the two-year-old New York City Ballet and Ruth all made their European debuts at about the same time. Ballet Theatre had already played a London season in 1946, but now, as it faced its first continental tour, it had adopted the clearly invasionary name of American National Ballet Theatre to indicate its sponsorship by the State Department. Ruth, who had been working toward a Paris engagement from the moment the war had technically ended, was the first to go ashore and accordingly bore the brunt of the landing.

She had been assured by all her official and unofficial emissaries that what Paris wanted to see was something typically American. Emerson Kailey had recommended putting together a single program after the pattern of the one Roland Petit had built so successfully around his *Carmen*. He suggested a theatre such perhaps as the Sarah Bernhardt, for a Paris run, to be followed by a tour. Some dialogue had also taken place with Georges Hirsch, director of both the Opéra and the Opéra Comique, for a season at the latter theatre.

And still hanging around was the ghost of that idea of a gala program that had been discussed with Boris Kochno for the Théâtre des Champs-Elysées.

Remisoff, when Ruth wrote him of her project, warned her to be cautious about Paris, where everything was competitive, and at all costs to avoid the Champs-Elysées, which "was always the most difficult theatre imaginable" and for her small company was "absolutely impossible." He urged her not to judge it by the success there of both Katherine Dunham and Josephine Baker, since Negroes were always successful in Paris, representing, as they did to the Parisians, something altogether exotic. He was not familiar with the Sarah Bernhardt, but he assumed that since it was a dramatic theatre, it must be more intimate.

In January Ruth and Tom went to Paris for two weeks to see for themselves. The Sarah Bernhardt had no orchestra pit, and most of the other intimate theatres were too intimate. Kochno's Ballets des Champs-Elysées, which had made a brilliant success immediately after the war as a youthful and revolutionary company, was momentarily disbanded, what with financial difficulties, dissensions and the departure of Roland Petit, one of its original instigators and chief assets. The theatre itself was in the hands of a receiver because of the financial difficulties of its former manager, and it was therefore available. So, in spite of Remisoff's animadversions, it was settled upon for a spring season of three weeks or so under the auspices of Gabriel Dussurget and Henri Lambert, directors of the Bureau de Concerts de Paris. They were not at all the typical commercial managers but were anxious to present new and interesting things. Angry as Ruth was with them from time to time, she admired and trusted them and came to have a genuine attachment to them.

In February Tom was busily checking on the productions of *The Bells* and *Billy Sunday* and arranging to get all the scenery and costumes for *Frankie and Johnny* from the Ballet Russe de Monte Carlo, since its rights had lapsed with its failure to give the required fifteen performances during the past year. It had managed fourteen, but lost by a nose when both Franklin and Danielian were ill on the night of the scheduled fifteenth. "Denham was furious with me when I took it back," Ruth wrote.

She was even busier, preparing a repertoire and engaging a company to perform it. With such a large theatre to fill, a single program was not practicable for a run of any length, and repertory became mandatory. Katherine Dunham had warned her to take a second program, for "the French public is completely unpredictable in its taste." The plan was even further expanded to include works of other choreographers, and the company was to be called Les Ballets Américains. Agnes de Mille, Eugene Loring, Valerie Bettis all proved unavailable as participants, but happily José Limón, whose *Moor's Pavane* was the first work she had thought of including, was both available and interested.

Late in March she was in New York casting and rehearsing and having to face, alas, some of those business problems with which she so distrusted herself. She and Tom had arranged with Limón—or rather with Pauline Lawrence, his wife and general factotum—to present both *The Moor's Pavane* and *La Malinche* and to bring along the three principal company members needed to perform them with him—Pauline Koner, Betty Jones and Lucas Hoving. Tom, however, had offered only $250 a week to be divided among Limón, Koner and Hoving, and Mrs. Limón was upset. Accordingly she went to Ruth to talk about the situation, because, as Ruth quoted her in her diary, she "can't get along with Tom! (That refrain again.) It made me sick to my stomach and I haven't recovered from it yet!"

But however the bargaining may have worked out, the Limón quartet went along and was entirely cooperative. They did not constitute "a separate entity by any means." Ruth had cast all the works very carefully, and she had seen immediately that Limón would make a fine King of the Ghouls in *The Bells* and that Pauline Koner would be a lovely Bathsheba in *Billy Sunday*. Betty Jones not only danced Desdemona in *The Moor's Pavane* and sang the vocalise in the pit for *La Malinche* but was one of the three singing Salvation Army lasses in *Frankie* and danced on point as a Golden Bell in *The Bells*. Hoving "was versatile enough to be able to step into about any part in 'Frankie and Johnny' in case of illness," and Pauline Lawrence herself sang nightly in *Frankie*.

Dancers, besides herself and Bentley Stone, whose names were featured on the billboards included Talley Beatty, Kenneth McKenzie, Helen Kramer, Dorothy Hill and Toni Grant. Toni was actually Tatiana Grantzeva of the Ballet Russe, who wanted to go along for the ride, as it were, but preferred to protect her official ballerina "rank" behind a suitably simple American façade. Most of the corps de ballet were soloists from other companies; this, Ruth admitted, was not perhaps the best way to make up a good corps de ballet, but she preferred interesting individuals to a line of Rockettes, and she knew that by the end of the engagement they would become a good corps. The way she had cast them for roles, large or small, met with their warm approval.

She had applied the same principles to the repertoire itself; *Frankie and Johnny* had been restored to its uncensored pre-Ballet-Russe form; *The Bells* had been recostumed, repolished and musically adjusted; *Billy Sunday* was actually completed, as it had not been for its contentious Broadway debut, and in the process it had inevitably been revised and recast. Ruth herself was doing Mrs. Potiphar and Bentley was Billy for the first time. Beatty and two other first-rate black boys, Alex Young and Albert Popwell, whom she had scoured the New York dance world to find, were now the three devils in the new version of the work.

Besides these major ballets she was taking along a new eleven-minute version of Gershwin's *An American in Paris* (here retitled *Les Américains à Paris*), in which she and Bentley and the three black boys were featured. This served as the climax to a series of miscellaneous divertissements under her old standby title of *Scrapbook*. It could be changed from night to night but was nevertheless put together in a kind of unifying production sequence, and made an ideal closing number for the evening.

Among the individual items in the series was a new version of her own Villa-Lobos solo, *Possessed*, made especially for Beatty. The little boy she had first known in the days of *La Guiablesse* now headed his own touring company and had developed a quality of movement that she found "really inspiring." As rehearsals went on she noted in her diary: "He is the first dancer who has made me weep since Pavlova and Kreutzberg and I would like to do nothing but make ballets for him."

She was naturally exhausted by the time they were all safely aboard the plane (along with Claudia Cassidy, incidentally, who was heading for a critical tour of the European theatre and came along as a guest). In addition to all the organizing and rehearsing she was facing an extremely heavy schedule of performing for a dancer of fifty, an age when ballerinas are conventionally supposed to be at least dallying with retirement.

As if that were not enough, another situation, of which at the moment she was naively innocent, lay ahead to be faced; she was taking along with her unbeknownst a stowaway—impersonal, intangible and invisible, a time bomb of Gallic fury. It had been kindled by New York's boorishly American rejection of Serge Lifar and the Paris Opéra Ballet a year and a half ago and had been smoldering ever since as it lay in wait for a suitable victim to explode upon. Into this role Ruth moved with fatalistic timing.

HANDS ACROSS THE SEA

L'affaire Lifar, indeed, must have been the most inept episode in the history of intercultural relations. For reasons far from clear, the ballet of the Paris Opéra was invited in 1948 to participate in a two-week International Dance Festival sponsored by the Mayor's Committee for the Commemoration of the Golden Anniversary of the City of New York—in other words, the anniversary of the founding of Greater New York out of the union of the five boroughs. Of the sixteen scheduled performances the lion's share of eleven was allotted to the French opera ballet, four fell to Ram Gopal and one to Charles Weidman and his modern dance company.

The event had been planned originally for the Metropolitan Opera House, which was manifestly the only suitable place to house it, but unfortunately it was already engaged for the fall season of the Ballet Russe. One would think that the Mayor's Committee might have been aware of this, and possibly it was, but things have frequently been known to go awry in such organizations as mayors' committees, and ultimately some other place had to be found. The place finally selected was the City Center; apparently the Mayor's Committee considered it officially fitting since it belonged to the city that was being celebrated.

Its other qualifications, however, were flagrantly nonexistent; it lacked not only beauty and elegance but also adequate working space and facilities. The stage was approximately one quarter the size of the Opéra's stage, for which all the productions had been conceived; its depth was 40 feet as compared with the Opéra's 120; there was virtually no wing space, no "grid" space and no room for the ramps and platforms and generally spectacular accouterments of the Opéra's repertoire. Much of the scenery had to be rebuilt or eliminated, and several of the projected ballets had to be abandoned altogether.

The season opened, however, with éclat, and the atmosphere was genuinely hands-across-the-sea. Outside the theatre it might have been Hollywood. There were giant spotlights on the sky, barricades on both sides of the street, and policemen every few feet to hold back the mobs of curious onlookers as the distinguished audience arrived. The Police Band, assisted by blaring loudspeakers, played in front of the theatre for forty-five minutes, including in its repertoire for the occasion "Mademoiselle from Armentières," in accordance with the American tradition of making ou-la-las at gay Paree.

Inside the theatre a half hour of welcoming ceremonies found the mayors of both Paris and New York on the dais; Marcelle Denya of the Opéra Comique sang the "Marseillaise;" Lucy Monroe, of course, sang "The Star-Spangled Banner," which had become more or less her exclusive property during the war years, since nobody else could sing it; Mayor O'Dwyer was decorated with the Cross of the Legion of Honor and an air of cordiality prevailed.

The merits of the ballet program that followed were of only secondary importance, for this was in no sense a dance audience, except, of course, for the top galleries; but whatever these *enfants du paradis* may have thought, the evening proceeded with decorum until the very end. Then came the curtain calls, and international unity took to flight; when Lifar joined the assembled company for a bow, he was greeted, against a general background of applause, with boos, in many cases singling him out by name.

This had nothing whatever to do with his art but with the persistent rumors that he had been a collaborationist during the Nazi occupation. The stagehands at the Opéra had refused to work if he performed, and he had accordingly been "suspended" for a year or two. After the liberation, however, he had been promptly reinstated in his post of ballet master, and the charges against him had been officially and vehemently denied by his superior at the Opéra, Georges Hirsch, who had himself been a leader of the French resistance and was in a position to know. But accusations once made are hard to unmake, and his status in the public mind at the moment was, to say the least, anomalous.

This afforded an excellent opportunity to the young political militants among the New York dancers, who were prone to protest at the drop of a hat, and once the police barriers had been removed after the gala opening, they staged a nightly picket line, ardent and vocal. In an effort to uphold the solidarity of workers, they tried to focus on Lifar alone and exclude his performing colleagues, but this was difficult, since the company backed him unanimously. (Ruth had asked a member of the corps de ballet, when she saw the performances in Chicago, how they liked Balanchine at the Paris Opéra, and she had answered, "*Il est bien, mais Lifar*"—and her eyes lifted up—"*il est pour nous.*") Furthermore, some of them, especially among the ladies, were involved even more deeply than he in accusations of consorting with the enemy.

So much for Lifar's political offenses, if any; his quite unrelated artistic ones could not be disposed of by any amount of official exoneration. Neither his ego nor his oeuvre was of a character to endear him to New York, as had already been twice proven. The first time was in 1933, when he made his debut in America with a little company of eight or ten dancers, a scratch orchestra and, as the chief number on the program, perhaps in the role of an historic landmark, the first ballet he had created when he took over as ballet master of the Paris Opéra three years earlier. This happened unfortunately to be the quite unchoreographable (by anybody) *Prometheus* of Beethoven. The other works were *Spectre de la Rose* and *L'Après-midi d'un Faun* (in both of which he donned "the mantle of Nijinsky") and a restaged version of Balanchine's *La Chatte*.

The second time was five years later, when he came as one of the stars of Leonide Massine's newly organized Ballet Russe de Monte Carlo, danced Albrecht on the opening night to the Giselle of Alicia Markova (it was her American debut) in his own staging of the work, received flowers onstage, tossing one rose from the bouquet to the conductor in the orchestra pit (a routine that in America was considered the exclusive prerogative of ballerinas), and very early in the season walked out of the company in high dudgeon and challenged Massine to a duel in Central Park (a gesture with all the dimensions of high camp).

On his third visit, ten years later, events at the City Center made it clear that, for whatever cause, Lifar was not for New York and vice versa. That scandal, in addition to its local embarrassments, caused quite understandable unhappiness and resentment abroad, for Lifar had a large and influential following. Certainly they had a legitimate grievance, for the ballet had been

shoddily housed and shabbily treated; they could not reasonably be expected
to understand a point of view that, even after making all allowances for
wretched working conditions, had found Lifar and his company guilty of
creative and stylistic breaches in the area of art, a category far more relevant
than bad manners and managerial ineptitude.

Now, a year and a half later, when Ruth and her company were figuratively sitting at the airport waiting to enplane for Paris, the Ballet Russe de
Monte Carlo, by this time long under the direction of Sergei Denham, opened
its spring season at the Metropolitan Opera House with Yvette Chauviré as its
guest star. An artistic protégée of Lifar, adored at home and endowed with
the popular sobriquet of "La Chauviré Nationale," she had had something of a
personal triumph even in the shambles at the City Center. But she had never
before danced with this company, which in spite of its title had become largely
Americanized in both personnel and style. Her own style could scarcely have
been more alien, and she had a far too limited time with them for any basic
rapport to be achieved. The opening night's *Giselle* (which of course she had
danced only in Lifar's version) was accordingly a schizoid catastrophe.
Throughout the entire engagement, for the same generic reason, she was never
seen to advantage. Though there were "raves" in the press again about her
gifts as an artist, her technique and her beauty, there was a general panning of
the works selected for her to bring along, and the tenor of her reception was
negative.

This was all that that symbolic time bomb required to speed it on its
avenging mission, and with Ruth's plane nearing the zero hour before flight, it
stowed itself away, as it were, in the undercarriage. The New York reviews of
Chauviré were taken up immediately by one of the most distinguished critics
on one of the most respected papers in Paris, who all bur burst into flame
with indignation. With unimpeachable data now in hand, he concluded that
the basis of the whole two-part debacle was a deep-seated chauvinism,
manipulated by one particularly venomous critic whom he referred to through
the hissing teeth of his typewriter as "ce Chauvin." The said Chauvin, who
apparently had a dossier of his own, prophesied lugubriously that the fat was
in the fire, and whatever American ballet company was next to appear in Paris
would not be received with outstanding grace. Which it was not.

April in Paris, justly famous for its beauty, can also be chilly backstage,
and a cold theatre formed the background for the trials and confusions of a
rehearsal period that bore no resemblance at all to the same thing in New
York. Rehearsals were apparently "on open invitation" to any photographer
or any reporter or almost anybody else, for that matter, who cared to drop in
at his own convenience. The company's carefully prepared publicity photographs were universally spurned; every photographer from the city's thirty-odd
newspapers and magazines insisted on taking his own pictures, choosing the

costumes he wanted and arranging his own poses. Visitors were constantly underfoot; there was no such thing as rehearsing alone and uninterrupted; "talk, talk, talk"—and the dancers were tired to death.

In the rehearsal room the piano was such a wreck that Simon Sadoff, as rehearsal pianist, had to sing along with his playing in order to make even the simplest of the scores recognizable to the dancers, and most of the scores were anything but simple. There was a studio in the top of the building with a reasonably decent piano, but the room had been adapted for recording, and the floor "was all squashy and soft" and impossible for toe-shoes.

According to revered French custom, musicians who did not choose to come to a rehearsal were allowed to send substitutes, with the result that the orchestra that turned up for a performance frequently contained musicians who had never been to rehearsals at all, and were sight-reading scores that were virtually unsight-readable. On Saturday nights half the instrumentalists were likely to be new. "On these occasions we shut our ears, counted and prayed." Since the practice was notoriously prevalent at this time, Tom had made sure in advance that the contract clearly stated that no such practice should prevail in this instance, but custom was more sacred than contract.

As for the managers, Dussurget and Lambert, "all their advice was bad." It was they who selected the numbers for the all-important opening program at a special "tryout" dress rehearsal. At this grueling session they "hated most of the costumes" and called in Georges Wakhevitch, who had designed successfully for Roland Petit, to redesign and reexecute many of them at this last moment. They thought Limón's costume for the King of the Ghouls was far too grotesque for "such a handsome man." Noguchi's original costumes for *The Bells* had already been replaced in their entirety by more amenable ones designed by Remisoff, but this particular one was considered not amenable enough. Limón's costume for Othello in *The Moor's Pavane* was considered much too plain, and it was only after a struggle that velvets and jewels were not added to it.

"A howl went up when we four girls for 'Americans in Paris' donned our costumes, which were designed by Remisoff as caricatures of four crazy American girls with foolish exaggerated costumes and hats. We all thought they were extremely amusing and very original, and our sharp Gershwinesque movements suited the extreme cut of the costumes." The French, however, automatically "read deeper meanings into what we had done as a light satire on the giddiness and homesickness of Americans in Paris . . . Our French friends considered these costumes an insult to the 'haute couture' of Paris. . . . American women, it seems, usually wear French clothes in Paris and these costumes they thought were a cruel satire on French clothes." So Wakhevitch came up hastily with "four tutus with big hats which were very cute but so completely French that I just *couldn't* do the American style steps in mine."

Park Avenue Odalisque at the Rainbow Room. (*Maurice Seymour*)

The Cambridge Ladies, danced to the poem by
e. cummings in the *Words and Music* program.
(*Maurice Seymour*)

Another *Words and Music* number,
danced to a poem by Carl Sandburg.
(*Maurice Seymour*)

Scene from *Frankie and Johnny*, New York, 1945,
with Pauline Goddard, Frederic Franklin and Ruthanna Boris. (*Gjon Mili*)

Ruth as "Frankie." (*Maurice Seymour*)

The Bells in its Paris production, 1950. (*Serge Lido*)

Billy Sunday in the 1950 Paris season. (*Serge Lido*)

Ruth and Bentley Stone in *Harlequinade.*
(*Maurice Seymour*)

Salome and Herod, with designs by Nicolas Remisoff. (*Paul Hansen*)

The *Merry Widow* in its Chicago production, 1955,
with scenery and costumes by Rolf Gerard. (*Paul Hansen*)

It was "a black tutu with long black full chiffon sleeves and a witch's hat." Somebody called her "the black witch of Salem." So they all wore the old costumes (most of the new ones had not been finished in time, but unfortunately Ruth's had) until she had time to coach an understudy to replace her.

Naturally, in dress-conscious Paris, the costumes played a crucial role, but not the only crucial role, for anything visual, choreographic or creative that diverged too far from the beaten track of French custom and that supreme and final criterion known as French taste got the ax at first sight. Several numbers from the *Scrapbook* were accordingly mowed down in short order at this managerial inquisition. Among them were the two Page-Stone comedy pieces, *Zephyr and Flora and Valse Cécile,* which had never been known to fail with an audience. At the other end of the spectrum, out went both of the sensuous tropical numbers—her always show-stopping *Tropic* (Cyril Scott), with its mask and its languors, and the Villa-Lobos *Possessed*, which she had taken away from herself and made over with such enthusiasm for Beatty. They were perhaps too unballetic and too brooding, for Paris had seen little or nothing of modern dance and, like its cousins across the British Channel, considered everything that was non-Petipa, non-Diaghileff, or done off *pointe* to be "Central European"—or to put it less politely, German. Limón's dancing was said by one critic to be Japanese, which was actually much nearer the point, if, as was likely, he was thinking of the dramatic movement of Kabuki.

In any event, in later programs three of these four rejected dances turned out to be "*real* hits," official French taste to the contrary notwithstanding. The fourth one, *Tropic*, Ruth "could never get up the courage to do."

The Bells had been brought over "in deference," as Ruth put it, "to Darius Milhaud the great French composer," but certainly in reference to his Frenchness as well. He was also to conduct it, but when he discovered that it was to open the program, he declined to do so. French audiences proverbially arrived late, and he did not intend to be walked in on. As a result, it was shifted to the end of the program, changing places with, of all things, *Scrapbook*. Such a switch necessitated an alteration even in this work, for if the audience came late, it would miss the number that the management had been most enthusiastic about in the tryout rehearsal. This was *Variations on Euclid*, dating from the Noguchi-Tchelitchev era, with its tapes and its sticks and its sack and its unusual designs in movement, which Ruth had made over into a six-minute number for Dorothy Hill. Thus, instead of being the first divertissement in the suite, it became the last before the *Americans in Paris.*

From another old friend in the musical division came further dissent at this moment of general agitation, for Gassmann, when he saw the opening night's printed program, wrote at once to Dussurget protesting its failure to give him credit for the music of *Billy Sunday*, which was announced for later in the season, and its generally second-rate treatment of the work. He also pointed out that the program notes on *Billy* were completely inadequate for a French audience. For these reasons he suggested that the use of the programs be discontinued at once and that the ballet itself be dropped from the season's schedule.

Though Gassmann had always seemed to be trying to prevent his own work from being performed, his bit about the need for adequate notes for the French public raised a valid issue, and later a French actor was engaged to explain from the stage the nature and substance of both *Billy* and *Frankie*.

At any rate, the curtain actually went up on May 8.

According to Paris custom, the opening performance was in the nature of an elite preview, to which the press was not admitted, and only the balconies were open to the paying public. The main floor was occupied exclusively by a congeries of brilliant guests of the management, who because of the enormous influence of their opinions, and their predilection for voicing them, were known as *les vipères*. They came from various sections of the sophisticated world—society leaders, artists, musicians, painters, poets, promoters of art "movements" and cults of all sorts, patrons and patronesses of their own jealously sponsored artists, self-appointed authorities in all fields, designers and heads of the great houses of *haute couture* (one of the major arts in Paris) plus the usual proportion of lion hunters, toadies and hangers-on. They were a law unto themselves, capable of killing or exalting whatever they saw, and their multiplicity of pronunciamentos had the finality of divine sanction—far more so than those of the press, with which they had no rapport whatsoever. Certainly, however, they did not sit as a jury; their verdicts were by no means collective, for in addition to the wide range of their fields of interest they were, with true French individualism, each buttering his own toast. For this reason it was customary to station members of the *Garde Civile* quietly throughout the theatre with especial care to prevent any such theatrical explosions of *le beau monde* as had occurred periodically from the days of *le Jockey Club* down to *Le Sacre du Printemps*.

The evening had hardly got under way when, to the consternation of everybody including those *vipères* who had arrived by that time, there was violent booing and whistling from the balcony, directed at every dance just before its final moment, so that the noise would drown out any possible applause from the main floor. Press reports reaching this country from Paris declared the boos and catcalls "unprecedented." Certainly they had not been equalled since 1913, when the première of *Le Sacre du Printemps* in this same theatre found a clamorous audience all but tearing up the seats. A major difference between the two demonstrations, however, was that the earlier one had been a spontaneous eruption of *les vipères* while the present one had been carefully prepared in advance by vengeful professionals.

The dancers were naturally shaken and distressed, but "we soon found out that the opera ballet had bought 250 seats in the balcony and that they had an organized booing against us. The Paris Opéra Ballet were treated so badly in New York that they decided to finish off the first American company in a big way. No critics were supposed to come till the second night, but the opera ballet had got in two of their cohorts"—including the fiery anti-chauvinist, no less. His review, which was "awful—unfair," was not only printed the next day, quite contrary to the usual practice, but also quoted on the radio immediately after the performance. (The radio critic was later to see the performance for himself and to declare in his own right that it was excellent and that everyone should see it, but the damage he did that night was considerable.)

After the performance "lots of people came backstage," including the architect and aesthete Le Corbusier; the painters and stage designers Michel Larionov and his wife, Nathalie Gontcharova; and Pierre Tugal, the eminent dance archivist; "all raving about the performance."

At the second performance there was, again, concerted hissing from people in two of the boxes, but it was drowned out this time by applause and cheering. After that "things cooled down and we got four good reviews, that were really fair." Jean-Jacques Etchévery, ballet master of the Opéra Comique, wrote Ruth a charming note acknowledging that he knew the whole thing had been planned in advance. Alexandre Volinine, Pavlova's onetime partner, invited them all to come to his studio for classes (which they did not have time to do), Escudero was "fiery" on their behalf, and many of the French dancers (obviously not members of the opera ballet) came backstage during the run to congratulate them.

"Milhaud conducted 'The Bells' brilliantly at the dress rehearsal and everyone was mad about it but he let the finale drop at the performance and played it so slowly that everybody got bored." They were also, as a whole, offended by the falling of the church, and the management made her take the ballet off for the next two nights. But the night after that she insisted on putting it back, and "it seemed to be most successful and now everybody likes it again!"

She had lunch with Dr. Tugal and Irène Lidova, who was one of the founders of the Ballets des Champs-Elysées as well as general secretary of the French Association of Ballet Critics and Writers and collaborated with her photographer-husband, Serge Lido, on his handsome dance publications. She told Ruth "why the French did not like certain things. *Frankie* is too realistic, too earthy and they are shocked to death by it." One of the French papers printed a list of ten things in *Frankie and Johnny* that shocked them and illustrated it with photographs. "The list was a great surprise to all of us. Here it is: 1. The daring manner of this dance (le côté hardi); 2. Frankie's red hair; 3. Johnny's purple shirt; 4. Dance with the coffin (a coffin is apparently tabu on the French stage); 5. The placing of the corpse in the bier (la mise en bière); 6. Nelly's lily wreath; 7. Macabre parody; 8. Frankie making effects with her legs over the coffin; 9. Salvation Army girls drinking beer over the bier; 10. All the dancers dressed in earth colors. So now at least we know what caused all the sensation. . . . The truth of the matter is that after talking to all these people it seems that what they want *entirely* is chichi, pretty, old-style stuff with *their* taste costumes. . . . I'm sure they will *hate* 'Billy Sunday.' "

However right she may have been in general, she could not have been more mistaken about *Billy*. By the time it went into the program the French actor had been provided to clarify it in advance and "the French audience took it right in their stride and didn't bat an eyelash." From that time on the management insisted that both *Frankie* and *Billy* be on every program.

The audiences were small, but they were by now "*extremely* enthusiastic," and "the season closed brilliantly. Letters, presents, very gala."

On her night off Ruth had gone to the Opéra to see *Le Chevalier Errant*, the new Lifar-Ibert work. "One hour and four minutes and about what? It cost a million," had many effects and singing, "but not one moment of *real* art. The first ballet was impossible and we didn't stay for the last. Paris is twenty-five years behind New York and even Chicago in dance."

She had not given the virtually obligatory party for the critics. Katherine Dunham had warned her of the custom, "but," she had added, "if you don't do it and get bad reviews, at least everyone will know you are an honest woman." After the first ten performances, however, "some of them asked to come see me and they came to our little sitting-room (at the Georges V) and we had champagne and sandwiches and a very pleasant time." She made "a terrible gaffe by saying that Paris had really not seen much that was 'new' in dance and the remark was resented. Why, Paris has seen *everything—everything* comes to Paris. I had not read what they wrote about me, so I was a little in the dark. Yesterday I started translating them and what a job! I am amazed at how good they are, but we certainly caused a revolution here."

They had unquestionably done wonders and with the odds all against them. They had succeeded in giving a season of twenty performances in a large theatre, where a year before, the Sadler's Wells Ballet, just before its epoch-making debut in New York, had achieved only ten and had been pronounced a failure because its décors and costumes were "*mauvais gout*." Now, during this present season, the Ballet Rambert was able to manage only ten at the "intimate" Sarah Bernhardt, with ballets by Antony Tudor, Walter

Gore and Andrée Howard. She had every reason, indeed, to feel that they had won a hard-fought victory in a significant battle, as she and her storm troops flew back to their home base.

She had hardly arrived in New York before Chujoy called her at the Plaza, where she was staying, to interview her, as it were, and she invited him to have dinner with her. The first thing he did was hand her a copy of his *Dance News* containing a report of her Paris debut. It was "a great slap in the face when I was so happy to get home. The whole story was told upside-down and so distorted that one would think to read it that we had been booed and hissed legitimately. I really was so mad that I just got up and left the table and went to my room and wept for a long time. Such complete unfairness—such complete misapprehension."

That kiss of death had not been lethal enough.

Revenge Can be Sweet

The year was epochal for Ruth not alone because of her invasion of Paris but also because it was the year when Tom's long labors in Texas began to materialize in terms of real money. Not enough, of course, to finance any world-shaking ballet companies, but quite enough to provide for certain personal expansions she had long dreamed of. Consequently her return to Chicago was designed to last only long enough for her to unpack her professional luggage, so to speak, before setting out again for Europe on a purely personal interlude.

One pressing professional mission, however, had to be undertaken at once. She was perfectly sure that, whatever happened, she would produce again in Paris, and with its challenge and its full flavor still in her blood she had already decided on the work she must do there. It was *Trovatore*, though not quite the one that she and Lehman Engel had laughed at so uproariously all those pre-Ballet-Russe years ago. Back in 1947, during the earlier ordeals of *Billy Sunday*, she had noted one day that the Metropolitan Opera's regular Saturday-afternoon broadcast was to be *Trovatore*, so, though she was in no mood to think about that ballet then, she had a recording made of the broadcast. (Much to her distress, it cost her $52.) Now she dug it out eagerly and listened to it. She was hearing it, of course, with Paris ears and seeing it with Paris eyes. Without having to watch the typically operatic "performing" of it onstage, she found herself "thrilled with its almost primitive force and intensity and immediately . . . started to conceive it as a dance drama based on the theme of revenge which forms the basic drive of the opera."

Lehman might very possibly not have been interested in her new attitude toward the work, but in any case he was far too busy with his conducting and recording activities even to consider it. So she wrote at once to Jerome Moross, asking if he would be willing to make a ballet score out of the opera music—without putting his own name on it if he preferred not to.

This done, off she hopped to Europe with Tom. What they were searching for was a house on the Côte d'Azur, in Italy or wherever else a tour by car (together with hints from friends) might turn up something desirable to serve as a European seat. She had "sat" too long in Chicago.

Among the most likely hinters were their Chicago friends, Leander McCormick (one of Tom's colleagues in the establishment of the Racquet Club) and his alert and lively French wife, Renée, who were beautifully domiciled in St. Tropez. Then there was Trudy Goth, dancer, writer and formidable organizer in both New York and Europe, who had a house on the island of Elba with her Hungarian mother and had already offered assistance in that area. So with their tale suitably told in St. Tropez, they set out in their little Vedette to drive down into Italy and wired Trudy of their date of arrival.

The wire, however, was never received, and when the boat from the mainland delivered them at Portoferraio, there was no one to meet them. Eventually they tracked down the Goths at their house, and Trudy transferred them into her own car, since theirs might not be able to cope with the steep drive up the mountain, and deposited them at the hotel at the top where she had arranged for them to stay.

It was the Fuente Napoleoni, extremely smart and with a magnificent view across the valley. The next morning they had breakfast in the hotel garden and were sitting in a swing there, looking at the tiny village far below, when a charming girl, beautifully dressed, walked past them several times and finally approached them.

"Aren't you Ruth Page?" she asked.

"Why, yes, I guess I am," Ruth answered in her best Americanese.

It was Margot Fonteyn. Only a few months earlier she had made her American debut in New York, which had established her immediately as a ranking international ballerina, but Ruth had never seen her offstage before. "Such a surprise," she wrote in her diary. "I never would have recognized her, but she did us. So we spent the entire day with her and her traveling companion." The four of them went looking for houses, had a picnic lunch and got back to the hotel about nine o'clock. They had turned up nothing that suggested Ruth's dream house, but she had found and sealed an enduring friendship with the young Margot.

Their luggage was still at the foot of the mountain in their car, "so Margot loaned me a dress. She is truly one of the loveliest characters I have ever met, as well as of course being the world's top ballerina. People at the hotel didn't even know who she was. She had to leave the next morning and about 5:30 she knocked on our door. They wouldn't let her leave the hotel because the check she was expecting had not arrived. So Tom of course said he would pay for her if it didn't come. So she left."

The following day the Fishers also left, only to find when they got down to Portoferraio that the boat never took cars on Thursday. She was "livid with rage," but back up the mountain they went in the Vedette—"didn't think she would make the climb, but she did." The next day they set out for Chicago—via Switzerland, Kreutzberg, Germany, Wigman, Paris, Mme. Nora and their respective summer schools.

Back in Chicago, repercussions from the Paris season were making it clear that the *scandale* that had been engineered to ruin the company had instead contributed to its success, if only in the matter of publicity. Propositions for its return were emanating from all sorts of European sources, until it was becoming difficult to decide which of them to accept, if any. Monte Carlo made an excellent financial offer, provided only that the company would call itself Les Ballets du Prince de Monaco. ("We shrieked with laughter over this. But it is a fine idea.") Another manager wanted them for Aix and Biarritz and Venice. ("Both want us for fall. So now we have to get ready.")

Getting ready, whatever else it may have included, certainly included for Ruth the new *Trovatore*. There had been no word from Moross, so she wired him at once: "Burning to know how Trovatore is progressing. Please write or telegraph." Apparently it was not progressing at all, for a month later she had also written to Fritz Wilckens, asking him to make the score, and he had accepted but "with too many provisos." So she turned to Isaac van Grove, who always knew what she had in mind, and it was he who finally came through with a fifty-minute score that was exactly what she wanted.

In September and October she had got the story into intelligible shape and was now hard at work on the creation of the ballet itself. It was her practice to invent, frequently with the aid of a partner, every movement and every phrase of each of the characters on herself, so that before she went into rehearsal, she had a more or less finished "script" both to cast from and to work from. Her immediate goal was another of those work-in-progress lecture-demonstrations at Mandel Hall in January.

Meanwhile the Sadler's Wells Ballet came to Chicago for the first time; in its only previous American season it had not made a transcontinental tour, as it was doing this year. Naturally, Ruth dropped everything to give the kind of opening-night party for Margot and the company that she knew they would like. She herself had "suffered through so many after-the-theatre parties on tour, where we had lemonade and cookies when we needed steak and red wine, I finally got to the point where I didn't accept any parties until I found out what they would give us to eat." She knew how starved dancers were on these occasions, so she arranged to have the dancers eat first. "This made a big hit with the performers." It apparently made a hit with the nonperformers as well, for "*le tout Chicago*" was there and the general verdict was that it was the best party of the year.

As soon as the ballet's visit was over, she dashed out to California for several days of conferences with Remisoff about designs for *Revenge*, as her *Trovatore* was now entitled. In this practical process he gave her enormous assistance in the further clarification of the complex story. Her immediate concern, however, was with the costumes for the Mandel Hall performance.

When that date in January came around, everything went well, for a change. Only excerpts from the ballet were presented, and with piano accompaniment. The ever-enthusiastic Mark Turbyfill gave a lecture, to hold the whole thing together, on the full sage of *Il Trovatore*, dating back to a legendary fifteenth-century folk drama that took eight days to perform.

In spite of her high regard for Remisoff's taste and talent, however, there were still some undefined new dimensions that she was feeling for in this particular, Paris-oriented creation. And it was not until mid-March that she found the ultimate designer—in Paris. He was Antoni Clavé, Catalan by birth but French by adoption, having come to France in 1939 as a refugee from Franco. He had first attracted attention in 1946 with his designs for a ballet by Ana Nevada called *Caprichos* for the then forward-looking Ballets des Champs-Elysées and had leaped into fame with his designs for Roland Petit's *Carmen* only a year ago.

Ruth and Tom arrived in Paris on March 18, a Sunday, and the next day they went to Montparnasse to see him. "This is something I will never forget," she wrote in her diary. "An enchanting apartment impossible to describe—so clean, so full of exquisite pictures, and his old mother sitting at a table painting. Such a beautiful old lady. Her right hand is paralyzed and she paints with her left. She has never painted before in her life and her work is unbelievable. It is easy to see where her son gets his talent. We sat in the room next to where she was painting and we could hear her singing as she painted. Her son Antoni is very quiet with great big rather placid eyes, squeaky shoes and a moustache. He says very little but listens very attentively. I played the Verdi records for him and told him all about the 'Revenge' ballet and he seemed to like the idea."

In its own altogether different way it was another meeting such as that with Margot on the heights in Elba, and the instantaneous friendship it sparked was just as enduring.

IMPROMPTU AU THEATRE

After a *Trovatore*-inspired pilgrimage to Spain she returned to Paris and on the last day of March had lunch with Jean Robin, the administrator of the Champs-Elysées ballet, which was having a struggle for survival. They were booked for a tour of Germany and the repertoire was in need of a short comedy ballet, which he asked her to create for them. Naturally she was interested, though totally unprepared. Emerson Kailey suggested *Gold Standard*, which she had set to Ibert's *Divertimento* in 1934. She did not remember a single step of it, but she finally agreed to do it if suitable setting and costumes were provided. This Wakhevitch was engaged to do, and four days later she started rehearsals, with Roger Fenonjois and his wife, Arlova, in the leading roles. Nine days after that she had finished everything except the passages for which props were required. She had never done a ballet so fast in her life.

This she accomplished in spite of the fact that, as she wrote to Dinah Maggie, the *sympathique* critic of *Le Combat*, "the French dancers are very different from the American dancers. The choreographer has to get used to their method of rehearsal. If there are eight dancers in the corps de ballet [as there were in this one] and they are all to dance the same step, the choreographer has to show it to teach one individually. This takes time and there is always lots of talk, for it seems that French dancers do not enjoy rehearsing. But once on the stage they are delightful performers and one forgets about the difficulty of rehearsals."

Nevertheless, after twenty hours of rehearsal with the corps and eighteen with the principals the ballet, under its new title of *Impromptu au Bois*, opened the program of the first performance of the company's tour in Freiburg. The tour was not successful financially and was cancelled after the Berlin engagement, ostensibly because of the unanimously bad reviews in Munich. Actually the German bookers had already lost so much money on all their French importations (the war, after all, had not been over that long) that they did not want to lose any more. Besides that there was political maneuvering among former members of the ballet company itself, and injurious stories were circulated against it from within, so to speak.

Ruth was particularly distressed by one such story, which had been printed first in *Le Combat*, then reprinted in the Berlin program and sent to all the Berlin critics, because of its inference that "an American millionairess" was supporting the company. "Neither Tom nor I," she wrote in her diary, "have given the Champs-Elysées Ballet one cent so it is all a little odd to say the least! In any event it is impossible for us to help them financially."

Of course she and Tom could not subsidize the company, if that was what she meant, but their ability to "help them financially" even without giving them one cent was to be proved very shortly. That she placed a high value on the company was clear in her letter to Mme. Maggie: "I think it is extremely important for French dance art to keep the Champs-Elysées company alive, because it is possible to be more experimental in this company than in Government-supported institutions. It is true that both the Opéra and the Opéra Comique have produced an extraordinary amount of interesting novelties, but the Champs-Elysées company gives the young choreographers a chance which is impossible in the two other companies."

It was exactly the situation in which she instinctively saw herself functioning at her best, and the present tour, abortive though it was in its own terms, undoubtedly paved the way to its realization.

ENTR'ACTE

While she was still rehearsing, Margot had turned up in Paris along with Frederick Ashton and John Craxton. They were all absorbed in the new ballet Ashton was working on for the Sadler's Wells company's forthcoming season. It was Ravel's *Daphnis and Chloe*, but created from an entirely different point of view than the mythological one of Fokine. It was to be set in contemporary Greece, though without abandoning any of the romantic overtones of the traditional legend. Craxton, who was familiar with Greece and spoke the language, had just completed the designs for the scenery and costumes. What the three of them were planning now was to hire a small boat in Athens and make a tour of the islands at first hand together.*

As soon as Ruth returned from the German tour, she and Tom joined them and they set out for Athens. This was before it was "in" to "do" the Greek islands, and Tom scoured the harbor before he finally found a boat that was for hire. In Athens they picked up two other British friends who were grecophiles and would make the cruise with them. One was Patrick Leigh Fermor, who had written many books on Greece, and the other was Joan Rayner, who took photographs to illustrate them for him. Both of them, of course, spoke Greek, which was absolutely essential. To make things more amenable, the old Greek hands hired a chef from the best hotel in Athens and a steward from the British Embassy who could sing all the songs and dance all the dances of Greece.

Of their two newly acquired grecophiles, Ruth wrote some years later:

> They seemed to adore each other, but I think his rugged austere life was sometimes too hard for her, and she liked to get back to England where she was a great favorite in London literary circles. Anyway, there were seven of us, and we were an adventurous group, ready for anything. Paddy told our captain where to go, and we went to all kinds of islands where no tourist had ever set foot. We usually had a donkey for Margot and some-times for Freddy and me, but mostly we walked and climbed and swam all day, and slept at night on the ship.

---

*According to Margot, the project was originated by Tom simply as a holiday lark. Ruth, thus reminded, agrees that this was the case. Thus its effect upon Ashton's subsequent works, including not only the immediate *Daphnis* but also the *Ondine* seven years later, was purely a by-product.

The Eliki was not exactly what you would call a swank yacht; in fact it was not a pleasure craft at all—just a small fishing boat. There was only one toilet, which was just off Tom's and my cabin. It usually didn't work, and everyone had to go through our room to get there, and the smell would have been a little too much, had we not imbibed a good deal of ouzo and resin.

At this time Margot and I started calling each other by our Greek names. She was Marigoula and I was Ruthaki, and we still use these names.

We had spent about three weeks wandering around the islands when we got into a terrible storm. The anger of Poseidon seemed bent on destroying us. Everyone acted very brave except Freddy and me, and we clung to each other trembling with fear, thinking to have a watery death in the Aegean Sea. We finally found shelter in a little harbor, where we abandoned the Eliki and reached shore, soaked but safe. There was only one house in this port, and I will never forget the hospitality of these fine peasants, who fed us and gave us dry clothes and then sang and danced for us.

Margot had to be in London for a performance at Covent Garden, and it was Tom's job to get her there. Like the efficient organizer that he could be, he somehow gathered together seven donkeys and a guide, and we all rode across the entire island and found on the other side a regular passenger ship that brought us back to Athens. It was rather an ignominious ending for such an imaginative trip, but Marigoula reached London in time for her performance.

RESUME SPEED

It was late in June when she got to New York on her way home, and as usual she had lunch with Kirstein. He was much interested in *Revenge*, though against his better judgment, since his company was in the throes of one of its frequent financial crises, and he still felt that he did not want to produce anything "on lease" but only what he himself could pay for and own outright. Nevertheless he still clung to the hope of doing something with Ruth, and what he now suggested was John Alden Carpenter's *Krazy Kat*, which Bolm had done years ago. It was small and inexpensive and American. He had provided himself with all the material on the subject and gave it to her to study at her leisure. Nothing could have been less to her taste or farther from her mind at this period. "But," she wrote in her diary, "he certainly is a sympathetic and interesting man and I *hope* this time we'll get together on *something*."

In spite of himself, he had not closed the door on *Revenge* and was interested in seeing the designs of both Remisoff and Clavé. The former he found practical but uninspiring, and Clavé's "frightened him to death." So, for that matter, did the Verdi music, probably because he knew how far it was from Balanchine's taste. However, the next time he and Balanchine met with her in New York they "both disappeared for a few minutes" and when Lincoln came back he said they definitely wanted *Revenge* for the February season. Jean Rosenthal, the company's technical director, agreed with him that Clavé's sets, with their platforms, stairs and wagons, made the production problem "overwhelming" on the quite inadequate stage of the City Center, but she reported that they were trying to think of ways to simplify them. "Clavé will not like it," Ruth opined to her diary. And off she went to Chicago.

But not for long.

The Ballets des Champs-Elysées was once again on the verge of expiring after several efforts to survive. As Ruth had told Dinah Maggie in her letter, it was too valuable a channel for fresh creativeness to be allowed to succumb; furthermore, it was just the kind of channel she herself needed, whether in France or anywhere else. The basic "lend-lease" policy of the Chicago Ballet Company had helped keep the Ballet Russe from becoming a hack repertory company, and it could conceivably perform the more important function of getting this already experimental company through its present period of financial crisis by supplying it with new works without having to finance them.

With Tom's gift for organization—what with Emerson Kailey on the ground rooting for him and almost certainly Irène Lidova, one of the original founders of the company, active on the sidelines—and both Jean Robin and Boris Kochno eager to keep going, *Revanche* had now been signed for production as the principal new work in a season set to open in Paris on October 3 at the Théâtre de l'Empire. Of course Ruth was primarily concerned with keeping alive such an ideal outlet for her own work, but she took a longer view than that. Not only did she bring the English choreographers, Walter Gore and Frank Staff, into the company, but she also "gave them their ballets," as she put it in her diary—Gore's *The Damned* and Staff's *Romany Romance*.

Late in August she was in London, where the Champs-Elysées company was playing a season. There was to be a broadcast of their work by BBC on September 6, including *Impromptu au Bois*, which was also to be in the Paris repertoire. As soon as she arrived she went to see their performance of it and thought it was "dreadful." It had been recast, of course, since the German tour and was not at all to her liking. Hélène Trailine was "too careful and not an actress at all," so she replaced her with Sonia Arova, who provided "a nice vulgar quality for it and acted it better." She polished it up generally, and when she finally saw the broadcast, she wrote in her diary: "I must say it looked very amusing."

The day after the broadcast she went to Paris for the start of rehearsals at the Théâtre de l'Empire, but, as always in Paris, there were dozens of distractions. She had no sooner arrived than she learned that Delacroix's one-time house was to be sold, so she and Tom went to the auction and bid on it in all good faith, thinking still of that European headquarters.

"It really would be ideal for us," she wrote in her diary. "We have offered to give it to the Louvre if they will let us live there till we die. They accuse us now of wanting to start a commercial dancing academy there—imagine that! The French just can't imagine anyone being altruistic or honest or kind." The government and the newspapers lit on them with both feet, even though, as she explained to Mme. Maggie (who had sent her the newspaper clippings), "we would have used the place a month out of every year and left it open as a museum the rest of the time. We even said it would be open a few hours every day while we were there. . . . People in France certainly think the worst of Americans."

Rehearsals at the Empire were difficult. "Each day the dancers are different," she recorded. "No one has a contract and everyone wants to be a star. Well, I've kept my patience until today when I was rehearsing with Dalba and Moreau and they started quarreling about who was to première 'Revenge.' And then Moreau said they should not learn the part at the same time, so I shall teach it to them separately. Poor old choreographers! Well, it certainly has been a hell of a week and I've gotten nowhere!"

The next day she "went to rehearsal . . . to work with Moreau and Dalba and Skouratoff but the two ladies (!?) got so disagreeable about who was to do the opening night that I finally walked out of rehearsal!" She had very much wanted Nora Kaye, in the first place, but after making every effort, Nora was unable to get away from her New York commitments.

That night she and Emerson Kailey dined with Kochno. "What an odd man—he kept telling me all through dinner I should *dance* as I had such an interesting face! . . . I wonder if we can pin him down to anything concrete. His new 'livret' sounds wonderful and I wish I could be the choreographer."

In the midst of all this Margot arrived in Paris again. She was about to join Alexander Korda and Laurence Olivier and his wife, Vivian Leigh, on a cruise on Korda's yacht to Greece and Constantinople, but she had come a few days early to indulge her passion for clothes with a few expensive sessions at Dior's and elsewhere. This was too strong a temptation for Ruth to resist, so she went right with her all the way. After the yacht had finally put to sea, Ruth recorded in her diary: "Hated to see her go but it will be better for my ballets."

Kailey went to the train to meet Frank Staff, and at the same time Leon Danielian arrived from New York to join the company. "I didn't *really* think Leon would leave the Ballet Russe but here he is." He was to dance in *Impromptu* and in several of the pas de deux in the company's standard repertoire.

Rehearsals at the Empire were getting no easier. "Another boy left the company, so again everything was messed up, and one boy came an hour late, etc., etc. I had to yell so that I lost my voice today. However, both Clavé and Kochno seemed to be enthusiastic about what I have done. . . . Gerard Ohn came at 11:45 to a 10-12 rehearsal. So I spent a half hour after rehearsal bawling him out and I really gave it to him. Voice still lost." By September 30 Danielian had hurt his leg and could "only rehearse things for the opening night," when neither of her pieces was on the program. "Saw Frank Staff's 'Romany Romance'—okay."

The season opened on October 3 and "they seemed to like it." There was a party afterward at Maxim's. On the eighth *Impromptu* had its Paris debut. "Ibert was pleased and so was Wakhevitch, and Kochno lit it well." Danielian was good in spite of his injured leg. Though the orchestra was bad, "for the first time I was really satisfied with the way they did 'Impromptu' . . . Rave review in Figaro, also a good review in Le Monde. Now that I 'remember' that I was a Cecchetti-Bolm product I seem to 'get by' in Paris."

On October 17 *Revanche* actually "got on as per schedule." Tom arrived from overseas at the last moment, but at least he made it. The program opened with *Impromptu* with Sonia Arova, Danielian, Gerard Ohn and Deryk Mendel; followed by a ballet without music called *La Création*, which David Lichine had made for the company several years earlier; then came the *Black Swan* pas de deux by Jacqueline Moreau and Skouratoff; and finally *Revanche*.

"The rehearsals were absolutely and completely grueling and by the time the big evening arrived I was almost completely unconscious. I sat in a box with Clavé and as each beautiful scene unfolded I nearly died of joy. The audience screamed and yelled and I bowed on the stage with Clavé and there wasn't anybody this time that didn't like it. It was a complete hit. We rehearsed all p.m. on the day of the performance. Getting the light right was so difficult. Kochno tried to help but Clavé was glad when he wasn't around because he says Kochno has only two colors, green and red."

When reviews appeared in the papers, she had scored "a complete triumph," for the dedicated antichauvinist himself, who had done his best last year to destroy her, "came out *completely* reversing everything he had said" the year before. Under a three-column head he declared that she had created a brilliant ballet worthy of the success of Roland Petit's *Carmen*. In her diary Ruth wrote: "I think 'Revanche' is a much better constructed ballet than 'Carmen' *but* I don't think it can ever be as popular because it has very little sex appeal." He admitted to having been one of the cabal that had maliciously attacked "the deplorable formula she had tried to force upon the stage of the Champs-Elysées last year," and he certainly did not recant. On the contrary this militant antichauvinist suggested that it was the good taste of Paris that had had such a salutary effect upon Ruth's art. At any rate, he declared *Revanche* to be a choreographic masterpiece, and that was reparation enough.

"The next night," according to her diary, "the ballet went even better than the first night and afterwards we had a party for the company at Chez Inez, a little night club on the left bank. I didn't like *anything* about it. The place was much too small and very ordinary. Emerson drank a whole bottle of cognac *straight* and lay all evening with his head on his hands on the table and every now and then lifted his head to say the only people he loved in this whole damn outfit were Wakhevitch, Clavé and me. About 4 a.m. all except about ten people left and then we started to have fun. I danced rhumbas and what not on the table with Clavé and we all got very gay and it was really fun from then. Kochno left with Frank Staff about 2 a.m. to dream up a new ballet and I really would have liked to see what went on in that seance."

The next day Marigoula arrived from the cruise with Korda and the Oliviers, which had proved to be a posh version of the *Eliki* disaster. The weather was foul, they never got to Constantinople and finally had to abandon ship in Italy.

Shortly after the première of *Revanche*, Ruth was invited to the United States Embassy for cocktails. The ambassador, David Bruce, "was very cordial and seemed to remember me very well from the Baltimore days when I found him such a fascinating and interesting young man. However, I was *not* invited to the Embassy last year when they considered me a failure."

The next day, in quite another field, she and Tom achieved one of their goals. Tom found in the paper the advertisement of a house for sale for $9,000, including $3,000 worth of furniture, and bought it on the spot. It was in Montparnasse and was owned by the Countess Isabel von Ostheim, a former Nielson from Chicago, "who was stunned, as she thought it would take her till December to sell it." It was small but quiet, and big enough, she thought, to dance in. "It is a real artist's studio and just a block from my idol, Clavé."

So much for the good news; the sad news was, first, that "Emerson and Robin were very depressed about the Champs-Elysées finances. In spite of the great artistic success of the season they have lost a lot of money and have not got enough to pay the artists. They think the whole company will have to break up now."

Secondly, she arrived in New York early in December in the snow and, according to precedent, had lunch at the Plaza with Kirstein (who talked only of his coming production of *Swan Lake*, with setting and costumes by Cecil Beaton, and not a word about *Revenge*) and left for Chicago.

Thirdly, and as always, it struck her afresh as a disheartening place. "Certainly there is no excitement (at least artistically) in Chicago. Nothing seems to have happened since I left and Chicago is so quiescent I suppose nothing ever will happen here. C. Cassidy reports 'Revenge' is having considerable success in Paris."

"Ballet Opérette Dansée" or How British Can You Be?

This dolorous return to the wasteland, leaving success behind in the green pastures of Paris, was indicative rather of a state of mind, like the dull ache after the glorious debauch, than of objective reality. In a matter of days, indeed, the Paris success began to pursue her into the midwestern wilderness.

Practically everybody on both sides of the Atlantic wanted her to do *Revenge*. Anton Dolin wrote her that he would like to have it immediately, with Alicia Markova as Leonora, for a Christmas season at Monte Carlo by his Festival Ballet and also for the company's regular season in London. Ruth had not given up hope of further performances by the Ballets des Champs-Elysées, in spite of its desperate finances, so she told him tactfully that she would rather do a new ballet for him based on *La Traviata*, which she was already thinking about.

Kirstein had by now got his sumptuous Beaton production of a one-act *Swan Lake* (with its pondful of artificial birds swimming about behind its stageful of impersonated ones) safely into the repertoire, to satisfy the pressures of the City Center management for something with automatic box-office appeal. He wired her, accordingly, that he and Balanchine and Jerome Robbins, the new associate artistic director of the company, all definitely wanted her to do *Revenge* for them. Robbins had seen a performance in Paris, though "a less good one," according to Ruth.

"The telegram," she wrote in her diary, "gave me a big thrill, but Tom thinks I shouldn't accept." With his professional disbelief in anybody's intrinsic integrity he had worked out another of his advance post-mortems in which he had convinced himself that since the Paris antichauvinist had praised the work, his opposite number in New York would inevitably damn it, "no matter how good it was," just the way Hatfields always shot McCoys and vice versa. "I am dying to do it," wrote Ruth, "but it would certainly be a shame to spoil all my marvelous European success."

Almost at once Sergei Denham joined the line of applicants, and a bit later so did the Marquis de Cuevas, whose company was now domiciled in France. But what interested Ruth most was the possibility that Henri Lambert, of the Bureau de Concerts, might take over what was left of the Champs-Elysées company for a season at the Théâtre Marigny, based on the established success of *Revanche*. If she could come up with another ballet of suitably contrasting character to make a balanced program, they might make a summer run of it.

It was Tom who suggested *The Merry Widow* as ideal for the purpose. Ruth was unresponsive; she had always looked down her nose at operettas, but he was eloquent and persistent and finally persuaded her. He found, however, that he had stepped into a trap of his own making, for the rights to the music, the lyrics, the libretto, the title were tied up in the most complicated international tangles. Some of the music was in the public domain and some was not; there were certain countries where it could be played and certain where it could not; English and American translations were in legal contest with each other; and in no case could the title, or any substitute for it that contained the word "widow" be used. Some thirty lawsuits were being prosecuted by the Lehár heirs against various alleged infringements. But that was just the kind of challenge Tom loved, and since he had convinced Ruth against her will, he clearly had to win.

She discussed the project at once with her two faithful advisers and collaborators, the visual Remisoff and the musical Van Grove, both of whom were also expert in the matter of librettos. Remisoff thought, like Ruth, that it was not her "dish," but Van Grove was enthusiastic about it and drafted a scenario for her, which she started to work on, though without any real commitment.

Meanwhile, besides her professional problems, there was necessarily a certain amount of simultaneous Chicago social life to be taken care of. One night at a dinner party she sat between the two painters Ivan Le Lorraine Albright and his twin brother. "Ivan was a little drunk," she records, "and kept insulting me. He apparently doesn't like celebrities at all and considers me for some odd reason a celebrity! However, his brother kept defending me and it ended up quite jolly. I drank a lot of champagne."

In less formal circumstances, Renée McCormick announced that she had found just the house for Ruth and Tom by the sea at St. Tropez. "Which sounds fine to me," Ruth wrote; that was what she had hoped would happen. From that point on, the project proceeded apace in the competent hands of Renée when she got back to France.

At the same time Clavé showed up in Chicago, fresh from Hollywood, where he had designed Roland Petit's *Golden Fairy* ballet for Danny Kaye's *Hans Christian Andersen* film. He was "stunned by his success there with Sam Goldwyn. Apparently Sam just liked everything he did and accepted all his work without a murmur." She took him sight-seeing in Chicago and proceeded to do the same thing for him in New York, where they went immediately. What she wanted especially to show him there was the stage of the City Center to see what he thought of the possibilities of a production there. "He didn't think it could be done on that stage. Also he didn't much like the company."

While she was there she spoke to Balanchine, but his attitude was not soothing. "He said, 'I don't want any more Verdi, Beethoven or Strauss for this company. Why don't you do a detective story for me?' . . . My God! I really give up!" (Which is exactly the reverse of what she did, for she eventually sent him the scenario for a detective-story ballet, though nothing came of it.)

She had taken his outburst too literally. She failed to realize that within the past year his company had presented Antony Tudor's *Lady of the Camellias*, adapted from *Traviata*, and his *La Gloire*, set to three Beethoven overtures, in addition to the Strauss *Till Eulenspiegel*, which he had staged himself under management pressure, and they had all been flops. She had hardly had time to return to Chicago, indeed, before Kirstein wrote that Balanchine wanted *Revenge* for the following November with Nora Kaye as Azucena. She had chosen Nora for it in the first place, and she was convinced that nobody else in the Balanchine company could handle such a dramatic role.

But November was still a long way off. She and Bentley and the company were booked for a short tour in June, and she had already started working on a daring experiment with a kind of pas-de-deux version of *Salome*, which intrigued her very much.

She had been flirting for some time with the idea of using the Salome story for a ballet one day, and had actually taken steps in that direction. Kurt Weill seemed to her the ideal composer for it, but he had shied off from presuming to play David to the Goliath of Richard Strauss, and the other composers she had approached declined just as emphatically. So there was nothing left for her to do but aim directly at the giant himself, and she assigned Tom the onerous task of securing the rights to the original music from the notoriously tough Strauss estate.

His insistence on *The Merry Widow* had already got him into one such campaign, but this second one was somewhat simplified by the fact that Boosey and Hawkes controlled the international rights to both works, and Betty Bean, head of the New York office, guided him as well as guidance was possible through both mazes.

She wrote at once to Dr. Roth, head of the London office, who was in frequent personal contact with Dr. Franz Strauss, representative of his father's estate, but Dr. Roth was dubious. It was very unlikely that Franz Strauss would consent, he wrote, "unless he could be sure of a substantial income. The old man [who had now been dead for three years] would never have consented. . . . My feeling is that for the right to misuse the music and libretto for a ballet a sum should be paid down apart from royalties and this is what I expect Franz Strauss to demand." A month later, after much correspondence, Betty Bean reported that even with this sop he "definitely refuses to use Salome as a ballet. . . . Terribly sorry but decision appears final." Of course there was no objection to the use of Salome's dance, on payment of a suitable royalty, since that would clearly involve no "misuse" of the music.

When Van Grove was informed of the impasse, he acted with dispatch. He very much liked the idea of the ballet and was eager to adapt and arrange the music, as he had done for *Revenge*. As a conductor for the old Chicago Grand Opera Company, he had conducted the opera and coached Mary Garden, Muratore, Baklanoff and others, and later he had staged and conducted the work for Jeritza several times. So, to Tom: "I am sending you herewith the original letter from the great master himself to me in his own handwriting, which is a prized memento, as well as substantial evidence of the artistic success of my Salome performance."

The next day Tom sent a letter off to Dr. Strauss at Garmisch, with appropriate enclosures, and very shortly received a courteous reply from the Herr Doktor, saying he would discuss the matter with Dr. Roth when they were both in Paris in April. At the end of that month Dr. Roth reported that Dr. Strauss "would not, in principle, raise any objection now to Miss Page and Mr. Van Grove adapting 'Salome' for a ballet, but he would like to see a script before agreeing formally. We would then have to settle the terms as well."

Since this was the first of May, however, with a tour opening the first of June, Ruth was already well along in her tour-sized version of the story, which she called *Salome and Herod*, involving only these two chief figures and two male slaves, set to the music of the "Dance of the Seven Veils." It was far too late to abandon it now, even if she had wanted to.

As long ago as March she had gone to California to consult with Remisoff about costumes and production, and they had worked out a system of "boxes" that were to constitute an adjustable abstract setting. But the only thing that had been finished and sent to her was her own costume, and she wrote Remisoff in considerable agitation. "It has really upset my rehearsal schedule terribly. Bentley and I both have the time and the inclination now to do 'Salome', and it is rare when we get in such a state. I just can't imagine what the boxes will look like, and I really don't know what Bentley is going to look like, so it is hard to give any style to the thing and we are both mad as hops . . ." (Not at him, of course, but at the makers of the costumes and props.)

And again: "I am scared to death of the 'Salome' thing. I certainly look interesting in the costume, but I am not sure people will understand our idea about her being a little doll-like creature and will think it looks musical-comedy-ish. However, I don't care what they think as I am going ahead with it. I think it looks very interesting. . . ."

And a week later: "Bentley and I have worked hard on the 'Salome.' But I can't say that I like it very much. My wig is lovely and very comfortable, and the costume is comfortable too, but when I dance in it, no matter what I do, I seem to look like a cross between 'Scheherazade' and 'Coq d'Or.' The costume is only effective when I stay on my toes all the time—which I do. . . ."

And in a letter to Kreutzberg and Wilckens: "I am now working on a short version of 'Salome and Herod,' but I think it is going to be a colossal failure. I hate it at this point."

It opened in Evansville, Indiana. Of course the little orchestra could not play it, so it had to be danced to a recording. There is no reason to believe that it was "a colossal failure," but its future had become unimportant; her vision of the larger work had taken over her imagination. The next step was to devise a scenario that Dr. Strauss would approve.

TIME OUT FOR PLAY

The minute the tour was over, she and Tom hopped on a plane for Europe, where they had made elaborate plans for the summer. Naturally *Salome* came along. Recordings of the full opera were in the top drawer of her luggage, so to speak, and as a third work-in-progress it officially joined the party.

Because their *Eliki* misadventure last year had been so successful, they had decided to do something of the sort again this year with the same congenial group. In April Tom had written to Ashton, asking him to consummate for him with Lord Grimthorpe at his Yorkshire seat an arrangement to lease for the month of July his Lordship's Villa Cimbrone at Revallo on the Amalfi coast, on astonishingly reasonable terms. Which Ashton had duly done.

But on the way to that sumptuous estate Ruth and Tom had a breathless mission to perform, for Renée had actually bought them a little house at St. Tropez and they had not yet seen it. When they did see it, their first impressions were profoundly depressing. It was known as Herbe Folle, for it had been owned by a mad-woman named Mme. Herbe. Ruth recognized that it was basically charming, but it was "too far from the sea and too close to the neighbors, who Renée tells us are communists. . . . Chickens and children all over the place." Not to mention flies and mosquitoes. The floors were of tile, which was impossible for dancing, and "of course nothing works." They stayed overnight and were off first thing in the morning for the airport at Nice. "Thank God I didn't have to stay any longer until it is screened!"

The Villa Cimbrone was something else. Ruth wrote of it (in retrospect) that it was "lovely, spacious and comfortable, its greatest claim to fame being that Greta Garbo and Leopold Stokowsky had lived there together. There was no road at all leading to it—only a footpath for about three blocks—but when you arrived, the view over the mountains and sea was overwhelming, and it was pleasant not to be on any highway."

Tom's description (at the time) was somewhat more detailed. It had "twenty-two bedrooms, four kitchens, four dining rooms, five sitting rooms, and enormous piazzas, crypts, cloisters, servants' quarters, etc., not to mention the most beautiful gardens, which are apparently world famous. It is about 1200 feet above the Mediterranean, and has a view which has inspired the poets. Wagner wrote the second half of 'Parsifal' nearby, and Ibsen wrote 'The Wild Duck' at its foot." Light, firewood, water, and fruit and vegetables from the gardens were cared for by the staff, and Tom had written to Lord Grimthorpe to "ask whether it is possible to use a reasonable amount of your excellent Cimbrone wine." (It was.) For all of this the rent was $500 for the month plus the salaries of a cook, a maid and three gardeners.

The party numbered eight this year instead of seven, for Margot brought along her sister-in-law, Adele, who had just been separated from her husband. Naturally only a small part of the house had been opened up for them, but Ruth found that the room she had chosen for her "studio" was "where Adele liked to sit and Croxton liked to strum on the piano, and that was where everybody liked to gather. So either I must clear another room or not work at all."

A holiday in which she could not work, particularly at this strategic period, would have been no holiday at all. Indeed, if *Salome* was momentarily only in the back of her mind, the *Widow* was intensely in the foreground of it; Dolin was breathing down her neck for it. And as for *Revenge*, the latest inquiry for it came from Janine Charrat, who was interested in it for her company.

On a side trip to Capri Ruth unexpectedly encountered Dolin, who somehow seemed to be first in every bidding. He now wanted the *Widow*, both for his regular London season and for the special Christmas season he was planning for Monte Carlo. He was most enthusiastic about it and wanted to play Popoff himself. In addition to the *Widow* Julian Braunsweg, Dolin's associate and general executive manager in the Festival Ballet organization, still wanted *Revenge* for the London season and wanted to announce it immediately.

But for all that business matters persisted in intruding, the month at Cimbrone was essentially a time for unwinding, as Ruth made clear in her later reminiscences. "The English really like to eat when they are on holiday. We used to go to the beach every day with a picnic. I told the cook just to give us cheese and fruit and wine (American style lunch [*sic*]). But our English friends balked at this—they wanted hors d'oeuvres, chicken, salad, ice cream etc. . . . We came back to the villa about 4:00 p.m., had a real English high tea, lots of conversation, and at 10 a big dinner. So we lived Italian style and loved it."

Donald Albery, the theatrical   producer, who was Margot's friend and business adviser, "came down to see if she was getting along all right, as I think he was suspicious of her wild American friends. He was a sort of crotchety English style person, who was extremely successful in producing all kinds of theatre ventures. [He and Margot were to be associated some years later in the production of the enormously successful musical comedy *Oliver* under the corporate name of Almar.] He was fun in a kind of brusque nasty way."

They were pretty well surrounded by people—largely "beautiful" ones and idle ones, titled and untitled.

"I was always curious to see Massine's island (L'Île des Sirènes) just off the coast of Positano. We hired a little boat and with Freddy and Margot took our picnic and arrived at the dock about lunch time. No one was there so we got off the boat and had a nice quiet lunch on the pier. The island seemed absolutely deserted. We walked all over the enormous rocks and finally got up the nerve to enter the big house. We tiptoed all over it, and finally there was Massine fast asleep in his bed with his arms crossed on his chest looking very ascetic and severe, but beautiful in this calm state of his sleep. I always loved Massine's looks—those big serious eyes and his small pale face. We giggled a bit, and then tiptoed out leaving a little note by his bed. We got on our boat, chugged out to sea, when we saw Mme. Massine rushing to the pier waving for us to come back. Margot and Freddy wanted to see the island, but did not especially want to see the Massines. They both like to get away from the ballet on their holidays, so we didn't go back."

Some time later they had a luncheon party at Cimbrone to which both the Massines came, bringing with them the eight-year-old Leonide Jr. [He was later to break away from his father for a career of his own, at which time he took the new first name of Lorca] and a house guest who was a professional colleague. Several girls and boys from the Sadler's Wells Ballet, who were holidaying at Positano, also joined them. The house guest, who was a Chicagoan and knew Ruth well, found occasion to whisper to her urgently to "send her some kind of telegram saying she. had to leave the island. She felt very trapped and isolated there and couldn't find a good excuse to leave. I thought the island very dramatic and rugged, and I think Massine's idea to build a theatre there and have a dance festival would be exciting but difficult."

EXIT VENGEANCE FOLLOWED BY A BEAR

During the months of high tension that rode the momentum of her conquest of Paris it was *Revenge* that held the center of the stage. It had won the day for her, and everything depended upon the immediate exploitation of its acclaim.

She and Tom were still playing cat and mouse with Kirstein about it, while he alternated between doubt and determination, in the pattern that had prevailed all along. In the January just past, the first after the Paris première and all the ensuing hemming and hawing, he had written Tom that he assumed they had given it to Dolin. (". . . anyway it would be better if Ruth started with us with a new work.") Tom had replied that, on the contrary, Ruth wanted only them to have it and proceeded to plug for Paris rehearsals and a European tour—which, of course, would protect it from the inevitable malice of the New York *"Chauvin."* Kirstein, however, reviewing once again all the familiar difficulties, had opined prophetically in response: "I cannot think that 'Revenge' will finally work out with us."

When April had come along, the pendulum had swung the other way, and he wrote with a certain amount of glee that "Balanchine very definitely does want you to do 'Revanche' for us, if you have not decided to do it for Cuevas in the meantime, as you have every moral right to do. [If it was not one competitor, it was another.] . . . We will have a five-week rehearsal period for the November season and I should think 'Revanche' could be done around the 20th of November. . . . I personally feel happy that we have got over the Verdi hurdle, and I know that with Jean Rosenthal you can get a good production. Nora, Melissa and Moncion will be excellent, and I feel sure you will have a success here as you had abroad."

But in August after the Cimbrone holiday, by the time Ruth was back in Chicago Nora had left the company and gone into a Broadway revue; Melissa was "weary" and "did not want to take on any more new roles than necessary"; and Maria Tallchief, whom Ruth considered to be another possibility, was getting married. Balanchine, however, wanted Ruth to come to New York anyhow before the beginning of their scheduled rehearsal period to talk to individual dancers in the company. "Verdi should be orchestrated by Hindemith"; *The Merry Widow* was just a potpourri of second-rate Viennese waltzes, and Richard Strauss was in outer darkness; nevertheless, she should get acquainted with the company.

To the Remisoffs she wrote: "Maybe it is a mistake to do it with that company at all. They are so stamped with Balanchine's choreographic style that maybe they could never do justice to it, and I hate to do it in this country until I am sure of a good performance. I am sure Nora Kaye would be marvelous as Azucena, and she said if I would wait for her until the February season she thought she could do it. So, I am waiting."

Kirstein, when so informed, scheduled the ballet at once for February; then Nora's show proved unsuccessful, and when Ruth phoned her in Boston, where it was playing its last weeks in November, she declared herself ready to do *Revenge* at any time; whereupon Ruth called Kirstein, who decided it should be done straightway. (In her diary she was moved to meditate a bit: "I told Dolin I would start 'Widow' in London December 1. Well, we'll see.")

Then with an explicitness that shocked her Kirstein wired that Nora was immediately available, that rehearsals were scheduled to begin December 6 for a December 26 première and that he had so informed the press. She exploded with indignation in the diary; then by way of summing up: "Anyway, I would have accepted in a second even with all the crazy risks, but Tom has really talked me out of it, as he did before, last year."

So, using Dolin's constantly shifting schedules of rehearsals and performances as a cover for their compulsive reluctance, they told Kirstein not to announce anything yet. That would have been difficult, since he had already announced something quite specific.

This was the actual, if not the formal, end of the project; which was perhaps just as well, for a collaboration so insecurely based could not have survived the ordeals that were to beset the accouchement of *The Merry Widow*.

As for the latter work, Ruth was still far from convinced of its merits and accordingly sought out her old and theatre-wise friend Hassard (Bobby) Short, to hear what he might have to say on the subject. To her amazement, he came forth with a radically new approach to counter her uncomfortable feeling that it was incurably out of date. "It is a completely modern version and very clever," she recorded. "I was completely turned upside down and couldn't sleep all night for thinking about it."

She gives no indication of what was so revolutionary about it, but a letter in the files from Tom to Kochno throws some light on it. In it he suggests that Kochno, possibly with the collaboration of Cocteau, write a strictly contemporary libretto: United Nations atmosphere, present-day Maxim's, American "dollar princess" looking like Rita Hayworth, with Aly Khan as her principal admirer, or possibly Margaret Truman, as the daughter of the chief disburser of American funds. That nothing came of it may have been due to Kochno, about whom Ruth had wondered if he could be pinned down to anything concrete; or possibly it was because, on careful rethinking, it seemed dangerously alien to the predilections of Viennese operetta fanciers. Certainly the final version of the scenario was substantially what she had worked out with Van Grove, but the very fact of her having been turned upside down by the discussion with Bobby seems to have overcome her indifference and set her to work with fresh enthusiasm.

Dolin's plan at the moment, after many shifts of date and place, was to start rehearsals in London on December 30, with the première to take place in Paris during the company's season at the Empire, scheduled to begin in late January. She had asked Cecil Beaton to design the production, since the Festival Ballet was British and so was its audience, but he had declined, and she had switched at this late hour to Wakhevitch, whom she wired at once to meet her in Paris on December 10 to work there on the designs until

Christmas. He had had very little time to think about the assignment, and
when she saw his first sketches, she was far from happy. "He has one or two
ideas, but certainly not many. I really have to give him all his ideas. It is
going to be quite a job." Which it was. They had to work steadily up to the
minute of her departure for London to get it done at all.

The only thing that served to brighten her life at this moment was the
news that the formidable Renée had "really gone through a big production"
and secured for her the old stone barn across the courtyard from the house in
St. Tropez. Its owners refused to sell the building but had finally consented
to a ten-year lease on the ground floor. They would not even consider leasing
the upper floor, which she wanted very much to make over into an apartment
for guests, since the main house had only two bedrooms. But the lower floor
would provide admirable space for the essential studio, and before she left
Paris for London around Christmas, she had arranged for the work to begin at
once.

In mid-January the rehearsals were shifted from London to Paris, to be
completed on the stage of the Empire itself. The *Widow*, now entitled *Vilia*
after its most famous song, was not scheduled to have its première until the
final week of the season. That, however, was the week that never was, for
the season itself had already collapsed in financial distress just before. *Vilia*
was still in a fragmentary state—the scenery and costumes not finished, the
music not ready and the choreography not set. The Festival Ballet was
booked for an immediate tour of Ireland, but so large a production could not
be included since all the stages were too small to accommodate it. As a
consequence, the *Vilia* première was now postponed until late in June at
Bournemouth. "Just long enough," said Ruth, "for everyone to forget it—
including me."

Ill and lonesome and frustrated, she phoned Tom in Chicago, and the
next day he was in Paris. It was a brief but recuperative interlude. For one
thing, it gave them a chance to go down to Lyons to look over the ancient
Roman theatre, where she had been engaged to do the choreography for a
production of Molière's *La Princesse d'Elide* in the Festival de Lyon in late
June. For another thing, Margot arrived in Paris for some engrossing hours of
haute couture.

But the climax of the whole holiday was yet to come: Leon Leonidoff,
the continental impresario, offered her a six-month tour with a company of
her own, which would number twenty-five and have Tamara Toumanova as its
star. The program would consist of *Revenge, Salome* and *Vilia*. The flight to
New York was on something lighter than air, for she was "thrilled" by the
prospect.

As soon as they got home, Tom flew to Hollywood to talk to
Toumanova and reported that she was enthusiastic. Ruth herself could

"hardly think of anything else." But in March when she wrote to the
Remisoffs, she had still not heard from her. "If she was a great success in the
last movie that she did, then she probably won't want to do this tour."

But there was another event that may have taken her mind off
Toumanova and thrilled her even more; she had just won the right to perform
Salome—everywhere except in Germany and German-speaking countries. She
(or rather Van Grove) had sent to the Strauss estate, at its request, a scenario
and a description of how she planned to use the music. There were three
scenarios that she and Van Grove and Remisoff had produced among themselves and worked over, and it was "the long one" they decided upon as the
best. Apparently it was good enough for Dr. Strauss.

The next order of business was to get back to the Festival Ballet on the
post-Irish part of its tour and try to get *Vilia* out of its state of suspended
animation. Her plan was to go to Paris on April 12, spend a week there
working on her Molière play and pick up the company in Birmingham on
April 20. She would have to spend the time between June 1 and 20 in Lyons
for the preparation and première of the production there and would rejoin
the company in time for the Bournemouth engagement, when *Vilia* was to
make its official bow.

"Am terribly upset," she wrote Dolin, "that the sets for *Vilia* have been
left all this time on the Empire stage. If you weren't going to take them with
you, you certainly should have had them sent to the warehouse or else to the
shipper. I hate to think what a state they will be in and how terribly
inconvenient for the Empire people who have always been so nice to me."

She was worried about the sets on other grounds too, for Wakhevitch
had put so much into them that there was not much room left for dancing.
"I think they will look absolutely stunning when we get the ceiling on and
the lights, etc.," she wrote, "but I do think the first two, especially the second,
absolutely ruin the choreography. The V-shape is no good for the round
waltz I designed."

The rehearsal movie she had made was poor and out of focus, but she
managed to make good use of it in giving Dolin details about cuts and
changes, as well as notes on how badly the girls wore their hair and their
dresses, how slovenly their toe work was and, above all, how poorly they
waltzed. She urged him to give as many performances as possible before the
London opening, because unless the performance of such a work as this was
impeccable and elegant, the whole thing would be a disaster. "Incidentally,"
she dashed off, perhaps a bit scornfully, "call it a Ballet Opérette Dansée if
you want to."

She arrived by train at Birmingham on the twentieth. She had inquired
of Dolin about the Royal Hotel, which was just across the street from the
theatre, but he had sent her instead to the Queen's, which proved to be

fifteen minutes away from it, because he had had a fight with the Royal and had sworn he would never go back. "Awful cold little room," she records. "Too late for dinner. Electric stove in room didn't work, a dreary cell."

At any rate, rehearsals were energetically resumed and apparently to good purpose. In Manchester, indeed, where the first public performance, though not the official première, took place on the twenty-ninth (which happened to be Lehár's birthday), she records: "Music bad but performance smooth. Audience loved it and it looked like a triumph."

This opinion was corroborated by Cecil Smith (who had come up from London where he was now a music critic on one of the papers) in a cable to Tom. Tom wrote her immediately: "I have your news from Cecil's cablegram that you had a big success for 'Vilia'. Can he *really mean* 'success of decade— everything wonderful—audience excited!' Well, you will never know how that message makes *me* feel. I nearly died with delight. You see, having suggested the 'Widow' and then somehow wangled the copyright through, and knowing every second what it has meant in creative effort on your part, I've never wanted anything so much."

After the Saturday matinee she records: "Dr. and Mrs. Otto Blau, who own the 'Widow' copyrights, or at least attend to them, came backstage and were enthusiastic. Said they would like to have it done all over the world and especially in Vienna. Only thing they did not like was use of 'Frasquita' for Dolin's solo. They said we would always have trouble with that copyright. Hated to change, but thought best to take it out." She stayed over an extra week in Manchester, chiefly to break in Nathalie Krassovska and John Gilpin as alternates to Sonia Arova and Oleg Briansky in the starring roles.

Back in Paris by May 10, she got to work on *La Princesse d'Elide* at her little house in Montparnasse. To her dismay she found that her Chicago friends, the Clinton Kings, who occupied it the year round except for the occasional week or two when she needed it, had waxed the floors, thereby making them useless for dancing. She had concluded, in any case, that the place was too small to dance in, what with all the furniture the countess had left in it, and managed to make arrangements to use the American gymnasium nearby to practice in.

On June 1, as scheduled, she went down to Lyons. The production was planned for the outdoor Théâtre Romain de Fourvière, under the direction of Charles Gantillon, using actors from Jean Louis Barrault's company and the corps de ballet of the Opéra de Lyon. The music was composed by Remo Bruni, and Wakhevitch had designed the setting and costumes. When she arrived, she records, she was "faced with twenty-four dancers, eight of whom aren't too bad but all the rest pretty impossible." When she went to look at the theatre, she found that Wakhevitch had "made an extraordinary design all over the floor which is very beautiful and interesting but of course changes all the choreography completely." Rain forced them to use "the awful stage of a dirty theatre" for the opening performance on June 19. Presumably the weather was kinder for the other performances, but she could not stay to find out, for *Vilia* was expecting her in Bournemouth on the twenty-third.

Dolin had phoned her earlier that he was not keeping Arova in the company and was trying to get Renée (Zizi) Jeanmaire to replace her. Zizi, accordingly, drove down to Bournemouth from London with Ruth and Tom. She was to discover shortly that she was pregnant, which effectively settled that matter.

They arrived at the Pavilion at Bournemouth just as the *Vilia* rehearsal was ending. At the performance itself the orchestra, which had had only one rehearsal, was "awful." And "Krassovska was just not the girl for 'Widow'."

They drove back to London with the realization that there was still a lot to be done between then and the London première at Festival Hall on July 20. This was, after all, the coronation season. Supper later at the Savoy Grill with Arova and Briansky was "lots of fun just talking and eating."

Tom went on to St. Tropez, and she wrote in the diary: "Dread the thought of two weeks more in London." However, she was working on *Salome* with the recordings, which provided balance, to say the least.

When the première of *Vilia* took place, it drew a bad review from the *Times,* but the other reviews, though short, were good enough. In view of the fact that the entire Marsovian scene had to be omitted because of the inadequacy of the stage of Festival Hall (which was built for orchestral concerts and was not really deep enough for theatrical productions), it is surprising that any of the reviews were good.

As soon as she could get away, she was off to St. Tropez. "When I saw my studio," she wrote, "I almost died with joy." The lower floor of the old barn had been transformed into a spacious room, half of it a sitting room and the other half a studio with a marvelous floor.

But not even that did anything to ameliorate her dissatisfaction with *Vilia.* The London Sunday papers were now out, and the *Observer* carried "a terrible review," but at the same time, there came a letter from London asking her to do a new musical, so it could not have been all that bad. Nevertheless, she invited Bobby Short, who was in Cannes at the moment, to come to St. Tropez for a two-week visit to consider the possibility of redirecting it for her.

Meanwhile, Hurok, who was also in Cannes, wanted to continue the preliminary talks he had had with her and Tom during the Cimbrone holiday, about a project he had in mind for Monte Carlo. He was in serious negotiations with the Société des Bains de Mer, which controlled the Casino and the theatre attached to it, for the formation of a new ballet company with that as its home base, and he wanted her to do all her ballets for him there. She would be one of three principal choreographers, of whom the other two were Ashton and Harald Lander, former director of the Royal Danish Ballet and at

present on the staff of the Paris Opéra. It was an attractive prospect, but she
would have to decide whether to do her "own show" first—that is, the
Revenge-Salome-Vilia combination for Leonidoff.

When Bobby Short arrived at St. Tropez, they got down to serious
business at once. He had seen *Vilia* in London, of course, and found many
things he did not like, beginning with the title. He also thought there should
be a complete reorchestration, and suggested that she go to Eze and confer
with the Viennese composer Hans May, who was definitely of the Lehár
school. Most of his suggestions she could accept as they went along, but Tom
chose to argue them all at some length and in detail. After two days Bobby
suddenly packed up and left. This had nothing to do with *Vilia*, he explained;
"he simply could not put up with any more of Tom's conversations." It was
a double blow that fairly staggered her, and when she and Tom went to
Cannes to talk to Hurok the next day, she made a point of looking him up.
"Bobby told me again with that steely look that comes into his eyes that he
just couldn't do 'Vilia' under the circumstances and nothing would persuage
him to stay. I burst into tears and dashed from the room."

CRISIS

Eventually she went to Eze as Bobby had recommended, but the time
had come, apparently, for something more than that—for reorchestrations all
around, indeed, and not merely those concerned with the arrangement of
musical notes. She had got herself into such a metaphorical state of contrapuntal congestion and unsolicited overtones that only some equally metaphorical
agency could explain her out of it. Which it proceeded to do.

As an unmistakable indication that she had crossed some symbolic
frontier, she had her hair cut. Throughout her dancing career she had
adhered, with whatever concessions to fashion, to the style Pavlova had
handed on to her. Now she emerged quite shamelessly with shaggy bangs à la
Zizi; "and," she noted in her diary, "I am very sensational."

Before she left St. Tropez early in September, she invited thirty people
to a cocktail party, and to her dismay a hundred and thirty turned up! Was
this simply a wordly "happenstance," or did it have symbolic implications—
like that inexplicable sound from the sky in Madame Ranevsky's garden in
The Cherry Orchard as of the breaking of a string?

Whether or not because of mystical forces, before she returned to St.
Tropez the following spring, none of the projects she had been working on
for the achievement of continuity in Europe had materialized, and she had
signed a contract that established her in, of all places, Chicago, which she had
left more or less forever four years ago. And she had signed it, what is more,
with the opera.

"Home to Our Mountain" with Arrière-Pensées

The reincarnation of the opera seemed promising. Instead of calling itself an opera company—grand, civic or what you will—it chose the title of Lyric Theatre, a much broader term implying an awareness of elements besides singing. Its newly formed team of directors consisted of Carol Fox and Lawrence V. Kelly, with Nicola Rescigno, with whom each of them had been associated before, as conductor. Their general concept obviously demanded a good ballet under imaginative and sympathetic direction in order to break through the cramping dimensions of conventional operatics.

Ruth was the logical person for such a project, partly because of her experience with opera ballet but more importantly because of her belligerency against its superimposed restrictions. If they were not already aware of this, Tom was there waiting to tell them. He had had a long association with opera in Chicago and well understood his wife's ideals and the practical requirements for fulfillment of them.

Some eight months after her return from St. Tropez, then, Ruth signed a contract in mid-May to become ballet director, beginning with the November season. Carol Fox was a good businesswoman and Tom was a shrewd lawyer, and no doubt an airtight document was produced that satisfied the minimum basic demands of both parties. Beyond these, however, lay the maximum potentialities of the situation, which could not be written into being. They called for the recognition of subtleties that transcended mere legalism; the interests of the two signitories, though they coincided over a considerable area, had substantively different orientations. The company's concern was with opera—broadened, to be sure, to an extent that would not be possible without the much greater participation of a much better ballet than was customary, but still opera. Ruth's concern, on the other hand, was with the ballet; not just a better "opera" ballet but a better "ballet" ballet, with the opportunity to function creatively in its own right simultaneously with its service to the opera.

The necessity for reconciling these two goals was fully understood and agreed upon. Ruth actually enjoyed creating opera ballets, her only reservation being that they were rarely allowed to be what they were capable of being. The directors, on their part, already had in mind the presentation of new ballets from time to time on the same program with short operas, in addition to experiments with the combining of singing and dancing in the same work. Beyond this they expressed a desire to develop "a resident Chicago ballet" as an integral part of the resident lyric theatre. Ruth was free to use the ballet rehearsal room for the preparation of works of her own that might not be performed in the regular opera season. They would serve her well on tours, which were contemplated as a matter of course at the close of the opera season.

Such off-season touring was essential as a step toward the developing of a resident ballet and would serve also to benefit the opera ballet. With an opera season of only five weeks, as was planned, the resident element could obviously comprise nothing more than the executive staff. The dancers in a ballet company, however, besides having to eat throughout the remaining forty-seven weeks, must also work together for a far greater proportion of their time if they are to acquire an ensemble sense onstage and, beyond that, ensemble identification and commitment.

In order that the small budget should all go to the dancers, Ruth took no salary, and neither did Tom for his legal services. For the same reason, when it was necessary to bring dancers from New York or elsewhere to replace those who had taken other jobs for better pay, longer terms or mere survival, she paid their transportation herself. Very soon she was to do the same for stars imported from Europe. To be sure, this was for the sake of using them in her "ballet" ballet, but it greatly strengthened the "opera" ballet as well. When she was able to establish an annual tour of ten weeks or more, as she was eventually to do, the higher rate of pay it called for made it easier to induce dancers to work in the opera season at minimum union rates, which was all the Lyric Theatre budget would allow.

Ann Barzel, whose critical faith in the Chicago-bred dancer was always deep and discerning, wrote: "One of the most important factors in the Lyric Theatre's dance plans is the ensemble of dancers. We have a fine one. Conditions in Chicago have produced a well-schooled group, more than ordinarily dedicated to their art." In the nature of things, defections are likely even among the most dedicated, but there was a substantial nucleus here ready to persist with something of Ruth's own conviction, even though, like Ruth, they might be continually asking for more of everything.

UNFINISHED BUSINESS

Meanwhile, before the new regime was even above the horizon, Ruth had brought home with her a great deal of work to be done. For one thing, there was *Salome*, the still uncreated ballet in her proposed Leonidoff trilogy. It had lost none of its fascination for her, and she devoted herself to it with characteristic energy. Remisoff's original Schéhérazade-Coq d'Or costume and the continuous toe work it demanded had long since disappeared into oblivion, for this fuller version bore no relation at all to the erstwhile pas de deux. It differed, indeed, from anything she had done before; there were no "ballet steps" whatever in it now, for it was less a ballet than a dance-drama, with a vocabulary that grew out of its own necessities. Its name was changed to *Daughter of Herodias* and again to *Retribution*; Herodias was the archvillain who motivated the plot, and the slaying of her daughter before her eyes was the just price she paid for it. Remisoff had designed a new production along the newly indicated lines, and the whole piece was difficult but engrossing to work out.

She was preparing it, according to precedent, for a tryout by the Chicago Ballet Company at her favorite hideaway, the St. Alphonsus Athenaeum, and besides Bentley and herself the cast included Barbara Steele, Shirley Harwood, Kenneth Johnson, Joseph Kaminsky and Etta Buro as soloists, plus a corps de ballet of twenty-five. On a Sunday afternoon late in January the performance took place; on the program with it were "Excerpts from *Vilia*" and a new piece by Bentley called *Little Match Girl*, set to music of Gluck.

It was a full week before she got around to catching up with her correspondence about it. On February 1 she wrote to Bobby Short:

> Well, Salome actually got on and your telegram gave us a good laugh, of which we were sorely in need at that point. This is one of those grim, dark ballets and it was terribly hard to do. We have stunning costumes, but they are full of long trains and great huge cloaks, and we are all congratulating ourselves that nobody got tripped up. The ballet seems to have great dramatic drive and the audience was wonderful. However, you cannot judge at all by the audience we had, as they were a mixture of everything. We did it in a wonderful theatre which I found here on the north side away from the critics where you can try things out, and this was definitely a tryout. It is a perfect theatre for dancing. It looks rather old and grimy, but the stage is a perfect size and it seats about 1000 persons. You can see from every seat, which is more than you can say for Covent Garden, the Metropolitan and Civic Opera. We had plenty of time to rehearse and that was a pleasure. Everyone who saw it seems to think the ballet is very sensational. . . . However, it is not a ballet that we should do with one piano, which is what we had to do at this performance.

Van Grove had actually made a two-piano arrangement, and there were plenty of pianists around to play it, but with such a score as that to begin with, one piano more or less could not have made much difference. As for the production, the result was naturally not what it might have been. This was, after all, "definitely a tryout."

The presence of the *Vilia* excerpts on the program served to emphasize the existence of other unfinished business, for *Vilia* was in the first stages of a thorough remodeling. On this same day of general correspondence, then, she wrote to Dolin on two separate topics but with one easily deducible attitude.

> I am most anxious to know whether you did "Vilia" in Monte Carlo. As you know, I thought it was very dangerous to take a chance on doing it there, and I am most anxious to know what happened.

His company had rights to the work only for the British Isles. Actually the Monte Carlo performances had been given, and quite successfully, but without Ruth's consent or even any notification afterward.

> It is important for us to know how many times and where you do the ballet, as you know we have to pay a royalty on this ballet and have to keep our accounts clear with the heirs or we will get into trouble, which we don't want to do. Your company is so very slow in paying the small royalty which we are charging you, that I must say doing business with you is quite difficult. However, I do not want to get mixed up in the business end of it.

(In this area Tom reported that the Festival Ballet took fourteen months to sign the contract and had paid royalties only up to the beginning of the past summer's London season. They still owed $2,000. *Vilia* had cost $22,000 and the royalty was only $75 a performance, out of which in turn a royalty to the Lehár heirs had to be paid. Tom, indeed, threatened to attach the Festival Ballet's box office when it came to Chicago on its scheduled Canadian and United States tour later in the year.)

Ruth's second topic was less peevish in tone but more to the real point. In the new *Vilia* she was planning, she wanted to cut all possible ties with the old one, which had been such an ordeal.

> You say "Vilia" has been successful on your tour in England. If that is so, would you rather I did not change it for London, if you are going to do it there next summer? As you know, Hans May is making a new orchestration, but he has made great, great changes which involve many choreographic changes also. I don't know whether you want to bother with all this if it is going well.

It was unmistakable that she did not want to bother with it.

In all her apparent concentration on the European tour of her three-ballet program there now appears an unexpected crosscurrent. In one paragraph of the *Salome* letter to Bobby Short (written from the Racquet Club, incidentally, where she was living and loving it) she said: "Would love to have my own company, where I could do lots and lots of ballets and not just try for one program, but Tom is very much against this. He thinks it is too much."

Of course he was right; not only would he be "mixed up in the business end of it," but he was also aware of how many far larger fortunes than theirs had been unable to meet the demands of such fanciful enterprises. He was also warmly aware of her compulsive creativeness, however, and since he too was creative in his own field, he proceeded to plant as strong a root as he could of an "own" ballet for Ruth in the fertile soil of the new opera company. By ingenuity and persistence he engrafted, as it were, the activities of the Chicago Ballet Company and its traditional system of operating into the structure of the Lyric Theatre.

Besides his very genuine interest in Ruth's career he had a strong personal motivation for his efforts; it was the transference of the center of her operations back to that very Chicago from which she had been trying for so long to flee. In spite of her Chicago persisted in being, as it realistically had to be, their official home, and the last four years had made painfully clear the impracticability of commuting overseas to work.

On the other hand, she had achieved a firm personal footing in the France to which she felt so strongly drawn; besides the pleasure of simply being there she was in touch at close range with painters and musicians of her own persuasion. She could even do a great deal of choreographic creation and preliminary rehearsing with European dancers and visiting American ones in the spacious studio at Herbe Folle. Again, on the more practical side, she was able to dress and mount her productions better and at considerably less cost in Paris than in America.

An ideal, at least, of balance had been set up; any real balance, of course, would be death to the creative life, in which imbalance is what makes the pendulum swing. In this situation, with Chicago at one extremity of the swing and Paris at the other, the still point was only a theoretical concept of physics to be passed through unnoticed.

It is apropos that at this moment Clinton King, the painter who lived at Les Trois Pastèques, sent her the portrait for which she had sat to him there, and her comment in the diary was: "I look very chic and tidy and not at all like the turbulent soul I am!"

Her turbulence was shortly to manifest itself in familiar disconsolateness. She had returned from St. Tropez brimming with plans, only to find that the first season of the so hopeful new opera project would not accommodate any of them. Already in September she had begun to suspect as much, for she wrote in the diary: "It seems as though Chicago Lyric Theatre will do no ballet at all, and I am breaking my neck for them in vain! . . . I should never have returned to Chicago. I feel now we can never do anything here."

There was only one studio in the opera house "and the singers always seem to be in it." It was obviously going to be the same old pattern of trying out works at Mandel Hall or St. Alphonsus and performing them where she could. *Salome* had already been tried out and was waiting to be presented; *The Triumph of Chasitity* was on the verge of being ready to go into rehearsal; and she was flirting very seriously with *The Barber of Seville* as her next ballet-into-opera. Although she was still working on it "only in my head," she wrote to Van Grove to ask if he thought it would "be possible to use the title 'Once Over Lightly'." If it was he who vetoed it, that was his only unforgivable act.

But if there was to be no independent ballet in the opera season, she was already setting to work, by way of compensation, on an outrageous idea for the incidental ballet in the fourth act of *Carmen*. She had done many of them over the years, and since Bizet had never intended to have any ballet at all in this opera, she had followed the general practice of using the incidental music he had written for Daudet's play *L'Arlésienne*. She had done it in authentic Spanish style, in conventional "operatic" style, in tutus and on point. She had considered and rejected the assembled bits from *Les Pêcheurs de Perles* and the Bohemian dances from *La Jolie Fille de Perth*, which others had sometimes used, and since Bizet died very young, there was not much else to choose from. (It is a curious trait of opera audiences to be bored by the ballet but to insist on having one inserted to be bored by even in operas like *Carmen* and *Faust* and *Tannhäuser* against the composers' intent.)

She had had in the back of her mind for some time the idea of doing a production of de Falla's *El Amor Brujo*, and Wakhevitch had already designed it for her; so, as a bold stroke, she decided to do it right here and now. She did not use the entire score and she ignored the extremely awkward scenario credited (or, more accurately, debited) to Martinez Sierra. (Actually the work had been conceived as an opera, and its destination had been shifted midstream.) Her own scheme of action was to have a band of gypsies assemble outside the bull ring to dance for the aficionados as they arrive for the corrida. Here they improvise a generally wild and gay dance in which the boys play at bullfighting and so forth before the mood shifts to a superstitious presage of tragedy, which somehow unites the predetermined ritual of the ring with the impending death of Carmen. It was the first time, she felt, that this fourth-act ballet, instead of being an intrusive divertissement, served after the manner of the Greek chorus to heighten the drama. After its first performance she wrote: " 'Amor Brujo' fitted into the fourth act better than I thought it would. . . . The ballet did it extremely well and it was exciting, although it was actually too modern and imaginative for the old-fashioned set."

The opera house had simply taken its standard production out of the storehouse, but she had used the new costumes Wakhevitch had designed. No two of them were alike, so that they avoided the appearance of a typical opera chorus and seemed rather to be a group of individual gypsies who had just come across the bridge from the Triana. The only visual detail that tied them together was the characteristic gypsy hairstyle of Andalusia. She had been uneasy about the offstage gypsy singing, but she found that "the wild gypsy voice in the de Falla score, surprisingly enough, seemed to heighten the Bizet music by contrast."

The critical response to this bold innovation was by no means uniform. Some of the critics liked it, according to Ann Barzel, and "some got apoplectic." But for all that the *Amor Brujo* innovation made a big splash, she was still unhappy about the future and the slim prospect it presented of her being able to do legitimate ballets.

As soon as the opera season was over in December, she made what might be called an "off-Wacker-Drive" presentation of *The Triumph of Chastity*, according to her familiar practices.

It should have been in the works much earlier, but in 1951, about the time of the *Revanche* production, Ibert had played the score he had written for it for the aging Fauvist painter Raoul Dufy, who had liked it. In spite of his chronic illness he had agreed to consider designing the production. In his own private fantasy he had immediately envisioned the Unicorn as a classic ballerina, which, not unreasonably, disturbed Ruth when it was reported to her. Because of his delicate health, however, it was almost impossible for her to arrange to talk with him about it. Finally in October she was admitted to his presence. "Talked to Dufy about 'Chastity,' " she was able to record at last. "He was supposed to be too sick to see anybody but he was sitting at an easel, painting. He still insists that the Unicorn must be a girl in white tutu, which certainly changes my story around a lot. He says he is too sick to do the ballet now but that if I will give him time he will *surely* do it as he is enthusiastic about the idea and likes the music."

The "idea" was based on the medieval legend that the unicorn is subdued to gentleness at the sight of a virgin and will come to lay his head in her lap, which is the only means by which he can be caught because of his swiftness and ferocity. Dufy's insistence on casting this role *en travesti* reduced the story to impotence. The whole idea of his participation was somehow tactfully sidestepped for the moment, and not much more than a year later he was dead. Ultimately, it was Leonor Fini who did the designing.

Ruth was so pleased with Fini's work that she asked her also to do a new production of *Salome*, which remained high on her agenda. With the Lyric Theatre now in the picture an orchestra of adequate size might bring it nearer to realization. Much as she liked Remisoff's scenery and costumes, the latter were hazardous to work in; just possibly she might also have found in Leonor Fini's style a certain tang that was missing in his. In February she had a reply. "Leonor Fini accepted to do 'Salome,' " she recorded. "She wants a little more money than she did for 'Chastity' because she has nine cats and one of them is pregnant and there are no rats to feed them." What happened to the cats is not a matter of record, but the production of *Salome* never took place; it drifted quietly out of the picture at last along with the Leonidoff project as a whole.

In November, even before the first opera season had opened, Tom had been negotiating for a suitable national management to book the projected ballet tours. Hurok, who would have been the logical one, was not available because of his contract with Ballet Theatre. The next place to turn was to

the Columbia Artists Management. Tom wrote to them accordingly, offering them not only the ballet but also, with the authority of the directors, the
Lyric Theatre's opera repertory. In mid-November he received a wire from
Kurt Weinhold, who headed one of the units of the organization: "Unable to
undertake Lyric Opera at this time. Must tell you that Page ballet is also a
proposition which although inviting we cannot undertake at present on account
of organizational difficulties." And that pretty much slammed the door on
the national booking plan "at this time."

No tour could reasonably have been expected for this first season of the
Lyric; now none was possible for the second; and unless drastic action was
taken, there would clearly be none for the third, since tours cannot be booked
overnight. Something had to be devised immediately if the whole scheme of
the return to Chicago were not to collapse.

The idea of booking independently again had to be considered, though
it was a backward step and a difficult one. Ruth wrote to Claudia Cassidy:
"As you probably know we cannot, unfortunately, get bookings outside
Chicago with just Chicago notices." New York notices were essential, and in
Tom's analysis that meant a fairly glamorous New York exposure for at least
a week at a Broadway theatre, with a striking repertoire, dancers of international fame and first-rate managerial auspices. He had already talked to
Hurok about something of the sort—a brief season at the Metropolitan Opera
House, perhaps, as a grand inaugural gesture to launch the Chicago ballet's
reemergence after a hiatus of four years. Since *Revenge* had won European
.réclame, and *The Merry Widow*, its natural counterpoint in the opinion of
several European impresarios, was still touring successfully in Great Britain as
Vilia, the striking repertoire seemed ready-made.

At that moment, however, and of more immediate concern, Ruth's
doubts about ever doing legitimate ballets for the Lyric Theatre were resolved
by the decision of the directors to give two performances during the 1955
season of opera-plus-ballet programs that would include both *Revenge* and *The
Merry Widow*, and the future took on a different hue. To assure an equal
success for her works in Chicago, Ruth suggested bringing over Alicia Markova,
Sonia Arova and Oleg Briansky. When Maestro Rescigno added a project of
his own to the programs in the form of an experimental production of a
Monteverde masque, Vera Zorina was added to the list of stars. Ann Barzel
remarked later in her announcement of the season, "Lyric Theatre's management is devoted to the star system, and when they say stars they mean stars."

As Ruth, in a personal letter, described the choosing of works by the
directorial triumvirate, she had "offered them a large selection of repertoire,
out of which they chose 'The Merry Widow' and 'Revenge.' When I pointed
out that they were doing 'Il Trovatore' as an opera during the same season,
they replied that the opera performances would be finished by the time the

ballet performances were reached. They went over the music for both ballets ... and they seemed most enthusiastic about their joint ballet-and-opera programs."

How enthusiastic Ruth was about reviving *Revenge* at this time is open to question, for *Salome* and *Chastity* were still in the front of her mind. The *Widow* was in a different category, for though she had not been pleased with the first version, she was already hard at working making it over on members of the opera's regular ballet company, including Carol Laurence and Kenneth Johnson. ("Carol is the perfect Widow in looks but has she the technique to do it and will she stay in Chicago?" To the latter question: no, she wouldn't.)

All that, of course, was for next season.

February 8, their wedding anniversary, found Ruth sick in bed with the flu. "Dinner alone with Tom and we talked about our thirty years of married happiness! And we still love each other and are not bored! Quite a record."

By the first of May she was in New York (en route to St. Tropez and a busy summer). In the diary: "Went to see 'Phoenix 55.' I had two tickets and as I couldn't get anyone to go with me, I invited my taxi driver. He turned out to be a young actor out of work and he was most entertaining and kept me amused with theatre talk all evening. He parked his taxi outside which was very convenient as it was right there to drive me home in."

It was to be a summer largely devoted to *The Merry Widow*. Bobby Short was now living on the Côte d'Azur and was very much back in the picture as director. Tom and his "conversations" were not around this early in the spring. She worked for weeks with Short at Antibes, while he made all the changes he had outlined before and added still others. For the scenery and costumes he refused to consider a remake by Wakhevitch, "who as an artist would not take orders from him as director," and they finally decided to start from scratch with Rolf Gérard, who had done a number of operas for Rudolf Bing at the Metropolitan Opera. His sketches, Ruth thought, were "not great art but they will serve the purpose of the ballet very well if well executed." To insure that, they were joined, at least in their conferences, by that superb executor from New York, Barbara Karinska, whose daughter, Irène, had executed costumes for Ruth in her own Paris establishment. (Barbara maintained that Irène was very good indeed, but not as good as she.) Bobby liked the sketches from the start, which made, perhaps, the final difference, and it was he who suggested the color schemes and the lighting.

During this time Ruth was working also at Nice with Hans May on his new orchestration, and what with his changes and Bobby's, she found it "hard to keep all the different versions straight." When rehearsals started in Chicago, Van Grove, the original arranger, was called in to make changes in May's changes.

One scene that had been added was a dream scene in which Danilo, having passed out on a sofa at Maxim's from too much champagne, sees an illusory, poetic vision of the Widow. Gérard had worked very hard on this whole episode, and when it was ready, Ruth wrote: "It is successful, I think. Tom gave us one of his arguments about its practicality but I guess he had some good ideas."

Her casting of Alicia Markova in the title role was a surprising tour de force. Some years later she wrote of it reminiscently: "She was the complete antithesis of everything that one expects from the alluring voluptuous Widow of Lehár. . . . She is delicate and fragile looking but with a body made of steel . . . and with her ethereal quality, she has a sense of tongue-in-cheek comedy. This was our cue for the interpretation of her Widow. In her first entrance she wore a brilliant red costume all covered with diamonds, and red feathers in her hair. This might have looked vulgar on anyone else, but not with Markova. She was the last word in Paris chic, and had at the same time a tiny touch of Fannie Brice. The combination was delicious."

She came to St. Tropez for a visit and it was there Ruth choreographed the Marsovian dance for her, "a very fast brilliant little pizzicato in which her feet looked miraculous." Contrary to her reputation, Ruth found her "very lazy (at least she was in St. Tropez), and if she worked an hour, she felt that was enough. As she never danced full out in rehearsal, it was difficult for me to tell how the dance would turn out. We used to go to the beach right after rehearsal. Markova would sit under a big umbrella, all wrapped up. She never went near the water and she always moved as little as possible. Her style was always understatement, and at this she was fantastically successful."

In the scene of Danilo's dream "she wore a little slip of a flowery costume. And she was about the most exquisite creature imaginable—like a will-o'-the-wisp, and absolutely unforgettable. In the last scene Gérard gave her a white costume decorated with big pink roses and an enormous black hat—a sort of combination of innocence and sophistication that was completely enchanting. I couldn't have asked for anyone better in this role than Alicia. She is certainly not an easy person to deal with. When I sat with her and her smart sister in a business conversation with Carol Fox, I was glad I was not Carol Fox. They are all three very shrewd, but after contracts were signed, Alicia's sister proved to be extremely helpful."

Stunning as the costumes were, they were, as Ruth had feared, a source of much difficulty in the execution. Finally Ruth herself modeled them all in long sessions, and Irène Karinska's bill for them was $21,000.

But there were other matters as well as the *Widow* that intruded upon the serenity of St. Tropez, some of them without any immediate relevance. For one thing, Clavé delivered his sketches for *The Barber of Seville*. "I put them up in my studio to study them and what a real thrill I got out of that."

Clavé could never be irrelevant. In addition, Tom Keogh, the young Paris-centered American artist, sent her a sketch for her long-projected production of Kochno's *"livret"* (which she so much admired) for *The Last Judgment*, with a score by Jerome Moross. "Isn't bad at all," she noted, *"so* lots of stimulation."

Then Vera Zorina arrived at Herbe Folle unexpectedly while Ruth and Tom were at Cannes, and had to stay overnight with no food in the house, to Ruth's grave embarrassment. She had come to discuss Rescigno's forthcoming production of the Monteverde masque *Il Ballo delle Ingrate*, which was to have a cast of mimes and dancers onstage and another cast of singers in the orchestra pit. Zorina was to dance the role of Venus while Ebe Signani sang it. "None of us knows what to do about the damned thing," wrote Ruth; and Zorina and Tom got into an argument—"all very disagreeable." But she was a wonderful guest. They "practiced" every evening, either together or separately, "and I actually did get one dance choreographed for her."

AN "OWN" BALLET

The two works were presented in Chicago in late November, but there was still no plan for getting that essential New York press coverage. Invitations were sent to the New York critics, and the few who made the trip wired back favorable reviews. The local audience also reacted with unmistakable warmth. The program had consisted of Puccini's short opera *Il Tabarro*, the Monteverde masque and *The Merry Widow*, and Rescigno had conducted both new works. The second performance later in the week was to replace the *Widow* with *Revenge* and did (with equally cordial response), but the audience had no idea how close it had come to nonappearance.

Ruth wrote the story in a long and explicit letter:

> You know how Italian singers are, not to mention Italian conductors. It seems that Maestro Serafin [who, earlier in the season, had conducted the opera version of *Il Trovatore*] made some kind of remark to Rescigno which seemed to imply that conducting for the ballet did not have quite the importance of conducting for the opera. At least, one of the orchestra members who overheard Serafin so told me. Although this happened only two days before the performance of 'Revenge', Rescigno refused to conduct the ballet as a result of it, and it was only after making attempts to find a substitute conductor, followed by five hours of argument and persuasion on the part of Fox and Kelly, that Rescigno relented and agreed to conduct the ballet. For obvious reasons, the music sounded at the performance even less well than it had at the prior rehearsal. Fortunately the audience loved it.

> What will happen next year, I don't know. But the problem of who will conduct the ballets will certainly have to be solved somehow, and with Rescigno more interested in pleasing Serafin and making a reputation in

Italy than anything else, we will surely have to have an entirely separate ballet conductor in the future. . . .

What particularly gripes the opera singers and the Italians generally is when the ballets have a success with the public. The Italians always hire a claque (there were two competing claques operating in our season this fall), whereas, of course, the dancers never have any claques. Also, the opera singers know that ballet outdraws opera in the U.S.A. much of the time, just as it does in Europe, and there is plenty of jealousy on the singers' part, which fortunately the dancers do not reciprocate or even understand.

When one deals with these Italians, it is plainly evident right away why there has never been any really good Italian ballet company, and never will be, so long as the singers have control of the opera houses and the public support.

But scandal or no scandal, the important thing was that Hurok, who had been interested in both ballets in their European versions, flew out to "catch" the Chicago versions and was impressed. In New York he had the Broadway Theatre under contract for Katherine Dunham and her company in December and the Kabuki Dancers from Tokyo after Christmas, leaving the house dark for the traditionally unprofitable preholiday week between the two engagements. It was possible, therefore, to offer the theatre to Ruth for that week, for better or worse. Since New York theatres were impossible to get during those years of theatrical prosperity, Tom accepted with alacrity. As Ruth wrote to Claudia Cassidy, "It is of course the worst week in the year for theatre business, but for us it was now or never."

It turned out to be definitely "now," for Columbia Artists Management, with their "organizational difficulties" apparently resolved, sent their representatives to the performances and signed the company at once for a tour the following season.

"We are very happy that we took the plunge," Ruth continued to Claudia, "for we now have a guaranteed tour for ten weeks next winter. As you probably know, I think Chicago should have a ballet company, and a ballet company, as you also know, cannot exist on five weeks work a year. This will enable us to sign the dancers for a longer period and maybe with this we will at least be able to stay together longer."

For all its happy ending, however, the New York engagement had not been without its own conducting crises. Because Lehman Engel had been so much a part of the *Revenge* adventure from the beginning, as well as being one of the best and busiest conductors in the field, Ruth had urged him to step in for this crucial occasion. With his customary good will he had accordingly arranged to take the week off from conducting the long-running musical comedy *Fanny*. But what with the strain of the apparently eternal *Fanny* and his heavy recording schedule, he collapsed from overwork and went to the hospital, and Robert Zeller rushed in and took over. Then Neal Kayan, their company pianist, injured his hand on a bad piano during rehearsals, and he also had to go to the hospital. Characteristically enough, the theatre being what it is, one of the New York reviewers wrote that the music sounded better than it had in Chicago.

It is curious that throughout the whole New York episode there was no sign whatever of Tom's morbid fear of those reviews of *Revenge*, and whatever "*ce Chauvin*" may have written, it produced no noticeable effect one way or the other.

Next year's problem of what to do about Maestro Rescigno solved itself unexpectedly without any help from Ruth. During the whole first half of the calendar year, indeed, the Lyric Theatre was engaged in a slam-bang legal fight between Carol Fox and Lawrence Kelly, complete with pleas to the court to appoint a receiver for the company, pleas to the mayor to prevent the appointment of one for the sake of the cultural life of the city, much general carrying-on in and out of the press and the ultimate dissolution of the company as such. It was well on into July before a new company, called by the somewhat tautological title of Lyric Opera of Chicago, was set up by court action, with Carol Fox at its head, and Kelly and Rescigno took their by no means inconsiderable talents elsewhere.

Until this date nobody knew whether there would be a 1956 season or not, but Ruth was busy with half a dozen other projects anyhow. Her chief problem was whether they would conflict with a 1956 season if one should materialize. Late in April she tried out her *Barber of Seville* at good old Mandel Hall under the title of *Susanna and the Barber*. In it she reverted to the use of spoken lines, this time between Susanna and Figaro. Tom reported that it "was a thrilling success."

She had by no means cut off her hope of making productions in Europe, if any should prove feasible, no matter how officially she had resumed residence in Chicago. She had already agreed in principle to do the choreography for a French musical comedy called *Minnie Moustache*, dealing with the California gold rush, which was set to open at the Gaîté-Lyrique in December. Wakhevitch was to do the scenery, and it was to star a group of nine French male singers known as Les Compagnons de la Chanson. They were a successful concert group who had done very well indeed on tour in this country under the direction of Columbia Artists Management. She had not even started to work under her own contract with Columbia, but they were eager enough to make each of their attractions boost the others when possible.

For months, also, there had been negotiations for another of those phantasmal take-overs of the Monte Carlo season. At the end of May she and Tom flew to London to attend the funeral of her longtime friend and champion Cecil Smith. Just before they enplaned, word came from Monte Carlo that the deal was off again.

"They are really such peculiar people," she wrote, "and now I see why Hurok worked two years on a deal with them and then gave up." What she did not realize was that the Monte Carlo Casino had no interest in the ballet per se. As Tom was to discover, one of the enormously rich Mediterranean magnates, who was addicted to large-scale gambling operations and owned a great number of shares in the Casino, was developing an ever-increasing animosity toward another major shareholder of similar addiction and was threatening to sell all his shares and open a competitive establishment on one of the Greek islands. In which case there would be an entirely new setup to negotiate with in the Société des Bains de Mer.

In the light of such a squaring off as this the rift in the Lyric Opera took on all the menace of a crack in a teacup. "But," wrote Ruth, who was an innocent bystander in both of them, "the Fox-Kelly-Rescigno battle goes on and on. . . ." In Paris there were meetings with the managers of the Gaîté-Lyrique to consummate the agreement for the choreographing of *Minnie Moustache*, and she continued to worry about conflicts with the still hypothetical opera season. Then she learned that that season was no longer hypothetical, and in no time at all she was back in Chicago—for the moment.

Early in August she had lunch with Carol Fox and a new non-Italian conductor who was very encouraging. He "seems to really know something about dancing and care about it, so maybe we will get to do some ballet after all." She was also delighted to discover that when Vasallo, the director of *Traviata*, asked for twelve couples, "he got them." It was a good omen for the new regime.

On August 31 she was in Paris again, ready to get to work on *Minnie*. She had already done some of her customary homework on the dances in Chicago and continued it at the American "gym" in Montparnasse. Since she was to have only ten or twelve rehearsals, spread over three weeks, her life can best be described as synoptic.

"To Dior's after lunch, then to the reading of the 'livret' of 'Minnie.' They seemed to like all my ideas but I doubt if I will succeed in getting them carried out in such a short time. Then to Joseph's for dinner at 8:30, invited by Josephine Bull [a Chicago friend] whom I met at Dior's. Interesting people with her, one Baroness Gunsbourg who seemed to know a lot about dancing. [Not surprising, really, since the Baron had consistently supplied Diaghileff with money to get his ballet going in Paris in 1909 and for much of the time afterward.] Went to the Gaîté-Lyrique just to get a look at the theatre. Very old-fashioned show but the theatre is wonderful—a bourgeois audience who seemed to love it. What am I doing in this atmosphere? It is really crazy but here I am and I will try to make the best of it."

First rehearsal: "What a terrifying experience—to face a new group in a new studio with a new pianist and with a new ballet to produce. I was a

nervous wreck and they probably all were too! Anyway I taught them two
dances. They are not good dancers at all but I think they will get by in this
sort of ballet. I hope so! Luckily I showed the first three dances to Robert
Manuel [the director] before I spent too much time finishing them because
they are not at all what he wants. I conceived the first entrance slow and
sexy and the men excited about the girls but the girls not excited about the
men. But Robert wants everyone excited and everything fast, fast, fast. . . .

"Rehearsed Friday and Saturday from 2 to 6 as usual. I actually made
a rough sketch of six dances and I think they are very amusing. They are
purposely 'corny' and I just hope the French public will not take them
seriously. Had a conference on costumes yesterday with Wakhevitch and the
lady who is making the costumes. How different from New York! Germaine
Royer just sits in her wonderfully comfortable office with a good secretary
and everything comes to her. They make all the costumes in the building and
the wardrobe mistress comes down with all the samples of material and the
art department comes down with all the sketches and models and it is so much
easier than 'chez nous'. I really am impressed."

She felt very lonely; rode the Métro because of the lack of taxis; ate
eggs and cheese at home. "Dior's is time-consuming and inefficient but
fun. . . .

"Had my very first rehearsal with the Compagnons and I really was
terrified. I had to do a 'Barbershop Ballad' which they sing, without ever
having heard the music or the words. However, I did it without even one
mistake—it all seemed to turn out well and they seemed pleased and I was
pleased—so at least we started out well together."

She had dinner with friends at St. Germain-des-Prés, then they all "went
to see 'Chevalier du Ciel' [the current show] at Gaîté-Lyrique. It is very
boring and very corny but I was glad to see the 'girls' on stage. We didn't
stay to the end. Tuesday at 2 I had the Compagnons and I must say I do
enjoy working with them.

"Doing the Square Dance was for some reason the hardest. I think it
was because we had to do it without music and only with counts and that
gets so monotonous. I did the whole thing in three rehearsals which I think
is quite a triumph as the Compagnons are of course amateur dancers. But
they are all very musical and very much 'artists' and it is much easier to work
with them than with the girls. The 'girls' are paid 25,000 francs a month so
how they lived I really don't know [*sic*]. I enjoy working with the
Compagnons more than with the dancers—they are such intelligent nice boys
and all of them talented. I like the 'movements' I did for them in their
Barbershop Ballad and they seem to like it too. But what these dances will
look like by December without me to rehearse them I can't imagine."

She was never to find out, for in December she was up to her ears in
the first tour of Ruth Page's Chicago Opera Ballet.

Tours and Detours

The Odyssey Begins

She arrived in New York on September 25. The plane was twelve hours late, during which Franco-American square dances, barbershop ballads and Rive Gauche forty-niners drifted off into outer space. There were hectic days of another sort awaiting her: interviews and conferences with Columbia Artists Management executives and publicity directors, all sandwiched in between tryouts and auditions for dancers. During the long period of dissension and uncertainty within the Chicago opera organization many members of the ensemble had fled to less doubt-ridden jobs elsewhere. For all her searching, she returned with only three new dancers to replace them.

Both Markova and Briansky also had to be replaced for her traveling company, since they had already made other commitments. To fill their roles in *The Merry Widow* and *Revenge* Ruth turned to Paris for stars of comparable glamour, and this time the gods were with her. After seven years with the Marquis de Cuevas, Marjorie Tallchief and her husband, George Skibine, were free until their new contracts as *étoiles* with the Paris Opéra went into effect next season. This meant, however, that they in turn would have to be replaced for the following tour.

For two months, then, Ruth was working full tilt not only with the present and future urgencies of her tours but also with the immediate requirements of the Lyric Opera itself, of which Ruth Page's Chicago Opera Ballet was a semi-independent unit. Fortunately the opera season was both brief and early. The first tour, for this and other reasons, was longer and earlier than any of the others that were to follow; it was, indeed, two tours, for it started at the end of November 1956 and (with a month out over Christmas) ended in the spring of 1957 after seventeen weeks of performing in ninety-two cities.

It opened in her home state of Indiana in the city of South Bend on November 26, with high hopes and the most careful preparation. To follow these breaking-in sessions more or less play by play is to gain a considerable awareness of the texture of the whole long-term enterprise, with its successes and failures, its petty irritations and major calamities, and for Ruth its creative satisfactions and perhaps more frequent heartaches.

For the strategic inaugural engagement arrangements had been made with Sister Mary Immaculate of St. Mary's College, Notre Dame, for the company to appear in O'Laughlin Auditorium without fee in exchange for the use of the hall for all the preceding week, in order to get into the swing of packing and unpacking, setting up equipment and hanging lights and scenery with a new crew, plus rehearsals by Ruth and the company on Saturday and Sunday for the première on Monday. Tom arrived on Sunday night, and so did Kurt Weinhold from the New York headquarters of Columbia, followed on Monday by Herbert Fox from Columbia's West Coast office. "The show went miraculously," wrote Ruth in her diary, "and the audience adored it. Of course there were a few mistakes but it went off with great dash. Our New York managers were delighted with it."

Her diary continued:

November 27—Midland Central High School (Midland Hotel in Bay City— awful—seventeen miles away from Midland). We drove today from 9 till 4:30 and got to the theatre at 6. It was a very discouraging performance because we couldn't hang *any* of our scenery and the lighting is *impossible*. In South Bend I made quite a little speech between "Widow" and "Revenge" as they had no programs, but tonight I made a very short one. We left Bay City at 10 and arrived two hours later at Port Huron, Mich. I drove in [the electrician's] car and we discussed lighting for our entire trip. The hotel is right next to the theatre here, thank heavens, and that really simplifies things a lot. The theatre is old and dirty and not attractive, but at least it is a theatre and not a high school auditorium. I went there immediately, then got a room and had a nap. (Harrington Hotel, okay. Desmond Theatre.)

To the theatre at 5:30 and we rehearsed an understudy, as Bonny Black is ill. Of course the stage was full of workmen as usual and we couldn't have class or anything. We rehearsed in the aisles. We started at 8:30 and every seat was taken. It was 90% better than the night before and I really got a thrill out of it in spite of the fact that nothing is really right yet. After the theatre at 11 I went with the Skibines to Mrs. Harrington's. She has a charming Victorian house on the river and the boats kept passing up and down and it was lovely. *But* nothing but whiskey and beer and *no* food and none of us had any dinner. So after we left we went to a chicken restaurant. To bed at 2 a.m. as usual. . . .

> Arrived Buffalo at 5 p.m. To Music Hall (Kleinhans Music Hall—good floor but no place to hang any scenery. Lenox Hotel, good). We had to wait a half hour in the snow to get in and only the *really* interested dancers brought their practice clothes. Betty Gour, our ballet mistress, gave us a short class and then we rehearsed with the Buffalo orchestra. Our stars didn't come so we let the understudies rehearse.

This was a day off; that is to say, there was no performance that evening and no travel the next day, so the company spent the day at Niagara Falls. The next night, however:

> The performance made me completely miserable. My dancers danced excellently but with no decors (except for a hideous summer-house set piece that was sent from Chicago) and dreadful lighting. I really suffered. However everyone seemed enthusiastic. I can't bear to see these two beautiful works murdered. However, the orchestra sounded marvelous and such a change from our ten-piece squeak!

> December 1—Sharon, Pa. Senior High School. We arrived at Sharon at 6 p.m. and started the performance at 8:30. We did the pas de deux from "Sylvia" with the two cupids.

This was an excerpt from a work she had long had in mind called *Soirée de Boston*, dealing with a salon in honor of Isadora Duncan in the home of Boston's famous Back Bay art patron, Mrs. Jack Gardner. It had a score by Antal Dorati, built on songs of the period, which Ruth had suggested to him, and a spoken text by Harold Acton, son of the English historian Lord Acton. This pas de deux used Delibes' music not in reference to his ballet *Sylvia*, but simply as an example of the sentimental divertissements in vogue in the early nineteen hundreds.

> We did it with piano as we didn't get in in time to have an orchestra rehearsal. It is very charming but I really think the program is better without any opener at all. The two big works are sufficient and when properly lighted and set make a perfect evening.

> After Skibine's solo in "Widow" he fell on the floor but walked off the stage. Kenneth immediately stepped into the part after Marjorie's solo and [Charles] Schick went into Jolidon, which was Kenneth's part, in his corps de ballet costume. I went back stage and found Kenneth getting into Danilo's costume and Skibine with a doctor from the audience. I went to the hospital with Skibine.

> What a job getting anybody in and out of a hospital these days! He had broken his Achilles tendon. They wanted him to stay in Sharon and be operated on, but I telephoned Irvine to have him brought to the Cleveland Clinic.

Her brother was head of that clinic, and he told her not to let Skibine stay at the Sharon hospital but to bring him to Cleveland—to the maternity entrance, actually, since that was the only entrance open at night.

We finally got him bandaged and took him back to the theatre, put him in the bus, waited for the bus to be loaded and were off at 12:30. We didn't stop to eat but went straight through to Cleveland arriving at 4:00 a.m. It was an awful trip—there was one hill the bus couldn't get up and we all had to get out and walk. That was the only pleasant thing of the whole day for me. I hate sitting still all day and night—this gave me a little exercise. Marjorie and I took George to the clinic and the company went to eat and to bed. Again all the red tape of getting in the hospital, and getting a room, etc. and seeing the doctor. Marjorie and I finally got to bed about 6 a.m. and I was up at 8.

At 12 I went to the theatre and spent till 3 getting the show ready and doing a barre myself. I must say the company came across magnificently.

The one bright aspect of the situation was that Cleveland happened to be the next stop on the schedule, anyhow, instead of being that many hours away in some other direction.

December 2—Cleveland (Music Hall, big, old-fashioned, good). Kenneth danced the two roles better than Skibine. He isn't as handsome as Skibine nor as appealing to women but he did very well indeed and I was proud of him. Cleveland is his home town and it all happened like a story book. His mother was so happy and proud. Tom arrived just before the performance and thank heaven he came. So many company problems. The stage hands and two wardrobe women refuse to go in the station wagon [a brand new one with gadgets, but it somehow broke down frequently] so the dancers gallantly stepped in. The electrician's assistant is very unpopular and is the problem child. We are overcrowded and the bus is very old and nothing works in it—lights, windows, seats, etc.

Left Cleveland at 12, December 3, and arrived at Newcastle at 4 p.m. (Scottish Rite Cathedral). I rode in the station wagon on one of the little seats that everyone complained of so, but I didn't mind it at all. I guess I am tougher than the young ones—most Americans now are so soft! Newcastle has an enormous Scottish Rite theatre—extremely unattractive but at least we could hang most of our scenery. Each performance is different. The music was *ghastly*! . . . Hotel Castleton quite nice but very unattractive town. Left Newcastle at 10 December 5 and arrived at Utica, New York at 8 p.m. The day passed quite quickly and agreeably. It was so nice to sit next to Bentley after the trivial boring conversation all day long of our wardrobe mistress.

Bentley had not been in any of the European productions after the first one in 1950, for he and Walter Camryn had started a school, with a burgeoning company, of their own. Though he was back in the fold now as guest artist, he frequently had to return to Chicago, just as Ruth did.

Went to the theatre at 3:30 (Stanley Theatre—big, 3000 people, old-fashioned, good. Utica Hotel absolutely ghastly.) to see if everything was under control. We always have union difficulties as they foist men to unload baggage and wardrobe women that we don't want and don't need and always the question who is to pay them! They didn't get going until 5 p.m. so of course only half the show was hung and there was no place to practice or rehearse or do anything! We had an audience of 3000—every seat taken. The lights were impossible—you couldn't see *anything* and the sets so improvised looked terrible and I thought the audience was very cold. I was really heartbroken about the whole thing until the manager of the Great Artists Series came back to see me swooning with joy and saying it was the best thing Utica had ever seen. But seeing these ballets of mine in the "road" versions is for me sheer agony. I walked home alone and went to bed weeping. I felt so lonesome and depressed.

The month's layoff at home had both its bright side and its dark. On the bright side was their purchase of a large apartment at 1100 Lake Shore Drive. On the dark side, Tom spent the whole of Christmas week in the hospital and did not go home until January 2. It was, Ruth noted, "not cancer or heart failure but some unknown virus in the intestines." She went to his office every day and took his mail to him.

On the Friday after Christmas she went directly from her visit to the hospital to the apartment ("our new home") with Tom's architect brother, Howard, and the two of them spent the afternoon discussing the necessary changes to be made. Naturally there were a great many of them, and what with her peripatetic way of life and her penchant for picking up objects of virtu from all her ports of call, together with an eye to "producing" an apartment as if it were a new ballet, it would be many months before it was completed. As a matter of course the installation of an ideal studio was the center of the whole plan. Its walls were ultimately lined with the mirrors from the old studio of Adolph Bolm where she had worked all those years ago.

As for changes that had to be made in the company before the tour was resumed, they were also considerable. To replace Skibine she had got in touch with Briansky, who had created the roles originally and was to return to them for the 1958 tour anyhow, and by some hook or crook he had arranged to step in now. Mireille, his wife, "a very charming girl," came with him. "She goes into the corps *only* because she wants to be with her husband."

Arova also returned, arriving on New Year's Day, which was the earliest moment she could get away from Ballet Theatre, in which she had been a guest artist. With her from the same company came her new teammate, Job Sanders, who was to do Popoff in the *Widow* and to stand by for Bentley as De Luna in *Revenge*. They insisted on beginning rehearsals at once, since the company reopened in a week, and in five days, Ruth noted, she had learned Leonora (she had done Azucena before) and he had learned both his roles.

There was also to be a new company manager, whom Ruth had known for years. "Have always felt he was a snake in the grass, but at least he is intelligent and entertaining, and after our last company manager, the fat old toad, he is a blessing."

The tour resumed, with all its personnel changes, in Cedar Rapids, Iowa, on January 7.

> The performance that night made me absolutely ill—lights all wrong, new dancers not really knowing their parts . . . I was ready to give up but the audience seemed to like it just the same. In "Home to Our Mountain" [one of the most affecting scenes in *Revenge*] one of the stage hands walked onto the stage and of course the audience laughed. It absolutely killed me.

Four days later she found herself, as a matter of simple routine, in Indianapolis and at the Murat Theatre, both of which were filled with memories. After a working session in the theatre all afternoon:

> Back to the hotel at 6, changed clothes and back to the theatre. I didn't take the class. I felt emotionally upset and I couldn't leap quite quickly enough from my old childhood world to my real world of the dance. I felt in between both and strange—like I used to feel as a little girl. . . . We had a big audience and big applause and I took a bow with the dancers. Rave reviews this a.m. But I am exhausted from the emotional tension of being in my home town! [An old local friend] wanted to take me to the Watsons' (who live in my studio) to see how wonderfully they have fixed it up and I just couldn't face it. The thoughts of Mother and Father were already too sad.

The next day in Louisville she rehearsed Arova in her old role of Azucena, which she had done for the first time on this tour in Indianapolis.

> She didn't do the role well at all last night. Emotionally she was okay but not correct with the steps. The rehearsal helped and she was wonderful. Her face looks exactly like a Clavé painting. "Revenge" was almost exactly right for the first time. I am proud of my company in every respect. . . . And now at last I feel that I can leave them on their own. It has been a hard pull.

Acting on that happy conviction, she left at once for Chicago, where Tom, scarcely recovered from his "unknown virus," had just had a hernia operation.

It was a good time to begin discussing the possibilities for the 1958 tour. There would have to be a second program, because they would be playing repeat engagements at many places where their present double bill had already been seen. There would also have to be a glamorous European ballerina, and they were toying with such names as Chauviré and Vyroubova. But Columbia would have to make the final decisions, and the new repertoire had not yet been chosen. Doreen Tempest of the Sadler's Wells Ballet had already been

signed to fill the place left open by Marjorie Tallchief's scheduled departure
for the Paris Opéra.

Ruth herself felt that, artistically, she "would be content with Arova as
leading star, but she is too pushy and insists on too much for Job, so I am
afraid they are both out since Tom does not like to do business with her. So
we'll see." Obviously she was not convinced. Her attitude toward Arova,
indeed, was curious in its development. As far back as *Vilia* in Bournemouth,
when Dolin dropped her from the leading role, Ruth had liked her performance
very much and had thoroughly enjoyed her company at their supper with
Briansky at the Savoy Grill afterward. She had noted in her diary, however,
along with these enthusiastic remarks, a self-warning to be wary of her over-
ambition. Nevertheless, she was ambivalent about letting her go, and in the
end she did not do so.

Bentley turned up in Chicago on a skip-out from the tour and "in a
somewhat liquory state told all the backstage gossip and what went on behind
my back."

On February 7 she was off to New York for a week of discussion with
Kurt Weinhold of Columbia and his associate, Tommy Thompson, about the
1958 tour. Tom, who had been trying a case in New Orleans, flew up to New
York to join in the conferences. There they were shown the batch of letters
and the local reviews from the current tour, which had been sent on by the
company manager. "My God," Ruth recorded, "what letters! I never read
such raves in my life."

After all the talking and counter-talking she was considerably let down
by Columbia's final choice of ballets for the next tour from those she had
submitted to them. They were *The Triumph of Chastity, El Amor Brujo* and
The Barber of Seville. "I am very much disappointed," she wrote, "not to do
'Salome.' "

At this inopportune moment somebody sent her the script of a Broadway
musical to consider. Though she found the music catchy, she thought the
book was terrible. "Difficult for me to refuse as I'm really doing nothing
much now of any importance. But my heart is not in this silly show." And
off she hopped to Dallas to join the company, and on with them to Fort
Worth, Houston, Port Arthur and San Antonio (with an orchestra of eighty).

Then a quick jump back to Chicago for a special personal purpose:
"Went to see the new apartment at 1100 Lake Shore Drive, and tried dancing
on the scraped floor. The view is so sensational that I could hardly do a
barre." And no wonder. The light, like that of Athens or San Francisco,
worked its transformations over sky, lake and sand, until it might have been a
vast projection from another world by Yves Tanguy, with the moving figures
on the beach far below as incarnations of those shell-like forms that inhabit

his canvases. After that, no matter how much she continued to rail against Chicago, there could not be any grave doubt about her staying there.

"Had to hurry back home, get our baggage, pick up Tom and go to the airport. We were supposed to leave at 11 but didn't leave until 2. Arrived in Tucson, Arizona at 6. . . ." Disgusted with performance. Dancers good but sets not used, light awful, etc. Gave hell to the new stage manager and stage crew. On to Hollywood (not forgetting Remisoff's new home in Beverly Hills), Santa Barbara, San Francisco. . . .

CATEGORICAL IMPONDERABLES

If she was "doing nothing much now of any importance," it is clear that importance is a subjective matter and muchness is strictly relative. Certainly that same kind of muchness would continue to keep her busy productively for the foreseeable future, as it had done in essence, if not in scope, since the day she was born. Fundamentally, in addition to her milder and gentler aspects, she was, and would continue to be, multifarious, intense, gregarious, forever peregrinating, artistically voracious, insatiable and indomitable.

Her life now fell into three major categories: (a) the tours with their predictable unpredictables; (b) the Chicago scene—a kind of layer cake consisting simultaneously of creating-rehearsing operations for the next tour, plus more of the same for the opera season, which had now grown until it occupied approximately three months of the year, plus her traditionally widespread social involvements, with her new home as the icing on top of it all; and (c) those blessed summers nominally at St. Tropez but branching out all over Europe, missing nothing that was reachable, teeming with people, and somehow getting all tied up with the ballet in spite of everything.

As for category (a), its long-term patterns were the most consistent; they were behavioral in nature, where the company was concerned, ranging all the way from irresponsibility and meanness to romance, laziness, indigestion and accident-proneness; they were logistic, including in that term travel, housing and sustenance; and they were creative, which is really what it was all about. This pattern concerned itself most consciously with the creating of ballets, but even at this early stage it was also creating quite unaware something possibly unique, namely, a company essentially of midwestern provenance, with a uniform style and a sense of ensemble. To be sure, the box office required something besides talented anonymity, and the addition of "names," both European and American, attracted an audience, without which a young company could not emerge and develop. The contribution of this imported glamour, however, was otherwise incidental and transitory.

It is interesting to note that fourteen years later, of the six then stars of the company four had been in the corps de ballet on the first tour—Patricia Klekovic, Dolores Lipinski, Orrin Kayan and Charles Schick; one, Larry Long, joined the corps on its third tour, and one, Kenneth Johnson, had been among the stars from the beginning. There were occasional defections of brief duration because of military service, or momentary pique, or rifts in company romances; but in spite of Ruth's perpetual auditioning, especially for boys, the record of stability in personnel and the resultant ensemble development was noteworthy.

As for the necessity for creating new ballets to make up alternate programs for the return engagements, nothing could have pleased Ruth more. The three she had created for the present season were, for various reasons, not to last long in the repertoire.

In *The Triumph of Chastity* the role of the Unicorn was difficult to cast. Perhaps in a sense Dufy had been correct in seeing it danced by a ballerina on point, for its speed and brilliance were hard to find in a man. She had selected a young boy from the corps whom she considered potentially wonderful, but when she saw him onstage, she realized that he did not have enough strength or experience to carry it off. She made a few cuts, of necessity, but still liked it very much as a ballet. Kenneth Johnson danced it on occasion, and it stayed nominally in the repertoire for three seasons, but it was seldom danced and never to her satisfaction.

El Amor Brujo she also liked very much, especially with its handsome sets by Wakhevitch, but it was unsuitable as an opening number, where she needed it, and was hard to place effectively in her present programs. It was not at all the ballet she had used so controversially in the fourth act of *Carmen* but a self-contained dramatic work built on the plot by Martinez Sierra on which De Falla had composed the score.

As for *Susanna and the Barber* she would have loved it if only for Clavé's designs. Van Grove had arranged both the music and the scenario from Rossini's opera and the play of Beaumarchais. As a return to her old dance-*cum*-speech formula she had had dialogue written by Ira Wallach and Ben Aronin, to be spoken by Rosina and Figaro, but this was a fatal mistake. For Ruth and Bentley speech had no terrors, but neither of them could be relied upon to be present for every performance. To make matters worse, about midseason Ruth developed Achilles-tendon trouble. Two sets of replacements were rehearsed and tried out in performance, but since few dancers have voices, diction or a sense of verbal projection, the results were not adequate. Even at best, however, the work proved to be too intimate for the huge auditoriums and acoustically poor college gymnasiums where they so often performed, and after this one season it was dropped from the repertoire in spite of its inherent excellence.

Mia Slavenska was the featured European ballerina finally chosen for the season. Because of her unavailability during the often protracted periods required for the producing of new works, she was in none of them. The best that could be done was to rehearse her in the already established roles in the old repertoire, such as the *Widow* and Lenora in *Revenge,* and provide her with other numbers to assure her presence in the new program. One of these was a little ballet for three dancers, called *Idylle*, composed by Skibine originally for the de Cuevas company to music of François Serrette, and the other was the familiar pas de deux from *Don Quixote.*

The season was not without incidents.

Item 1: In New Orleans the performance was a matinee in "the largest, most unattractive auditorium I have ever seen." It seated 5,000 and was completely sold out, so that Ruth, along with the parents of one of the boys in the company as unexpected guests, had to climb up to the top gallery and stand more or less against the back wall. The box-office situation that had produced this sad inconvenience so delighted the local manager (as the program itself did too) that she phoned Columbia at once and asked for a return engagement next year, for three performances instead of one.

Among the local newspaper reviewers, one young woman apparently did not share her enthusiasm. By an odd coincidence she happened to be a friend of a somewhat obstreperous boy in the company whom Ruth had offended that very day by telling him that his performance in the *Don Quixote* pas de deux was not as good as Erik Bruhn's. His performance a little later in the afternoon with the lady reviewer, however, proved more successful, for he was the only dancer she mentioned in the paper the next morning.

Item 2: Ruth had wired ahead to Armand's in New Orleans to arrange for a big party for the company at 6:30. The members of the staff and the musicians arrived punctually, but the dancers, what with resting after the performance and dressing up, got there very late, and by that time the other guests were already "a little drunkish!" The company manager, who was witty and adroit (and at this point somewhat mellow), stole the show with his excellent toasts. But, not to be outshone, the young man who was not as good a Don Q. as Erik Bruhn toasted Ruth as "the woman I hate" and leaned over at once to whisper in her ear: "I am going to have an affair with you."

He had been making himself markedly unpopular offstage throughout the season, especially by his constant "swearing" in hotel lobbies and other public places, where he attracted unfavorable attention. As Ruth noted, "this was before swearing was chic."

Item 3: After dinner some of the company went along with Ruth to a nightclub to see Sally Rand and her four girls. She did her famous fan dance to Debussy's *Clair de Lune*, and "I must say," Ruth noted, "she still looks young and beautiful, and she is an extraordinary woman." After her performance "she came and sat with us and we talked and talked. She knows quite a lot about dancing. She talked about her 'work' so sincerely that one begins to believe that stripteasing *is* an art. [As a matter of fact, Sally was by no means a stripteaser.]   Her conversation was really extraordinary, and, I must say, amusing."

By this time, however, the company manager was "quite in his cups" and Ruth did not know what to do. "But Sally did. From her complete nudity (except for the fans) she was now in a dress so enormous that when she took us to a coffee-house next door her dress filled the entire shop." They finally got the erstwhile toastmaster somehow medicated through the collaboration of Sally and the waiter, and folded him into a taxi headed for the hotel.

It was 3:30 when Ruth got to bed, and she was up at 7 to take a plane to Valdosta, Georgia. "We made ten stops en route but finally got there."

Item 4: Briansky was having a terrible time with an injured knee and became less and less able to dance, until he finally had to leave for New York before the season was over. The situation bred quite a bit of bad blood, not only among the dancers he partnered, but also with the management. He maintained that he had hurt himself during the season; they claimed that he had joined the company knowing that his knee was bad. It was especially unfortunate because Ruth thought "he was wonderful when he was in condition."

Ocala, Florida—high school auditorium—brand new—no current, so lights could not be used—no place to fly scenery—not enough rake to the floor to allow the audience ever to see the feet. "These American architects who build all our unattractive, impractical, impossible theatres should be run out of the country. In spite of the fact that Briansky was not there, that Mia did not dance on account of a pain in her knee, and that Doreen Tempest fainted in the middle of 'Revenge,' the performance seemed to be a big success."

Item 5: Because of some transportation mishap Ruth complained that she hated to have to go alone next day on the public bus from Lynchburg to Danville, and one of her boys remarked "in all seriousness, 'I'm sure no one would mind if you stood on our bus'!" She took the public one.

As for category (b), the Chicago sector of her life was comparatively short this year before the departure for St. Tropez but all its departments were in full swing, with the new apartment as a dominant background. She was working at it with an artistic concentration that made her understand how people could be carried away by the fascinations of really creating interiors. The workmen were taking over for the summer, but in the meantime she was making the best of it. She had brought home from Florida a collection of magnificent seashells and was planning to have a round dining room with something of the suggestion of an aquarium.

She had already done stretches and the like in the enchanting studio. She had also had three rehearsals there for a dance she had been induced to create for the Goodman Theatre's student performance of *A Midsummer*

Night's Dream. Neither the music, which was by Purcell, nor the make-do costumes inspired her, but at least she went through with it conscientiously with the equally uninspiring dancers. She had always been interested in the Goodman Theatre and was to continue to be through all its changing phases, for the concept of Chicago as a producing center for the theatre arts was one that she cherished with a deep, if cynical, passion. A production there of a dramatization of *Billy Budd* during this stopover at home elicited from her in her diary a pointed summation of her attitude toward the theatre as a whole: "It always takes me quite a while to get used to people on the stage just talking. It always seems to me they should be singing and dancing."

On a Sunday in May her niece, Ann Finlay, came to lunch at the apartment with all her children, including a six-month-old baby. "Our first lunch in our dining room. Effie cooked it for us and it was really great fun." The faithful Effie had gone into retirement, but she emerged from it now, no doubt with a proprietary interest in these new domestic burgeonings.

CATEGORY (C)

The summer, which went under the general name of St. Tropez, was entirely typical, including everything from the World's Fair in Brussels to a new maid named Josephina at Herbe Folle who could not speak a word of any language but Italian and was an incredibly bad cook even after Ruth bought an Italian cookbook; but she was young, sturdy and clean, which was something.

In Paris Ruth had lunch with Clavé's mother in her new apartment just around the corner from Les Trois Pastèques. Her son had found an old place and fixed it up "enchantingly" for her. Maria Nieves, her devoted maid and friend and a marvelous Spanish cook, was taking care of her, as she would continue to do as long as she lived. "It was such fun seeing her again. She has not changed and still disapproves of Toni's Madeleine [he was separated from his wife] and will not see her at all. I stayed with them till five o'clock trying to explain my ideas for 'Camille' to Bazarte, the cousin of Clavé, who is going to try to design them. His French is about like mine." Clavé himself had turned completely away from the theatre and was devoting himself to painting.

In St. Tropez guests from every quarter of the world peopled Herbe Folle until every couch was occupied, and the peasants, who still owned the loft over her studio, stamped on the floor to protest the noise of music and dancing below at all hours of the night.

But [Ruth wrote late in July] our most extraordinary guest was Clavé Bazarte, le cousin de Clavé. He arrived four days ago at St. Raphael and we went to meet him at 8 a.m. We had coffee at St. Raphael and the second we arrived at Herbe Folle he got out all his sketches for 'Camille'. I was awake all the night before worrying over them. I knew he had done so much work on them and I was so afraid I wouldn't like them. But finally I *did*. I was really enthusiastic. Of course we had to make a lot of changes. But still the great mass of the work was splendid. We worked all a.m. on the ideas and then we went to Pampelone for lunch and took him with us. It did not take me long to realize that he was a Spaniard and did not like to be in the sun and swim, so the next two days we left him at home to work. It was a big job for both of us and I was exhausted when he left and I am sure he was too. He stayed three days and we really worked constantly on it.

The final diary entry of the season, written on board Pan Am en route to New York on August 2, epitomizes what was clearly par for the category:

We left St. Tropez Thursday about 4 p.m. We had difficulties all day because our English Austin just wouldn't start and the telephone (as usual) didn't work so we couldn't get the garage. Tom finally bummed a ride to town to get the garage men. We had our farewell picnic all alone on the rocks, a wonderful swim, a perfect day. Only person swimming was Brigitte Bardot, her doublure and her entourage of boys. She looks lovely at a distance, and I hope to never meet her as I like her at a distance.

Madeleine was supposed to arrive but she was late and we didn't get to see her. Clavé was to arrive the next day and they will stay at Herbe Folle for August. We went to Cannes to see about getting our Austin on the train to Paris and there premier danseur Scheepers from Amsterdam found me. (He came over to St. Tropez on a scooter the other day to see me as he wants to join my company. He didn't have any ballet shoes so he did some, I must say, very good entrechat-six in his bare feet!)

He was having a drink with Romanoff of Ballet Theatre, so we joined them and heard all the Ballet Theatre news. A lot of their scenery and costumes and all their personal clothes were burned up in a camion! Nora Kaye and Lucia Chase joined us, the latter busier looking than I've ever seen her. Jerome Moross made all the arrangements with Oliver Smith to do our "Last Judgment" for the New York season on September 24. Lucia was supposed to see me about it in Cannes to make final arrangements. All she said was it was impossible to do it at all because there was no rehearsal time, and not another word! As I didn't want to do it anyway, I didn't care.

The *Last Judgment* episode had its origin back in 1951 during the difficult period of rehearsals for *Revenge*, when Ruth had had dinner with its author, Boris Kochno, and wondered if he could ever be pinned down to anything concrete. He outlined his *livret* to her and she thought it sounded wonderful and wished she could choreograph it. A bit later she actually bought it from him, even though not a word of it was written down. When she returned to New York, she got in touch at once with Moross, who seemed the ideal composer for it, and together they filled in the whole scenario from only her memory of what Kochno had outlined. At the end of 1952 she talked to Kochno again and showed him the score, which he liked. "I told him it was a very New York Jewish version—therefore most interesting and very different from his which is so completely French. In any event, he didn't object." In the meantime several designers had worked on it, including Miles White and Tom Keogh. Moross never lost his enthusiasm for it and only recently had "sold" Oliver Smith on the idea of an immediate production in the next New York season. As codirector of Ballet Theatre, Smith had arranged for Lucia Chase to make a formal ratification with Ruth at Cannes. After all its curious history the work was never produced.

> We took Le Train Bleu at 8:30, had a big French dinner and arrived in Paris at 9 a.m. Went directly to Les Trois Pastèques, found Clinton King, had a short talk, and immediately to Dior's where I arrived at 10. The usual madhouse and inefficiency, but so much fun that nobody cares. At 11 I started my fitting. I bought three dresses and a coat for about $1500 and they are all wonderful. Then to the Boutique and bought blue wool dress ($135), a velvet skirt and two blouses ($200). Lunched with Tom at Relais, back to Pastèques, practiced an hour, packed, unpacked and back to Dior's at 5 and watched the new collection till 7:30. Too long but very beautiful. Drank champagne with the buyers afterwards, then to Gaîté-Lyrique to see "Chimes of Normandy." We left after Act 2—it was so long and so ordinary that I just couldn't sit through it. Such a lovely old theatre. How I would love to have that setup for a ballet company! Serge Lido met us and took us to a dinner of pig's feet at Les Halles. I drank a great deal of red wine so slept like a top. Breakfast at a little restaurant near us and then spent three strenuous hours explaining Bazarte's "Camille" costumes to Mme. Tussia, Irène Karinska's assistant. She is so wonderful and understands dancers' costuming so well that it was a pleasure. . . .
>
> So now our vacation is over. Tom seems well and happy so it was all worthwhile. We had a fine time and now I am anxious to get back into my ballet world!

Effie was around again to open the house in Hubbard Woods when they got back from St. Tropez. The weather was "lovely and hot," the way Ruth liked it, and she was "certainly grateful" that Effie had been so thoughtful. Ruth had acquired a Mexican maid named Felisa, who at this point could speak very little English. But Ruth liked her very much.

LA DAME AUX CAMELIAS

Before long Ruth was working intensively on *Camille*, which was to be next season's major work, with Marjorie Tallchief in the title role. She had started to concentrate on it as soon as the tour was over last spring, working with Klekovic and Orrin Kayan and especially with Kenneth on the many difficult lifts that were in the choreography.

Her original casting decisions had somewhat remade themselves just before she had left for St. Tropez. All through the winter some unidentified man had been "hanging around" her company at the opera house apparently offering them jobs for a new American-based ballet he was forming to operate in Europe during the coming summer. It seemed to her "a very shady operation," and before long she found that Arova and Sanders and one of her other boys had decided to go with him. There was no reason why they should not do so, since none of her company was hired on a year-round basis, but she did not like the apparent surreptitiousness of the proceedings. She had been upset by Sanders's personal behavior in general ever since he had joined the company and at the end of each season had threatened not to reengage either him or Arova, but because of her admiration for Arova's work she had always weakened. This time she decided to stand firm; and she did, though she had nobody in mind as a replacement.

A month later, while she and Tom were in New York preparing to take off for Paris, she had dinner with Veronika Mlakar, a Yugoslavian dancer who had come to this country the year before with Roland Petit's company, and took her to see Zizi Jeanmaire in the *Folies-Bergère*, which was playing a Broadway engagement. They both found it boring and ordinary, but they had a long talk and Ruth liked her. "She would fill Arova's place in my company *very* effectively I think. But will she?" She would.

With *Camille* Ruth probably came nearer than she had ever come before to creating a ballet for a particular dancer. To be sure, choreographers who are also dancers inevitably create all the central roles unconsciously for themselves no matter who is to dance them. Ruth, in particular, actually worked them all out on herself before the beginning of rehearsals. But this may have been a little different.

She had had the idea of doing *Traviata* for several years and had even offered it to Dolin at the time of the great success of *Revanche*. Now when she started to work on it specifically, it was with a certain trepidation, since she felt it had been done so badly so often. Nevertheless, "the romantic spirit seemed to be there from the beginning," she wrote. "Maybe it was because I went to Père Lachaise cemetery and wept over the grave of Marguerite Gauthier . . . and maybe it was because Marjorie Tallchief seemed to be born to dance the role of 'Camille.' The whole company wept when they first saw her perform it on stage in rehearsal just in her practice clothes and under the hard white working light of the theatre."

Marjorie was not a bravura dancer like her older sister, Maria, but when the latter was making her first successes in New York under Balanchine's direction, Bronislava Nijinska, the first teacher of them both, had nodded knowingly and said, "Wait till you see Marjorie." But if technique was not her specialty, neither was it at all a problem for her. "She has strength," said Ruth, "a fluid line, high extensions and a poetic quality that I find irresistible. . . . She never says a word at rehearsal and she does whatever you tell her without any questions, and she does it easily, quickly and beautifully. She can also do all kinds of stunts if required." Ruth devised for her in one place, for example, what she calls a "fouetté stunt," which has caused trouble from time to time to real virtuoso dancers who have followed her in the role.

The whole work, for some reason, objectified itself in difficult technical forms, with many trick lifts, and the company consequently hated to rehearse it, which made matters no easier. The solo she planned for Armand proved exceptionally hard for her to evolve because of its apparently unavoidable demands. When she had finally finished it to her liking on Kenneth, he was able to perform it excellently, but she was very much afraid that Skibine would not be.

Skibine, of course, was back as one of the stars; he and Marjorie were on leave from the Paris Opéra. The other stars were Veronica Mlakar and Bentley, who was always listed nowadays as "guest artist." He was so deeply involved with his own school and its choreographic activities that he was becoming more and more reticent about touring. The music was again in an arrangement by Van Grove, who had collaborated on the scenario as well.

The ballet was a great success with audiences from the start, and took its place at once as a major attraction.

GIOTTO TO ORFF VIA MENOTTI

During the summer overseas that followed, the little English Austin set what must have been a record for mileage. Being naturally generous, friendly and hospitable, Ruth and Tom had invited two of their dancers, who were both in Europe for the first time, to join them for a bit of Italian sight-seeing. They picked them up at Monte Carlo by arrangement and set out on a week of Italy-hopping for all the world like a caricature of American tourists on a binge. They were an hour late in getting to Monte Carlo because they had stopped at an antiques shop and bought a cart that had once belonged in an old French circus. "It is amusingly painted and will be fun for us to sit in in our courtyard."

They motored to San Remo for dinner and spent the night at a magnificent new hotel, with their two guests occupying a room together. The young man, however, was not interested in romancing, and the young woman definitely was, so there was more to the trip than traffic problems.

The next day they had a tough drive to Milan, for they did not know that the heater was on in the car. Once there, they spent hours at the American Express arranging their young friends' flight home, and proceeded to "do" the town. Ruth had a business appointment at dinner to meet Margarethe Wallmann, the stage director who was to direct *Carmen* for the opera next season. She was to bring along the costume designs to show Ruth, but she arrived late, dinner arrangements were disrupted, and she had brought almost no sketches. The few she did bring struck Ruth as commonplace and Italianate, and the whole mixed-up meeting was not worth the effort.

From then on, their itinerary was an echo of Cole Porter's troupers' song in *Kiss Me Kate*. They went to Padua, Venice, Vicenza, Arezzo, Perugia, Assisi . . . On the road they passed a sculptor's home and bought "three stone cupids for our well and two stone poodles for our entrance room in Chicago. We had been looking for a sculpture for our St. Tropez well for five years and were very happy to have found something amusing and something we could afford!"

At Florence they stopped off to see Mrs. Goth, only to find that she had been injured in an automobile accident and was in the hospital—"for the first time in her life except when Trudy was born." She was delighted to see them. Trudy had gone to Spoleto, which was also their destination.

This was their first visit to Gian-Carlo Menotti's Festival of Two Worlds; for some reason they had not made it there the summer before when it had begun. The car got stuck in a narrow street and "it took half the village to lift it out." They could not find the place where they had been booked to stay, so they went straight to the theatre. Ruth thought it not only beautiful but marvelous for dancing—not too large, not too small. The program, however, left her with mixed feelings, and some of it made her "ashamed to be an American." They had dinner at the Festival Restaurant with Trudy, but the American jazz was too loud to make conversation possible. "Spoleto is such a charming little town but I'm sure our American 'civilization' will ruin it." There was no hotel available, but they managed to stay with a private family.

The next day they put their young protégés on the plane for Rome (St. Tropez was not on the schedule) and were "sad to leave them. They were both wonderful guests. We really turned ourselves inside out to give them a good time and show them Europe and we were both worn out when they left. I think he was too; she tried very hard to lure him in every way and I think he just didn't want to be lured. They slept in the same room every night and one night in a double bed, but I'm afraid nothing happened. Poor girl, she tried so hard. He even took to drinking a little as that seemed to make his life with her easier!"

Worn out they may have been, but they did not so much as stop for breath. When they got back to Florence, they decided to go on to Munich, and after "a lot of wild telephoning to St. Tropez" Ruth talked to her house guest at Herbe Folle. He was Marius Constant, the composer, whom she had asked to write a score for her, and what she wanted now was for him to agree to stay there longer (which he could not do). "We hate to leave our maid, Mme. Borget [poor Josephina apparently never learned to cook], all alone—we are afraid she will be so lonely that she will leave!"

Nevertheless, they loafed on up to Verona, left the car there and took the train to Munich. They arrived "dead tired" and went straight to bed. But she was up early in the morning, "found a tiny corner in the room to do my barre" and was off to the Prinzregententheater to see Heinz Rosen. He had been a pupil of Laban and a member of the Kurt Jooss ballet and was now both a choreographer and a stage director at the opera. When he had finished his rehearsal, they had coffee in the theatre canteen, and she left to "do" the museums until time for the evening performance at the opera house.

"The big thrill of Munich was Carl Orff's 'Trionfi I and II' (Carmina Burana and Catulli Carmina)—the music is new and original and to me deeply moving, and Heinz Rosen's staging of it is splendid—chorus and dancers so well integrated. I would love to do this work for Chicago. I couldn't do the chorus parts better than Rosen (if as well) but I believe I could do the choreography maybe a little bit better."

It was her most important experience of the summer.

. As soon as the curtain was down, they were off to the train, had a sleepless night, picked up their car in Verona (after having lost the key and, in the last stages of despair, had it returned to them by a policeman; "we had dropped it and he had picked it up and kept it for us—bless him") and started the long drive home.

"We were both dead—what a long trip of one-night stands! But how inspiring—I need time and repose to think it over. Instead we were greeted by an enormous stack of letters. I practiced this a.m. in my studio, unpacked and spent a couple of hours on the rocks nearby swimming and picnicking with Tom alone. B. Bardot was on her little beach swimming and looking like a mermaid. Spent p.m. writing a long letter to Carol Fox. . . . How hard it is to get started on business again. I'd rather dream about the Giotto frescoes in the Scrovegni Chapel at Padova or of the Certosa of Pavia and *all* the lovely churches.

A COUPLE OF CARMENS

For the next season she decided to add to the repertoire, of all things, *Carmen.* Her very first go at opera-into-ballet had been *Guns and Castanets* back in the WPA days, and she had staged countless varieties of interpolated fourth-act ballets for the opera itself. To complicate matters, in this very opera season she was to stage still another one for Margarethe Wallmann's production, which came along while she was working on her own independent project. (In her notes she referred to them as "Carmen" and "Carmen-Page.") But the idea interested her and she went at it with enthusiasm.

She had asked Remisoff to do the designing and Van Grove the arranging and, according to long custom, was collaborating with them by mail and telephone. Now at last, however, she rebelled against this one-dimensional form of communication and flew out to California where she could thrash things out with them both in person.

This year for the first time she was not importing any European stars, though Mlakar was returning for a second season. Her featured newcomers were the Canadian-born Melissa Hayden, and John Kriza, who was not only American-born but near-Chicago-born. She had borrowed the one from the New York City Ballet and the other from Ballet Theatre. But Hayden, after the pattern established with Slavenska, was not to do the new *Carmen* at all; she was to take over *Camille* and *The Merry Widow*. Mlakar was to be the Carmen and Kriza the José (as well as Armand and Danilo). Ruth virtually commuted to New York to work with them all there, separately and together, at their convenience, since they could not come to Chicago during their seasons.

One Saturday in New York, when she was unable to rent a studio, she went to Melissa's apartment to work with her alone. "We worked in her living room from 11 to 1:30 on 'Camille'. I must say she is most conscientious and wants to do everything the way the choreographer wants—how unusual for a star of her rank. I adore working with her."

She was also delighted with Mlakar and Kriza. It was a pleasure to work with people who were actually to dance the roles, instead of with their understudies in Chicago on whom she had to build them. By this awkward method of rehearsing, however, each of the principals knew only his own isolated role without ever having worked with the full cast. To take care of this situation as well as possible she rented the old Eighth Street Theatre, which was a wonderful place to rehearse, for a full week before the season's scheduled opening in Dubuque.

Mlakar arrived on Saturday and they worked very hard on her role over the weekend. The wardrobe women, however, who were supposed to come on Friday, did not show up until Monday, when Ruth was already in full rehearsal, which, since she had the wardrobe and the packing problems dumped into her lap at the same time, "about killed me." To complicate matters still further, the scenery arrived simultaneously with the dancers, making a three-ring circus of it all.

She "got very excited working over all the sets." Of course she had to change a great deal of the action to fit them, instead of the other way around. The costumes likewise demanded changes in the movement. They had been made by Barbara Karinska in New York and were consequently much more expensive than the things Irène Karinska made for her in Paris. So she decided to save money by making the shawls herself. To that end she bought up all the lace curtains she could find, sewed them together, dyed them—and "had a hard time teaching the girls to use them. But in the end they looked stunning, so maybe it was worth all the work." Early in the action she discarded the tutus Remisoff had designed, and for the finale she dug out the old costumes for *The Bells*; it would be interesting to know how Remisoff felt about these emendations, if he ever saw them.

As for the ballet itself, it "really began to come to life with Mlakar, my dream of a 'Carmen', Kriza just exactly right as José, and Klekovic an angel as Micaela."

Melissa was not supposed to arrive in Chicago until after her performance with the New York City Ballet on Tuesday, and Ruth accordingly set aside all of Wednesday to concentrate on *Camille*. But Wednesday morning Melissa phoned from New York that she could not get there until late in the day, which threw the already tight schedule into disarray. "When she finally arrived, she didn't know her roles *at all*, and couldn't remember anything. She is a very interesting girl and I very much enjoyed having her stay with us. But she was tired and worried about her roles, and rightly so. I couldn't give her my undivided attention because I had the packing of the costumes to attend to and all the millions of details for the tour. I would sell my soul for an efficient wardrobe woman!"

To cap the climax, "my faithful Bill Maloney broke two bones in his foot and couldn't go on the tour." Nobody knew his roles, for he had never missed a performance or a rehearsal, so at this eleventh hour she had to try out more boys and get them into shape. In desperation she sought out Bentley, who was planning to skip this tour altogether, and somehow persuaded him to help solve the casting dilemma by coming along again as guest artist, at least for the time being.

In spite of the prevailing chaos, the company arrived in Dubuque in time actually to have a dress rehearsal onstage at Clarke College.

> Sister Xavier supervised everything. She was practically having a nervous breakdown at the monetary demands of the stage hands' union. She worked with us from 8 a.m. to 8 p.m. and she admitted to being exhausted. I told her she should have a union and she replied "I have a union of my own," and looked heavenward. It was so lovely. . . . The sisters invited us to dinner and we were looking forward to talking to them, but when we arrived there were places set for only two, so Tom and I were served by the nuns and each one as they passed the food would discuss things with us.

> Time for the première *finally* arrived and Carmen unfolded before my eyes and practically everything seemed to be just right. It was really thrilling. It is not at all a chichi spectacular production like Roland Petit's, but it is truer to Carmen. It seemed to me simple, effective and moving.

It was only a happy interlude, however, in a still tumultuous situation, for it took a little time for the repertoire to shake down.

One of the designs for *El Amor Brujo* by Georges Wakhevitch. (*Frank Derbas*)

A set for *Revanche* by Antoni Clavé, 1951. (*Frank Derbas*)

One of Leonor Fini's designs for *The Triumph of Chastity*.

A design for *Fledermaus* by André Delfau. (*Frank Derbas*)

Mephistophela, with designs by André Delfau. (*Frank Derbas*)

Guns and Castanets, Federal Theatre production, Chicago, 1938.
(*Minni Photo by Candid Illustrations*)

A design by Nicolas Remisoff for a 1959 production. (*Frank Derbas*)

A 1961 production with designs by Bernard Daydé. (*Frank Derbas*)

THE FOUR *CARMENS*

Two of the many costume designs by André Delfau for the Caribbean version created by Ruth in 1972 for the Dance Theatre of Harlem. (*Frank Derbas*)

Sketch of Ruth by Noguchi. (*Frank Derbas*)

Some Postscripts from the Future and a
Coup or Two

The 1961 tour was to have two new ballets and, most importantly, a new designer, who stepped in on short notice and, like the man who came to dinner, remained as a quasi-permanent fixture in the artistic household. His name was André Delfau, and Ruth found him quite by accident in a crisis.

The larger of the two new works for the coming season was to be *Die Fledermaus*, musically arranged by Van Grove and with settings and costumes by Rolf Gérard. Late in June, however, Gérard found at the last minute that he was unable to take on the job. It was Irène Karinska who met Ruth's panic by suggesting Delfau as a replacement.

Ruth had never heard of him, which was surprising, since she had always heard of everybody; but she got in touch with him at once and was much impressed. Before long he was ensconced at Herbe Folle, working on both *Fledermaus* and the other new number for the coming season, a small piece called *Concertino pour Trois* (later renamed *Three's a Crowd*) composed for her by Marius Constant at St. Tropez. It entailed the designing of only three costumes.

Because he was to become a vital part of the organization, it may be worthwhile to step out of sequence and record at once Ruth's summation of him in a little sketch she wrote after twelve years of working with him:

> He is completely sufficient unto himself. He does not need you, or me, or anybody, or anything. His private life is very private. He reads everything, except newspapers and magazines. He eats a Cordon Bleu meal with great pleasure, but he is equally content on a monk's diet. He drinks very little and he adores sweets; he likes to nibble candy all day and he is never hungry. We had a long wait for something or other one day, and just to make conversation I asked him what he had had for lunch. (He told me he had been to a very interesting, charming party.) "I don't know," he said. "How can you be interested in such a subject? It makes no difference." Of course he is a person who does not give parties and doesn't understand the difficulty of making menus.

> He once told an English secretary of mine who was annoying him, "You are middle class," and this was the biggest insult he could imagine. He is maybe too refined; he is also antisocial, and yet if you take him to a party he makes a real effort to be entertaining and always is. I enjoy his company tremendously and so do most of my friends.

> He knows exactly what he likes in art and the theatre, and, like the critics, he thinks he is always right. I usually agree with him—but sometimes not. I adore Ashton's choreography tremendously. André thinks he and the whole British Royal Ballet are a bloody bore. He loves New York and London and Bombay, but mostly he hates all big cities and modern life. He likes exotic places like Polynesia, Easter Island, Bali and Morocco. These places seem to inspire him.

I find him an excellent collaborator. He listens carefully to your ideas and then adds his own, to be accepted or not accepted. He is a good critic and I always listen to what he has to say—almost always. If you really took his advice all the time you would do nothing. He naturally does not like compromise and unfortunately it is rare in the United States that you don't have to compromise.

We have a great deal in common—we laugh at the same things, we are not ambitious or pushing, we like blacks and exotic races, and we tend to leave the world alone and go our own sweet way. His talent has not been sufficiently appreciated, although he has done scenery and costumes for a great many companies.

I love to go shopping with him, as he has an eye for finding lovely things even in a pile of garbage. He leads by preference a lonely but reflective life, and one of these days he will probably just disappear without any fuss.

What she does not record is that he can be so upset by noncomprehension or disapproval of his work (as, for example, when dancers start tearing costumes apart) that he can walk out of a rehearsal and vanish into thin air for days. Also, that when he retreats into one of his exotic haunts, he leaves no address and can be communicated with only by extra-sensory perception.

The 1961 season had a number of casting changes to contend with. Melissa Hayden returned for a second season, but because of her obligations to the New York City Ballet she could not join the company until its second week. Maria Tallchief most accommodatingly replaced her in *Camille* for the opening week, after which she in turn was required for the opening of Ballet Theatre, of which she was a member. "I had never seen Maria in a role anything like Camille," wrote Ruth, "and I thought she was wonderful."

Neither Mlakar nor Kriza returned. (At last Kenneth stepped into the role of Armand which he had worked at so hard in its creative stages and which he danced really better than either of his predecessors.) To make up for some of these defections Arova was back in the fold for the first half of the tour. Her return was in no way surprising, for Ruth, in spite of everything, had the greatest admiration for her as an artist and very much enjoyed her as a person. Sanders, of course, was among the missing. Her partner this time was Milorad Miskovitch, a Paris celebrity from Yugoslavia. He also brought along the prima ballerina of his own small European company, the Brazilian-born Yvonne Meyer.

Then in mid-season Melissa discovered that she was pregnant and departed amid management suspicions that she had simply invented the whole thing as a device for getting out of her contract. Nature in due course proved otherwise and the ill feeling ultimately disappeared. In a summer or two Melissa, with her husband, visited Herbe Folle and cooked marvelous fried chicken—five of them, as a matter of fact, for a party—and Ruth wrote in her notes, as if nothing unpleasant had ever happened, that of all the ballerinas, she had always liked her the best personally. It is not so clear how she felt when Meyer also left the company with Melissa's complaint; pregnancy is apparently endemic to ballet companies.

As far as the repertoire was concerned, she found herself facing a new problem. The *Carmen*, which she had liked so much choreographically last season when it was new, had proved extremely troublesome because of the necessarily rapid costume changes and the difficulties of packing and transporting the scenery. But there were new and less physical objections, which were more disturbing. When the ballet had made its debut in Dubuque, she had found it "simple, effective and moving" and "not at all a chichi spectacular production like Roland Petit's." Since Petit's production, however, had been designed by Clavé, her "idol," it was certainly not he she was criticizing. The work had just now been revived, after ten years, by Petit himself for the Royal Danish Ballet. Can she have felt that by comparison her beloved and indispensable Remisoff was just a bit old hat, and that she must meet Petit's competition with something more piquant? Certainly she had no intention of abandoning the work itself, which she valued highly, but just as certainly she felt the need for a new production, perhaps to shift the balance of smartness in her own favor.

Delfau had not yet assumed in her mind the aspect of permanence that was soon to attach to him, and for the last time she turned to somebody else. This was Bernard Daydé, one of the most striking designers of the French avant-garde. In March, accordingly, before the tour was over, she wrote to him in Paris:

> I think we have a marvelous Carmen, but frankly I am not satisfied with the scenery and costumes. They are in very good taste and *very* artistic but not daring enough, and they are too complicated for traveling. I have twenty-six dancers (including principals) so we have to do a lot of fast changing. . . . After Clavé's wonderfully imaginative scenery and costumes, I feel that it is better to go in the opposite direction and be startlingly simple and modern. We travel by bus, and scenery should be only simple set pieces that pack easily and take up very little space. We have black curtains or blue. . . .

Late in April he replied. He had talked to Arova and learned about the way they traveled and the kind of places they performed in. The problem did not seem too difficult to him, since he had already made décors for Miskovitch and Béjart and others that would all but fit into a suitcase. But if he was to put the least possible on the stage, it must also be the best possible, and he would have to do it himself, not from any advance sketches, but on the spot. He would do it over fifty times if necessary, but he must go to Chicago for a week and work with the actual set in place.

Thus a virtually new *Carmen* was born, up-to-the-minute and perhaps a bit more, both visually and stylistically, while remaining, except for minor editing, exactly the same choreographically. It was the only new production on the 1962 tour. Not that others were needed, as it developed, for things were to take a far more newsworthy turn than any new work could have provided.

For the first half of the season the guest stars were Josette Amiel and Flemming Flindt, both *étoiles* of the Opéra, and Arova came back for the second half. Flindt was a product of the Royal Danish Ballet who had taken advantage of the privilege accorded to all the soloists of that organization of leaving Copenhagen for long periods to dance with other companies while still retaining their Danish franchises, so to speak. He was the first of the Danes to appear in Ruth's company and accordingly the first to bring into the repertoire an excerpt from one of the famous Bournonville ballets. This was the pas de deux from *The Flower Festival at Genzano.*

CAPTURING A COMET

About the end of January, with the customary seasonal procedures of touring underway, Ruth cut across routine with a startling coup; she grabbed the newly anointed *dieu de la danse*, Rudolf Nureyev, for his American debut in a single performance with her company.

Only about six months before, in June 1961, he had defected dramatically in Paris from Leningrad's Kirov Ballet at the beginning of its first tour of the Western world. This was a defection not entirely of his own choosing. He had made all plans to depart for London with the company at the end of the Paris engagement as scheduled and discovered only at the airport that he was to be put instead onto another plane and sent back to Leningrad because of official disapproval of his social behavior in Paris. With undeniable flair, indeed, he had violated all the Soviet regulations for traveling artists. The probabilities are strong that he was planning to defect, but not until the company got to New York. In conversation with some Americans in Paris he had exhibited an intense interest in Balanchine, whose work he had never seen but whose reputation was surprisingly familiar to him. His questionings were persistent to the point of unmannerliness. However little conception he had of Balanchine's artistic procedures, he was clearly eager to find out about them at first hand, and if possible as a member of his company.

Ruth met him for the first time shortly afterward at the international dance festival at Nervi, where he had gone with Margot Fonteyn. He had been dancing since the great *scandale* chiefly with Rosella Hightower in the company of the Marquis de Cuevas, and now Margot had invited him to make his London debut, also with Rosella, in October at the annual gala of the Royal Academy of Dancing, of which she was president. Whether or not this was what suggested to Ruth the idea of inviting him to make a similar debut in New York under her auspices, that was exactly what happened, and Tom, with his customary zeal and ingenuity, managed by the end of the year to get all the complex arrangements signed and sealed.

On March 10, 1962, accordingly, Nureyev appeared with Ruth Page's Chicago Opera Ballet, dancing the *Don Quixote* pas de deux with Arova on the company's already scheduled program at the Brooklyn Academy of Music. *Le tout New York* was there, Brooklyn or no Brooklyn, and not since the early days of Frank Sinatra had there been such swooning in the aisles. This was not just because of his brilliant technique and ballon. There were, as a matter of fact, half a dozen other premiers danseurs in the audience who could, and often did, dance the number just as well and sometimes more stylishly. It was simply as Ruth said: "His sheer animal magnetism swept us off our feet." He had shown himself, indeed, to be, roughly speaking, the Brigitte Bardot of his medium.

"That was a very strange night," Ruth wrote reminiscently. "He and Sonia Arova danced the old chestnut from 'Don Quixote', but they did it so brilliantly that one forgave him for his choice of 'pas de deux'. My spotlight man was ill, so I had to spend the entire evening at the top of the balcony directing a new operator. One of my star dancers, also, was ill and couldn't dance and there had to be a couple of changes for the corps. But it couldn't have mattered less, as everyone had come only to see Rudy. Arova danced just as brilliantly as he did but virtually no one even knew she was there. . . . Rudy is not particularly prepossessing. His legs are short (I will never understand how he is able to partner tall girls so skillfully), and he is not good-looking in the conventional sense." None of which, of course, made any difference.

Perhaps the "strangest" thing about the whole evening, however, was the smallness of his fee; "he was paid $500 for the performance" in addition to plane fare both ways. Tom and Columbia tried their best to engage a Broadway theatre for a second performance, which they had under option, but there was no place available, and consequently the only other appearance he made in the country was on the Ed Sullivan TV show.

But the year was yet young. Before Ruth left for St. Tropez, arrangements had been made with the Lyric Opera for a gala all-dance performance in October, and at the same time for his and Arova's appearance with the opera company in the Polovetsian dance scene in the four already scheduled presentations of Borodin's *Prince Igor*, with Boris Christoff singing the title role.

In May Ruth wrote to Arova, making plans to get together if possible with her and Nureyev to work on *Prince Igor* during the summer. "I know the Fokine version," she wrote, "but it should be 'fancied up' for the two of you. What version does Rudy do, and has he danced it in Russia?"

When the events materialized in the autumn, they were sensationally successful. In the gala the two of them danced Ruth's *Merry Widow* and the pas de deux from Bournonville's *Flower Festival at Genzano*. The role of Danilo offered Nureyev no opportunity at all for his spectacular aeriality; nevertheless it was he who walked away with the show, in spite of Arova's already well-established gifts of personality and her general excellence in what was legitimately the stellar role.

He had learned the *Flower Festival* pas de deux from his colleague and, by now, devoted friend, Erik Bruhn. Like most of the Bournonville pas de deux, this one offered more brilliant opportunities for the man than for the girl, since in Bournonville's approach the ballerina was always treated as the modest maiden (she was, indeed, rarely even on point), while her partner, like the traditionally dominating male, exhibited his skills and prowess by way of courtship. Nureyev, of course, danced it to the hilt.

But "he didn't like the costume [which was the one Ruth had 'inherited' from Flemming Flindt] and he started to throw it out the window into the river. [The Civic Opera House on Wacker Drive backs on the Chicago River.] I grabbed it just in time, and while I saw to it that he got a costume that pleased him, I certainly didn't see any point in throwing Flemming's excellent costume into the river. . . . The only other time I ever saw a costume being treated so rudely was when I was with the Champs-Elysées Ballet in Paris, and Violette Verdy's mother tore up a costume so that her daughter would not have to wear it. I often wonder what would happen to a dancer in Russia if he started destroying costumes, and some of them really should be destroyed!"

As for *Prince Igor*, she need not have worried about fancying it up; Nureyev could be counted on for that. In the Allied Arts days she herself had danced the Polovetsian girl with Adolph Bolm, who had created the leading male role fifty years earlier in Fokine's original production of the work, but since she was not familiar with the important ensemble choreography except in a general way, she took infinite pains to learn it from the best available sources. "Enrique Martinez came to Chicago for a week and showed us exactly Fokine's version, and Tommy Armour very kindly sent us all his notes." The stage was too small to accommodate more than twelve boys, and she put one of her girls, Dolores Lipinski, into the role of "the wild Polovetsian boy," because she knew she would dance it brilliantly and authentically. Nureyev, true to form, did much as he pleased with Bolm's old role. He had no qualms at all about disregarding Fokine and substituting "more spectacularly athletic steps. . . . His animal quality as usual reached across the footlights as he jumped higher and higher. My only criticism was that he stopped between his great leaps to get his breath, and I don't think Fokine would have approved of that." He also "had his costume cut back so that his middle was bare."

He stayed with Ruth and Tom during the rehearsals and the perform-ances, and she pronounced him "one of the easiest house guests I have ever had. As long as he got a steak, plenty of tea, a little whiskey, a massage, a chess game [with Tom] and a telephone to call Erik in Australia, he was very undemanding. His telephone bill was over $1000, which he paid immediately!"

MORE RETROSPECTION ON THINGS TO COME

But for the intervention of what is sometimes irreverently called an "act of God," the history-making *Nutcracker* would have gone into rehearsal just about now. Tom had already been negotiating with Nureyev and Arova for its forthcoming Christmas week, which, as it turned out, never forthcame. That it did not materialize as scheduled, however, did not prevent its elaborate preparations from constituting a large part of the year's activity.

As a project it had first come into consideration as long ago as the middle fifties, when Ruth and Tom met Edward G. Lee at the home of their friend Arnold Maremont, who thought they should know each other for more than social reasons. Lee had been brought to Chicago to be the director of McCormick Place, a huge, virtually inaccessible structure on the near South Side, which was a combination of convention hall and supermarket of industrial displays, with the usual variety of incidental eating places. An enormous barnlike auditorium, called the Arie Crown Theatre, was designed hopefully for performances, if any could be found with dimensions large enough to establish contact with an audience either visually or acoustically.

Ruth was impressed with Lee straightway as "an extraordinary man— powerful and sympathetic at the same time." He had had a great deal of experience in the "performing arts" but had got out some time ago because of the financial stresses and personality clashes that made it such a harum-scarum world. How he was induced to go back into it is a question only he could have answered, but the inherent stability of a large Chicago enterprise with the name of McCormick and the challenge of an entirely new set of problems may have had something to do with it.

Certainly one of the least responsive of these problems was proving to be how to find attractions to put into the big auditorium that would not be preordained flops. Everything, including rock concerts and "black" shows, had failed pretty consistently to fill the house. Trust Ruth to bring up the subject of the ballet. Not that it had not already been tried, along with all sorts of other normal-theatre-sized performing arts, but Ruth thought that it might be an excellent idea nevertheless to put on an annual Christmas season of the full-length *Nutcracker* with hordes of children in the cast. Balanchine had done just that in 1954 at the New York City Center with great success. So great, indeed, that it packed the house for a month or so every year and was to become a quasi-perpetual institution.

Somehow the idea hit home with Lee. But it was obviously an expensive project and a far more difficult one to organize than Balanchine's, since it lacked his established company with its successful school and its loyal audience. In fact, it took some five or six years for the Chicago enterprise, starting from scratch, to get all its disparate elements integrated sufficiently to settle on Christmas 1962 as the time to start the annual performances.

From the beginning it was understood that Lee, in the name of McCormick Place, would be responsible for the financing and the sponsorship. He also wanted the designing of the scenery to go to Sam Leve, the New York designer, who he knew from experience would be able to handle the large and unwieldy theatre. Ruth, who was to cast, choreograph and direct the production, chose Rolf Gérard, on the basis of his *Merry Widow* achievement, to do the costumes. Just about the time when all the sketches by both artists were finished and ready for execution, Lee discovered that he had throat cancer and removed himself promptly from the scene. The project was of necessity abandoned in this very autumn of 1962.

Nobody could have dreamed that two years later Lee would have recovered and taken up just where he had left off and that by Christmas 1965 *The Nutcracker* would become exactly what they had planned it to be. Or did Ruth still cherish an unreasoning hope? Certainly late this very September she wrote to Chujoy of *Dance News* that though the production would not go on as scheduled, Gérard had provided the costume sketches and McCormick Place had paid for them, and she felt that ultimately they would use them.

But for all practical purposes *The Nutcracker* had simply joined the ranks of *Salome* and *The Last Judgment* and *Soirée de Boston* and the other cherished works that would never be done. And she transferred all her concentration to her coming spring tour.

This year there were to be two new productions. The smaller one was a "ballet bouffe" called *Pygmalion*, with music adapted by Van Grove from Franz von Suppé's operetta *Die Schöne Galatea*. It involved only three dancers in addition to the sculptured figure of Galatea and various isolated torsos, legs, arms and heads floating above in space, alone or in amusingly related groups. ("Klekovic was a lovely Galatea, Kenneth her perfect partner, and Orrin, an excellent comedian, was truly funny as the sculptor's assistant.")

The other ballet was considerably more ambitious. It grew out of Ruth's reading of a libretto written in 1847 by Heinrich Heine for Benjamin Lumley, director of Her Majesty's Theatre in London. Walter Sorrell had dug it up and *Dance Magazine* had published it under the title of *Dr. Faustus, a dance poem*.

The devil in the story was not the conventional Mephistopheles but a woman, which of course was what awakened Ruth's interest. The work had never been produced, even by so temerarious an impresario as Lumley. "The transformations were too complicated even for those days," Ruth wrote of it.

"Witches had to change themselves into coryphées, the devil with her wand changed everything in the room, and at the end of the ballet she changed herself into a snake, and all in front of the eyes of the audience."

She was fascinated by it, however, and sent a copy of it to Van Grove for his advice and collaboration. What they worked out together Heine might not have recognized as anything more than a mild plagiarism, but it was almost equally unproduceable on the gymnasium floors and in the high school auditoriums where it was presented. It was now entitled *Mephistophela*, and Van Grove had conceived the idea of using music from the three nineteenth-century operas that had been written on the Faust theme: *The Damnation of Faust* by Berlioz, the *Mefistofele* of Boïto and Gounod's *Faust*.

If she had suffered agonies over the way her ballets had been mauled and manhandled in inadequate theatres, it is no wonder that this one, with its added mechanical and electrical requirements, should have compelled her in self-defense to take it out of the repertory after two seasons of sheer torture.

The imported guest stars this year were again of Royal Danish Ballet origin, but this time not by way of the Paris Opéra but directly from the Royal Theatre in Copenhagen. They were Kirsten Simone and Henning Kronstam, who proved themselves to be so excellent in *The Merry Widow* (among other things) as to make it virtually their own. Pas de deux, both Danish and "standard," were now a regular feature of the programs. This was partly because visiting stars knew them and did not require rehearsal time for them and partly because provincial audiences were coming more and more to prefer the decorative acrobatics of the pas de deux to anything more demanding on their background and attention.

As usual at the end of a tour Ruth was reediting the new works before she forgot what she wanted to change for future use and digging into next year's novelties. At these periods St. Tropez loomed ahead as a haven of refuge. Generally speaking, the prime function of that delightful place was to cater to the social rather than the creative man, though, in all conscience, she did plenty of creating there. But this time what it had to offer was quite outside the customary giddy and diversionary pastimes and struck a more deeply social note. Clavé, indeed, had bought land a hundred yards down the road from them and was building himself a house—not just a vacationing place but a home.

Several summers earlier, when he and Madeleine had spent August at Herbe Folle after Ruth and Tom had departed for the season, he had fallen in love with the Cap St. Pierre. Now his mother had died, and with Madeleine and Maria Nieves as his family he was turning his back on the chichi world of the Paris theatre, which he did not like, and setting himself up in a place where he could devote himself exclusively to his painting. He had designed a

large Spanish house overlooking the bay with two studios where he could
work all winter and a swimming pool for the summer, so that there would be
no occasion for him ever to go back to the little house in the Rue Chatillon.

A year or two later, after the house had achieved permanence, Ruth was
to write of it: "He almost bends over backwards to have simple friends in all
walks of life. He loves to entertain them with Maria Nieves' long Spanish
meals, sometimes with fish caught in the bay by Madeleine and Maria Nieves
in his boat (named Maria after his mother). . . . Sometimes I wonder what
effect this rather bourgeois life will have on his art. He seems almost too
comfortable in it." But she reassured herself by the uncomfortable fact that
"his nerves keep him from sleeping and he still suffers. And don't all artists
have to suffer?"

But that was a year or two later; as yet she had not even seen the place.

Thunder on the Left

For those who go in for post-hoc mysticism, with signs and portents and the
esoterica of numbers, the stage was prophetically set at St. Tropez to mark a
critical moment. The ballet company had completed seven tours and, though
nobody knew it, was to make exactly seven more before disbanding. As if to
give premonitory emphasis to such a foreordination, the intervening winter
had come up with a mistral that brought the sea's water over the rocks and
the roadway and into the studio, wrecking the precious dancing floor. Ruth
and Tom got to Herbe Folle late in June, tired out by several hectic days in
Paris, and were gratified that their good Mme. Borget had aired out the house
and had luncheon waiting for them. But the studio "was a wild mess—the
floor . . . all hills and valleys and ruined for dancing. Je suis désolée!"

As in any good theatre piece with undertones of tragedy, however, the
summer was to be on its surface a farcical madhouse with touches that only
Feydeau could have written. Visitors, as usual, scarcely waited for their hosts
to unpack before they began to barge in, and wonderful hosts that they were,
they offered hearty and genuine welcome in spite of fatigue and household
disasters.

They had been there only overnight when Jeanne Armin, one of Ruth's
best dancers, phoned from Paris that she wanted to bring down her latest
boy friend to audition for the company. They would take the night train and
arrive at St. Raphaël at 9:30 in the morning, but Ruth and Tom, good hosts
or bad, were too weary to drive over there to meet them. Which was just as
well, since they missed the train. When they finally arrived later, they had
had neither sleep nor breakfast, and auditioning was momentarily out of the

question. The obvious solution was to stay overnight, but Jeanne calmly announced that she had the German measles, and since Melissa Hayden and her husband were due to occupy the guest room the next night and could not be exposed to such a contagious disease, the young dancers, after an approximation of a tryout and some characteristic Fisher hospitality, were politely carted over to St. Raphaël to take the night train back to Paris.

The next day Ruth and Tom drove to Cannes to meet Melissa and her husband, and their weekend started right there; it continued with sight-seeing and entertainings of all sorts and ended with Melissa's memorable fried-chicken supper for the assembled guests at Herbe Folle. With the common urgency of all ballerinas she and Ruth "practiced" daily on the wretched floor, on which, however, "no one can dance full out without breaking a foot." Milly "gave the barre" and Ruth "the middle. But we can't do too much on the very risky floor."

It was a summer, however, in which "much" had to be done, though the floor ran through it all like a bad cold in the head. She had new productions of both the *Faust* and the *Tannhäuser* ballets for the opera to discuss with directors and designers, in addition to a new ballet of her own—a musically difficult one called *Combinations*, which she had been working out on the company very diligently in Chicago for quite a while. All of them, of course, eventually involved Delfau, who had thus far done nothing for the opera.

Then, as a contrapuntal theme, there was her young nephew, Christopher Page, who phoned her from London that he had a "classic" MG a dozen or so years old in which he would drop in on her at an unspecified date on his one-man tour of Europe. He arrived for the first time the day after Melissa left, in the midst of an afternoon tea party in the courtyard which involved some of St. Tropez's most eccentric characters. He was an engaging twenty-two-year-old, way-out innocent who was to continue to pop in and out, sleeping perforce on a couch in the living room since the only guest room was inhabited by either Delfau or a sequence of quotidian itinerants who occupied it on what might be called an end-to-end basis. This time he brought with him a German boy on a hitchhiking trip to Italy, whom he had taken on at Aix; on a later visit he appeared with an unshake-off-able French-Greek girl whose hitchhiking had no apparent goal but him. Soon his things were strewn all over the studio wherever a dry spot emerged from the mildew. He had "about two words of French" at his command, but he got along wonderfully with everybody and thoroughly enjoyed himself.

Water, as if it had not already done enough, also supplied a nerve-racking background of noise, for Clavé was having a well dug for his new house. It was all but literally right under Ruth's bedroom window. The workmen arrived at 7:30 and kept at it continuously except for their lunch break, which came at the time when the household at Herbe Folle always went to the beach.

As soon as there was a moment between guests, Ruth and Tom, urged on especially by the flood in the studio, went to visit madame the peasant who owned the building, for their ten-year lease had only one more year to run. "It is a most complicated situation," Ruth wrote. "Her son who is just married and has a two-weeks-old baby [*sic*], wants to live in the empty room over the studio and use my studio for his camion. If they do this, my pleasure in St. Tropez is finished and I don't want to come back. We talked to them about two hours" while Madame was cleaning fish. "She is a fascinating character right out of Marcel Pagnol. I did my best to make friends with them! So we'll see."

Delfau she summoned from Paris to help her solve the problems of the *Faust* costumes. The director whom Carol Fox had engaged to make the new $30,000 production had come down from Paris presumably to show her the sketches, but all he brought was a few ideas that were themselves on the sketchy side. He was planning to take them to an economical costume maker in Milan, who would presumably be able to whip up a little something that would do. Ruth, with her devotion to costumes, was distressed at the thought of such procedure, and doubly so since her opinion of the Milan costumer was not very high. Accordingly she and Delfau did their own "sketches" and sent them along to Milan, where in due course Delfau would follow them to see that they got under way.

The *Tannhäuser* costumes they determined to make themselves, for Carol Fox had budgeted them at only $20 per costume. Of course visitors continued to drop in, but between all the luncheons and dinners the two of them managed to work on both the designs for *Combinations* and the execution of the Venusberg costumes. For the latter they bought materials at Toulon and Cannes, and "we draped thirteen costumes on me and I pinned and sewed them together. Quite a job but lots of fun. It took hours."

Delfau was scheduled to go to Milan on the last Sunday in July, and Tom accordingly bought him a ticket. But on Saturday "he was sulking about something or other and wouldn't work on the costumes or do anything. He scarcely even spoke to anybody." He said he was sick and soon he simply disappeared for the day. What was actually wrong was that he felt they were trying to get rid of him by sending him to Milan, whereas they were simply expecting him to go in the natural course of events, which was not quite the same thing.

On the strength of that perfectly routine expectation, they were preparing for a visit from Kurt Weinhold of Columbia Artists and his wife, who were in Europe and had been invited to stop over during Delfau's absence on their way from Paris on Sunday night. Ruth spent all Saturday afternoon taking personal belongings out of their bedroom and moving them into the guest room, so that Kurt and Liz could have the larger and more comfortable room after their long motor trip. Delfau was not scheduled to go until early the next day, so all his things were still in the guest room, which was "a wild mess," and it was perhaps not altogether surprising that he felt de trop. The studio was "an even wilder mess, with all of Christopher's things [Christopher too was fortunately scheduled to leave the next morning], plus all the costumes that Delfau and I are making for 'Tannhäuser', plus the wavy floor and a rowboat to cover the most dangerous spots."

She had been in touch with the Milan costumer by phone, and this afternoon she called him again to remind him of Delfau's scheduled arrival the next day. But he protested that it would be useless for Delfau to come until later in the week, since he had no time to give him at the moment and, much to her surprise, did not intend in any case to start making the costumes until September.

"We couldn't find Delfau anywhere so we went to the port and canceled his ticket. He can't do anything practical for himself. When he finally turned up and heard the good news, he confessed that he thought we were trying to get him out of the house. Well, certainly with the Weinholds arriving it was most inconvenient having him here too. But finally we let him stay in the guest room and Tom and I spent two nights at Clavé's. We didn't want Kurt and Liz to know we were giving up our room for them and we wanted them to think Delfau was sleeping in the studio, so we had to go through a lot of complicated planning. It was really terribly funny. I think Liz and Kurt probably thought the three of us were sleeping in the small double bed in the guest room. The Clavés have no screens and I was kept awake all night with mosquitoes. But I got up a lot and walked around on their terrace and this was really so inspiring—the view in the moonlight and the soft air and the peace is something I will never forget. The noise in the daytime is absolutely infernal."

Sunday was full of traipsing about and partying and ended with "a delicious 'loup' dinner at Mouscardin's, and home about midnight. Delfau didn't seem sick at all after he found he didn't have to go to Milan right away." The next morning Ruth and Tom "slipped out of Clavé's house at 7 a.m. and managed to get to Herbe Folle just before Kurt and Liz got up. André was still sleeping in the guest room but we tiptoed in. We talked with Kurt and Liz during breakfast and they left at 9:30. . . . We had a marvelous weekend with them and I think Delfau enjoyed it too."

As for the floor, it was Nureyev who finally gave it the coup de grâce. He and Erik Bruhn were driving down to Monte Carlo, where Nureyev had bought a $69,000 house "with three and a half bathrooms and a chauffeur's room with bath. . . . Rudy had a funny striped hat on that made him look more St. Tropez than the Tropezians." They were driving in a small open car and "the Tropezians at the port recognized Rudy right away shouting his name and following the car" but no one noticed "the unsensational Danish star" in spite of the fact that he is "usually considered the top male dancer of Europe."

She showed them the studio and they sat in the middle of it in the rowboat. There were even a few mushrooms growing out of the floor, and "we were all laughing at our plight. Rudy wanted to practice but with his first leaps the floor caved in and he finally had to give up." It was afternoon when they arrived and she thought they probably wanted to stay overnight, but there was not a bed available anywhere, since both Delfau and Christopher were back. "Anyway I think our place is much too simple for Rudy." Furthermore, she and Tom and Delfau and Christopher were all going to Aix to hear *Idomeneo* and had to drive as fast as they dared to get there on time.

When the day finally came for Delfau to go to Milan, they took him to the airport at Cannes, "which gave us an excuse to go on to Monte Carlo where Margot Fonteyn was dancing. En route "we stopped at La Turbie to see Rudy Nureyev's house. *What* does he want with a grand villa like that? A capitalist at heart!

"The last days at St. Tropez were absolutely mad. We put everything both from the house and the studio into our tiny little guest room, so that some major surgery can be made both on the house and studio. The studio has to have an entire new floor, be repainted etc., etc., and for the house we plan a new bedroom underneath a tower, a new bathroom off our room etc., etc.

"We had to make three more trips to see the owner of the studio. She absolutely will not sell and she absolutely will not let us have the upstairs but she finally agreed to give us a ten-year lease on the downstairs. She wouldn't tell us at what price and gave us nothing in writing; however, her 'word' is said to be as good as a contract—we'll see!

"Clavé got a mason from Grimault to come to see us and we made a trip to Grimault to see him. But of course no 'devis' from him. If he does anything for us at all it will be only because Clavé will be there to egg him on! Anyway, we're hoping for lots of improvements next year."

In Paris before enplaning there were: first, the usual socializings. ("We took Sonia Arova and the Clinton Kings to dinner at a pretty park with a little lake where I had never been. We had a fairly good dinner and lots of fun. I just couldn't afford to take Sonia [into the company] this year and I will certainly miss her."); second, the usual auditionings. ("Two Canadian dancers, Mr. and Mrs. David Holmes, came from London to audition for me. They have just spent three years in Leningrad. They said the school was marvelous—also the ballet company, but they *hated* life in Russia."); and third, the usual shoppings. ("This a.m. to St. Laurent's and picked two dresses—one suit and one cocktail dress—very expensive and I hope they will turn out okay without *any* fittings. Just had time to stop at Vivier's for a pair of shoes, pack and get to the airport. We made it and no overweight! Tom is absolutely marvelous in picking my clothes—he is so interested and unbelievably helpful!")

MONEY, MONEY, MONEY

On the bright side of things back in Chicago her good friend Yvonne Payerimhoff from St. Laurent's, who had a summer home in St. Tropez, came to New York and Chicago on a business trip, bringing with her as scheduled the dresses bought in Paris without a fitting, and they were perfect.

By that time the apparel situation was in need of a bright side, for when the *Faust* costumes arrived from Milan in late September, "they could not have been made more poorly and were impossible to dance in," so that much of the limited rehearsal time was spent in trying to fix them up. Delfau's idea of having Mephistopheles conjure up "an imaginary court scene with stylized fifteenth-century costumes, made very nudish," was a fine one, but for the men's costumes he needed fur, which the budget did not provide for. Carol Fox came up with the brilliant scheme of asking some of the opera's guarantors to contribute their old fur coats, and they gladly complied. But none of the coats ever made a stage debut, for they were commandeered by the wardrobe women and the dancers, while the dancing men disported themselves in the cheapest fur that could be bought. Nevertheless the scene worked marvelously, though the music critics, who "actually know nothing about style," panned it along with the rest of the production.

It was apparently an inauspicious season for operatic bacchanalia, for the Venusberg scene in *Tannhäuser* she feared would not go down in history as one of her proudest creations. The space was so small between platforms that there was no room to dance. This was made no easier by her own decision that somehow "Three Graces didn't seem to be enough," whereupon she added six more, replacing, as it were, the Graces by the Muses. The stage was so darkly lit by the director in an effort to hide the hideousness of the old scenery that the dancers were barely visible, and the dress rehearsal was thoroughly discouraging. But in spite of everything, that night "the final result was superb. The floating veils were lovely, the swift running, the high lifts—the general effect was stunning. The Three Graces were very dignified, and I finally got them to dance together." All nine of them, presumably.

So much for the traditional ups and downs of contemporary opera ballet; the equally familiar financial difficulties were becoming ominously greater, not only ruling out any possibility of increased activity but even threatening the modest artistic standards that prevailed. Ruth, who had long been a curious combination of Calamity Jane and Pollyanna, was now adding the more heroic despair of Cassandra, sensing an inexorable inching of the situation toward the area of questionable survival, without being able to do anything about it. Not that she had any intention of accepting such a situation and yielding to fate; she would continue to exercise her wits, her social graces and her deep commitment, if not upon the gods themselves, at least upon those who administered for them.

As long ago as the previous May, after her 1963 tour she had invited Carol Fox (with her husband, Larkin Flanagan), Donati, the musical director; and Chris Mahon, the general stage manager, to dinner to discuss the ballet's desperate state, of which they were markedly less aware than she was. "We really had a delicious Mexican dinner [by this time Felisa had become a pillar of the household in spite of her periodic hoppings off to Mexico] and lots of fun, but actually decided nothing." On the strength of the full ballet evening with Nureyev Carol wanted to do a dance gala, "but she will not do it if it loses *one* cent (they lose $12,000 a night on the opera). It was quite a strenuous evening. Donati, of course, does not say a word as he doesn't speak English, but he is certainly the power behind the throne."

In mid-June she had spent an entire afternoon in Carol's office. "*Nothing* for me is more depressing than an afternoon with the opera directors—no money for the ballet, no ambition for the ballet, no acceptance of ideas for the ballet. I came away almost wishing I could give the whole damn thing up."

Almost . . .

Now, four months later, there came, virtually out of the sky, the possibility of a kind of dance gala that might or might not pay for itself but would in either case be of enormous value in terms of prestige and precedent. After she had had a few days to recover from the première of "the sad production of 'Faust' ", she attended a performance of the Bolshoi Ballet, then giving a season in Chicago, and went backstage to see Simon Semenoff, the former dancer who was now serving Hurok as coordinator and interpretor for the foreign companies he brought to this country. Simon had sent her word that he had good news for her, the gist of which proved to be that he had seen Konstantin Sergeyev, director of the Kirov Ballet in Leningrad, and "he would like to come over to do a full-evening 'Don Quixote' for me. . . . Simon told me exactly how to go about it; he was extraordinary." He was familiar, of course, with the customary Soviet red tape. She followed his instructions and very shortly there came a cable from Sergeyev confirming Semenoff's message and saying that a letter was on the way.

She proceeded at once to entice Carol Fox and her husband by means of another dinner, to try to get the customary private-enterprise red tape rolling. "So now," she noted, "if his letter is satisfactory, we have to go round raising money. I have never been able to ask for money for myself, but maybe I will be able to ask for others. I *hate* the idea."

When the letter arrived and proved to be "satisfactory," she "made an appointment with Van Gorkham, president of our Lyric Opera, at 8:30 a.m. downtown. I got there on time (with difficulty) and he came in soon after. Such a swank modern office, with of course, some large 'modern art' book on the desk. If you have a 'modern' office you have to have modern art around, I suppose. Van Gorkham is an extremely attractive man. He admits knowing nothing about ballet and he apparently has no interest in knowing. I told him my project and I asked him to let me see if I could raise $40,000 for it. He was anything but encouraging. He kept saying 'this is an opera company and not a ballet company.' Well, I went away with all the wind taken out of my sails." The next day she talked for an hour over cocktails with "the opera money raiser and she was much more encouraging than Van Gorkham but she has to have the opera's permission to even try. Doing any serious dancing with Lyric is impossible."

A week or so later at a party in the home of a wealthy patroness of music, she asked her hostess to give some money to the ballet, and "she almost laughed in my face. . . . In any event I won't need help as I just received word from Van Gorkham that we can do *nothing* with the ballet at Lyric. At this point I suppose I should really give up. The Fords have just given millions to Houston, San Francisco, New York, Philadelphia and Boston—and not a cent to Chicago. The competition without money is impossible. There is no point in my trying any more. How I hate to see all my beautiful ballets die."

Money problems were beginning also to worry Columbia Concerts Management. The wolf was not yet scratching at the door, but he had begun to sniff around the keyhole right after that quasi-mystical seventh tour had ended.

A year ago, indeed, when according to annual custom the next tour was under discussion, it had been suggested by the management that the name of the company be changed and all Chicago Opera connotations, which had once given identity to a young company, be dropped. The increasing number of European ballets imported under the government's international exchange program had begun to make the Chicago Opera a provincial liability. It was to offset just such a possibility that Columbia had insisted from the very beginning that European guest stars were essential to proper exploitation. The idea of the change of name met with hearty approval from both Ruth and Tom, and the latter suggested calling the company simply the Ruth Page Ballet, but no decision was reached.

At stake, indeed, was something more than just a change of title; what Columbia really wanted was "a major ballet company like Ballet Theatre."

Unlike the Lyric Opera they wanted not to cut down on scale and costs but to increase them. This Tom could not accept, for the increased costs would fall not upon Columbia, which was primarily the booking agency, but upon the Chicago Ballet Company (alias Ruth and Tom), which owned and produced the repertoire.

But it was inevitable that the subject should arise again, for Columbia was facing a steadily growing competition from the nonprofessional "regional ballet" movement. This had been organized into a kind of unity the very year of Ruth's first tour by Atlanta's distinguished teacher, choreographer, longtime dancer and practical idealist Dorothy Alexander, under the collaborative goading of Anatole Chujoy. In the early forties she had started an Atlanta Civic Ballet School, together with an Atlanta Civic Ballet consisting chiefly of its pupils, which had given periodic performances ever since. Other "civic" ballets began to spring up in various communities along the same lines, and the bringing of them all together in a Regional Ballet Festival in 1956 had spread the movement to still more communities, large and small.

An excellent movement in itself, more or less after the pattern of the many locally based professional companies-*cum*-schools all over Europe, it was unfortunately not foolproof, and it soon gave rise to a widespread practice among individual dancing teachers of claiming for their immemorial annual pupils' recitals the new and more pretentious status of "regional" or "civic" ballet productions. Not many of them, however, were Dorothy Alexanders in either performing or choreographic experience or, for that matter, in talent or altruism. The gimmick seemed like a good one, but actually, instead of uniting the activities of each potential center in truly civic concentrations, it served more frequently to splinter them. In one southern city less than half the size of Atlanta there were at one time fifteen such soi-distant "regional" or "civic" ballet companies, made up entirely of students with the occasional addition of a professional guest artist or guest choreographer. Nothing could have been more injurious to the "image" of the ballet. If only because of its technical requirements, the ballet is an exclusively professional art, and there can really be no such thing as a nonprofessional ballet any more than there can be a nonprofessional surgeon.

None of these dubious activities served to diminish the response of either the public or the press to Ruth's performances; that had been phenomenal from the beginning, even in communities that had to see them in those wretched school auditoriums, gymnasiums and convention halls that broke her heart almost nightly with their built-in distortions of her conceptions. Communities that were so ill-equipped physically, however, could obviously never have seen well-mounted, theatrically viable ballet performances; consequently when (or if) they were persuaded to undertake performances of their own, these might easily have seemed just as satisfactory.

If their dancers could not jump as high or turn as fast "yet," they were "graceful" and, above all, they were their own.

These very communities had originally been developed by the Community Concerts Corporation back in the twenties into a circuit to be catered to according to their specific off-the-main-road status, and they still provided the raison d'être of the tours they had inspired. If the one ballet company per season that they could support was now to be taken over by themselves, what was to become of a professional company that had been created especially for them in terms of their own particular dimensions; that is, population, sophistication, possible fees and so forth? It could not simply be transferred to a different circuit geared to larger attractions; the difference was not essentially qualitative at all but quantitative, so to speak. The only solution seemed to be the transformation of the present small-community company into a "major" ballet, as Columbia suggested.

Nothing would have pleased Ruth better, but Tom's financial negation was well founded. Soon all the unions, including AGMA, the dancers' own union, were to begin making steadily greater demands. That these, especially in the case of the exploited younger dancers, were justified, Ruth well knew. She had even gone to Carol Fox and threatened to quit on the spot unless the minimum of ten girls that she needed in the ensemble was retained and the salary of Jeanne Armin, who was now dancing solo roles, was raised to at least the equivalent of what she earned in Ruth's own company. And she was to continue to do the same sort of thing as time went on. In the higher brackets the foreign guest stars were following the lead of Nureyev and Fonteyn (who now demanded $3,000 and eventually even $5,000 apiece for each performance) by doubling the fees they had been asking. Then there were the musicians, the stagehands and all down the line, until the very survival of the company on its present scale was being threatened.

COMBINATIONS AND DISJUNCTIONS

However dark the future might look, current activities could not be panicked to a sudden halt, and plans for the 1964 tour proceeded according to pattern. Kirsten Simone and Henning Kronstam were again to be the guest stars, and the single new work was to be *Combinations*.

This was quite enough, for apart from the confusions of the environment in which it was created, it constituted a complete departure from Ruth's characteristic approach, and it proved to be inherently difficult to put on. It was based not on a "literary" idea but on a set of musical variations composed for her by Van Grove on the theme of the old French folk song "*À vous dirai-je, Maman*," which American children sometimes sing as "Twinkle, Twinkle, Little Star." It was strictly a musical abstraction, employing fugue and canon and other formal devices to challenge a composer's ingenuity, and it was no doubt its similar challenge to her own ingenuity that led Ruth to do it.

Unlike Balanchine she had never treated her dancers as sheer instruments of musical movement; to her they were always persons, quite aware of each other as such, moving musically in dramatic relationships. She had even planned in this instance to put aside her customary employment of costume as a collaborative element and stage the work in quasi-practice clothes.

When she came to discussing it with Delfau during the summer, however, it was already "getting complicated"; Balanchinesque "cool" was being tempered by Pagian "warm," and on Delfau's recommendation she added "a few suggestions of costumes." Few and fractional and merely suggestive they indisputably were, but they canceled out the neutrality of practice clothes; they consisted, indeed, of sundry amusing appurtenances, snapped on, as it were, over basic leotards and tights, to point up the particular flavor of each variation. They contributed effectively to the theme-and-variations concept, though not to an essentially musical one.

Whatever its original intention may have been, the work finally emerged with the faint skeleton of a dramatic plot, though one that functioned quite outside the content of the music. It concerned itself rather with the way a particular choreographer met the challenge of a particular composer, never losing the playful overtones of a children's game. It had only two named characters: "the combiner," who was the protagonist, representing Ruth in the person of Orrin Kayan; and "the muse," who was the antagonist—that is, the challenger—who stood most flatteringly for Van Grove in the person of the atrractive Ellen Everett.

For those who were, so to speak, able to read while they ran, the text of the souvenir program set the whole thing forth with appropriate ingenuity in a witty parallel of just this challenge:

Combinations

Are Sometimes Fascinating
To Those Who Create Them

To musical variations by Isaac van Grove
Doors and costumes (a long way) after André Delfau
Combined by Ruth Page

1. Children love the alphabet long before they love words
2. By putting them together
3. To solve perpetual motion
4. Making two canons better than one
5. With what dreams are made of
6. Though harassed by the telephone

7. One can sense the cast
8. And get going faster
9. Before we end it all

Offstage the real combiner was having her troubles. Much as she loved the alphabet, it was enough to have to put it together to solve perpetual motion with what dreams are made of, without being harassed by the telephone and appalled by the realization that the more she sensed the cast the more she had to get moving faster if she was ever to end it at all. The cast, in short, was cutting up.

They were indeed one big happy family with common artistic and financial problems, working together, bus riding together, eating together and in some cases sleeping together; and accordingly when one of them was affected by obstreperousness, they were all affected. Even such a personal matter as the breakup of a romantic liaison could, and almost invariably did, throw everybody off the close emotional balance they sought automatically to maintain. Sometimes it was opera directors, costume designers, insufficient salaries that threatened the equilibrium; again it was learning new works for the tour while simultaneously relearning old ones with new castings; and always there was the overcast of touch-and-go temperament.

Combinations was as far off their beaten track as it was off Ruth's, and, what with one thing and another, a general state of irritability prevailed. At one point she wrote in her diary: "This disagreeable week finally passed. I hate the feeling of discord in the company, and the relation of Larry to me was extremely strained all week." Larry, of all people, whom she secretly held in her mind as her successor one of these days. Before the tensions relaxed, she had managed to clash with practically all the closest members of her team, including ultimately even Chuck, whom she considered a genuinely close (though in no sense an amorous) friend.

Then suddenly Orrin, "for and on whom I am doing this ballet," skipped off to New York briefly at the call of romance. Larry found the role much too hard, "so I am teaching it to Ken. Ken doesn't like the role, but anyway it is good for him to learn it, and he's helpful in the pas de deux." Ken was good at lifts, in which the choreography abounded.

So the new ballet struggled along against various resistances and inertias as well as its inherent difficulties, but somehow progressing nonetheless.

Videlicet: In May she reports having worked with Orrin and Ellen, with Neal Kayan at the piano, "mostly on the girl's solo. It is very bravura and if anyone can do it, I think it will be exciting." Again with the same three she worked for two hours on the third variation, "which is a fugue—Bachian in style—a difficult dance." Then Van Grove sent her the "finale," so Neal came and "for three hours he practiced the damn tape thing and then made a tape for me. It was very unsatisfactory. Though he is a brilliant pianist, he can't play it well yet and the tape keeps breaking. We tried to figure a way to count it. It is very, very complicated and I hope worth all the trouble!" . . . On the other hand the lyrical pas de deux with Orrin and Ellen "is turning out well, I think (fingers crossed!)."

In June, after Orrin had left for his New York tryst, she worked with the rest of the cast on "the finale" (actually Variation 8, since Variation 9 had not yet materialized). "They just can't learn it and it is so difficult to make steps to such choppy music." . . . Then there was "a solo dance—a sort of Perpetuum Mobile, very difficult"; which it must have been indeed, since, solo or no solo, it required on this occasion the services of Dolores, always the brilliant technician, Larry and Ellen for three hours. On the verge of departure for St. Tropez, she got Ann Barzel to take a movie of the part of the choreography that was finished.

In August when she returned from St. Tropez, things seemed brighter. Her first demonstration of joy was: "How wonderful to have a studio with a decent floor!" Then on a shopping expedition she finally found the half dozen or so toy telephones she needed for Variation 6 at Woolworth's, and to cap the climax Van Grove sent on a new tape of the music. "I find it very inspiring. I can't wait to see the ballet finished!"

In September she was working with Orrin on Variation 9, which was a solo that followed the so-called finale. She had tried to do it before, but both Kenneth and Neal were so against including it in the ballet at all that she had "just got nowhere. To do justice to the dance it takes a great *artist* to perform it."

Now it was the turn of the other Kayan brother to go off on a jaunt to New York. In late September he announced that he was going to join Ballet Theatre for three months but of course would be back in time for the tour. Recently he and Kenneth, who had been close friends and roommates, had begun to quarrel, sometimes loudly and publicly, and whether or not this had any bearing on his departure, it was a blow to Ruth. She was indignant. "Besides conducting for them he will play Mendelssohn's piano concerto [for William Dollar's new ballet called *Mendelssohn Concerto*] and he spends every spare second practicing it, so even in our ten minutes, one can never relax or think at all—same all through lunch hour."

One afternoon late in October, Orrin drove her out to a teachers' college where they were to do the, by now, finished piece in a tryout on a program with several other companies that night.

"We found a brand-new theatre with of course a slippery floor over concrete, exactly two dressing rooms (one for boys and one for girls), an inadequate lighting system and freezing cold! Well, anyway we rehearsed, and then hung around while everyone else rehearsed, and finally at 8 the 'show' went on. It was a Ballet Guild performance and my 'Combinations' went on first. . . . Actually it was a very interesting evening and very professional. I have no idea what to think of my ballet! I can't decide until I see it properly presented. The costumes arrived the day before, so there was no time to experiment with them. There are only a few and I think they add."

In November she was still working on the number with all the little telephones. "The music is very difficult but the idea is interesting. I really need a group of modern dancers, however, to do it justice." She was also trying to cut the work as a whole, "as it is too long for an in-between ballet and too short for a big ballet. The cutting is very difficult." Naturally it would be, for it was based on closely self-integrated musical forms.

But her musical troubles were only beginning. In mid-November Neal wrote her that he would not be coming back for the tour after all, since "Ballet Theatre was so pleased with his work that they had offered him a permanent contract." Her first idea was to replace him with their present concert master who knew the repertoire, but he was leaving the company himself. Finally she sought out Simon Sadoff, who back in 1950 had gone over to Paris as José Limón's musical director in *Les Ballets Américains*. He duly arrived toward the end of December and stayed with Ruth and Tom while he tackled the learning of the repertoire and the rehearsing of it in an already troublesome orchestral situation.

"What a mess the whole Neal situation is," Ruth lamented. After all the adjustments had been made, she estimated that "the change in our orchestra has cost us about $10,000." The irony of it was, however, that Neal's "permanent contract" did not materialize, and before Ruth's tour even opened, he was out of Ballet Theatre in a complicated ruckus that had nothing at all to do with Ruth. But by this time Sadoff was all signed up and over his ears in work.

Then along came the end of the opera season. "On Sunday I had the company party. They arrived about six and some of them stayed till 2 a.m. Felisa and a Mexican friend cooked a marvelous dinner for us and you can always count on dancers to eat. We showed our film of 'Fledermaus' and of course there is no better way to entertain dancers than to show them pictures of themselves. Most everyone left after the film, but about twelve stayed and danced. I love to see them dance. They did the finale of 'Combinations' to regular jazz (on a record) and I must say it looked wonderful."

The day after New Year's they started rehearsing the repertoire with orchestra. "All kinds of problems with them as usual. The trumpet didn't show up and so I had to call an extra rehearsal." It turned out that the poor chap had got the measles at the last minute and could not go at all. "With ten minutes out of every hour [union requirements] and some time wasted, a 5-hour rehearsal is a *long* way from five hours. *But* I do love Van Grove's orchestration of 'Combinations', and even if it is a big flop, *I* love this ballet."

It was not a big flop. It opened the program on the first night of the tour in Wawatosa, and "I thought Van Grove's music was excellent and my choreography fresh and inventive and I thought the dancers did it well. The audience seemed to like it." After they had had a month of performing it, she exercised her creative authority with proud aplomb by putting the "finale" (otherwise Variation 8) on point, "which I've always wanted to do but got talked out of."

Throughout the tour she was to talk herself back into other things that she had dropped, but persistent musical battles and company bickerings were anything but helpful. The trumpet with the measles was duly replaced, and eventually the bass player had a stroke and for a while there was a different bass player every night, but these were merely incidental "acts of God" against a continuum of diversionary unpleasantness.

The lighting, which as early as the second performance had become fairly monstrous because of a crucial backstage defection, improved during the week, but the music, what with a new conductor and a partially reconstructed orchestra that objected strenuously to extra rehearsals, did not. And as for between-performance personal inconvenience, a new high was achieved by a 16 ½-hour bus ride from Bowling Green, Ohio, to Charleston, West Virginia. "I really don't know how our bus driver ever did it, nor how we ever survived it!" For her the ordeal was somewhat tempered by the fact that Simon Sadoff sat next to her and she found him "an extremely interesting seat partner—we really have lots of fun together."

After about two weeks the tour had shaken down sufficiently for Ruth to bid them a temporary farewell. She rejoined them, as scheduled, at Jacksonville ("How I hate to leave Tom and Felisa and a nice comfortable home!") and bused with them to Daytona Beach. They had expected to find the Riviera Hotel "a lovely resortish hotel," but "it turned out to be an old people's home, and when we entered, the lobby was full of them all staring at us as if we had just arrived from Mars. It was about two blocks to my room and *no one* to carry any luggage. I can carry my big suitcase (full of music, which makes it so heavy) for a little bit, but this time it was almost too much. Then there was no place to eat, unless you had ordered food a day in advance, and everyone was starved." The company manager, after some telephoning, decided they should all move downtown to the Daytona Plaza, "so everyone got their luggage, got back in the bus and went to the other hotel, except me. I just couldn't face carrying the luggage again, so I stayed, in spite of the fact that I was ten miles from the company [and there was no telephone in the room!]. I felt deserted." Eventually she did carry her luggage the "two blocks" to the door and signed in at the other hotel.

Her bus ride to West Palm Beach the next day was a wretched one. Her congenial seat partner, Simon, "spent almost the entire trip saying how miserable he was in our company. He said the work was just too hard for him. Probably with the companies he has been with he never had to give a performance every night, or maybe they gave the same program every night. Also he hates riding on the bus because of all the talking. He says when I am not there Larry Long spends most of his time talking against me and the company in a loud voice. Finally I got so depressed that I haven't recovered yet." For the next day's trip she arranged to ride with Simone and Kronstam, who had rented a car of their own, "so I was able to give Simon two seats to himself and he didn't have to sit with me. He doesn't like to 'talk shop,' and of course the only reason I go on the bus is so I can make corrections and discuss our problems with the dancers."

There was no place to eat in "the very unchic little hotel, so I walked about four miles and found a little joint where I ate a horrible lunch alone." The high school where they played proved to be one of the worst theatres they had ever performed in—"absolutely no space at all and dreary and impossible. I got more depressed than ever. Two of the corps dancers were ill and the morale of the company is low when we are in these small theatres. However I managed to live through the performance somehow. I took class, although there was so little space, I stood way off in a corner so as to give all the space to the dancers. How I wish I were not so polite!"

The Sadoff complaint continued to rankle, and some two weeks later, when she was again about to leave the company after a performance in Memphis, an opportunity arose that was too pat to be resisted. The company bus was to depart at 8, and she got up early to wave them off and had breakfast with Larry at 7:30. She told him ("maybe very stupidly") that she had "heard" that as soon as she left them, "he started saying things against me in the bus. He denied it completely and said he was the only one in the company really interested in the company! So we both felt very badly, and I must say I am very happy to be away from them for a while. There is too much discontent all the time—too hot, too cold, too early, too late, and *nothing* ever seems to please them. The only satisfaction is that the audience absolutely adores us (even the critics do!), and that we are the source of inspiration to everyone who sees us and we are always invited back!"

One of her luckiest endowments, however, is that she finds it impossible to hold personal grudges. Though the orchestra remained for her not so much a group of persons as a collective incubus, she was soon sitting next to Simon quite happily again. The diary served as cupping glass, parish priest and analyst's couch, and once she had unburdened herself there, however bitterly, of resentments and hurt pride, it was as if they had never happened.

She rejoined the company at Peoria. The performance was to be at nearby Camden, where "Ken gave a nice class which I took and then watched the 'show.' I must say when I've been away from the company for a few days and then come back the performance looks *marvelous*."

The big event that night was that Chuck went in for Orrin for the first time in *Combinations*. He was "absolutely electrifying. He danced it far from perfectly technically but he had exactly the right zany approach to the character of the ballet, and he met with instant 'rapport' with the audience. They laughed and clapped at all the right places. . . . I found it very refreshing and original. . . . There are some companies that are always excellent but not exciting, but we are always exciting even when not excellent."

She had been working steadily on *Combinations* during the tour, chiefly taking Orrin, who was the chief figure, out of this number and putting him back into that one, feeling that he was in too many of them. Chuck's brilliant try manifestly awakened fresh interest and new purpose. She called an orchestra rehearsal especially to have a go at Variation 9, which she had dropped during the original rehearsals because it required "a great artist."

> But a terrible thing happened. Our dear orchestra players found out that we had "bootlegged" a tape of "Combinations" during a performance . . . [and] said they had to be paid for it. Even this I wouldn't mind, but they spent so much time discussing it (when we should have been rehearsing) and they got me so upset, that I finally got to weeping so hard I had to leave. Finally they got around to playing the number for twenty minutes, but by that time I had lost all interest and was far too exhausted to think of anything "artistic." Simon told me they complained like crazy because they had to rehearse twenty minutes! . . . I could have asked [them] to rehearse six hours. . . . The truth of the matter is that I have never met any men in the orchestra who have any interest whatever in music! It is just a business for them.

To make the day consistent the performance that night was "terrible," in a "dreary movie house with no stage facilities whatsoever, no lights, and worst of all, only a handful of people." It was not a Community Concerts booking but an outside date and had had none of the local promotion that was inherent in the Community Concerts setup. "Our company simply does not draw at all on 'percentage dates' and our expensive guest stars don't draw even one person into the house." The program included a new version of *Mephistophela*, which she was trying painfully to cut to half its normal length for a CBS television film ("Every time we make a cut it is like taking off a finger or an arm."), and the television director, who was fortunately her friend, was there to see it. She herself "saw it through very blurry eyes."

She had planned to go along with the company on two more dates, but advance reports were that the next town's theatre was "one of the worst! Also I hated to see those unsympathetic, uninspired, materialistic orchestra men for two more days in the bus." So she took the plane back to Chicago along with the TV director.

When the film was finally shot, she doubted that it "would look like much, but I suppose I should be thankful that we had a chance to do it at all!

Now I am sending this ballet to the warehouse and there it will stay forever until I have a chance to do it *properly* in the theatre."

Tours of one-night stands, indeed, were making it more and more impossible to do anything properly, and she had come to the point where she wanted to quit touring altogether. What with the union difficulties and the across-the-board increase in costs in general, Tom was quite ready to go along with such a decision.

Then, late in March, when they were in New York together, they went at the request of Jean Cerrone to see Rebekah Harkness to talk to her about some changes she was considering in her own touring procedures. ("Jeannot" was everybody's favorite company manager; he had worked for Ruth and was now working with the Harkness Ballet.) It was a long talk; "Tom said afterwards I had said everything on earth to discourage her, and he thinks I did it because I unconsciously don't want to give up my company. Maybe he is right."

His grounds for such a conclusion were strong, for she was going right on working on a new ballet for next season. It was one for which she had anything but high enthusiasm, and if she had really wanted to quit, this would have been the moment. It was *The Chocolate Soldier*, and though she had read everything in the library about it, her indifference persisted. Possibly it was because the opera-operetta pattern had begun to wear thin for her, especially after her gratifying experience with *Combinations*. But she had finally come to terms with it, had got a scenario set with Van Grove and was dealing with it choreographically.

Tom was with her in New York not on recreational pursuits but on legal business. He was working much too hard these days, to her great distress. Perhaps even more distressing was his new determination to sue the Ford Foundation as a monopoly. Needless to say, they had both been chagrined at the omission of the Chicago Ballet Company from the grants, totaling nearly $8,000,000, that the foundation had made in December to certain resident ballet companies over the country. The Chicago Ballet Company, to be sure, was "resident" only insofar as its office was concerned. It had no performing entity there, no school of its own, and its members rarely had an opportunity to perform in Chicago at all except as part of the opera establishment. It was perforce a "road show," and not even that under its own name. But it was sorely in need of money to survive and would be delighted to be able to become a truly resident company.

Why Tom actually considered such a plan is difficult to understand on its merits. He was far too knowledgeable to believe that any funds that might by some miracle be forthcoming could possibly materialize in time to keep the company alive. His motive might rather have been merely to make a brilliant protest, not in words alone but in terms of action that could not be ignored. Certainly the grant had aroused considerable anger throughout the dance world, and he was being egged on vigorously by some of the other companies that felt themselves aggrieved.

Ruth herself, however, was in complete opposition to such a procedure, realizing not only its futility but also the damage it would inevitably do to her in the public mind. Happily, it was her point of view that prevailed.

". . . *Yielding Place to New*"

The calendar was moving along toward St. Tropez time, but Tom was working nights, days and Sundays and was far too busy to set even a provisional date for departure. Ruth was eager to go, not for the pleasure of St. Tropez (which this year involved the far from pleasant unfinished business of Herbe Folle) but for the necessary sessions with costumers for both her own tour and the opera season.

She was by no means idle, however, for there was all the preparatory work to be done on next season's *Chocolate Soldier.* Things were becoming brighter in that sector, and in mid-May she records that "I love working on it, much to my surprise." Most of her company were off on either summer jobs or holidays, and she had only Ken and Kleck to work with and not even a pianist. After having done both *The Merry Widow* and *Fledermaus,* "to find new waltz steps seems almost impossible. Jazz and modern dance choreography is *so* much easier because 'anything goes,' but an old-fashioned waltz presents problems of elegance and simplicity that require a great deal of subtlety."

They were at Hubbard Woods, this being summer, and since Felisa had left on her annual trip to Mexico, Ruth was "learning to take care of the house. I thought it would be difficult, but it is easy—just time consuming." Which may have been an advantage under the circumstances.

One day Tom "worked from 8 a.m. till 11:30 p.m. without a break except for a quick lunch and dinner which I cooked." She had packed and unpacked at each of his hopeful hints of a possible departure date. They had reluctantly wired Claudia Cassidy and her husband, "Bill" Crawford, who were already in Europe, that they would not be able to join them in a proposed week of touring in Sardinia. Toward the end of June Tom decided that probably he could not go at all, then on July 2 he said he was finally ready to go. ("He is pooped at last," she wrote with grim glee.) But the day after that he said again that he probably could not go at all. She was losing her mind with all the uncertainty. Then at 6 p.m. on Saturday, July 4, when she got home from a movie chosen hopefully as an anesthetic, he made his Declaration of Independence; they "packed like mad," and at 3 the next afternoon they were in the air en route to Paris and Les Trois Pastèques.

A REST FOR TOM

They had decided, under the circumstances, not even to open the house at St. Tropez. Instead they were heading for, of all unexpected places, Corsica. The prime purpose was to provide Tom with a rest. First, however, there were some pre-Corsican duties that had to be taken care of in Paris, which proved to be difficult, since "everybody 'weekends' in Paris now from Friday to Tuesday." In addition to which it was raining cats and dogs most of the time, and taxis were impossible to get.

She always felt "90% unconscious after that all-night flight," so as soon as they got to Les Trois Pastèques, they went to bed and slept until 1:30. Then after two cups of coffee they had revived sufficiently at least to get going. And going they got—at a pace that was to accelerate throughout the summer. If Tom did not need a rest at its start, he assuredly would at its end.

That night they went to see, of all things, *Swan Lake* at the Opéra, because Josette Amiel and Flemming Flindt were dancing in Vladimir Bourmeister's version of it. Bourmeister was ballet master of the Moscow Art Theatre ballet (or, more officially, the Stanislavsky and Nemirovich-Danchenko Lyric Theatre), and for his *Swan Lake* he had gone back to the original score as it had been done at its première in Moscow in 1877. They got the last two seats in the house "in a box almost exactly on the stage." At that close range many of the French dancers looked bored by the attempt to Russianize them, and she was "not at all thrilled by the performance." Afterward they took Josette and Flemming to supper, and they, in turn, brought along Chazot, "the dancer-choreographer that Auric fired from the Comédie Française. . . . As usual with Josette and Flemming we had a very gay time. To bed about 3 a.m."

Clavé was in Paris, fixing up his mother's old apartment to give to his son as a wedding present, and they dined with him the next evening. "He really is the best friend we have in the world. He offered to design (for nothing) a new house in St. Tropez for us to build on our property next to him. For such a busy man to do all that work and supervise it is *really* being a friend!" Apparently this was to assure them that no matter what happened to Herbe Folle, they would have a place to live right on the water. The reason they had bought the land, which was just across the small road from Herbe Folle, was to provide against somebody else's building there and cutting them off from the sea.

In the morning at eleven she had a fitting at St. Laurent's, went to Repetto's to buy tights, trousers and "especially swim suits," dashed to lunch with Irène Lidova to hear all the dance gossip and listened to so much of it that she did not have time to go home and change, as she had planned, before her appointment at Karinska's with Delfau to discuss the *Chocolate Soldier* costumes. When she and Tom got there, Zizi Jeanmaire was also there, "looking as gamine as ever," and Jean Robin had made a special trip there, of all places, to see them; "which was really very nice of him," since there was no other time or place to do so, even though they were able to do little more than say "hello and good-bye." At 7:30 after a hasty cup of coffee all around Karinska drove the two of them and Delfau in her car to the Opéra because of the downpour. Ruth was still in her "black and white St. Laurent sport suit, carrying bundles, and both of us looking like tramps." Gilles, the stage manager at the Opéra, gave them "two wonderful seats and we bought one for André." The performance was Béjart's production of the Berlioz *Damnation of Faust*, but they were too tired to have any opinion of it.

"After the theatre we took André to supper and got home about 2 a.m. Packed up at 6 and off on the 7:30 plane to Corsica. How strange (after twelve years) not to be going to St. Tropez. I am as excited as a child going on my first trip."

Fortunately, her enthusiasms and her enjoyments were as absorbing as her sufferings and her despairs, and in Corsica she did the Napoleon bit with as much eagerness as any other American tourist. The scenery was breathtaking, and even their little car had the grace to have its puncture in a town instead of on a mountain pass. In Propriano they stopped for lunch ("bad fish soup, asparagus and a little cheese—all very expensive") and had a swim. "Quite a mistral blowing all night and all day so I only waded while Tom swam in the big surf."

Often she was exhausted. One night she went to bed at nine as soon as they reached a hotel, but Tom talked to her until one about what to do with the house at St. Tropez. There were times when she was bored, and only a chance book that Josette had given her by Jacques Chazot ("in very difficult French") saved the situation. "I want so much to go to Nervi to see the Béjart Ballet, but Tom hates festivals and just wants to sit in the sun, so here we will stay just sitting in the sun. However, this is much better for him, so I am happy to do something for him!"

Nevertheless, a week later Nervi is where they were. Where to go next? "We have never had a 'fancy free' life like this." Finally, the choice was Spoleto, where they would just be able to catch the last performance of *Raymonda*. But all planes to Rome had been canceled by a strike, so they settled for Bayreuth—"much to all the dancers' disgust."

From the Munich airport they motored to Seefelt in Austria "to see our old friends Lotte and Fritz Wilckens. We had a hard time finding them but finally discovered their charming little house, and as I had expected, Fritz was having his afternoon siesta. . . . Fritz finally has his life's dream—to do *nothing* and literally nothing. They just eat and sleep. He has his piano there and hasn't played one note since his last concert with Kreutzberg." (This was in 1959, when Kreutzberg made his farewell appearance as a concert dancer in Frankfurt.)

When they got back to Munich, they phoned the Wilckens's daughter, Marita, who was married to Otto Suitner, one of the conductors at Bayreuth, to ask her to get tickets for them for *Parsifal* and to engage a room for them for the night. She told them the latter was absolutely impossible, but they went anyhow "on the wild chance that we could get in somehow." They headed directly for the little hotel where Claudia Cassidy and Bill were staying ("a horrid little place but with apparently charming people running it"), and Bill got them a room with no trouble—"no bath but perfectly all right."

> To the opera at 3:30 in a taxi ordered in advance by Claudia and Bill. . . . Marita got two tickets for us in a box right in the middle of the theatre and there were only two other people in the box that seated twelve. I had heard so much about the uncomfortable seats but those in the box were wonderful. Maybe the extreme heat kept people away, or maybe if you wait till the last minute you can always get seats! So finally we were there and it started. I nearly died of joy the entire afternoon. I just sat back and listened and for once in opera the looking was as good as the listening. The flower maidens could have been much better but the stage was so dark you couldn't see anything all evening and I liked this because it made everything seem like a dream. You couldn't see the orchestra or the conductor or the singers' faces and there was no applause and I thought the effect was overwhelming. Serge Lido had told us not to go to Bayreuth, that it was all a great big bore for old ladies. How wrong he is. It was one of the great experiences of my life. Vickers, London and Hotter—such men—such voices. I was transported. I loved the dark lighting—the abstraction of the sets.

Tom's version in a letter to Tommy Thompson was somewhat different in accent:

> The hotel where we stayed with Claudia Cassidy is across the street from the railroad station and it seemed that all night the camions were running between the beds. There is one nice hotel on the edge of Bayreuth but you can't get into it unless you reserve your room a year in advance and I think it is extremely expensive. However, there is one new attraction in Bayreuth for me and that is that they have just built and opened another of those marvelous German swimming pools in which Germany excels. In fact, there are actually four separate pools in this enclosure in Bayreuth. Since one starts the opera in evening dress at 4 p.m., I can imagine swimming and sunning all day in the Bayreuth pool and spending half the night in the Festspiel House every night. That is, if I could stand so much Wagnerian music for so many hours in such dark surroundings.

The effect even on Ruth may have been somewhat more violent than she realized, for as soon as they got back to Munich the next day, she went to the dentist with an abscessed tooth. The little Austin, for its own reasons, developed the automotive equivalent of a toothache and had to go to the repair shop. So they hired another small car at once in order not to interrupt the already established tempo of their restful holiday, which was approximately that of the Indianapolis speedway.

Its final ten days, indeed, were an extension of the " 'fancy free' life" to the pattern of crazy-quilt improvisation:

Salzburg—two nights—pouring rain and heavy traffic—sight-seeing, the Mozartian bit this time—much shopping for clothes, including a Loden cape for next season's tour—a puppet performance of *Fledermaus*—dinner with Antal Dorati's family at nearby Strobl. (He himself, according to Tom's account, was away "in the Alps above Garmisch-Partenkirchen having his back massaged by a masseur upon whom all the conductors in Europe as well as the violinists seem to rely to keep them going from year to year.")

Back to Munich in late afternoon for another visit to the dentist—night at the airport hotel to allow for an early-morning flight to London. A quick glimpse of the school of the Royal Ballet—a visit with Ninette de Valois at her new house on the Thames—both matinee and evening performances by the Ballet Rambert at the Sadler's Wells Theatre—night at the London airport hotel, where they almost missed the plane back to Munich because the hotel failed to call them.

In Munich they picked up the Austin and were off to Bregenz on the Bodensee to see Lehár's *The Land of Smiles*, performed on a stage built out in the lake with the audience seated on shore. "For some strange reason," Tom reported, "the stage director cut the lights as soon as the ballet appeared and at the same time shot off quantities of fireworks behind the stage." The performance lasted two hours and twenty minutes without a break, and, good though it was, Ruth wrote, "I just can't sit that long."

From Bregenz to Zurich, where Tom tried vainly either to leave the car or sell it so that he could fly back with Ruth to Paris for her final projects there. Instead he had to make the seven-hour drive alone and met her next day at one o'clock at Karinska's, where she had gone with Delfau to try on *Chocolate Soldier* costumes through two wearying hours of standing.

To the Dior boutique for several purchases, but her old friend, Jeanne, the *vendeuse*, caught a glimpse of her and ushered the three of them into the "collection" (against Ruth's inclinations), seating them proudly in the first row, where they could not get out for another two hours. Ruth found it hard to sit that long even at a "Collection."

Tired though they were, there was a new ballet at the Opéra and there they landed, again in the front row. The new work, called *But*, was a "*sportif*" piece—"a sort of basketball game with teams"—and was not very good.

In the two days that followed there were more dresses to buy, more long sessions trying on costumes at Karinska's; a most rewarding visit to Delfau's to see his paintings and to buy one, *Le Lever du Rideau*; the better

part of one day picking up all the various purchases, a difficult business in
which Tom impressed her deeply by his ability to find his way around Paris in
the Austin; a visit on a glorious night to the *Feérie de Notre Dame*, the
illumination of the details of the church with music and "completely inaudible
narration" plus more standing up. . . .

Saturday noon, seated in the plane and communing with the diary
before she forgot: "Now waiting to leave. If all goes well we should arrive
one month from when we started. What a month! Nicest memory is Delfau's
'Le Lever du Rideau'."

In New York it was still early Saturday afternoon, so from Kennedy
Airport they went to the New York World's Fair for three hours—African
Pavilion and Zulu Dancers—South-Sea Polynesian show—Japanese Pavilion—and
for the rest of the time "just walked around looking at the architecture. It
all seemed very honky-tonk and sort of ordinary."

By taxi to the Long Island Festival, which Ruth had been invited to
participate in, but had to decline. . . . Royal Winnipeg Ballet performing—tent
theatre most unattractive—no scenery possible—inferior lighting arrangements.
Ruth sat near her one-time patroness, Winthrop Palmer, whom she had not
seen for years and who was now a member of the faculty of C. W. Post
College of Long Island University. . . . Taxi back to Kennedy Airport for the
midnight plane to Chicago, and home at Hubbard Woods at 2:30 a.m.

Said Tom in his letter to Tommy Thompson: "We had a real rest on
the island of Corsica, but the rest of our time we dashed about from one
festival to another."

NUISANCES—FAMILIAR AND UNFAMILIAR

It can be distinctly disheartening to come home after four such hilarious
weeks, which by reason of their very fullness seem longer than they are, to
find that the house is filthy and the status of everything else is quo ante.
Some of it was pleasantly so, however—the beach, for example, with Chuck
and other company members who were not still on vacation coming out every
day from Chicago for a swim and a barre; the various Fisher families and
North Shore neighbors with their lively social and artistic activities; and the
already emerging plans for the busy season ahead.

The opera was providing its routine headaches; there were only five
members of the corps de ballet returning from last season, which meant more
of those harrowing auditions ("many girls and four boys and no talent"). To
make working conditions a little less inadequate, Betty Gour, who had been
the first ballet mistress of Ruth's company, now generously gave her the
barres from her own studio, which she was closing, and though it cost $60 to
move them to the opera house, Ruth accepted them eagerly, for the opera
had never provided her with barres and certainly never would do so. She was

also delighted with what Larry was doing as her present ballet master in bringing into top shape the almost entirely new ensemble.

On the last day of September, when she had just started the actual opera-ballet rehearsals in Chicago, Clover Roope and Antoinette Massie of England's Western Theatre Ballet dropped in with a letter of introduction from Ted Shawn, and she invited them to dinner, along with two members of her company, that night at 8. When she got home about 7, she saw no signs of Tom and assumed that he had not yet come in. She found him, however, in the bathtub, obviously very ill. He had had some kind of seizure at the office about 2 o'clock and had managed to get home but not the strength to call the doctor. This she did at once, and since it suggested to her a possible heart attack, she asked him to bring along a heart specialist. After an examination they found it was not a heart problem at all but an unidentified "bug he had picked up in Texas." The guests dined alone and Ruth joined them only after Tom had fallen asleep. The doctors, who came into the living room with her for a short time, "seemed to enjoy our crazy dance conversation"; in a social situation she was unflappable. But naturally she spent a sleepless night and the next day did not go to the theatre at all. "It was the first time I've ever missed a rehearsal except when I had my broken rib."

Tom did not go out of the house for four days, and weeks later she recorded that "his 'bug' is still giving him fever, so he can't do much and seems very exhausted." Once in a while he went to a performance with her, but more often he did not feel well enough. This was a new development for him, for he enjoyed being in circulation as much as she did.

She had been seriously worried about his overworking, but she so detested all matters of business, and especially his "legal" business, that she had no curiosity about what he was overworking at. Toward the end of the year, indeed, when Tom resigned from the active management of the Texas ranch to relieve some of his pressures, she did not even mention it in her diary.

The opera season, for all its hardships, did offer her two compensations. For one thing there was a revival of Donizett's seldom produced *La Favorita*, and the fifteen-minute ballet she made for it gave her genuine satisfaction, not only for her own part in it, but also for the work of the company. The audience loved it and so did the critics and all the European artists in the cast, but she "was not asked to take a bow with the 'creators' and the artists." This oversight, though perhaps not deliberate, was at least character-istic, which may have been what infuriated her most.

The other bright moment came toward the end of the season when she went to a conference with Carol Fox, Donati and Bartoletti, the conductor, and "to my utter amazement they suggested our doing 'Carmina Burana' with

'L'Heure Espagnole.' I nearly fainted for joy." It was for next season, of course, with much water to flow under the bridge in the meantime; but the joy was genuine while it lasted.

Among the other long-familiar nuisances was her forthcoming tour. *The Chocolate Soldier*, now retitled *Bullets and Bonbons*, was giving her trouble. When in early November she had had her first run-through, she reported that it was "rather a mess" and added, "Thank God Van Grove is coming as it needs fixing in a lot of places." The music did not "flow together" yet, as eventually the maestro would make it do. When the costumes arrived from Paris, she walked in to find Kleck tearing hers apart in typical dancer fashion—"a costume designed by Delfau and made by Karinska!" Another costume had to be made in such a hurry (a better one, as it turned out) that Tom was forced to go to the airport at the last minute and grab it in order to get it safely to the opening performance.

But the major threat to the tour, which was scheduled to begin on January 12, was the Columbia Artists was bringing Zizi Jeanmaire's show from Paris for an American tour lasting until February 6, and they had politely taken over the entire crew of Ruth's company to man it. Tom was, if possible, more distressed than Ruth about the consequences of a tour with an all-new staff. The new company manager met with everybody's approval; it was at the other end of the scale that the trouble centered, for Bob Boehm, who had started with the company as a dancer before he went into the costume department, was the only man alive who knew their wardrobe and how to handle it.

There were also more and more union problems, with special cantankerousness emanating from the musicians, which put Tom into such a state of desperation that he heartily recommended quitting the whole touring business.

The imported guest artists involved further complications. They were Irina Borowska, now a member of Braunsweg's Festival Ballet in London, and Karl Musil, leading dancer of the Vienna Opera and at the moment Borowska's partner as guest artist of the Festival Ballet. Because they were both needed up to the last minute in the London season, they did not report for duty until noon on January 10, which by anybody's calculation was very tight scheduling indeed. But, Ruth noted, "they learn fast and are both musical so it is not too difficult." They were to do the *Black Swan* pas de deux, which of course they already knew, and they were rehearsing day and night under the coaching of Ken and Kleck for *The Merry Widow*.

On the bright side, Larry Long had for the first time created a ballet for the repertoire—*Bagatelle* (Beethoven), done fortunately in practice clothes—and she thought it was "a lovely ballet" though too short for easy programming. And at the eleventh hour, as a sudden beam of sunshine through the organizational thunderclouds, Bob Boehm was able after all to take over the wardrobe.

The orchestra situation however, produced no such ray of comfort. A ten-hour rehearsal was only fair to middling at best and considerably less than that in the playing of *Carmen*. Nevertheless, they opened in Springfield on schedule, and Tom went along—in case. The scenery for *Carmen* fell over at the beginning; the guest stars had not got into their stride with the *Black Swan*; and Tommy Thompson phoned from New York as soon as the final curtain was down to inquire nervously about the music. The only criticism the office had ever had about the company concerned the orchestra, and things were getting no better.

All the old traveling troubles were again in vigorous operation, with a few new ones added. Bob Boehm, who was still at heart more a dancer than a crew member, liked to sit in the bus instead of the station wagon, but the new concert master had commandeered his seat and said he would return to New York before he would give it up and sit in the back with the other musicians. When the company arrived in Denver, one of the new girls, who had been acting troublesomely, confessed that she was pregnant, as Ruth had suspected. She did not dare tell her mother, so she stopped off in Denver, promising to return "in a few days." Said Ruth, always the grim Pollyanna, "Now Bob can have her seat, thank God!"

She made her customary trips back to Chicago from time to time, and on one of them she found a letter from Van Grove, suggesting enthusiastically quite out of the blue that she do *Billy Sunday* again with a suitable score by him. She obediently dug out the old movie and sent it to him. "I looked at it and I really don't know how I ever had the nerve to do such a daring ballet! I hate to re-do old things and I'd have to do a lot of thinking before I could re-do that one."

She rejoined the company at Nashville, where she found them rehearsing *Widow* at the Grand Ole Opry House. She had come this time because there was still work to be done on the new version of *Camille*, which, much to her distress, she had had to cut from one hour to twenty-nine minutes for another of those TV films, and she was to see it the next night in Lexington with a second cast. She made the trip from Nashville in "a rented car with Irina and Karl and Chuck and Simon. These are the nicest people in the company and I really enjoyed tremendously the ride with them. The rented car was very comfortable but of course not as nice as our old Oldsmobile," which, alas, had recently cast itself in the role of the one-hoss shay and had to be abandoned somewhere in the desert.

When she got home at last, her assessment of the season was bitter and familiar: "The New York musicians ruined the tour. For once, all the Chicago musicians stuck together. There were endless union quarrels between the two factions. If only they would quarrel over music."

But at least the tour was over.

NUTS REDIVIVUS

The most unexpected of all possible events occurred early in March. "Much to my surprise we had a letter from Ed Lee saying he is spending $60,000 to have Sam Leve do the scenery for 'Nuts' at McCormick Place and could we take over the rest of the production? So we are trying to persuade Lyric to take over the rest of the expenses. However I feel sure they won't." And of course she was right. Nevertheless, Ed Lee had miraculously recovered and was planning to go ahead with the production "this Christmas!"

How the money was to be raised for the *Nutcracker* costumes was the great question, for McCormick Place had agreed to put up $60,000 for the scenery and nothing more. When the estimate came in for that, indeed, it amounted to $250,000, which meant that Sam Leve would have to cut his original plan to the barest skeleton. Nevertheless, Ruth, doubtful but dauntless, saw to it that Rolf Gérard's costume sketches were sent to Irène Karinska in Paris to get the inevitably bad news from her. Nobody was remotely visible over the horizon to foot the bill, but at least she had taken the next logical step.

Then Ed Lee, quiet and resourceful, asked her to come to a special meeting with "his entourage," as she put it, at McCormick Place on May 13. To her surprise it proved not to be his McCormick Place "entourage" at all. "What a revelation that meeting was! Ten very important business men and me! I really couldn't believe my ears—they really want 'The Nutcracker' and will pay for the costumes." She did not in the least realize that the presence of those "ten very important businessmen" was an indication that the *Chicago Tribune* was in fact sponsoring *The Nutcracker*. Ed Lee had been doing his homework.

What made the meeting especially exciting was that only the day before there had been a thoroughly depressing meeting with Carol Fox and "her entourage" at the Lyric on the subject of *Carmina Burana*. Ruth was already sufficiently disturbed about that project, for Lyric in the natural course of operatic procedure had invited a European director—Josef Witt of the Vienna Opera—to direct it, and the more she worked on the score the more she realized that it had to be directed by the choreographer. With a dancer's innate muscular awareness of danceability, she sensed (if she did not already know) how profoundly Carl Orff and his music had been influenced by dancing—first by Mary Wigman herself and later by his close working association with the school of Dorothea Günther. Neither of the two of his *Trionfi* that she had seen could be treated according to conventional opera-house thinking, simply as opera with choreographic interludes. And now at this particular meeting Lyric came up with a set of Italian costume sketches that dealt the whole production the coup de grâce as far as she was concerned. "They are very good *opera* costumes, but definitely *opera*. My interest in 'Carmina' has completely cooled off."

She had already written to Witt, at his request, to tell him what her choreographic ideas were and had somewhat offhandedly suggested Harald Kreutzberg for the Death figure. "I just sort of said in one of my letters that he used to be marvelous in such roles. Witt got very excited about the idea and arranged for a meeting with Harald. So, we'll see. Carol Fox was as surprised as I was about Kreutzberg being interested and wanting to come." So, with none of her original zeal, she was to go to Vienna and talk to both Harald and Witt late in June.

She had already reconciled herself to the situation in a characteristic way; she would accept the opera's production as "definitely *opera*" but go right ahead planning a nonopera production of her own. She knew perfectly well how critical the situation was with Columbia. She had already talked to them about the next tour and had agreed to go along with their very practical suggestions, which certainly did not include anything remotely like *Carmina*. But she was impelled to work on it, whether or no. Not only that, but in the back of her mind was the even bolder determination to do *Catulli Carmina* also one day. The first time she had seen either of them was in Munich when they were performed together, and they had remained somehow together for her ever since. (Fortunately Heinz Rosen had not produced the *Trionfo di Afrodite*, the third member of the *Trionfi-Triptychon*, until the year after she was in Munich!) If the time and circumstances were still unclear, the intention was not. "So," to borrow her favorite phrase, "we'll see."

Her final meeting of the season with Carol Fox, Donati and Chris Mahon did nothing to win her further to the opera in general. "I made no progress with them at all. I just can't get a 10% raise for anyone and *none* of the things I want. I can't even get them to give me a pianist for class. For ten years we've been doing class without a pianist and I am so tired of it. I really should leave Lyric—it is *impossible* to make progress."

Her immediate concentration now, however, was per force on the miraculously salvaged *Nutcracker*. She had already been working on the "Snowflakes" pas de deux with Kleck and Ken, and on the "Waltz of the Flowers" with Dolores and Larry. "Expected to spend all of Sunday 'creating'—instead spent entire day and night over Nuts costume 'devis' from Karinska in Paris and Grace [a longtime assistant of Barbara Karinska] in New York. Very confusing."

The annual European pilgrimage began on June 21 in Vienna, where Ruth had flown, without Tom, for her meeting with Josef Witt at the Wiener Staatsoper. Trudy Goth had engaged a room for her in a pension, and she went at once to pay her respects to the Herr Professor. She explained to him in detail her entire plan for *Carmina*, and later, when Kreutzberg arrived at the opera house, she went over it all with him. She was naturally overjoyed to see Harald again and excited that he was going to play the roles of Death and Winter in Chicago, but she was worried about his age. As a matter of fact, at sixty-three, he was two years younger than she.

Her next stop, of course, was Paris, where she had to see what Karinska was doing with the *Nutcracker* costumes. Les Trois Pastèques was occupied (it had changed tenants since the Clinton Kings had returned to Chicago) and she stayed at a hotel. It was there that she was joined by Tom, very tired from the journey.

On the last day of the month they went to St. Tropez for the first time in two years. The dismal state of things they had left behind had been changed as if by magic. The studio floor was perfect. The newly acquired "upstairs" was marvelous. "Our angel Clavé had got the lease for ten years." It had been transformed into a self-contained apartment, with its own kitchen, bath, bedroom and large living-dining room overlooking the water.

All these rooms had still to be furnished, of course, and at once, for Delfau was due very shortly to become their first occupant. Though he would have no new ballet to prepare for the coming tour, his indispensable professional function would be to discuss with her at length her proposed ballet version of *Carmina Burana*, which automatically included a great deal of designing.

She was well aware that her company was much too small for her large-scale ideas and that the music, with its chorus and soloists (including a countertenor), offered insuperable problems. This was the same area in which she had met defeat at the hands of Richard Strauss years ago. Nevertheless, there was an irresistible compulsion to bring her conception of the work into some kind of elementary viability while she was feeling so belligerently creative about it. She realized early that her first compromise would have to be the use of tapes instead of live music, and she put Tom to work at once on what proved to be a long and tough struggle with the musicians' union and the publisher of the score. But with Ruth an obsession was not to be put aside, even if fulfillment required temporary compromises with visionary goals.

It was a busy July at Herbe Folle. Rolf Gérard came over to go into the many details of the *Nutcracker* costumes. At one time on their beach were Delfau, Gérard, Clavé and Bazarte—a clear majority of her designers since she had emerged from her wildly adventurous skirmishes with Americana into the audio-visual sophistication of Madame Fichère. "I sleep so badly here in St. Tropez. I have to go to bed very very late so I can sleep at all. But I work well late in my studio when everyone else has gone to bed."

On the first of August, well past midnight, when Tom was in bed and asleep, Anton Dolin dropped in, with appropriate apologies, on his way elsewhere. He was anxious to do Drosselmeyer in her Chicago *Nutcracker*, which was fine because she was anxious to have him do so. The next day

Delfau left for Italy, and the day after that she and Tom set out for Paris, where there were chores still to be done. Among them was the exhausting one of standing for hours, trying on sixty-one costumes at Karinska's.

From Paris they were off to Copenhagen for the weekend, where they talked to Kirsten Simone and Henning Kronstam about *Nutcracker*, in which they had already agreed by cable to dance the "Sugar Plum" grand pas de deux for ten performances. The real reason for going there, however, was to see a performance of Flemming Flindt's ballet *La Leçon*, based on Ionesco's one-act play of that name. He had done it first for Danish television, had later staged it at the Opéra Comique with Amiel (who, as a great friend of Ionesco's, had got permission for him to do it in the first place) and had now staged it again for the Royal Danish Ballet with its original setting by Bernard Daydé. After nine years of free-lancing with other European companies he had returned to this, his parent company, to become its director on January 1, though that had not yet been officially announced.

COLUMBIA CRISIS

The Copenhagen visit was actually motivated by Columbia Artists Management, with whom their situation was increasingly serious. As usual, when they got back to New York in early August, they went together to the office for their customary session with Tommy Thompson. Among the many ideas discussed was the possibility that they join forces with another company under Columbia's auspices. What seemed more feasible, however, was to continue as an independent company "but using my name and not the Chicago Opera name. I am very flattered that they prefer my name. He suggests 'Ruth Page's Dance Theatre', but I don't like this idea."

More immediate production matters, however, were primarily on her mind at this moment. She had brought back with her from Karinska's some *Nutcracker* costumes to be delivered to Vlady for alterations and rectifications when the time came. (Vlady was the nephew of Barbara Karinska and had taken over her business in New York when, under the Ford Foundation grant, she was engaged by the New York City Ballet to work exclusively for them.)

A few days after they got back to Chicago, Tom received a letter from Tommy, dated August 15, reporting a meeting of the Columbia directorate after their departure. It was a very long, sympathetic and tactful recapitulation of the state of affairs, in which all the subjects they had discussed in New York had been pulled together into a practicable plan for survival. What it consisted of was, in a nutshell, the phasing out of all Chicago Opera connotations not only in the company title but also in the repertoire. Though Ruth's innovative opera-into-ballet creations had been, and still were, eminently successful, the time had come to quit being unique and individual and to barge into the international ballet situation and beat it at its own game.

To this end, since everybody was doing *The Nutcracker*—Ruth's forth-coming McCormick Place production being the latest example—a new one-act arrangement of it by her would undeniably be attractive.

For another thing, there was Kurt Jooss's modern classic, *The Green Table*, which would have a strong appeal in revival. It was Columbia that had first brought *The Green Table* to this country in 1932. In the summer of that year Kurt Jooss and Frederic Cohen, its creators, had entered it in an international choreographic competition in Paris sponsored by Rolf de Maré and his Archives Internationales de la Danse, where in its first performance by their newly organized Jooss Ballet it had won first prize. With its eloquent antiwar theme it achieved worldwide acclaim and a permanent place in the repertoire as long as the company existed. Jooss restaged it in 1948 for the Chilean National Ballet, and Columbia had booked that company for an American tour only this past season of 1964-65. Thus it was again fresh in the public mind and certainly .with its antiwar eloquence by no means dimmed.

It was Columbia, also, that in 1956 had brought the Royal Danish Ballet to this country for the first time, and in line with his continuing admiration for them, Tommy noted that "Columbia would be decidedly pleased if Ruth wished to add Flemming Flindt's new ballet … . which I understand is highly desired by several other American companies." He further suggested that Kirsten Simone and Henning Kronstam be brought back as guest stars.

Tom's reply to thé letter was an enthusiastic one. He said he agreed with "practically every word you say!" He had immediately written to Kurt Jooss about *The Green Table* for the 1967 season, had already sent a contract to Flindt and would try to borrow some *Nutcracker* costumes from McCormick Place.

As it was finally worked out, there would be one more tour of Ruth Page's Chicago Opera Ballet as already planned, and the proposed change of name and the switch to a nonopera policy would take place with the 1967 tour. The 1966 tour, however, would include as many as possible of Columbia's suggestions. There would be at least a set of variations from *Nutcracker*, and a larger and more formal suite would be readied for the 1967 tour. Simone and Kronstam, however, would not be available until next year's tour, since they would be touring with the Royal Danish Ballet itself. This would not affect their already-contracted-for appearances in *The Nutcracker* for ten performances during Christmas week.

Flindt and Amiel would come over immediately and he would stage *La Leçon* for the tour. She would appear in it, by permission of the Paris Opéra, but he could not do so, since he was taking over the directorship of the Danish company at once. The two of them would nevertheless make two appearances in *The Nutcracker* before he left.

DIRECTING IN TRIPLICATE

Ruth's immediate schedule of operations could scarcely have been more complex. Besides the preparations for the forthcoming Columbia tour, the opera season and its rehearsals came along right in the middle of the organizing and producing of the momentous *Nutcracker* première.

In September there was an audition for local children, who were to constitute one of the important features of the McCormick Place production. Notices had been sent to all the dancing schools, and nearly five hundred youngsters between the ages of nine and thirteen showed up. Ruth had the happy idea of asking Edna McRae to take complete charge of the children. One of the most celebrated of Chicago teachers, she had had long and productive experience with children, and only recently she had closed her school and given up teaching. Perhaps for this very reason she accepted the invitation with enthusiasm.

The auditioning was, of course, more heartbreaking than usual, for there were so many more hearts to be broken; only forty children were to be chosen. When the actual rehearsing began, Edna McRae "was marvelous—the second I did anything [for the continuous children's scenes throughout the first act and for their part in the second act] she wrote it down—I was really impressed."

Ruth had worked out the role of Drosselmeyer, which was of course entirely involved with the children, with Dolin specifically in mind and had even engaged Marshall, the magician, to invent suitable tricks of magic for him to perform. Since there were two alternating casts of children for him to work with, the rehearsals were necessarily demanding on both him and Edna McRae—not to speak of Ruth, who actually managed somehow to be at every rehearsal with Dolin until the choreography was finally set.

As usual she had rented the large studio in the basement of the Eleventh Street Theatre to accommodate some of her rehearsing before the opera house was available, and after that she was forever dashing back and forth among these areas of activity and McCormick Place. She had only a week to devote herself exclusively to the *Nutcracker* before the Lyric Opera rehearsals started, and the *Nutcracker* problems followed her there as a matter of course.

As if the opera were not able to produce enough of them on its own! One director of the standard repertoire, for example, had a penchant for changing his mind at the last minute and even adding whole sections after rehearsals were finished. Just as she was trying, in this postscript manner, to choreograph a charioteer with four horses for him into the Amneris scene in *Aida*, a note arrived from Vlady about *Nutcracker* costumes. She had deposited them with him in New York for ultimate adaptation to the shapes and sizes of the dancers she was hiring in Chicago, and the measurements she had sent him for one of them puzzled him somewhat. "The chart says his chest measures 18″–should it read 38″? Please, Ruth, do not hire dancers with 18″ chests. They must be too sick for words!"

In October Ed Lee had a fresh inspiration. He thought the time was ripe to organize something to be called the Ruth Page Foundation for Ballet, which he was convinced could "become the assembly point for the creative and performing arts of the dance in this community." The announcement of it in connection with the *Nutcracker* production, he thought, would "achieve public interest to maximum advantage all around." Tom was immediately enthusiastic and suggested many ideas for the charter. Such a corporation was duly chartered before the end of the year, though it was never actually organized. At Lee's suggestion, however, a nonprofit organization was created by the *Tribune* for the purpose, first, of carrying on the *Nutcracker* for ten years and, second, of producing a new work along similar lines for Easter week, which, if successful, would likewise be repeated for ten years. (It did not take Ruth long to decide that *Alice in Wonderland* would be the ideal subject for this purpose, and she already began to visualize fantastic designs by Delfau.)

As far as the opera season was concerned, *Carmina Burana* was naturally her main interest. Now that she had her own ballet version of it established among her creative purposes, she approached the opera version with a less agitated state of mind. By the end of October, when Kreutzberg arrived, she was well along with it.

At the same time she was creating a new Bacchanale for *Samson and Delilah*, which proved to be a bit too bacchanalian for Carol Fox, who made her tone it down. Ruth was afraid Witt would think she was putting "too much dancing" into *Carmina*; which he did, but his only action was to follow Carol's precedent and tone down its exuberance, for basically he was pleased with it.

The actual trouble with *Carmina* came later when stage rehearsals got under way. The chorus, which was massed behind the dancers, could not see the conductor, so, much as Witt liked the dances, they had to be juggled around and the dancers moved about or taken out. The platform on the stage limited all the movement and hampered all these adjustments. "Not until after the dress rehearsal was it removed! What a week! Thought I could not live through it." Nevertheless, the première was triumphant. "The audience cheered long and loud. . . . I bowed (in my off-shoulder St. Tropez black Hindu sari dress) with Witt and Fournet [the conductor]–two very handsome men.

"After the performance we dashed home and had forty-five people to supper–a real supper. The only nondancers were the Witts and their son and two friends. We had a marvelous supper (Felisa and two Mexican friends cooked it). Bob Joffrey, Lisa Bradley and about ten of his people joined us so it was really a mob. . . . We got to bed at 4 a.m. and the apartment was a shambles. Someone threw up all over the living room."

In mid-November Kreutzberg left for home, happy with his visit, and the season closed early in December, much to her relief. But not before she learned from Carol Fox that one of her opera boys had "garneria"! What would Lyric come up with next!

Throughout the final *Nutcracker* rehearsals, after the opera season was over, she was having trouble from the third area of her simultaneous concern— namely, the tour. Flemming Flindt, in his staging of *La Leçon*, insisted that it was "impossible for him to do anything without Daydé in Chicago to confer with him. Apparently the set was the most important part of the ballet." He was also asking for "impossible things in his contract." The *Nutcracker* opened on December 26, and the next day Daydé arrived, and she talked business with him. "Very unpleasant. What we thought would be a little inexpensive pas de trois I think will turn out to be the most expensive ballet in the repertoire." Amiel and Flindt duly danced their two performances of the *Nutcracker* pas de deux before he flew off to his new duties.

Neal Kayan, who had been somewhat at loose ends since his Ballet Theatre debacle, had been called back to share the conducting of *The Nutcracker* with Simon Sadoff. Simon, however, was not planning to go on the tour again, which made it good for Neal, who moved back smoothly at last into his old job.

The *Nutcracker* engagement ended on January 2. Every performance had been sold out, thanks to the active support of the *Chicago Tribune*. The production was not reviewed by most of the other papers; indeed, there was no reason in the world why they should promote their major rival's promotion scheme. Nevertheless, it was a huge success, and the *Tribune* ran a full-page ad announcing another season next year.

Ruth left at once for Urbana to open her company's tour, with a parting note to Tom to behave himself in his dealings with Ed Lee. "I only hope you won't be too critical of him," she wrote, "and that you will be able to stay friendly. It seems to me that in your character you are always either bawling your friends out or being overeffusive."

Behaving himself was exactly what he had not been doing; indeed, he had made the whole season distinctly unpleasant off stage. In a measure, Lee may have been at fault, for early on he had called on Tom for assistance in various areas and Tom was not by nature an assistant in any project. Now, two days after the season's close, he wrote Lee a fairly caustic summation of their differences. To this Lee replied the next day with his characteristic poise. He was sorry, he said, that this first season of *The Nutcracker* would carry so many scars; it was just such unpleasantnesses that had "chased" him away from the performing arts after twenty-five years' experience. But after reflection he realized that Tom's "memorandum" came quite close to what he had expected him to say. After touching on all the matters Tom had broached—finances, public relations, artistic policy—what Lee summed up as "the aesthetics and economics of our Nutcracker"—he wanted to go on record with a clear statement of his own attitude toward the undertaking. He had worked on it because he believed it would be good for Chicago and for McCormick Place and, most importantly, it would provide pleasant family entertainment for the community. He had visited Ruth to wish her luck before the first performance and once more after the final performance to congratulate her for a fine job. Beyond that he had no personal interest of any kind. He had worked to provide the money, facilities and audiences, and he could rest his case with the belief that all those concerned had given the best of their abilities. "If the Nutcracker is to survive," he concluded, "I believe we will have to give more thought and fuller efforts to avoid the kind of troubles we labored through the first time around."

Tom replied to all this with a kind of wide-eyed innocence, but he could not have been much surprised and may even have been pleased. He had participated in this venture, as in others, as neither aesthete nor altruist but all-out attorney dedicated to winning. There was no avarice involved; neither he nor Ruth took any salary for their labors. But he would promote his client-wife against colleagues, patrons and, if necessary, even her own wishes.

As for the tour, its only imported star was Josette Amiel, and its only new ballet was Flindt's Ionesco-based horror play *en pointe*, with music by George Delerue and its "indispensable" set by Bernard Daydé. Ruth had also revived *Camille* for Josette (she "learned very fast"), and there were, besides, *All's Fair in Love and War* (which was *Bullets and Bonbons* under a new title), the *Widow* (who had never yet missed a tour) and other more or less standard works of the repertoire.

Urbana—high school auditorium—tiny stage—cement floor—no dressing rooms ("a nightmare!")—looked awful in the "tan-colored drapes," those dismal drapes so much in vogue in nontheatres, which had been causing her anguish for years—audience seemed to like it as usual—"I suffered agonies. Literally couldn't sleep all night."

Fond du Lac—bad movie house—absolutely no heat—wait in freezing cold while stagehands remove enormous loud-speakers—too cold to do any real rehearsing—made up and dressed in hotel—full house—nobody danced very well—"Larry Long conked out toward the end of 'Concertino.' Said he didn't know why."

Et cetera, et cetera, per saecula saeculorum . . .

" . . . As the Sparks Fly Upward"

New Face, New Woes

The transition from Ruth Page's Chicago Opera Ballet to her rechristened International Ballet was simple enough on the face of it, and even the change of policy it implied was accomplished painlessly. Only *The Green Table* failed to materialize as scheduled; by the time Tom's request for its revival reached Kurt Jooss in Germany the City Center Joffrey Ballet had already contracted for it.

Its loss, however, proved to be a boon to Ruth. As if by providential forewarning, she had *Carmina Burana* well along in preparation, which to her delight could now be slipped patly into the gap. Her unreasonable insistence on completing it had been justified after all. Its score was high in public favor and fell into the category designated by Russell Lynes as "middlebrow" that was exactly what Columbia was seeking.

When she finally saw Joffrey's *Green Table* revival in New York after her own tour was well under way without it, she was reassured that fate had been beneficent. For all its undeniable excellence, she could not have helped sensing that it was not really her cup of tea. Its stark earnestness was at a far remove from her natural grace.

The intervening summer at St. Tropez, then, had necessarily been dominated by her concentration—and Delfau's as well—on *Carmina*. Thanks, perhaps, to Anna Marie and David Holmes, who had lived in Leningrad as guest artists with the Kirov Ballet, she had discovered in Paris, where Karinska was not available on such short notice, two expatriated Russian nobelwomen,

Marie Molotkoff and Marie Gromtseff, who were expert at the execution of costumes, and Delfau himself undertook the supervising of the process. The production as it finally emerged was probably the smartest and certainly the Frenchest the work had ever known.

Tom, to be sure, had still not obtained all the interlocking permissions required for the use of tape instead of live music and did not do so until the eleventh hour. Only in December, three weeks before the opening of the tour, did he receive final approval from Associated Music Publishers, Inc. The letter announcing that welcome news concluded with a pleasant little fanfare: "It would have been nice to meet you at long last to offer our personal congratulations on your resourcefulness, vitality and imagination."

Not even these admirable endowments, however, together with his unremitting persistence, had solved the problem that imperiled the future— namely, the rising cost of operation induced by the ever stiffer demands of the unions. He knew that Sergei Denham had recently organized a company called Les Ballets de Monte Carlo under Monegasque laws; in fact, Denham had asked Ruth to associate herself with it, as both Massine and Lifar had done. So Tom wrote to appropriate sources in Paris to ascertain if it would be possible to incorporate Ruth Page's International Ballet (nonprofit) in France to avoid "devastating" contract increases from AGMA. Such increases, he pointed out, were generally not applicable in the United States to foreign organizations; but did this mean that the incorporators must be French citizens? He also investigated the chances of creating a corporation, either profit or nonprofit, in the Bahamas. Without something of the sort in the immediate future, no amount of policy changing by Columbia would ultimately save the situation.

Nevertheless, activities started at Hubbard Woods as usual as soon as Ruth and Tom returned from St. Tropez, and they increased in scope as her dancers began to reassemble. In accordance with the built-in pattern, the opera rehearsals and the *Nutcracker* rehearsals would be concurrent, housed inconveniently far apart and further complicated by preparations for the tour, which intruded upon them both and involved many of the same people.

This year's opera schedule provided only two novelties, neither of which excited her at all. One was Casella's ballet *La Giara*, in which Carla Fracci and Erik Bruhn were to be guest artists. Ruth was to provide only the choreography, while the work as a whole, notorious for its intractable scenario by Pirandello, was to be directed by Fracci's husband, Beppe Menegatti. The other was Bizet's first (and seldom produced) opera, *The Pearl Fishers*, and it, too, suffered from serious libretto troubles. Otherwise there were only the run-of-the-mill opera ballets for her.

Typical of the overlappings of her three departments of activity, Bruhn was also to be one of her European stars for *The Nutcracker*, dancing the grand pas de deux with Josette Amiel; and Amiel, without him, was then to be one of the imported stars of the tour—the first tour, indeed, of Ruth Page's International Ballet. Simone and Kronstam were also to come back for *The Nutcracker*, but no matter how indispensable Columbia might consider them, they could only do the first half of the tour. When it came time for them to go back to Copenhagen, John Gilpin, of London's Festival Ballet, was to join up as stellar partner to Amiel. Having three European stars for the first half of the tour was expensive, especially in this period of stringency, but unavoidable. New to the program, besides *Carmina Burana*, would be the enlarged *Nutcracker Suite*. It would still use the borrowed costumes from McCormick Place but would have a new setting by Delfau.

The financial clouds, however, that hung so formidably over the survival of the company were soon to be reduced to insignificance by the preposterous union of extrinsic forces, unrelated even to each other, that were steadily closing in on Tom in an ironic confluence. The tragedy is Greek in its inexorableness.

Ruth's diaries, whose province is almost organically private, do not recognize the approach of the ultimate catastrophe at all at this point. Not until it can no longer be brushed aside automatically as belonging to that hideous world of business, which is Tom's area of operation, does it gradually acquire substance, and even then from a remote and impervious stance at first. But the breaching of the dense texture of her life, as it does occur, takes on a reality in the diaries' own first person that no objective report can approximate. So, at whatever risk, it is the diaries, cut as close to the bone as possible without destroying their essential workaday values, that must be allowed to tell the tale as fully as may be.

THE VIEW FROM WITHIN

To the diaries, then, or at least to relevant excerpts from them.

It is Hubbard Woods, toward the end of August:

> Chuck has been out every day and yesterday he actually practiced with me. We had a short but very good practice—however he did not show up today. Such a lazy boy and so juvenile but so much fun. We took a long walk on the beach with Margaret. He and I worked on the branches for the Delfau "Carmina"—it seems like an endless job. The way they were made in Paris they would have fallen completely apart after one bus ride. . . . The weather is hot like I like it.

Margaret Fisher, Tom's younger sister, an excellent and sensitive painter, lived alone in the old family home in Winnetka. She was close not only to Tom but also to Ruth, who ranked her very high among her favorite relatives. If they are seen in the following pages to have their differences, these were such as could exist only between people whose feelings for each other were fundamental and indestructible.

September

Went to town last Monday. Did errands downtown till eleven. Then practiced with Orrin and Patricia [otherwise Kleck]. At 2 p.m. I went to David Fishman's with Chuck and Patricia and we took pictures of "Carmina" all p.m. It was an exhausting job. Orrin and Patricia came to H. W. Thursday. We practiced at noon, then worked on a pas de deux for "Carmina" and late in the evening went swimming.

Friday I went to town early, went to the dentist, then worked two hours with Bill Hughes [the pianist] on counting for "Giara." Had an interview with Raya Lee [a new member of the company] at 2:30. She wants to be Larry's assistant as ballet mistress. I would like to let her try it, but I haven't any extra cash.

Today Patricia, Orrin and Chuck came out. We practiced at noon and then worked 2 hours on "Carmina." The little pas de deux I think will be quite charming. To the beach for a swim at 5. And now an evening to read. Am fascinated with Capote's "In Cold Blood."

Had a lovely but exhausting Labor Day weekend. A dinner party for Tom's birthday with all the Fisher family. It was too cold to eat out, so 8 of us ate in our tiny living room and 4 in the dining room.

To town Thursday. Orrin, Kleck and Chuck came and we did class and then did some rehearsing on "Giara." At 5:30 I met Edna McRae and all the children from last year who wanted to return for the "Nuts" performances this Xmas. Most of them do want to do it again, and they didn't seem to have grown too much.

Sunday we had the children's auditions at McCormick Place. While the children are refreshing and sometimes inspiring, it is still an agony for me, as we can only take a very few and there are so many who have to be disappointed. It was a long seance.

Moved to town on Tuesday—as usual absolutely exhausting. We started rehearsals Friday at the Eleventh Street Theatre basement. We gave over most of the week to "Nutcracker" for McCormick Place. We had all the extras every day. I don't think the corps of extras are as good as last year. McCormick Place paid for the week's rehearsals. Saturday was our day off so I worked all day with the soloists at 1100 [the Lake Shore Drive apartment]. Saturday night I went over to McCormick Place to help Edna select children for Danse Arabe.

We rehearsed Sunday through Thursday at Eleventh St. and moved to the opera house on Friday. We rehearsed there Friday and Saturday from 4 to 11:15—absolutely a killing time to rehearse. I just can't get used to those hours. The usual madhouse at the opera—no space—dirty—but still lots of fun. When I got home last night I was absolutely pooped.

This a.m. I spent 3 hours getting the list of tights ready to order. I have to get them all in Paris as no one here makes tights with calgoules. Anyway I finished the order.

Got about ten minutes of "Giara" ready and it doesn't look too badly, but I can't say that I am very inspired by this ballet.

October

Thursday after a long hard day at the opera, we took Fracci and Menegatti to the Racquet Club for dinner . . . and I must say we had a lovely evening even though I was very tired.

Friday I rehearsed till 6 p.m. then dressed for the opening night of the opera in my little room. I just barely got dressed in time—I had to borrow makeup. I didn't have time to eat anything but we did get to the opera in time. It was "Boris Godunoff." I wore my new dark blue and silver St. Laurent dress and I felt very chic and elegant. I love the Boris opera and sitting in the front row I really felt a part of it. Ghiauroff was absolutely stunning and believable. The sets were old-fashioned but quite good and some of the costumes stunning. The "polonaise" scene bad—big hill, so we practically could only do one step and I missed this lovely dance. We literally just walked on and off but my dancers looked very chic and handsome.

After the opera was the usual ball. This is the thirteenth I have been to and they all seem pretty much the same. Everybody is all dressed up and we all come marching in and bow while Carol Fox makes a speech about us. I usually walk in with Lepore [chorus master] (Chorus and Ballet). The chorus is the best paid chorus in the world—the Lyric ballet is the worst paid in the world! We got home at 3 a.m. . . . Fracci was invited to the opera ball but *not* Klekovic or Johnson or any of our dancers. It made me furious.

Did nothing all week but rehearse. "Giara" is coming along slowly. The music is difficult and it is hard to put over the story. While I like to work with Menegatti in a way, he gets very "operatic" at times and wants "properties" of all kinds which I am against. Also he wants Carla and Erik in every scene and now instead of having too small a role they each are on the stage almost too much. If we had more time, everything could be easily adjusted but now there is so little time.

All week we worked on "La Giara"—Lyric gave us plenty of time with the orchestra, as the score was just as difficult for them as it was for us. It certainly sounds a hundred times better with orchestra than with piano and at times the music is very exciting. The trouble with the ballet is the story and the fact that the construction of the music is not good for ballet. It is really an impossible task for *anyone* to make a success of this ballet.

In any event, we finally got it on last night, but with what difficulty. The *day* of the dress rehearsal Carla Fracci had to be operated on. She is of course still in the hospital and will not be able to dance for quite a long time. Erik couldn't dance the stage rehearsal because he hurt his back. He found all the lifts too hard for him to do, and also the jumping too strenuous, so *after* the dress rehearsal—the day of the performance, we had to change everything for him. He just is not in shape to dance—he barely got through it last night. Kleck got through the role quite well and it is extraordinary how well she did it considering that it was Fracci who did all the rehearsing. The corps danced exceedingly well and with real passion and acted well. I was proud of them. Catusso's set was quite good, although one critic said it was the worst set he had ever seen! How little music critics can see. Carol Fox invited all my dancers (except Orrin Kayan) to supper at the Italian Village afterwards, along with the singers for "Cavalleria" [the other half of the double bill]. It was a very nice party but completely spoiled for me because she did not invite Orrin Kayan, even though the last minute Orrin had to go into the tarantella as it was just too much for Erik.

November

Last night was our last "Giara"—if only the first night had been as good as last night. Erik really danced the ballet for the first time. He still can't do the lifts. Maybe he feels (and rightly) that Klekovic is too big for him, but he was with the music last night and he did the pantomime well. But actually, wonderful as he is, he is not a good choice for this ballet. Fracci got home from the hospital yesterday and she came to the performance last night.

The music for "Pearl Fishers" third act ballet is so ordinary and just gives no "inspiration" for dancing at all. I got the idea to do the dance as a symbolic human sacrifice, but it seems a bit "corny," like the music. Crevelli, the director, seemed to like my ballet, though it is still a mess.

We had the opening of our "Pearl Fishers" last Friday and to me it was an extremely pleasant surprise. The idea of the story and the music are both so naive and French that the work has a great deal of charm. The music of course is 100% better with orchestra. The ballets all looked charming and added a great deal to the action. I didn't like Peter Hall's costumes very much—the sets were all right. One of the critics thought the ballets looked like Minsky's, but he must have been referring to the costumes and not the dances because the dancers' movements were what I remembered from India and Shankar. Another critic liked these ballets and it is the only time he liked us all season. The critics all seem to be crazy and don't seem to know what they are talking about. Crevelli added a whole new section for the dancers *after* the dress rehearsal. Carol Fox had new trunks made for the boys as she thought they were too naked!

All through this busy week I was preparing for the wedding of Felisa's daughter Celia. The groom, Guerrero, arrived last Wednesday and is staying in our guest room. He doesn't speak a word of English. I think he will make a good husband for Celia. He seems like a substantial attractive sensible man of about 36. He has a good sense of humor, and after the wild affair Celia has been carrying on with her very young cousin, I think Felisa is very relieved to have her marry Guerrero. [Celia, it seems, was the fruit of an indiscretion of Felisa's, and was to be saved at any cost from the same youthful mistake.]

Tom gave the priest at the cathedral (Church of the Holy Name) $100 and he prepared a lovely wedding ceremony for us. I had to go directly from rehearsal to the church. I wore my cerise and black St. Laurent boutique dress. [Felisa, incidentally, was wearing one of Ruth's Diors.] Tom gave the bride away and she looked lovely in a brand new wedding dress with a long train, with a darling little girl to hold it up. We all knelt in front of the altar for a long time. The most beautiful part of the ceremony was when the priest put the bride's veil over the groom's shoulder and the maid of honor then entwined the two of them in a long crystal rosary. It was very moving.

After the ceremony we gave a big party for Celia—all the Mexicans, Margaret Fisher, Ann Barzel, Edna McRae, Rose Wergoth (my hairdresser and a life-long friend), Menegatti and Carla Fracci and Chuck Schick. We had lots of champagne, lots of pictures and a delicious supper. I had planned to leave the party to the Mexicans and go to see the last performance of "Pearl Fishers" with Ann Barzel, but it was just *impossible* for me to get away.

First of all, I had gotten out all my amusing dance and party records and then for the first time in history something happened to the victrola needle and we couldn't have *any* music. This made me absolutely sick. Then the big wedding cake that I went to so much trouble to get didn't arrive. I was supposed to pick it up at the pastry shop but they forgot to tell me so and I of course supposed that they would deliver it. Of course I called them and no one answered. Finally they called me at 10:30 and brought it over! They all stayed till after midnight and I really was too tired to sleep.

This a.m. had breakfast with the bride and groom. Felisa wouldn't let them sleep together, because she said Celia belonged to her till they left Chicago, which, thank God, is Monday night. Much as I love them, it is really too tiring with all the work at the opera.

Tom has to go to Texas today—lots of long distance phoning this a.m. and now I have to go to rehearsal.

OYEZ! OYEZ!

Tom had to go to Texas for one day. Something happened to his plane coming back and he had to motor 280 miles and he arrived home absolutely dead and sick to his stomach. Then he had the Atwood trial yesterday a.m. and the court is making it very hard for him and are threatening to put him in jail for "contempt of court." He was too sick to do anything on Thanksgiving so we stayed home all day. It is good to have a day off but I had to work all day getting the programs ready for the tour and writing business letters.

My rehearsals for "Carmina" at the opera are not going well. Klekovic and Schick were just impossible the other day—she showed no imagination at all and he didn't understand what I am doing. They were very discouraging.

Was very ill all Friday a.m. Felisa and Tom were both sick too—all of us throwing up! I felt very weak but dragged myself to the theatre about 3 and worked for an hour and a half. The finale of "Carmina" is very difficult to arrange. My "Carmina" is for a very large company and my company is so small that they all have to make quick changes like mad. The trees (in place of scenery) are difficult to handle also. My great friend Chuck Schick was very insulting to me and that made me *iller* than my stomach upset.

Then Tom has had so much trouble with the Atwood case that that made us all sick. The judge wants to put him in jail for "contempt of court"! He is very sick so is going to the Cleveland Clinic to see what is the matter. . . .

So finally "Traviata" got on. Menegatti's staging was very flashy and brisk and he kept things moving but he made a lot of mistakes and on the whole I was disappointed.

I still felt sick today so didn't go to class but rehearsed for 3 hours. "Carmina" cleared up a bit today. Had dinner alone and spent the evening correcting programs for tour and making program for McCormick Place "Nuts."

December

A wild awful week I had and thank God it is over! Tom has been in Cleveland all week at the Clinic getting looked over. He can't return to Chicago so I am very lonesome and having an awful time with all the business affairs. Am finally getting the contracts from McCormick Place for the dancers for "Nuts" and have finally arranged for the Lyric to let us rehearse in the Civic and getting out the insurance, etc. etc. etc.—a million details.

Sunday I went with Albertine Maxwell to the Francis Parker School to see the "young dancers" of Chicago—from about all the schools—and I must say, it was a dreary afternoon.

Went with Orrin and Patricia to the Stadium to see the Italian festa and I absolutely adored every minute of it. Such interesting dances—such beautiful horses with knights riding them, a Sicilian puppet show, a chess game with people. It would take five years to see all that if you were in Italy. Had dinner with K and K and Orrin afterwards and home late.

Rehearsed every day all week and after my rehearsal at Lyric took a taxi and went to McCormick Place to see what Edna was doing with the children. Got home at 9:30, had dinner and went right to bed really exhausted.

Thursday I made a lovely and touching dance for Judith Thelen for the swan [in *Carmina*]—she inspired me and I choreographed the dance very easily—I really enjoy choreographing for her. I used to love to choreograph for Schick, but now he cramps my style completely. I can't stand to even have him around.

I was very tired after rehearsal today and decided to go out and have a bite to eat before the opera. Bentley and Walter were in the restaurant so I ate with them. But I wish I hadn't. They kept saying how terrible everything the Lyric does is—*everything* was awful according to them.

Tuesday I thought would never end. We had class at 10 a.m. and rehearsed till 5, then I went to McCormick Place and rehearsed with Edna and the children.

When I arrived home my brother Irvine was there to spend the night with me. Margaret Fisher, Ann and Ray Finlay and 5 of their children and

Narcissa King came for dinner and we really had a lovely time. Irvine is one of those inspiring people who make you think that life is worth living. He talks fascinatingly on almost any subject.

The children put together a rickshaw that I bought so that kept them occupied. But at the end of the evening, about 11 p.m. Margaret and Ray were still there after the others had left and they got to discussing Tom's situation. I pretended to be very steely, but the whole conversation made me very sick and I just couldn't sleep all night. Irvine left early in the morning.

Today we rehearsed with the children from 5:30 to 9:30 and I got to McCormick Place at 4:30, but the rehearsal was so interesting that it seemed to me like no time at all.

It is difficult for me now without Tom as I have to do all the business. I spent the *entire* day Sunday telephoning dancers for the rehearsals. Then Monday before rehearsing I had to go to Tom's office and spend a couple of hours getting business done—how I hate it.

Another wild, wild week—I need about 6 secretaries. All I do is telephone and write letters and programs and attend to business and *nothing* for pleasure!

We are half rehearsing at McCormick Place and half at opera. Dolin arrived and we gave him two long, full rehearsals. We have three groups of children for him to work with this year instead of two and it complicates the rehearsing a lot.

Had trouble with a black child whom we let go because she missed rehearsals and just couldn't do the work and Edna said her mother was impossible. All hell broke loose because she was black. We only picked her because she was black and there were lots of white children at the audition infinitely better than she was. Edna and I both stuck to our guns, but Ed Lee telephoned today and said we just *had* to take her back. So, I'm afraid our discipline will go to hell from now on.

Today was also very hard. I missed class because of telephone calls, but got to Civic Theatre for rehearsal. We had a run-through of "Carmina" in costume. I have seen it so much now that I don't know what to really think about it. The spring scene seemed to come off best.

Had to pack up all my things at the theatre and take them home with me— tape recorders, projector, costumes, clothes, etc. What a mess.

The weeks get wilder and wilder. We had our final dress rehearsal yesterday with of course the usual problems. The Tribune was trying to get pictures at the same time we had the light rehearsal and the orchestra rehearsal plus costumes, etc. and it was just too much.

After a dress rehearsal from 12:30 to 5:30 on Tuesday without a break, we still had a television to do for CBS that night of the 2 first-act doll dances plus Danse Arabe (without children). Vicky Fisera [a member of the company] and her new husband took me in their new white Cadillac and we had a flat tire right near 1100, so we came to the kitchen and had a quick dinner. Felisa wasn't there, so I got the dinner of just cold stuff in the ice box and it wasn't too bad. Barry Edson [another member of the company] was with us and we had a lot of fun. It was then that we did the television and when I came home the kitchen floor was flooded with water and I had to get an engineer in the middle of the night.

Next day Margaret Fisher called me and said our studio in Winnetka had been broken into. What next! This is certainly *not* my year. If my luck doesn't change next year I'll give up.

Tom is still in New York and can't return to Chicago, so besides all my own worries, I worry about him a lot.

. . . Xmas was very hard for me this year. We actually had the day before Xmas free and I spent the day preparing for a party on Xmas day.

We opened "Nuts" the 22nd of Dec. and repeated it the 23rd. Only two newspapers reviewed our performance—Tribune and American. The other newspapers (Sun-Times and Daily News) just refused to come at all. Well, we are a tremendous success without them. Eighty thousand tickets sold and not a seat to be had for *any* performance. Even Xmas day was sold out!

We had a matinee at 4 p.m. and afterwards my company (the Lyric, touring version) came to 1100 for supper. Margaret Fisher came and fixed a tree for us. Ann Finlay and the children also made me a very amusing tree and then I had one of my own, so we looked very festive. I had 42 people and gave them a delicious supper. They left about 1 a.m. and I was dead. I do hope they enjoyed it as it was a lot of work.

I was too tired to go to the matinee today so stayed home and attended to business *all* day. Life is horrible without Tom—I couldn't enjoy the Xmas party at all without him.

. . . Erik and Josette danced their 6th and last "Nutcracker" this afternoon. She dances the Sugar Plum Fairy very well.

Delfau arrived Thursday. I came home from the matinee and he arrived just after me. I took him to "Nutcracker" and he seemed quite impressed. His favorite dance was the "Arabe."

I had a truly wild and exhausting day on Friday. All the contracts are wrong and I am trying to untangle them, with no success. On top of all my troubles the Tribune decided that they wanted to take color pictures. Friday Delfau and I spent all a.m. at Becker's working on scenery for "Nuts" for tour. Delfau was very disappointed with what Becker had done and we had quite a morning. I went from there directly to the theatre and had quite an afternoon. Taking the pictures was sheer agony— we had two hours to take both acts and everyone was tired and disagreeable.

New Year's Eve, Delfau sick in bed, Felisa in bed and I hope I won't be enticed out to any parties!

January

A wild, wild week trying to get our ballets ready for the tour. Tom·is still in "exile" in New York at the Harvard Club, and I am very lonesome and helpless, but learning fast how to take care of everything. No time for myself at all. . . .

OFF TO THE STICKS AGAIN

A whole week of performances finished last night. I really didn't think I would live through it, but I did! Our first performance was in Waukegan. It was not a Columbia date; we were engaged by the Abbott Laboratories; our manager, a lady from Chicago, Mrs. Marks, brought us here.

Saturday Jan. 7 Delfau and I took the train to Waukegan and arrived at noon and went directly to the theatre, which thank God was very nice and new and attractive (which always surprises me in a new theatre). We stayed at the theatre till 7 p.m. trying to get the lights set. We had intended to light "Carmina" on Sat. and "Nuts" on Sun. but we didn't get to "Carmina" at all. We have four new men for the crew and a new stage manager. André is not much help on the lights—he knows what he would like but doesn't know how to get it. It was all very wild and crazy. We spent the night at a lovely motel, the Waukegan Inn. We had not planned to spend the night, but just thought it would be easier.

The company arrived the next morning and we gave a matinee of "All's Fair" and "Nuts" at 3 p.m. It was the very first time we ever gave "All's Fair" with the full set, and it certainly did make a difference. It really looked stunning and was most amusing. Delfau said he loved it.

We came home in our car, which is being driven for the tour by Orrin Kayan and carrying Kirsten and Henning. They brought us straight to 1100. I cooked dinner for André and then I worked all evening trying to get "business" attended to—programs, rehearsal schedules, etc. etc. Left by the company bus next a.m. at 9.

When we got to Kalamazoo there was Tom to meet me and was I thrilled— life without him is just impossible. We had the lights for "Carmina" all afternoon, but with the new crew, all the lights were not set up till almost time for class. So Delfau and I did the lights while class was going on—this was the wildest light rehearsal I've ever had. The evening seemed to be a triumph, although I was so tired that even "Carmina" left me a bit cold. Tom took us to supper at an old railway station converted into a restaurant and it was really charming. Next a.m. Tom left. The review said we "captivated the audience," and that we had danced in Kalamazoo 3 times and this was the best, so maybe we are improving with age!

The theatre at Kalamazoo was pretty good, but the Benton Harbor theatre was a disaster—yet with no lights and facilities at all, Carmina was very thrilling. Klekovic is just exactly what I want for this ballet. Johnson was much better than I ever thought he could be and was even better than Chuck in Act 3. In any event, Delfau and I were both thrilled.

We came back in the bus with the company to Chicago and arrived at 12:30 a.m., so it wasn't too bad. There were too many people on the bus, so I sat in the back seat with the musicians, while a corps de ballet boy sat in my seat!

Arrived Friday at Minneapolis at 2:30. They gave me a wonderful big room at the Pick-Nicollet Hotel but I had no time at all to be in it. Dressed quickly and we left for the theatre at 5. At last a good stage— excellent floor and nice and big. Completely sold out house (at least 5000 people) but not a good theatre for ballet as you could really only see from the last ten rows. I sat in the 3rd row and could hardly see at all. We gave a very curious performance. . . . I thought it was not a good program at all but everyone in the audience seemed delighted.

"All's Fair" was a big hit. We have given the last performance of it (only four times) and never again. It seems tragic to drop it. I have only seen it twice with all the scenery and what a difference it makes in the success of the ballet to have all the paraphernalia. It was really a hit. Saw Chuck after the performance and he said he would never dance his role again— stupid, stupid boy as it is one of his best roles. Larry Long hates his role too, so I let Lloyd Labit do his part. I'm so fed up with dancers and all their nonsense.

What a grim two days I had in Chicago. The big apartment was very lonesome without Tom and Felisa. Monday I spent getting cleaned up and attending to correspondence. I spent all my spare time listening to records—oh, there are so many exciting things I would like to do if I had the money and the place—I was teeming with ideas, but none of them very practical I'm afraid.

February

Rice Hotel, Houston . . . tried to find a movie but with no success at all. However, I was glad to have an evening in my room alone and wrote all my necessary letters. Boring. Did barre in my small room yesterday a.m.. Tom Fisher arrived in p.m. and was I thrilled to see him. Tom had a business appointment this a.m. so I practiced in the room.

Our performance in Houston was a tremendous success in spite of the fact that it was too long. But the theatre is so marvelous and what a difference that makes to the presentation of my ballets! They looked absolutely sensational and we had superb notices.

We packed hurriedly, dashed to the airport and got a plane to New Orleans at 11 a.m. Went directly to the Sheraton Charles Hotel—we had a tiny little room that I hated. I remembered staying at the St. Charles before Sheraton got hold of it and adoring it. Horrible theatre in which everything looked *awful*. Also, I made the show much too long. I had to make it this long to give the 3 guest artists plus my own artists a chance to be seen. But I should forget about my dancers and just think of the show! No one in the audience could see anything and I don't really see any reason to perform at all in such a theatre.

We took Henning and Kirsten and Orrin to supper after the show at Brennan's. We had duck all covered with sauce which I hated. We said goodbye to Henning and Kirsten and they left the next a.m. Kirsten had $650 stolen from her hotel room—John Scott [the very congenial company manager] had nearly $1000 stolen (of our money) and one of the musicians had $50 stolen. I hated the new part of the Sheraton Charles. Tom left the next a.m. also.

March

We had a long bus ride from St. Louis to Carbondale and arrived tired (as usual). The backstage of the theatre is very crowded and no wing space, so we had to cancel "Lesson." But the auditorium I adored—just the right size, small and one could see from every seat, and our company never looked more beautiful than it did in Carbondale. A man (a stranger) sitting next to me in the balcony said "I have never spent a more beautiful evening in my whole life than this one." I really think I agreed with him. And it is a remark like his that makes me keep going under such difficult circumstances.

We had another long ride the next day to Indianapolis. I wanted to go to class but felt I should go to see Edith Clewes, whose husband financed Clewes Hall, as she is ill and can't get out of bed. She seemed to really appreciate my coming and I was glad to see her.

Went directly to the theatre. I sat in about the tenth row for the performance and was disappointed in the sight lines. The theatre is not nearly raked enough—otherwise it is fine. I bowed after the performance as the manager, Borshoff, asked me to. I didn't see any of my old friends at all. I don't really like to go back to Indianapolis—it makes me sad. I never did like Indianapolis when I was young and I still don't like it. Mr. and Mrs. Borshoff took us out to supper afterwards—Gilpin and Josette went along and we had a nice time. To bed late and up early and took the 9 o'clock plane to Chicago. I feel as though I have done everything I can for the company and I am wasting my time to stay with them any longer.

I was really thrilled to get home, but Tom is still in "exile" and Felisa is in Mexico, so the apartment seems big and lonely. I spent all day and most of the night cleaning up the place. This a.m. went to class at Walter Camryn's and really enjoyed that.

Telephoned the opera and heard the dreadful news that we will have no opera season due to the musicians' union's extreme demands. *What* will this do to us! Then telephoned Petersen at McCormick Place and it will be a long time before their theatre is ready. No "Nuts" there this Xmas. So Chicago is fraught with tragedy for me—maybe it is the end for me—and just when we have never been so beautiful.

Quite characteristically, she does not mention the fact that McCormick Place had burned to the ground shortly after the close of the *Nutcracker* season.

Took the plane to New York on Sat. a.m. and went directly to Plaza Hotel, where Tom met me. It was heaven to be with him. Tom is living at the Harvard Club but he stayed with me at the Plaza. We spent all Sunday just talking.

For the next four days and nights they really "did the town" before she had to return to Chicago.

Monday a.m. I left with the company [they had been playing in the Chicago area] for Madison. It is somehow depressing to return to the company and hear all the complaints and troubles, and I had looked forward to coming back to them.

I like the small Madison theatre for "Carmina" but "Nuts" did not fare so well. We had to leave Snow scene out because Patricia and Ken couldn't dance that and the grand pas de deux the same evening. It is too hard for them to do both, even with intermission between, although it is not too hard if I would pay them extra. . . . Had a crisis with Bill Hughes yesterday. He refused to run the tape recorder unless we gave him $750 (75 per week for the whole tour). He is already getting $285 weekly plus extras. Always problems. . . .

Saginaw . . . another unattractive theatre, a sort of arena where only the people who sat in the balcony could see and they were too far away to enjoy it. However, the performance went very well and we got a very exciting writeup the next morning. Had a lovely big clean redecorated room but no bath, only a shower. In my usual manner I got up about 3 o'clock and took a shower, thinking it would have the same effect as a bath, but instead of putting me to sleep it woke me up and I never did get to sleep.

It was our day off yesterday. I lunched with Josette, then went with the local dance teacher, Miss Marsh, to Delta College and had a television interview. They showed it to us afterwards and it was extremely interesting. I looked old and fat but what I said was really to the point, and I was surprised at how intelligent I looked. I certainly did a lot of talking and to my great surprise it made very good sense.

Miss Marsh took me to Bay City and I got there in time to go over costumes, etc. How I hate the end of a tour, and all the terrible problems it entails.

Tom [he had flown out again, probably to assist at the end-of-tour obsequies] and I went to the airport together and I took the plane at 5:30 for Chicago and he left for New York. We had hardly any time to discuss any of our problems.

Had Goldie, Tom's wonderful secretary, Wed. a.m. from 10 to 11:30 and it is great being able to dictate all that time. Rest of the week listened to a lot of music to decide what I want to "create" for next season (if there is any). What "inspires" me the most is Vivaldi's "Four Seasons," but it is for string orchestra and our poor 2 violins, 1 cello would sound a bit feeble, I'm afraid.

Trying to clean up the terrible mess in the apartment. Felisa finally arrived Thursday. She now isn't happy because "Celia is not mine any more." I am certainly happy she is here.

Lunched with Albertine Maxwell today and she told me a lot about her "regional" ballet. Quel horreur!

Went to Clinton King's cocktail party at his new studio on Wells St. Easter Sunday. It is the first party I ever went to where guests were met at the front door by a black policeman (or any policeman). It is a dangerous neighborhood so it was probably a good idea on their part. It is the first party I've been to at the Kings' where they had no black guests. After the party I took Felisa to see "A Man for All Seasons" which I found fascinating, but Felisa slept through most of it and I think the English was too much for her.

Was very upset Monday when I was served a summons to come to court next Monday—all these legal affairs scare me to death.

April

Saturday Raya Lee and Orrin Kayan came here and I started "Catulli Carmina." They are an ill-assorted pair, so it is a little difficult, but anyway I got started. Today I worked a little this a.m. and then Margaret Fisher picked me up and I took her to Ballet Folklorica at the opera house.

The Lyric Opera has announced that there *really* will be no season this year. It is due, they say, to only 6 or 7 musicians who are causing all the trouble.

Such a dreary week—such a dreary city—not even a movie worth going to! Monday I went to Walter Camryn's class and in the afternoon worked with Raya and Orrin on "Catulli." Orrin and Kenneth and Patricia, Bob Boehm and his boy friend, Bob Spaur, came to dinner. Tuesday to Keith Allison's class which would be good except that it is so slow you almost fall asleep. Thursday to Walter Camryn's class. Today rehearsed with Raya Lee and Orrin instead of going to class and at 2 I went to the Boston Symphony. Ate dinner with Felisa and worked at my desk all evening.

There was a horrible article in the Tribune this a.m. about Tom's case—a big long one with everything misrepresented and it made me sick with all our troubles.

Talked to Carol Fox who just returned from Bermuda and she says she doesn't even know if they can have a season for 1968! Chicago is a discouraging place to live and I am ready to kiss it goodbye forever.

Rehearsed with Raya Lee and Orrin Mon., Wed., and Fri. on Catulli. Sometimes I think I am wasting my time—it is such a great big work and needs more "staging" than dancing. I really would like to direct and choreograph it for Lyric, but I'm afraid just as a ballet it will not be sufficiently interesting.

Last night I spent 3 hours downstairs at a meeting of all the owners of the apartments in this building. They all want to sell except the Gallerys and us and I'm afraid we will lose. It is a complicated situation.

I went early Monday a.m. to Tom's office to dictate a letter to Delfau about "Catulli." I got into a nest of vipers. Apparently Mrs. Ford and Goldie, Tom's 2 secretaries, don't get along at all. When Tom is there it is okay, but without him it is agony for all of us. . . . Haven't slept at all for 3 nights so am very tired. Now about to board plane for New York to see Tom.

And, as usual, theatres, movies, art galleries, ballets, dance studios and friends.

Back to the Wellington, got my luggage, took Tom to the Harvard Club where he is living and am now flying back home to Chicago. I will be glad to get there after my very uncomfortable stay at the Wellington.

Poor Tom seems very harassed and worried and his case is not going well. I lie awake every night worrying about what will happen.

. . . Have been home nearly a week and busy as a bee. Went to class Mon., Tues., and Thurs. and rehearsed with Orrin on Tuesday afternoon. I felt in a very "creative" mood, and in one hour and fifteen minutes choreographed a beautiful dance for Catullus—"Nothing endures time's ravages"— it is very deep and profound and I *hope* he will be able to dance it in a great manner. We both loved it but usually when my dancers like their dances right away they don't turn out well! We'll see, but the dance did seem exactly right.

Another talk fest yesterday when I went to Evanston to Northwestern University to be on a panel of four to discuss "Chicago Culture" for some budding young journalists. Silas Edman represented Chicago Symphony; John Reich, Goodman Theatre; Jerry Ross, the mayor's cultural committee; and I, Chicago Ballet. Two hours of talk and everyone seemed to agree that the Chicago situation was pretty hopeless.

Took a taxi and stopped for tea at Mark Turbyfill's. That was most interesting. I had never seen his old house and I must say I loved it. It looked so interesting and so full of character and his really very unusual paintings were all over the house.

Wednesday I went to the Art Institute to see Wyeth's exhibit and was a little disappointed. After that I went to Tom's office and dictated a lot of letters to Goldie. Her house blew away in the cyclone and her car was smashed—the gods are really against us this year.

May

Was pretty dead all day Thursday and as usual so many letters and so much business to attend to after I have been away.

She had just returned from another of those four-day visits with Tom in New York.

I went to Tom's office at 9 and stayed till 11. Wrote letters—had conference with Tom's lawyer. Tom's case seems hopeless to me. . . . Justice! . . .

Had a grim day Monday. To court at 10 a.m. where I sat alone with ten men and they asked me questions. It made me very nervous and unhappy. . . .

The next day she took the plane for Montreal and Expo '67 where Tom joined her, and they "did" the fair with typical insatiability for a few days; then to New York, where they "did" that perpetual "expo" with equal intensity.

I suggested a lot of ideas to Tommy Thompson for our company but he didn't "spark" to any of them—he just likes to stay in a rut. . . . The evenings are marvelous here but I hate the days. I hate having no place to work.

Tom is working very hard trying to straighten out his very complicated business. I just wonder if he will ever be able to come home!

Chicago, May 28—Today is Margaret Fisher's birthday so I drove out to Ravinia. We had lunch at Peggy and Walter Fisher's. Margaret got some amusing presents, then she drove me to H.W. to see our house, which has been broken into and apparently lived in. It was a mess but nothing seems to have been stolen. Margaret drove me to town and I got here about 6 p.m. It was a rainy cold day and I missed Tom and did not enjoy the day.

June

Went to Oak St. beach all alone last Sunday and sat on a bench and watched the people and read the newspaper. Met a few friends bicycling and it was quite amusing although lonesome without Tom.

Went to the farewell party for the Allevaerts at the Alliance Française. It was fun to see so many charming people, and also I got some news. I saw Gertrude Guthman [of the Board of Education] and she said she had 40 lecture-demonstrations for me and a small group of dancers for the schools. She says she will give me $10,000 for the 40—I hope I don't have to give it all to the dancers as it will be a lot of work for me.

Rehearsed Tues., Wed. and Thurs. with Orrin and Klekovic. "Catulli" is really a tough nut to crack and I am very doubtful about being able to put it over.

Terrible news for Tom. Tom's lawyer thought he could get the judge to let him come back to Chicago till his case was finished but hard-boiled Barrett and all the other lawyers said "no." Another big article in the Tribune filled with complete lies. So I try to drown myself in work and other things. But it is increasingly difficult for me without Tom.

Very sad letter from Wakhevitch telling me all his troubles.

Sunday we had our audition at 2 p.m. at Civic Theatre. I arrived at 1 p.m. to see that everything was all right and to start getting acquainted with the dancers. With 85 dancers (all girls and *one* boy) it is difficult to know which is which. Larry Long gave a few warm-up steps and then everyone had to learn Marzipan as that is the hardest dance in "Nuts." Finally after a long seance I chose one girl, Mary Hanf, from California, for the regular company and 15 girls for "Nutcracker."

We had girls from California, Seattle, K.C., Dallas, N.Y., Boston, etc. It was quite extraordinary. I *really* suffer agonies at these auditions. One girl was such a beautiful girl from the waist up, but I just couldn't take her on account of her short ugly legs—not too bad but just not good enough. She doesn't have a cent and came all the way from Seattle with her mother to be rejected. I brought her home with me after the audition with Mary Hanf (the winner) and talked with them for almost 2 hours—it almost broke my heart.

Tues., Wed., and Thurs. I worked with Orrin and Patricia on "Catulli" and Thursday Ann Barzel took a film of it in the studio at 1100. We had to be at one end of the room so were totally cramped for space but at least it will help to remember the steps in the fall, if I ever find a place to do the ballet!

Took a long walk last Saturday on the beach all alone. The beach wasn't very crowded and I enjoyed the walk.

Bill Hughes came Tuesday and we worked all p.m. putting music together for my new ballet (I hope), "Ballet Scaffolding or Warm-up."

July

I unexpectedly left Chicago at 3 p.m. last Thursday. I had expected to leave Friday but I couldn't get a plane, so I had to pack and get ready very fast. Tom met me at the Plaza Hotel in New York. We went to see John Butler's "Catulli Carmina" at Caramoor [Katonah, N.Y.]. We fortunately got seats in the front row or I could have seen nothing. Maybe it is a good theatre for music but an impossible one for dance. Tom didn't read the explicit program notes and had no idea at all of what it was all about. I don't think I could tell the story clearly either, but that is not so important as to make the action interesting. I like my ideas for production much better, but again I do wonder after seeing it if it is worth the time and the money.

. . . Have been very busy doing nothing of any importance. Am living half in town and half in Hubbard Woods. I asked Bob Boehm and his boy friend, Bob Spaur, to live in the studio and Felisa lives in the guest room at the house. I *hate* being in H. Woods without Tom. I somehow feel less lonesome in town. The beach is disgusting with the stinking smell of the alewives. I got into the water only once, and just for a second, it was too cold.

Friday I got into town to have breakfast with Sam Leve at the Palmer House to discuss "Nutcracker" sets.

She has not mentioned the arrangement already made to produce *The Nutcracker* during the Christmas season at the opera house, since the musicians' strike has forced the cancellation of the opera season this year, and it will take at least another year to rebuild McCormick Place after the fire.

Rehearsed twice with Raya Lee and Bud Heideber on a strange new "thing" I'm starting—a sort of class for lecture demonstrations. I don't quite know what it will turn out to be. I'm putting the music together myself.

I keep thinking Tom will call and say we are going to Europe. I'm sort of half packed and feel quite restless. But now I doubt if we will go. The indecision is terrible.

Hubbard Woods—My 2 Bobs and Felisa are spending the night in town so I am all alone and missing Tom. I think of him all the time—his situation is so unfair and so tragic. He is staying in Hammond, Indiana, and can't come to Chicago.

. . . Finally all settled in H.W. and I hate it here without Tom. I have 2 Bobs, one for the daytime and one for the night—they are both such nice sweet boys but 2 Bobs are not worth one Tom. Tom telephones me twice a day but the separation gets harder all the time. And nothing but terrible indecisions.

Got myself all set to go to Paris alone for 2 or 3 weeks. It took me 2 full days to pack and now I can't get a reservation back, so I am sitting here on pins and needles. Nothing seems to be right or go smoothly for us any more.

At least, however, I got the "lecture demonstration" barre figured out carefully and I love it. I had Klekovic and Bud Heideber for one rehearsal in town. The middle section I have all figured out too but they didn't have time to learn it. It is all very difficult but I am enthusiastic about it.

AUX TROIS PASTEQUES

Margaret Fisher motored Felisa and me to the airport last Tuesday at 2:30 and my plane left at 5 p.m. and Felisa's at 4:30 for Mexico. I went "economy flight" $406 round trip. I thought I would have to sit three in a row but I had three whole seats to myself so I could stretch out and really sleep. I drank 2 bottles of red wine with dinner and really passed out—first time I was ever able to sleep on a plane. We arrived on time at 7 a.m. and I came directly to 17 Rue Campagne-Première. Everything seemed pretty well in order. But it took forever to find things and get straightened out and it took me 4 trips to the plumber to get him to turn on the water.

Delfau came and we did a lot of talking of course about our problems. We finally found my victrola, but impossible to make it play and we finally gave up. We hiked what seemed like miles all over Paris. I bought a rain-coat and a "smoking" coat at St. Laurent Rive Gauche, but was quite disappointed in their Boutique. We walked all through the Luxembourg Gardens talking about Catulli, had dinner in a little bar near our house. I bought a little cheap victrola which so far works all right and I played Catulli for Delfau and we discussed it from all angles. I'm really sure it is a bad choice for a ballet but I somehow can't give up the idea. . . . Catulli is the one opera that I would really like to do with real singers and I think I made a mistake to do it as a ballet. Anyway, I started very seriously so I guess I'd better go on with it. Parts of it are so wonderful and then dramatically it bogs down. Well, we'll see. Delfau was working on it all day. . . .

Up early this a.m. and was just starting to practice when Delfau arrived with some sketches for "Catulli." The idea for the set is stunning, but I didn't like the costumes much. Maybe I am getting now so I just don't like to see everyone in tights. I didn't really think I would ever come to that—but each costume that Delfau showed me seemed a little "surchargé." . . .

August

Another very hot day and no air conditioning anyplace in Paris where I have been. Had a quick shampoo this a.m., then practiced, then to see

Mme. Toussia at Karinska's, then to the bank to get some money and finally to St. Laurent's to get Marika Wakhevitch to take her to lunch. Tried on a couple of dresses but they are much too expensive for me. I would love to have the 18th century velvet suit for my lectures, but doubt if it is worth the money. [Nevertheless, she broke down eventually and bought it.] Marika and I went to the Marquise de Sévigny's tea shop for lunch and Marika told me the sad story of her marriage to George and how the two boys just ran away from home. Whose fault is it?—Marika's or George's?

Yesterday I practiced a bit after breakfast, then André came and brought me a sketch for "Bolero," which is very saucy, I must say, and quite intriguing. After we had discussed that we walked through the enchanting Luxembourg Gardens to St. Laurent's Boutique. We were very lucky as I found 4 lovely dresses for $310 plus a pin and the atmosphere was most sympathetic.

Took a bus to the Museum of Modern Art where we saw an extraordinary exhibit of moving art objects—really exciting (like Expo in Montreal). I was really thrilled with the objects—it was like walking in outer space. I was exhausted afterwards and came straight home and rested a while.

Serge Lido came at 7 and we went to see the Grand Music Hall of Israel— which I really hated—noisy and tasteless and the audience went wild about it. We only stayed for half of it and then met Skibine at L'Orangerie where we had dinner. Stayed till 1:30 a.m. talking.

Couldn't sleep at all last night—I think I drank too much wine and I also had mosquitoes in both beds for the first time. Got up at 6, made a horrible cup of coffee and then wrote to Tom. Did a short practice and at 11 a.m. Delfau came and 11:30 Hector Pascual and photographer Brody. Hector came to see the Catulli sketches and to make an estimate on masks, etc. . . .

Wild day today. Practiced early then went to Repetto's where I met André. I bought some tights and stockings to try for Bolero and then we went to Gromtseff and worked on a costume for Bolero. I modeled for a *long* time, then we came home and had a bite to eat at Camilu next door. Serge Lido came to get us at 3 p.m. and we spent the rest of the afternoon at Joinville which is the place where all the television shows are made—a very ugly place but everyone was so nice to us. . . . Watching was quite boring as they work so slowly. We have to do my ballets (a half-hour ballet) in *one* day and they take from 4 to 6 weeks for each ballet (paid for by the government). Talked to Claire Motte and she would like to come on half of our tour with Bonnefous. . . . André and I ate a lot of cakes in a marvelous pastry shop in Joinville so we didn't eat any dinner and worked all evening on a costume for the leading girl [Lipinski] in Bolero. I am completely dead and so tired of modeling.

. . . Did my barre and at 10 went to breakfast with David and Anna Marie Holmes at Camilu next door. They really seem crazy to come as guest artists with our company. I am dying to do my new ballets—every day they get more interesting.

The Holmes took me to Gromtseff's and I met André there and we worked on a costume for Dolores for a long time. Rather tongue-in-cheek and foolish. . . . My biggest problem is not knowing what ballets I can afford to do—if any! So I'm really working in the dark.

Tom writes very discouraging news about his case. He couldn't manage a settlement so it will be tried Sept. 26. There is no chance of his winning at all. We are in a *horrible* situation.

In the afternoon I went to see Youly Algaroff. Someone suggested that we do our "Nutcracker" in Monte Carlo at Xmas. They all seem very anxious to have it. *But* everything can be taken care of *except* transportation, and as we are not "subventionné," we could never raise the money to get there, so I might as well stop thinking about it!

Couldn't sleep all night even with 3 baths. Up very early, practiced, went to Camilu for breakfast as I am really sick of my Nescafe. Went to St. Laurent Boutique and bought a few things—then met André at Gromtseff's and we had a seance with the costumes. Worked from 3 till 6 p.m. André took me and what was ready of the costumes to the house—we had a drink together and he went home.

Soon after Josette Amiel arrived. I asked her right away about Flemming and she said that was finished long ago and "of course" she had someone else! She wants to bring on tour an Italian dancer at the Opéra Comique but for a completely unknown dancer he wants much too much money. She left at 8:30 and now I am really packing seriously.

Paraphernalia for Survival

Delfau took her directly to Orly the next morning and put her on the plane. When she checked her baggage, she was ten pounds overweight, which would have cost her $39, but the TWA girl said she was "in a good mood" and let it go. Then she and Delfau had a nice lunch and "a lot of fascinating conversation" and she took off under gracious auspices.

To my great surprise and delight Tom met me at the airport and we went directly to Margaret Fisher's and spent 2 nights with her. He is taking a terrible chance to do this, but it really was essential for us to see each other. It is so tragic that he can't stay with me in our darling little house by the lake.

I slept in Tom's mother's bed, where she lay sick for so long and I couldn't help thinking about her. The next day we spent mostly writing business letters and talking. Margaret gave us a nice dinner and I slept better last night. Lots more business this a.m. and at noon he left me to go back to Hammond, Indiana, to work all by himself. He doesn't stand a chance with his case and yet he has to spend hours and hours preparing it. I am exhausted. The ballets (Bolero and Catulli) I feel sure I will not be able to do—anyway I am ready to do them if I ever get a chance.

. . . I can't get used to being in H. Woods without Tom and I must say I hate it. Orrin and Patricia came out yesterday and I finally started "Bolero." It is an interesting problem. I must say I got quite a lot done on it—I felt sort of "inspired."

Bob Boehm spent 2 nights with me and so did Patricia but last night I was alone and it is quite scary here alone.

I talked to Tom on the telephone and he is terribly depressed about his case—nothing is going right and they want to fleece him. It is horrible. . . .

A dancer wanted to try out for me on Sat. so she came and got me at H.W. and motored me to 1100. I spent an hour working with her.

Patricia and Orrin came at 1:30 and we did an hour barre and then worked 2 hours on "Bolero." We did the same yesterday and the same today. I must say my "Bolero '68" is entirely a far cry from my original version—I only hope my new version will be half as successful as the original! I am only doing it because Tom Thompson suggested the idea—I thought I was through with "Bolero" *forever* but I guess not! I still don't want to do it very much, but maybe it will work out—who knows?

Life is just as dreary at 1100 without Tom as it is in the country. But somehow I just don't feel like going out there—I left all my clothes and left the front door unlocked, so I hope nothing happens.

I couldn't sleep all night even with my usual 3 baths. Had breakfast at the drug store, shopped a bit, then class and rehearsal at home. I got almost to the end of "Bolero" and it looked promising today. But what will I think of it tomorrow!

September

I got so lonesome in the country and it was so cold that I called Bob and asked him to come help me move to town. He came at 11 a.m. and I got to town just in time to rehearse. The apartment is terribly dirty without Felisa, but I am glad to be in town. I feel much less lonesome here. Had three good rehearsals on Bolero and I'm beginning to like it, and have really enjoyed working on it. It is certainly very different from my old version.

Petersen from McCormick Place telephoned that he could get a studio for us in Fine Arts Building for $350 a month. I was so thrilled at the thought of a studio just only for us that I dashed immediately down to see it. I was so disappointed because there was just no space at all, so I came sadly home.

I spent the evening cleaning house. Felisa was supposed to be here long ago and I've telephoned twice to Mexico and no word from her at all.

Tom is having a terrible time with the Continental Bank case. Their treatment of him is completely scandalous.

Klekovic, Kayan, Anna Baker and Raya Lee came at 1 today and we did barre and then rehearsed. It was a very unsatisfactory rehearsal for some reason. I got a headache from writing too many business letters I think and I didn't go out all day. Very blue and lonesome. . . .

Honeymoon passport picture, 1925.
(*Restored by Frank Derbas*)

Tom and Ruth
snapped playfully by Serge Lido
on the Pamplone beach, 1954.

With Effie Beals at Hubbard Woods.

The house on the lake in Hubbard Woods. (ca. 1932)

Margot Fonteyn, Ruth, and Frederick Ashton in Greece,
with the fishing boat "Eliki" in the background.
(*Photographs by Tom Fisher, montage by Frank Derbas*)

Ruth in her lecture-demonstration costume.
(*Maurice Seymour*)

Foyer of the apartment on East Lake Shore Drive with murals by Delfau.

I rehearsed Friday with my little group of dancers—I am beginning to like Bolero 68 very much—am really excited about it.

At 4:30 I went to the opera house and Edna McRae and I met all the children from last year who wanted to be in "Nuts" this year. We had 20 little boys and about 30 girls. It is tiring but fun to see them. . . .

Sat. p.m. we had the "child stars" plus all their parents at 1100 for a rehearsal. They arrived at 2 p.m. and left at 6. I was a wreck! But it was an interesting afternoon.

At 6:30 I went to H.W. and spent the night at Margaret Fisher's. I didn't sleep well, but it was nice to be there and we took a walk on the beach. Sunday a.m. I came to town right after lunch as I was restless. I came on the elevated and subway but it doesn't go to the loop on Sunday so I finally had to get out and call a taxi. I thought I'd never get home. . . .

Went to Keith Allison's class yesterday, then rehearsed all p.m. on our program for the lectures. Was really tired last night. Dusan Trninic and Nono Yoshido came for dinner and I did really enjoy them. They are here with "Land of Smiles." I saw it Wed. night. I went alone and I must say I was very interested in it. Di Stefano has aged a lot since his glamorous days at the Lyric but still he is exciting.

Just before dinner I rehearsed with Edna and the children in room 100 at the opera house. It is really fun to rehearse with them. Rehearsed at 1100 before lunch with the dancers for the lectures.

Spent a lot of time this week looking at space for a studio with no good results. I don't think in my lifetime I will ever have an adequate studio. It is very discouraging.

Every day I talked to Tom on the phone in Hammond. The judge won't let him come to try his case in Chicago and there is no chance that his lawyer can stand up against Barrett. I just hope Tom's morale doesn't break.

Sunday was a day of agony for me. I went to the Civic Opera House at 1 p.m. and left about 6 p.m. We had expected about 50 children for an audition and over 350 came. Edna McRae, Larry Long, Bernie (very experienced with children) and Melba Cortez (also very experienced with children) and I were there. Out of the 350 we only needed 30 children so there were 320 broken hearts. It couldn't have been a more fair audition, but of course 320 children plus parents thought it was unfair. Some of them came backstage after the audition and practically shot me. It was *horrible* and I haven't recovered yet.

This morning there was another *long* blurb of publicity detrimental to Tom in the Atwood case, which is to be tried tomorrow. None of the settlements worked out and the judge will not let Tom come back to Chicago to defend himself. It is horrible.

Then my sister-in-law, Mary Page [the widow of her older brother, Lafayette] died today. On top of this we started our lecture demonstrations.

THE STRANGE NEW LECTURE-DEMONSTRATION "THING"

Larry picked up Kenneth and me at 8 a.m. and we went directly to Roosevelt School. Our first experience was great. Dr. Zimmerman greeted us with open arms and did *everything* for us—even gave us a lovely private lunch after the demonstration. The audience was divine and clapped and laughed in all the right places. The next lecture was at Van Steuben—a small stage, slippery floor and no place to dress. And the principal, Mr. Dolnick, dismissed the whole audience because they were noisy. He said we would be paid but we needn't give the lecture. Then in 15 minutes he came back and said he had a new audience for us. So we did it, but the audience was a little squelched!

Sept. 26—Another wild day in the life of R.P. Last night Charles Blake and his friend from Puerto Rico, Angelo, and Orrin and Kenneth came to dinner. Felisa made us marvelous enchiladas and I tried to relax. But knowing that Tom's Continental Bank case was going on this a.m. *without* Tom, I was very nervous. Went yesterday p.m. to the Arts Club opening tea—I went because I'm too nervous to stay home. It was nice to see our friends and I think they are as worried about Tom as I am.

Up at dawn this a.m. Larry and Dee picked up Kenneth and me and we arrived at Sullivan School at 9 a.m. We have had slippery floors in our careers but *never* one like this and when I went onto the stage they were waxing it. I told Dr. Erzinger I couldn't let my dancers dance, so he said, "just give the lecture without them"! Well, we ended up giving a sort of "happening." My dancers did everything in bare feet. I ad libbed like crazy and it really was our best lecture so far. We lunched and then did another at 2 p.m. at Mather, a very modern high school. But I was tired and didn't do as well as in the morning.

Margaret Fisher is spending the night with me. She went to Tom's trial today and said Tom was being defended *very* badly. I can't bear to even think about it. We will be ruined, I'm sure.

We rehearsed "Bolero" Wed. p.m. and did a barre before rehearsal. I did not rehearse well—nothing went right and I didn't like Klekovic and Kayan in it. They haven't got the spirit of it. Margaret Fisher came for dinner and Kenneth Johnson is staying with me so he ate with us. Margaret went to Tom's trial again and there was a lot of disagreeable publicity about it.

Up early this a.m. and Larry picked up Ken and me at 8:30 and we did our first lecture at Foreman at 10:26. Rather small theatre but a very exciting audience. Lunched with Larry and Dee and Bill. Our second lecture was at Steinmetz, where we had a *marvelous* theatre. *But* Dr. Connery made me very nervous because he said we had to finish exactly at 2:02. Our lectures always start a little late so our performance has to be a little under 40 minutes. I ran our "show" so fast that we finished 3 minutes too soon, so we had a question-answer period of 3 minutes. It was rather fun. Dead when I got home.

The forty lecture-demonstrations were a lifesaving digression, lasting until the beginning of November. They occurred several days a week, twice a day, at highly inconvenient hours—just after breakfast and just after lunch—and very few dancers indeed can force themselves to enjoy "the light fantastic" at 10 a.m. They were far more pleasing for Ruth, however, than her ordinary rehearsals because they involved her in actual performing, even though she did not do the dancing.

They were also constantly providing the unexpected and rarely came up with the same situation twice. The schools were located all over the city, with modern and decrepit buildings, stages of all sizes and degress of practicability, with and without dressing rooms, sometimes integrated and sometimes not, sometimes well-mannered and sometimes dangerously tough.

In one instance "so many of the teachers came backstage to tell me how thrilled they were, I really never felt so 'wanted' in all my life. The music teacher said I had done more in 40 minutes than it takes him a whole semester to do." A day or so later in a "real tough place—half white, half black"—just as they were about to start, the fire alarm went off. It seems that a "dropout" had slipped in and pulled it.

Another day the floor was so slippery they could not do a grand pas de deux, so substituted the "Flower Song" from "Carmen." "It is not a very good one for teenagers," said Ruth; "it is too sexy and sex always seems to make them laugh." One girl, before the performance, came backstage to see how they got up on "tipsy-toes," and another girl after the performance said she was going to beat up her teacher for not having told her there was to be one.

One high school that had been integrated for twenty-five years had a fine audience, but the first lecture was at 8:44 and "it was hell for the dancers, and Orrin Kayan refused to do the beat section of the Mozart. Anna Baker, bless her heart, did it for him." They were then fed coffee and cake and in forty minutes they were at it again. As Ruth was walking through the corridor in her "St. Laurent knee breeches, which I always wear for the lectures," she heard somebody ask, "Is that a boy or a girl?" At another school "at least one quarter of the stage was being rained on and nothing could stop it so we roped it off" and went right ahead.

On more familiar ground: "Board of Education hasn't given my check yet so I can't pay the dancers and they are wild."

The only performance that "our boss, Gertrude Guthman" came to was naturally the weakest one they had given. Ruth had let Kleck and Ken go to St. Paul to perform, and it was too early in the morning for Orrin to do the lifts, so they were omitted. Though he did consent to do the "Sleeping Beauty" with Dolores, they missed the ending.

Occasionally Ann Barzel or Margaret Fisher or some other interested party dropped in to watch. One school, reputedly "one of the toughest in the city," was "a miserably dreary place" but with "a very refreshing spontaneous audience." To that one Narcissa King came to see them, "and of course this is the kind of place she likes. I was so glad she came."

STOCKINGS, CHAIRS AND A DASH OF SPICE

If these and less closely related activities served as a partial background of escape from the ordeal of Tom, there was also a background beyond the background, so to speak. This was the apparently hopeless search for stockings or tights or both, plus ten chairs, suitable for *Bolero '68*. If this seems an unlikely combination of things to search for, *Bolero '68* was an ·unlikely ballet. Ruth herself was progressively surprised at the shape it was taking and how far removed it was from her original *Bolero,* alias *Iberian Monotone.*

Ann Barzel was to describe it in her review when it came to performance as "a satire on sex . . . funny sex, not creepy." It was not only funny and satiric, but since Ruth's mental state was what it was in these troubled days, it was also sardonic. It starts, logically enough, with ten girls seated in a cuadro-flamenco semicircle within a semitransparent white "room." They are dressed in maillots, with black lace mantillas over their heads and shoulders, and sequin-sprinkled stockings gartered at mid-thigh. They are busily knitting as they wait for "gentleman callers"; it is, indeed, what used to be politely called a "parlor-house." When a gentleman caller arrives, however, he proves totally indifferent to their obvious allures and stands glancing over a sheaf of pornographic newspapers. But when a figure (Dolores Lipinski) enters clad from head to floor in everything but an Arab tent, with sunglasses completely hiding her face, the gentleman loses his mind. The real action starts with a colossal do-it-yourself striptease and concludes with the entrance of other gentlemen and a grand Ravelian debauch seen through the sophisticated screen of deep-seated wit. It would be safe to say that this was not exactly what Tommy Thompson had in mind.

But to return to the diaries:

October

Went to Oak Street Beach all alone Sunday a.m. I like walking alone there—it is certainly one of the most amusing places in Chicago. The "underground" walk to the beach has very amusing (some grim, some dirty) graffiti written on the walls.

Monday I practiced with Klekovic and Kayan and at 2 had 10 people here to rehearse—it is really too many for this small studio.

At 7 Dr. Jules Wasserman and Mrs. Dennis Freund came to dinner. We had "pork à la Page" (my recipe that was printed in Tanaquil LeClercq's cookbook) and it was delicious. After dinner we discussed my lecture for them which will be Oct. 10 at the Arts Club. They don't know what they want, so it is difficult for me. I'll just give them what *I* think they will like.

Tuesday I went to Bentley's to class and I really did enjoy having a real class but it was tiring. . . . We went to my storeroom at the opera to pick up some costumes and I got home about 4 p.m. Did all my telephoning. Dinner in the kitchen with Felisa and Lucia and we talked Spanish and had a very nice time.

Tom's case has been put off for a month, so at least we will have a breather.

. . . My Arts Club performance for the psychiatrists took place tonight. Mrs. Geraldine Freund paid me $500. I had to pay 9 dancers and my pianist out of that, so I didn't make any money, and I really gave my all. I was *really* sick all day today—sick to my stomach—and I wasn't sure I would make it, but I did and *everyone* seemed to think it was a brilliant success.

The program took one hour and 5 minutes and we did scene from Court of Love [*Carmina Burana*], then Orrin's dance from "Catulli," then Spring from "Carmina"; then Larry and Anna and Raya Lee improvised to 3 of Jules Wasserman's compositions and I even entered into the improvisation, and it was fun. Jules played the violin from the stage. Then came Flower Song from "Carmen" (with Ken and Dolores) and we ended with "Bolero." From the reaction of the audience I think we have a big success with the "Bolero." Well, anyway, Mrs. Freund seemed tickled to death. My dancers, *all* of them, were marvelous. I haven't eaten anything since breakfast and it is now after midnight. I just couldn't eat, and I still feel sick.

. . . Today I went to the Junior League to talk at a symposium on "the living and visual arts in Chicago." Paul Zimmerman (Mayor's Cultural Committee), William Hartmann (architect), Louis Sudder and, of all people, Claudia Cassidy. Again a lot of boring talk. I am useless at these functions and I am much too frank and outspoken and I'm afraid I only make enemies for myself. The others all had their speeches written out and I hadn't prepared anything at all. Claudia gave her usual "line" about how Chicago should have only the greatest, and her concern is not money at all—she's only interested in bringing the greatest artists to Chicago and who pays for it is not her concern.

. . . Ken and I went to McCormick Place headquarters and picked up Duane Petersen and went to see our new studio. It is much too small, but I'm happy to have anything. . . .

I had dinner with Tom and was I glad to be with him again even for a few minutes. He is the man for me and after all my "fairy" visitors, it was wonderful to be with a real man again. If only he could come home.

They had set up a kind of surreptitious system of meeting at obscure restaurants, which proved to involve none of the risks that she had feared at first.

November

She had been invited by Larry Kelly to go to Dallas to stage a dance in the production of *Figaro* that he was making there.

Orrin came to get me at 1 p.m. Friday and took me to the airport in our station wagon. I arrived in Dallas about 5 p.m. . . . . They took me to the Dallas Woman's Club where I was to choose the dancers from 11 till midnight. As there were only 6 couples there was no one to choose. For once the boys are better than the girls. The girls are pretty bad.

Yesterday I rehearsed from 3 to 6. The Figaro "fandango" is quite a tricky little dance, but I got it all done and finished off today from 1 to 4. I could have had 5 hours each day but that is too long for one dance. I worked them very hard, but so far they can't do it very well. Mozart is difficult for them. . . .

Went yesterday to Neiman Marcus as I had heard so much about it, and it is very nice—mainly because it is small and compact and tastefully arranged, and polite salesmen. I bought a velvet "smoking" jacket and a blouse and a pair of gold stockings for "Bolero."

. . . I am disappointed that Kelly is not more interested in modern ideas—he and Rescigno seemed married to the past. I wanted to persuade Kelly to put on Carmina and Catulli but he is afraid of an all-Orff evening and wasn't even interested enough to see the designs which I had brought with me. Well, I guess all opera people are more or less alike. Kelly wants to put on "Sleeping Beauty" with Margot and Rudy! Now that is really something interesting to do.

I rehearsed last night from 10 to 11:30. I really have had 3 times as much time as I needed. This a.m. I had a shampoo in the hotel, and watched the teenagers' convention whirling batons, rolling the hoops around them and a vulgar jazz dance—really now!

Rehearsed from 9 to 11 at the Music Hall—a *typical* opera rehearsal—I can't stand them and I really hope I never have to do another opera ballet. A real waste of time. I rehearsed "Figaro" so carefully and at our first stage rehearsal 3 boys were sick and the 2 understudies didn't know the dance at all—I was disgusted. However, we stayed after the rehearsal and they learned it.

Took the plane for Chicago at 8:50 a.m. and was home by noon. So much mail, so many telephone calls—back to the madhouse! . . .

Really never lived through two worse days. We finally got together for rehearsal. I gave class at our new studio (at 120 S. State) for the girls. Larry gave a boys' class at the opera. I rehearsed the girls' part of Bolero for almost 3 hours and got it all done up to the boys' entrance. Then at 5 p.m. the mob arrived for Snow. Today Larry gave the class at 120, and Ken worked with a new girl for "Nutcracker" at 1100 and Orrin worked at the opera with Dee and Chuck. So we had 3 rehearsals going on at once.

Tom's lawyer came to the studio and I signed a lot of papers for Tom. Oh, if only Tom were here everything might be different.

. . . Just before I left for Dallas on Monday [the performance there was to take place on Thursday] an African gentleman named Fodé phoned me from the station and asked me where he should stay in Chicago. As I had had a letter from John Crane about him, and as I was leaving, I told him he could stay at 1100 until Thursday. He arrived 15 minutes before I left—very black and quite attractive—with about 12 marvelous African sculptures he wanted to sell (he is apparently an art dealer). He put them up in my studio and they looked wonderful—I almost missed my plane.

We had our final dress rehearsal Wed. night in Dallas. Peter Hall's scenery and costumes are in good taste and pleasing but actually nothing new or interesting—just operatic taste of the conventional but good kind.

When I returned to Chicago Fodé was still here and is still here [Sunday]. He says he is leaving tomorrow. I actually enjoyed his company very much. But *very* tiring to be always thinking of a house guest when I have so much work to do. . . . I invited Arnold and Adele Maremont to come see our African sculptures and Fodé sold them a beauty. Fortunately before I left I called Rue Shaw and Narcissa King. Rue was very nice to him—so he really has done well but he is a lot of trouble for me as Felisa doesn't like blacks. He cooked a delicious African stew for us but Felisa said he was not clean in the kitchen!

My biggest problem is the 2 awful corps boys I have to replace. . . . A black boy arrived, recommended by John Barber in N.Y. and he is our best new boy. I told him I would take him and then Tom Fisher said *not* to take him without a telegram from Tom Thompson saying he agreed with my taking a black! After I had already told him I would take him, Tom Thompson said absolutely not to take him unless I wanted to get into a lot of trouble! I felt terrible and Duane Petersen saved me. He said I could take him for "Nuts." So now I have too many boys and the only one I like is the black one.

Had dinner with Tom Fisher in a restaurant. If he isn't allowed to come back to Chicago soon, I will go mad. It is really awful.

Carol Fox and Larkin Flanagan came to dinner one night and it was like old times. We really didn't get to talk any business but we had a lot of fun. Carol seems to think there will be an opera season next fall, and she seems to want me but not all my soloists. I bought a splendid porterhouse steak for dinner and Felisa thought it was roast beef and cooked it like roast beef and it was ruined.

December

Monday we had our [*Nutcracker*] rehearsal at the opera on the big stage, and everything went well. Am still having lots of corps de ballet boys problems.

I talk to Tom every night on the telephone. He has been in "exile" now for more than a year. It is horrible.

The guest stars in *Nutcracker* this year were to be Gerd Andersson and Erik Bruhn, and once again, Kirsten Simone and Henning Kronstam.

Gerd Andersson arrived from Sweden Thursday p.m. Erik Bruhn asked me if she could stay with me and in a weak moment I said yes. Strange to take a person you have never met to live with you! However, she couldn't be nicer and again I am breaking my neck to make everything nice for her.

Today I went to the Clinton Kings' studio for a brunch party. We had
Bloody Marys and interesting people, but I had to leave before food was
served. I went to the theatre and did my little jobs, and then went to
studio 100 and did Kronstam's barre, which made me feel better. Watched
[*Nutcracker*] rehearsals of Act 1 from the wings and Act 2 from the front
and then Gerd Andersson and I came home and I cooked steak for her and
then we worked on her entrance steps in "Nuts." Bruhn was supposed to
work with her tonight but his plane was late so they have only tomorrow
to rehearse.

At 7:30 I went to a party and it turned out to be a madrigal singing group
strolling around singing Xmas carols and I was in no mood for that. I
came home, had a little talk with Gerd and expect to spend all night at
my desk.

Kirsten Simone arrived and we finally opened Wednesday. The lights were
not exactly to my liking but everything really went smoothly. I was very
pleased that Ed Lee and Dolly came backstage to congratulate us—I really
appreciated that. [This performance was, after all, not at McCormick
Place but at the Lyric Opera.] I wore my tuxedo of black velvet that I
bought in Dallas and I bowed with the dancers and everything seemed very
gala. . . .

Monday was our day off but it wasn't much of a day off as I had a million
things to do. Tuesday at 6:15 we had "Nuts" and Erik and Gerd danced.
I think I was even more nervous than Gerd. She is exquisite in the pas de
deux. She is not very strong technically but she has an exquisite presence—
very aristocratic but with a warm lovely smile.

Delfau arrived from Paris in p.m. I sort of hinted to Gerd that she go to a
hotel but she didn't take the hint! I had a little party for her and Erik
after the performance.

Wednesday we had a performance of "Nuts" at 10:30 a.m. free for school
children and we were paid by the Board of Education. There were
speeches and pictures afterwards and it was all very gala and really lots of
fun. We had another performance at 6:15. [Because of the smaller
capacity of the opera house, there were two performances daily during this
season.]

In between parties and rehearsals I have been shopping for Bolero. I don't
think I've ever done a ballet where the costumes were so much trouble.
We bought a lot more stockings today and we looked at every chair in
Field's and came out with only a new hat for me!

I finally told Gerd she had to go to a hotel. I really was afraid André
would leave if he had to stay any longer in that little room next to Felisa's.

Sat. Dec. 23 I had Walter Dunner Fisher and their 3 children to dinner. It
was quite an effort on my part but I enjoyed them very much indeed. Tom
and I were planning to go to Evanston and have Xmas dinner with all the
family there, but the children talked so freely about Tom's problem that I
was afraid to let him come. I was very disappointed but it was just too
dangerous. So on Xmas day André and I had dinner all alone with Tom.
He seemed in fine condition, full of optimism and looking young and

healthy. I was really surprised and happy to see him. Oh, if he could only come home. A real man in the house would certainly be wonderful.

At 5 p.m. I had 35 people to dinner. It was really a strange assortment of people. I had all the dancers from the company that didn't have family or friends to go to and then other people that I just telephoned to Xmas a.m. thinking they might be lonesome. . . . We had a very good dinner and Simon Sadoff entertained us with French popular songs—he sang and sang and each time the songs got better and better. He sings like Edith Piaf, only with a sly sense of humor about it all—he really was great and just made the party for me. However, it was exhausting getting the party ready and it was exhausting cleaning up afterwards!

Went to Carol Fox's to a Lyric party last Thursday night and it was fun to see all the Lyric office workers. Everyone is glad there will be a season. Had a 2-hour session with Carol Fox this a.m. but with this season I can't see any hope for the ballet. I absolutely don't want to choreograph Masked Ball, Otello or anything she suggested. She doesn't want *any* of my stars— only Nureyev or Fracci or someone foreign—only big stars from Europe—no interest in the productions at all.

This a.m. Delfau and I were at Field's at 9:30 and shopped till 12 for things for Bolero. Then to buy sequins for Bolero stockings. I thought I would die from all the shopping and every day we've been shopping for Bolero—I really don't think I can stand any more of it.

Planned to go to N.Y. for 2 days to complete and make corrections on our souvenir book but had to give up the trip at the last minute as I just had too much to do! I was disappointed as I really felt like getting away. Spent most of evening at my desk—troubles now with contracts for tour. It is so difficult for me to do all the business, and I am really tired.

Dec. 31—Had class with the company yesterday. Saw the 2nd act from the front. I went to see "Elvira Madigan," the Swedish film—it is so beautiful and sad. Had dinner with André and Felisa in the kitchen and then André and I spent all evening painting 10 Bolero chairs. Such a time finding them but we finally did—they arrived and now, all painted, they look wonderful.

To company class today and watched the performance backstage which is fun. Lots of problems as usual. The manager of all the stagehands complained to me about [one of the character dancers] chasing some of the stagehands and he is afraid one of them will hit him. I went to tell him but a lot of people in his room so I asked [a dancer whom he had "chased" successfully some years before] to tell him.

André and I had dinner with Tom and then André and I came home and spent a quiet New Year's Eve at home.

January

Larry Long was sick all week and so I had to do all the rehearsing as well as all the business. I didn't really think I would live through it. We still are minus 2 for our crew [for the approaching tour, for which, incidentally, she had engaged David and Anna Marie Holmes as guest stars]. Our new company manager, Chas. Blake, is after me on every little detail of the business. . . .

He solved one of the perennial problems, however, by procuring a transportable plastic floor, and "all the dancers seem to love it, thank God!"

. . . Delfau is wildly impractical. However, he's a wonderful companion to have around and I always enjoy talking to him.

When I got home last night I was really completely dead, so I called Antal Dorati (who came to see me the night before about 10:30) to tell him I just couldn't come to his concert. He seemed so disappointed that I finally got myself out and went to Orchestra Hall all alone. I never heard Mahler's Sixth before and it was so pleasant to sit back in the box and hear all new sounds—such exciting ones. Mahler is so strange—sometimes so very poetic and sometimes so ordinary. Anyway I enjoyed it thoroughly. I was very worried about getting home as the temperature was below zero. However I found [a friend] and just asked him if he wouldn't take me home and he did.

Up early this a.m. and was downtown by 9 a.m. getting a haircut, and after that still shopping for Bolero stockings. I bought a lot more as the ones that cost so much money to sew jewels on, were all ripped and it made me sick.

I finally more or less finished the Bolero. The corps de ballet is absolutely stunning in it.

Very full of problems—still missing 2 stagehands. We just can't get anyone to go.

LABOR (UNOBTAINABLE) AND
SEX (UNFORGIVABLE)

Stagehands, indeed, this year replaced musicians as the collective enemy. Though their absolute minimum for the road was $350, apparently all the young men had abandoned the craft, and the tour actually started out with only two men instead of the customary four, both of them old and neither an electrician.

The first weeks were largely spent in tracking down two others, old or young. Denver was the first large city that might logically produce them, so Ruth flew ahead and spent hours on the telephone to no avail. At last she located two "expert electricians" in Salt Lake City who agreed over the phone to come, but when they arrived in Denver, they were found at the last minute to belong to the wrong union, and she had to send them back at a cost of $100. She managed somehow to hire two local boys for $80 for the night, and the immediate show was put on. From then on it was necessary to stop off, or even go off-route to pick up any prospect, expensive or not. Eventually she had to send to New York, and the two who arrived turned out to be "trouble makers of the first order," much as their musical predecessors from New York had been.

As usual, she flew back to Chicago from time to time when she felt that things were sufficiently under control for the moment (though Larry Long maintained that the minute she departed the company fell apart). Not only did she have to avoid falling apart herself if she stayed, but there were also business matters to be taken care of in Chicago—or New York or elsewhere— and of course there was Tom.

When she returned to the company on the West Coast after one of these interludes, she found evidence that Larry was right. The "brilliant crew" had left behind somewhere (or otherwise disposed of) the black velvet cyclorama that Columbia had lent her to avoid those deplorable "tan-colored curtains" that had long been standard school-auditorium equipment and were guaranteed to kill anything that was set up in front of them. All the tools also had disappeared, along with all the gelatines and Neal Kayan's dress clothes. Delfau's set for the "Nutcracker Suite" was completely ruined by rain, and "our brilliant property man had let people steal" the pornographic newspapers created by Delfau as props for *Bolero*.

In the midst of all this depredation, Tommy Thompson phoned from New York to report that it was no longer possible for him to get bookings for the company because the local auspices were required to pay fourteen men to unload the scenery. "So now," she lamented angrily (if such a thing is possible), "no more tours."

It proved not to be quite as final as that, and the skies brightened considerably when Tom joined the tour in mid-February in Los Angeles and stayed for a full week. Furthermore, when he saw *Bolero* for the first time, he loved it.

Bolero, however, was already the season's greatest troublemaker next to the stagehands. In the general confusions of the tour's opening performance in LaCrosse, Wisconsin, Ruth felt that she would have to see it again before she really knew what she thought of it; but what she did know at once, even through the haze, was that it was not a ballet for small towns. The farther west she went the more convinced she was, and in Grand Junction, Colorado, she felt the audience "was quite shocked."

By the time they got to southern California things had come to a boil. One night, while Tom was with her, they stayed in the hotel suite instead of going to the performance at Anaheim High School in Fullerton, because she had an enormous amount of telephoning to do and Tom had brought along work of his own. "We should have gone," she reports, "as apparently all hell broke loose." The audience was "shocked to death," the sponsors were furious, and there was talk about canceling all further *Bolero* performances. All the next day she was on the telephone, but Columbia insisted that it be removed at least from all Community Concerts bookings.

She tried her best to make it less shocking, and, ironically enough, she chose Las Vegas for her first attempt at bowdlerizing. (They did not play on the Strip, of course, but in a little theatre in the city itself.) Now for the first time she put the girls in colored tights up to the waist instead of the stockings with garters, and she hated it. As luck would have it, one of her old girls, who was now in the Folies-Bergère on the Strip, came and saw it in this sorry state of compromise, and Ruth wished she had postponed her efforts to placate Columbia for just one more night. "I admit," she wrote, "that it is not for children, but I hate to take it off the program." But take it off she did after one final go at Tucson, and she was "sick about it."

Obviously this was the moment for another flight from the company, even though Chicago meant the ordeal of letters, bills and "boring" papers. There was a great surprise awaiting her at the airport, for there was Tom. She had no idea how he knew she was coming on that plane, but it made for "a happy homecoming," if only for the usual restaurant dinner and "a big talk" before he had to go back to Hammond.

"*Nothing* has changed in Chicago," she wrote, "since I left, and this is really a boring city. No one even knows our company is on tour—no one has heard anything about "Bolero" and no one cares! At least it is marvelous to have dinner with Tom at night, although God knows we are sick of restaurants."

The same thing, night after night—"Dinner at Union Station Golden Lion with Tom—very poor dinner. . . . Went to Walter's class this a.m. which I enjoyed even though I can't do much. Dinner with Tom and then kissed him good-bye. This separation is ghastly." One night he brought her the long brief he had written for the Atwood case, and she found it "absolutely amazing . . . clear, concise and interesting every second. [Later she was to say, "Even I can understand it!"] What a mind he has and how right he seems to be on every single point. If this doesn't win him his case there aint no justice in the world! What a lot of work he has put into it and how sick he must be of living in Hammond, and yet I have never heard him make a complaint."

Tommy Thompson, in spite of all his apparent finality earlier, had not given up trying to book next year's tour, and had suggested that she do the Tchaikovsky *Romeo and Juliet Fantasy Overture*. Now she began to think seriously about it for the first time, but it did not interest her in the least. If she had to do a *Romeo and Juliet*, she would much prefer to use the richer and more expansive Prokofieff score, which was composed for dancing. But Tommy wanted her to do it, for he felt that both Tchaikovsky and *Romeo and Juliet* were "selling names." Kleck and Ken also wanted her to do it for them, so she decided to try to go along with it, though she couldn't say her heart was in it.

She returned to the company toward the end of the tour. Charles Blake had come up with a "glitter" curtain to substitute for the somehow purloined black velvet "cyc," but it did not please her. "This road version of 'Nuts'—'mini-Nuts'—really needs a nice set."

They had a scenically marvelous drive from Portsmouth, Virginia, to Clarksburg, West Virginia: "a very wind-y dangerous road but such a beautiful day. However, everything was spoiled by an argument afterwards with the dancers and musicians about overtime. We had two days to make the trip, but no one wanted to get off and spend the night anywhere. Charles Blake tried to please everyone and do it all in one day.' But that extended the "day" far beyond the specified number of working hours. "So in future we'll just follow union rules and get off in any old dump, as the overtime amounts to a great deal."

Then she had a fight with the faithful Bob Boehm because whenever they did the alternate program, consisting of *Carmina* and *Nuts*, which involved many quick changes of costume, he took three wardrobe women, and as far as Ruth could see, they helped no one to dress and were very expensive. "I feel ready now," she wrote, "to give up the company—the wardrobe, the musicians, and the stagehands ruin everything." That night she had to take three sleeping pills.

Before the end of the tour *Bolero* emerged from the doghouse, for there were some sophisticated dates in the East that were not on the Community Concerts circuit. In Dayton, Tommy Thompson and six men from the Columbia office came from New York, and though the program concluded with *Bolero*, nobody exhibited any symptoms of shock. She thought, indeed, the Columbia contingent was very impressed with the performance.

The last night in March, when the tour closed, she gave the annual company party at 1100. She had skipped her own show in nearby Harvey in order to go to the Harkness Ballet performance in Chicago, and that started so late she did not get home until the guests had already arrived. She had invited the whole tour personnel and many of them had brought friends. She had seen personally to the buying of food and drink and, knowing dancers' appetites, had made sure that there was enough "to feed an army." But for unaccountable reasons, "when the stagehands and truck drivers arrived there was *nothing* left. Fortunately I had a little canned ham, but I was very embarrassed—in fact the party was a nightmare to me. I had Felisa and Lucia and Beatrice, but it was not really enough help for the 60 or more people who came." To make things worse, Ken, protesting that he was still hungry, proceeded to upbraid her not only for the immediate food shortage but also for all the problems of the just-completed tour, including unpopular members of the staff whom she had engaged for it. "I usually enjoy my own parties tremendously, but this one I didn't."

NEW LAND TO EXPLORE

Late in May she was packing to go to Portugal. She had been invited by the Gulbenkian Foundation, which had headquarters in Lisbon, to attend the

Gulbenkian Festival, including the Gulbenkian Ballet. Besides her passion for festivals, she was motivated also by the fact that the foundation was wealthy beyond belief, and with her present financial woes no possible channel could be overlooked. She had bought a three-week round-trip plane ticket that allowed her only forty-four pounds of luggage. "I think I repacked 25 times."

When she got there (one of the few places in Europe where she had never been before), she found herself noisily housed in the wrong hotel, badly fed in self-chosen restaurants and generally unhappy. But "everybody" was there, from Paris as well as London, and it was all very-very.

At the opera the first night the only person in the audience she knew was Serge Lifar and he hardly spoke to her. "He apologized (when I saw him backstage afterwards) because he said he was talking to the King of Italy (whoever that is). Everybody was all dressed up—very swank audience and they clapped a lot and Lifar and everybody was photographed a lot and everybody seemed very happy about everything. Quite chichi and boring I thought."

Eventually countless friends turned up, including her adored Margot (with Rudy, of course); and Walter Gore and his wife, Paula Hinton, whom she admired very much; Darius and Madeleine Milhaud, Tania Grantzeva, and others from various eras of her career.

Among the new friends she made was "a charming and cultivated" Portuguese gentleman named Philippe de Sousa, and they liked each other at once, which just about saved the situation for her. He came for her on Sunday and drove her out to Copa Rica. She was not prepared for the beach, but she took off her shoes and stockings and "we had a wonderful walk with the wind blowing in our faces, and at last I was happy in Portugal." At least for the moment.

There were performances and sight-seeings of all sorts—operas, concerts, ballets, cathedrals (with and without organ programs), ferias (with and without fados) and ballet classes—to watch, though unfortunately not to take ("My body is falling apart with all this laziness here"). She herself taught a class for the Gulbenkian Ballet. "It is difficult to give one class with all strange dancers and a strange pianist and a strange language. The dancers all seem to speak a little English and a little French, but most of the time when I was talking their faces seemed to be completely blank. Some of them have fairly good legs but all of them seemed inexpressive."

She also had an appointment at noon with Senhora Perdigao of the Gulbenkian Foundation. She arrived on time and saw her for a few seconds, but spent most of the time talking to one of her secretaries who was a musician. "He was very nice and agreeable and obviously knew a great deal about music and nothing about dance, so I'm afraid all my efforts were wasted. In all it was a very discouraging interview."

A week later she wrote: "I can't believe I am still in Lisbon, and I can't wait to get out of here!" Margot phoned and wanted to go to the beach for lunch, so Ruth was trying to organize a party; she was also trying to reach Delfau by phone in Paris to make arrangements to meet him in London on her way back; she was also trying to reach the Gulbenkian Foundation, whose phone was always busy. Of course, if only to keep herself occupied, she bought some clothes here and there.

One afternoon she went to a rehearsal of Béjart's company and was surprised to see the dancers dancing "full out." "It was quite interesting to see them in their practice clothes. The boys absolutely fascinate me with their long hair, their very good acting and expressive dancing. They are perhaps a little short on classic technique, but they are certainly moving well. Béjart's style reminds me of my own."

She had dinner with Philippe de Sousa and Maria Cidrais in a quaint little restaurant in the old part of town. "So I had sardines grillés for lunch and again for dinner. I like them, but not twice a day." After dinner she went with them to the Coliseo to see Béjart's characteristically offbeat production of *Romeo and Juliet*. They had "perfectly terrible seats, in the first row but almost underneath the stage, so I couldn't see the choreography at all." Some of it she liked, and some not. "The ending was a trick, but not actually a bad idea, especially to get applause—'make love, not war' in all languages. Lots of applause and Béjart came out and made a speech including a minute's silence for Bob Kennedy, 'a victim of the fascists and the dictators.' This certainly surprised me but no one made any remarks about it." Nevertheless, his performance scheduled for the next night was canceled and the entire company was given twenty-four hours to leave Portugal.

The next night she drove around Lisbon with De Sousa and "saw the beautiful old part of the town and then he took me to a very chic hippy restaurant for dinner and we talked till midnight. Came home and packed [her forty-four pounds of luggage were now augmented by five blouses, two dresses and a sweater, which could not have made the job any easier] and couldn't sleep all night, and today I am off for London, thank God. I can't wait to leave. It was really a completely wasted trip."

She had engaged a room at the Savoy in London. David and Anna Marie Holmes met her at the airport there and helped her find Delfau; according to their telephone arrangements, that was where he was to be picked up to go along with her to the Savoy. The object of their meeting was to discuss her hoped-for production of *Alice in Wonderland* as an annual Easter attraction at McCormick Place. Nothing was as yet signed, but the *Chicago Tribune* man who was the pivotal figure in the matter, had indicated genuine interest; which meant that she had to be prepared when and if the project materialized. Delfau had to leave for Brussels after three days but "at least we got our ideas sort of straightened out and we had a good time together. But it is not the same thing as working at St. Tropez and doing everything gradually and peacefully."

She would have liked to stay over another night in London to see a particular ballet and then go to East Berlin with the Holmeses, "but Tom wired me to come home, so I am doing what he wanted. He says he can't go to St. Tropez and I am so disappointed."

From her almost casual reaction to his wire it is plain that he gave no reasons. Actually he was desperately ill and knew it.

> Had a very easy flight coming home—three seats all to myself and the day flight is so much easier than the night flight.

> Tom met me at the airport and took me directly to Margaret Fisher's where we stayed from Thursday till Monday. It was so lovely to be home, but it was a weekend of horrible decisions. Tom is not well and his case drags on and on. He still can't come into the state of Illinois and all is disaster for me. Maybe Margaret Fisher has the right idea—just live alone and have very little contact with people. A ballet life is so completely involved with hundreds of people.

> Well, my ballet life has come to an end. We will have to cancel our already fully booked tour from first week Jan. till end of March. We have not told the news to anybody yet [not even Columbia Artists] and I don't know what will happen. Margaret and her house and life are so peaceful and it was nice of her to take the exiles in, but in all this peace I am torn apart—my life is finished. And I must take care of Tom—he seems for the first time in his life utterly lost and hopeless.

> We will not go to France at all and how I will miss it. But we are trying to find a nice place by the sea where he can rest. I went to my studio yesterday and I am so happy to have a studio to dance in. Our lovely little house is still there, but all is desolate—nothing but weeds in the garden—the grass all grown over. The place looks sad and beautiful and brings back all the memories of our past life there. If only we could spend the summer there, maybe our lives would be all right again. . . .

> A dreary week in Chicago. Went to class a few times. Had dinner with Tom every night at a different restaurant—we just can't find a single one that we like at all.

> He is in desperate physical condition—maybe it is all mental but he thinks it is something physically wrong with him in spite of the fact that 2 doctors have said he is in marvelous physical condition for his age.

> We spent the weekend again with Margaret. I don't think she likes having us at all—in fact when we brought her to town this a.m., she said she was not going to have any more guests, and Tom said, "not even Ruth and me?" and she said "not even you," so now we know she doesn't want us. It makes me miserable.

> I spent most of the week trying to find a room for us somewhere, but everything is taken. So Tom finally said we had better go to St. T.,

especially as we had a letter from Mme. Borget saying she wants so much to come. Well, we'll see if we ever get there.

Tom finally wrote a letter to Columbia Artists saying we just had to cancel the tour. They worked so hard on it and it is already booked—I just don't dare think what is going to happen. In any event my career is completely ended.

I had a long talk with Carol Fox finally, and she agreed to take all my soloists except Kenneth Johnson and Charles Schick, so I had to break the news to them. [Actually this decision was not final.] Anyway I'm glad to hear from them. I had two seances with La Fox, so I hope things are more or less settled, but it is a lousy season for us—just nothing. After I've spent a musicless week with Margaret, I feel just starved for music. I did not go to class today but came home from downtown and just listened to records all p.m. This is a terrible mistake for me as then I keep getting such marvelous new ideas for ballets none of which I can afford. I would just as soon be dead as not to do new ballets!

The tour was not to be called off so easily as that, in spite of prohibitive costs and Tom's well-justified fears that he would not be able to handle any of the business end of it. Columbia could not simply drop a fully booked tour with a polite "excuse it, please" to its clientele. It was not very long, therefore, before Ruth had resumed her producing activities, which actually she had not really abandoned.

The Last Mile

The trip to St. Tropez was an unmitigated nightmare. High winds had disrupted all the air schedules; their 6 o'clock plane to New York was three hours late, the airport there was in utter confusion, and they and six other passengers for Nice missed their flight. Finally at 3 a.m. they got a flight to London. It was crowded and Ruth had to sit in the window seat, which always gave her acute claustrophobia. At 3:30 they were served breakfast ("Quel horreur!"), and three sleeping pills only succeeded in waking her up more.

It was 2 p.m. when they arrived in London and 3 or later by the time they managed to book transportation for Nice. So they went to the airport hotel and slept until 9, had dinner, slept again until 8 in the morning, and finally enplaned at 10:30. At Nice they waited three hours for their luggage, rented a little Renault and arrived at Herbe Folle, thoroughly exhausted, at 6 p.m. on Saturday.

To their dismay, they found that Mme. Borget, for all her eagerness, was not there and that the house had not been opened. In the hope that the Clavés might have a key, they went to their house, but nobody was at home, so they set out on a desperate search for their "guardian," whom, by the grace of God, they found in the *parc* playing *boules*. When they got into the house at last, it was just as they had left it, and Mme. Borget did not arrive until Tuesday.

After that, life was easier.

Anyway I did the best I could so Tom could rest. He sleeps all the time and eats well enough but something is very seriously wrong with him and we just can't find out what on earth it is. We go to the pier every day and stay a couple of hours and he does a little swimming, but that is absolutely all. He doesn't want to see anybody or do anything. . . . We see the Clavés every day for swimming and once in a while we go to town so I can do the shopping for the house.

Yesterday Yvonne Payerimhoff had an enormous cocktail party for the opening of her St. Laurent boutique in her tiny garage facing the Place des Lices. Tom wouldn't go to the party but he took me and waited for me in the car. I couldn't enjoy the party without him. If he had been there I would have had a lot of fun. I wore a little black suit that I bought at the St. Laurent boutique [in Paris]. One of the boys had on the same suit. I wrote quite a long article about the party and the clothes as Peg Zwecker (fashion editor of the Daily News) asked me to and I will send it off today I hope. . . .

Last night B. Bardot had an all-night binge that started at 10 p.m. and was still going at 5 a.m. when I fell asleep. I must say the music was marvelous— I would like to know who was playing. Certainly it sounded like American blacks or real Africans—very primitive and a marvelous drummer. But I can't enjoy myself at all in St. Tropez with Tom in such a terrible state—I just worry about him all the time. I try to work every day. It would be easier if I had the Holmes or Delfau but Tom doesn't want any guests at all, and this summer I will do everything he wants. . . .

Nevertheless, in the middle of July Claudia Cassidy and Bill Crawford came for the weekend.

She is a fascinating creature and he is a saint. He does everything for her and while she works hard I think he works harder just taking care of her. Claudia and Bill never go near the water so they are not easy to "entertain" as there really is nothing to do here but swim, eat and go to the beach. However, she loves to talk and she is always entertaining, so I can really say we spent practically the entire time talking, and such talk. She really says what she thinks. She didn't seem to want to see anybody or do anything so we just sat and talked and talked. It was nice of them to take all the trouble to come here—I think she is a good friend and is sympathetic with Tom's problem and so is Bill. Well, they couldn't have been more simpatico. . . .

After the Crawfords left we went down to the port for Tom to get his injection and to get the newspapers. Tom is no better and each day he is getting weaker and weaker in spite of all the rest. It is very depressing and I don't know what to do with him. . . .

The days pass and we seem to do nothing at all. Tom mostly reads newspapers all day—we have to write a lot of letters, both of us, and I manage
to practice every day. Have arranged a nice set of exercises for myself to
music so it is easier to get through them alone. They are hard exercises.
Am reading Proust's "A la Recherche du Temps Perdu" at night. The wind
blows and blows and then blows more—a real mistral for almost a week
now so we can't swim. Last night we went out for the first time in a long
time. Clavé called for us in his car and we went with them to Port
Grimaud for dinner. Good food but noisy and crowded. The new port
(built in old-style St. T.) is attractive and done in good taste by an
Austrian architect. But the night was so wild and terrible that we couldn't
walk around with any pleasure. . . . I give myself a concert every night on
my victrola—Alceste, Oedipus Rex, Rossignol, 7 Deadly Sins, Golden
Apple and my favorite, Le Quattro Staggioni—how I would like to do a
ballet to that music. . . .

When the weather cleared up, they made "a big effort" on several
occasions—a neighbor's cocktail party, a beach party ("a really dreamy day
and interesting French people to talk to on the beach"), a little visit to
Yvonne Payerimhoff and her husband . . .

Everything would be lovely this summer *if* Tom were well and if I had a
few dancers to work out some ideas on! Tom is not a good invalid and I
spend all the time worrying about him. I try to get him to rest all the
time but the rest seems to do him no good at all. We go to Dr. Fayard
every day for some sort of piqûre but nothing seems to do him any
good. . . . Besides the swimming what I enjoy here the most is reading "A
la Recherche du Temps Perdu" every night in bed until very late—that is a
true pleasure.

One day about noon Dolin drove over from Cannes in a chauffeured car
with a young student from Rosella Hightower's school there, and he gave her
all the gossip about the Harkness Ballet. He took them to lunch at a very
expensive place, and there he met a friend, Elvira, a Russian dancer with a
fourteen-year-old daughter who was about to go to Russia for four years "to
become a ballerina." They had arrived from Cannes in her speed boat and she
invited Dolin to go back with her in it. Accordingly she brought the boat up
to Herbe Folle and joined in an afternoon of talk and drinks before she took
Dolin and his guest aboard and sped away.

So we had quite a gay day and I think it did Tom a lot of good. But he
still says he is fading gradually away and I am worried sick—I can't think of
anything else. We spend most of the time reading newspapers. I'm afraid
the Avignon Festival will be canceled before I get there—The Living
Theatre seems to be what is ruining it. . . .

Well—I finally got to Avignon. Tom got me so terrified of going any place
and we spent so much time discussing "to go or not to go" that I finally
gave up my 2 day sojourn to Paris completely. After waiting 10 days for

my reservation on the train to come back from Paris to St. T., I finally got
it and then gave it up. So no Paris, no new clothes, no Delfau.

Anyway my main object this summer is to get Tom well and it seems I
have not succeeded in spite of the fact that I have made him rest and rest
and rest and it was no good. He got a cable last week saying he lost his
mortgage case [on the ranch] in Ocala, Florida, so we have to go home
and get the money to pay it and see if we can buy the Florida ranch back
when it is foreclosed and put up for sale. I really don't understand it very
well, but in any event it is better to go back to U.S. and put Tom in
Cleveland Clinic as none of his "piqûres" seem to have done him any good.
He had an inoculation of something or other nearly every day.

She did get to the Avignon Festival, though it was not easy. She had to
take an hour's taxi ride to St. Raphaël and wait two hours for a train, but she
arrived eventually at 5:30 on Friday afternoon. Tania Grantzeva, who was
teaching a class there, took her in charge and saw that she had tickets and so
forth. The weather was bitterly cold and the performances were outdoors,
and Ruth reflected somewhat ambivalently that AGMA would never have
allowed dancers to appear under such conditions. Nevertheless, she sat
through performances that night and the next night by Béjart's company,
which always seemed to have an irresistible fascination for her.

Sunday morning Grantzeva phoned her to tell her the news:

The stage by the Pont d'Avignon where they were to give a free performance for 20,000 people blew down the Rhone last night and there is
nothing left of it except a few pieces of wood standing out of the water.
What a place to dance—on top of a river and no seats for the public—just
standing around. I wonder if they will have time to build a new stage
before tonight. And also I wonder why the festival wants Béjart's company
to perform for nothing when they refused to let the Living Theatre
perform for nothing. Everything seems screwy in Avignon. . . . They
invited me to go to Les Baux tonight to see the Charrat company but I
was afraid to leave Tom alone. The travel agent gave me the wrong time
of my train's arrival. I've already been waiting (standing up) for an hour
and I'm still waiting.

In spite of her earlier lamentations, there were to be Paris, new clothes
and Delfau. They closed Herbe Folle almost immediately, took the plane
from Nice, and settled in at Les Trois Pastèques. For two days she shopped
with Delfau, which was "always fun," and managed to get some bargains.
Tom stayed at home in the daytime, as the shopping would have been too
much for him. At night they ate at St. Vincent's, since it was just a block
away and Tom could not walk very far. One night the three of them went to
see an old Buster Keaton film.

It was fun staying in our little house. We had toilet trouble (*why* can't the
French make a toilet correctly) and we had to have a plumber one whole

day. How I would love to get our place really nicely fixed up and live in Paris a while. I still adore Paris even if it is démodé to say so. The Luxembourg Gardens never looked so lovely and with no one in them I felt as though they were my own private gardens! It was marvelous having Tom in Paris with me and it was a real sacrifice for him to come.

Their first night back they spent with Margaret Fisher in Winnetka, and Tom went very shortly to the Cleveland Clinic. Ruth stayed only overnight and plunged at once into the complications of unpacking, housecleaning, taking care of the accumulation of letters and the like at 1100. To make things no easier, it was very hot and the air conditioner was out of order—"the one time in my life when I've really needed it."

It was not long, however, before all three branches of her supposedly disintegrated career were in full and habitual swing. She had talked to Petersen about the *Nutcracker* (the new problem there was that since there was to be an opera season this year, they would have less time to rehearse on the stage); she had auditioned a hundred girls and seven boys for the opera; and she had worked with Bill Hughes, the pianist, on the music both for her newly planned ballet, which was to emerge as *Dancers' Ritual*, and for *Alice*. At home she was spending "80 percent" of her time on the phone "contacting dancers and planning 'Nuts' and the opera" and was "really getting telephonitis."

On the surface all this was merely a return to routine, but there was a new undertone of franticness, which had first appeared perhaps at St. Tropez. In Chicago it was accentuated by the necessity of facing friends and colleagues who must not be allowed in on her private tragedy. This necessity to present an impeccable front was due partly to her instinct for performing, and partly to that aspect of gallantry that belongs to good breeding. Behind all surfaces, however, was a desperate battle for self-preservation, a grasping for the restoration of normality—familial, professional, artistic; social, urbane, fashionable; even irksome and contentious.

In the opera auditions, of the hundred girls five were "possible" and of the seven boys only one was possible—a black, Charles Neal, whom she decided at once to take. "Auditions exhausting as usual. I kept thinking of Tom and really wept when someone just asked about him. I hate to break down in front of people."

As far as sheer absence from Tom was concerned, it was not much greater than it had always been. What with her tours and his long periods in Texas or Florida or New York, they were quite used to being apart. They had, indeed, built altogether separate and demanding lives in totally unrelated fields, with only the male-protective, female-dependent relationship to provide a specific connecting link. Yet there had never been any weakening of their mutual respect, their enduring companionableness or their romantic devotion.

It was the pattern of their separateness that had now changed; their two independencies were being uncoupled, and they were reaching for each other in space.

Ruth, who has always put more into a day than it would hold—creating, "practicing," seeing everything in all the arts at no matter what cost, going to parties and giving them, *haute couture*, shopping, traveling—now sought to maintain her equilibrium by pursuing all these interests with added intensity. She was in no sense negating Tom; if she had, as it were, stopped breathing, it would not have helped him to breathe.

His physical condition was steadily worsening. After he returned from the Cleveland Clinic, he went again to Margaret's in Winnetka. ("He goes to Billings Hospital soon. If only he could come to 1100 to live. His doctor has refused to let him do any work at all. *What* is going to happen to us!")

When her friend Ingeborg Heuser phoned her from El Paso and asked her to come there to stage a ballet for her regional ballet company, she said yes, "really to get away from the telephone." It would also give her a chance to work out her ideas for her new ballet. Even with a group of amateur dancers, who, for all their delightful ardor, could not begin to sense the subtle comedy that pervaded the work, she got some sort of groundwork laid. Also, the weather was marvelously cool after sweltering Chicago, and she was delightfully entertained. One night they went across the border to Juárez, where "we saw some enchanting Mexican dresses but couldn't get any to fit us."

When she got back to Chicago, Tom, who was still staying at Billings Hospital for observation, took her to dinner one night at The Bakery and the next night at Su Casa.

> ... Each night at a different restaurant—all quite good but one doesn't have the desire to return! Tom came in to get me in the car Sunday noon—we went to our darling little house in Hubbard Woods—it looked so sweet and sad and lonely. Tom found my engagement ring on the floor in the guest room. When the burglars came they ransacked everything and when they found nothing of real value they just threw things on the floor. I wanted to go down the bluff but the walk is now too much for Tom so we sat on the porch for a while.

Then they went to Winnetka for a sandwich and a movie and, after a visit with Margaret and a good restaurant dinner for a change, they drove back to town.

> Tom went to Billings and of course I came to 1100. . . . Always busy— otherwise my troubles would be just too much. Tom gets weaker and weaker all the time and our meetings are so quick and sort of frantic. I went out twice to Hubbard Woods to spend the night with him, but Margaret doesn't like me to come out there, so I feel very strange and uncomfortable. We went one day over to our little house and sat on the

porch and I never felt so sad in all my life. Tom helped me get my "Alice" libretto into good English. It took a long time.

I had a meeting with Ed Lee, Petersen and Ernie Farmer from Shawnee Press at 9 a.m. and we discussed music for "Alice"—composer's fees, etc., etc. It was really a tough session for me and I don't know whether I got any place or not. We'll see. The night before I had Ernie Farmer and Petersen and their lawyer to the Racquet Club for dinner. ·It was a very nice party but tiring and I didn't get home till 12:30. I did my best to sell the Alice idea. . . .

Only went to class once and had very little time to practice. David and Anna Marie Holmes arrived last Thursday. I really did not know whether they were coming or not. I had dinner with Tom and left word for them to come, but we just missed each other. I finally met them on the street— we had an ice cream together and then talked till about 2 a.m. They are lots of fun. We did a barre the next day and worked on "Romeo and Juliet." We got along quite well with it. . . . The Holmes are wonderful guests. They can cook, clean, and the other day David took the studio curtains down and washed them and put them up again. The professional cleaner wants $82.50. . . .

Monday and Tuesday I spent all day on a television "commercial" [for Great Books] of Trepak [from *Nutcracker*] at St. Alphonsus Theatre. I was asked to use 6 boys and got them all. At the last minute Sunday, Wilding Studios telephoned and said we must have a black. So I telephoned Charles Neal, the boy that I engaged for the opera. I called him at 7 p.m. Sunday and he got there that night and we put him in it on Monday a.m. I had to more or less change the formation. He learned fast but he couldn't quite do the steps—however I don't think he will spoil it. We had two very grueling days—the poor boys were dead.

Monday I was one of the guests of honor at the Chicago Drama League's luncheon at the Blackstone. All honored guests represented the "performing arts"—12 very distinguished Chicagoans. No one told me we had to make speeches so I wasn't prepared at all. We were taken alphabetically and P came very close to the end. The speeches were all very good but very long so I modestly made mine very short and really didn't say anything interesting at all. However, mine had 2 paragraphs in the Tribune and the others only one line. . . .

Tuesday I rehearsed "Masked Ball" a lot and Larry rehearsed his new divertissement [for the tour] to Donizetti's "La Favorita" music—so the day passed. . . . Met Tom at Harvey in the station and again we had so much business to attend to that we couldn't have much fun talking. My poor Tommy gets weaker and weaker every day and every time I see him I am heartbroken. Life without him will be completely unbearable for me. . . .

Usual class and rehearsals every day. I can't say that I'm very thrilled to have only Ballo and Falstaff to do. We [the opera season] finally opened last night. I spent all day in the theatre. We had a Snow call for "Nuts" from 3 to 7:30 p.m. and the curtain went up on "Salome" at 8:30, so it was quite a rush, especially as I had to get out of my dressing room because

the singer who sang Herodias' page had to be alone. She had about 2 lines
to sing! Well, I try to be agreeable so I packed up all my stuff and went
upstairs and dressed with Dolores. I wore my white ostrich pants with the
white satin overdress. The feathers shed a good deal but otherwise I was
very comfortable in it. I slipped into the auditorium by the stage entrance
to avoid all the crowd and the pictures etc. . . Went to the ball afterwards
with all the artists in the bus. Before we made our "Grande Entrée" we
had to wait outside the ballroom for about 2 hours for Felicia Weathers to
arrive. I drank a lot of champagne so I didn't feel too badly. At supper I
sat next to Astrid Varnay and Michael Manuel and enjoyed them both very
much indeed. Home about 2:30 a.m. I missed Tom so much—I feel so sad
without him, but I try to act as gay as possible. . . .

I spent Sat. and Sun. nights at Margaret Fisher's in Winnetka. I felt
unwanted as I know Margaret is furious that Tom doesn't leave her. I told
him to leave but he just can't bear to go back to Hammond, and he keeps
thinking his Atwood case will be settled. He feels he is dying and it is all
so sad. We spent all Sunday at our house in H.W. I worked a little in the
studio and sat the rest of the day on the porch. Was I glad to get back to
1100!

Last night Irvine Page spent the night with me and Tom took us to dinner.
Irvine can't think of any solution for Tom's illness. Had a wonderful talk
with Irvine. I didn't even know he had received the Shean award as "the
outstanding physician of the year" (with $10,000). He gave a lecture this
a.m. on "heart transplanting" and then left for Cleveland. He is such a
wonderful person.

October

Monday we had class at quarter to one. The girls rehearsed "Rossignol"
from 2 to 4 and the boys from 4 to 6. Novaro was sick so Larry took the
rehearsal.

Luciana Novaro, guest director from Italy, had started as a dancer and
choreographer and now staged operas in their entirety. She had staged
Poppaea in Chicago two seasons ago.

I tried to rehearse the "Romeo" boys upstairs in room 100 but the wardrobe people were ironing so I couldn't get a line so that we could have
music on the tape recorder. I finally gave up. I always feel like a boot-
legger when I get a few seconds squeezed in for our non-opera ballets.

Today Tito Gobbi came at 12 and tried to explain to us his ideas on
"Falstaff" last act. He only wants about 2 steps of dancing but the
mise-en-scène and costumes are complicated. And suddenly they want 15
children. If only I could have chosen them during "Nutcracker" auditions
it would all have been so simple. But, as usual with the opera, everything
at the last minute! This is the last season I will ever do at the opera and I
will leave with no regrets whatsoever. . . .

The Atwood case was brought up for retrial yesterday and Tom's name is
all over the newspapers and radio programs. Everything false. It all makes
me sick. I hope after this year we can leave Chicago forever.

Sunday I went to the theatre at 11:30. Consternation because there was a mixup in the call for children, and many too many came. So the same heartbreaking experience as in "Nuts." We got them all into costume and ready on the stage at 1 p.m. and worked straight through to 7 with an hour's break. Everything we set had to be changed because of the star singers, and a white horse, and the chorus having to see the conductor, etc., etc., etc. It was a very long and tedious day. So exhausting for the dancers and so little money. Oh, how I wish we didn't have to do opera!

I didn't watch many of the "Rossignol" rehearsals—I love the music and the story, and the costumes and scenery look absolutely beautiful. It is very good for the dancers to have to work with Stravinsky's uneven counts. Novaro is very slow but she makes the dancers do her steps as she wants them. Larry is a big help to her. Klekovic's legs are bad again and after one rehearsal she decided not to do it. I have a feeling also it is because the part is so small!

Wed. a.m. I went to the theatre planning to give a lovely class and when I went into the Civic the stage was all filled with the "Oedipus" set. I had already promised the upstairs studio to the soloists, so we stayed downstairs and did the best we could under the circumstances. After class the director of "Oedipus" arrived, Gian Pietro Calasso, and he talked to us 2 hours about the Sophocles play. Calasso is a real intellectual and I enjoyed his talk very much, but I would like to know if our dancers were really interested. I somehow doubt it. . . .

Last night Carol Fox, Ardis Krainik and Luciana Novaro came to dinner. It was our day off so I did the shopping and we had quite a nice dinner and an agreeable evening. Luciana told us the story of her life and I was glad to know more about her. . . .

Monday night after the rehearsal I met Tom and we had dinner and a long talk. His condition seems so hopeless—I came home and cried and cried and cried. If only he could stay at home so I could take care of him. His case is being retried, so there is more disagreeable publicity and all that work all over again. . . .

Very busy day yesterday. Went to the theatre earlyish because I was nervous about all the physical "arrangements" of rehearsals etc. We couldn't have class on the Civic stage because it was all set for a talk fest for the school teachers of Chicago to learn about opera. Goldowsky started to talk about 9 a.m. and I was glad I went early as he is a very entertaining, informative speaker. He also was moderator of a panel discussion, which was more of the same old thing and naturally quite boring to me, so I didn't stay till the end. I went across the street to lunch, waited a half hour, and then left and got a sandwich from the food machine at the opera. Impossible to eat it.

Raya Lee gave class at 12:45 and I thought she gave a very good one.

Dress rehearsal for "Falstaff" was all afternoon—the usual wild mess. In Gobbi's version the dancers do practically nothing but "supe," so it is not very interesting for us, and very tiring—and the poor dancers, after the dress rehearsal, had to rehearse 2 hours with Calasso on "Oedipus"—it apparently takes him hours and hours to set one or two simple movements.

Dolores and Orrin came to my apartment for dinner, then Orrin took us to see the Pennsylvania Ballet. The evening was not one to be inspired by, but maybe they are on their way to something. They had an orchestra of 19 men. Oh, how I would like to have 19 men! . . .

Last Monday I went to Edna McRae's rehearsal with the children and nothing is more fun than that.

I had dinner with Tom Fisher and then went to see "Falstaff" alone, and sat in my usual front row seat. I really enjoyed every minute of it. Gobbi was superb and every role was brilliantly sung *and* acted and every comedy point was made. Zeffirelli's realistic production was effective and the last act with all the dancers and children was stunning. I thought I would have preferred it with more nymph-y costumes for the dancers to suit the music, but somebody told me that Zeffirelli purposely made heavy realistic costumes to make the effect with the light poetic music seem amusing. Well—anyway it was effective. . . .

Went at 4:30 to rehearse the children with Edna—so refreshing and inspiring to see them. Dinner with Tom and very much grim conversation. Our affairs go from bad to worse and there seems no hope at all.

Saturday I didn't rehearse until 5 p.m. We were supposed to rehearse "Masked Ball" in room 100 but Sanzogna and the singers were working there and asked me if I wouldn't rehearse in the Civic. So I went to the Civic and Calasso was rehearsing "Oedipus" with the corps and asked me to give him 5 minutes. He took 15 minutes, then the corps had to have a 10-minute break, so we only had 25 minutes to rehearse.

Then I rushed into my black velvet tuxedo and went to the Swiss Chalet in the Bismarck Hotel to have dinner with Ruby Mercer. The maître d'hôtel wouldn't let me stay in the restaurant [because of the trousers, of course] so I had to go to the ladies' room and take them off. Fortunately I had tights on, so returned to the restaurant in tights!

November

We had the dress rehearsal of "Ballo" on Friday. They used the dreary old sets from the opera here and my dancers wore long dominos and masks so they couldn't be seen at all. They were very ugly colors—oh, well—opera! Klekovic and Orrin did a little bit of a dance and even under the masks and dominos their elegant movement showed. But it was a long kind of boring "old hat" evening. How I wish I could do some of the new productions instead of only getting the little tidbits of nothing!

By the first week in November, though she gave a daily class to the corps, she had "given up all rehearsing till 'Rossignol' and 'Oedipus' go on. The rehearsal schedule is frantic—we never know where our class will be—if it is announced upstairs we have it downstairs and if announced downstairs we have it upstairs."

The diary itself takes on something of the same incoherence; a recurrent theme runs through it of a party she has decided "in a foolish moment" to give after the opening of the two Stravinsky operas. It is to be chiefly for

Fracci, Novaro, Calasso and the singers—not the dancers. Through a maze of activities we stumble on data about how much harder it is to put on a party than a ballet, how much shopping she and Felisa did, how long it takes to clean up both before and after.

In and around all this she went with Ann Barzel to see the Paul Taylor company and the Dancers from Ghana. She went to a piano costume rehearsal of the Stravinsky program, but she got there when *Rossignol* was half through, so she missed the pas de deux by Fracci and Kenneth, and she had to leave halfway through *Oedipus*, but she stayed long enough to see that "the dancers do so little movement that the chorus could have done it." A few days later she took Margaret Fisher to an invitation dress rehearsal of the program, but had to leave early to be a guest of honor at a "Know Your Chicago" party at the Casino, and hurried away early from that to meet Ann Barzel for dinner and the José Limón company's performance.

On one of their days off she "was idiot enough" to accept a lecture-demonstration at a school way over on the southwest side, at the request of a science teacher whom she greatly admired because of his desire to get his neighborhood interested in the arts. She had become, indeed, a virtual convert to her own Billy Sunday's sawdust-trail preaching—not to "the saved" but to those who did not even know there was such a thing as "salvation." This would also give her a chance to break in parts of *Romeo and Juliet* before an honest and innocent audience. But Kleck had hurt her back, and practically everything went embarrassingly wrong; "so I had to talk my head off to make the thing go at all. I really gave my all and I am exhausted today." It is possible that these exhaustions helped to preserve her sanity.

When the Stravinsky evening opened:

> I saw "Rossignol" from the front row so it was very difficult to judge, but it seemed to go quite smoothly and it is a very agreeable ballet. The story is not well told and not at all moving but the music is lovely and poetic. It is all sort of a combination of Coq d'Or-Firebird-Gilbert-and-Sullivan. The ballet-opera was well rehearsed and our dancers did very well. The nightingale's role for Fracci was very conventionally choreographed but she is an enchanting dancer, and maybe there are no new ideas for bird-girls.

She did not stay for *Oedipus* because she had to go home to prepare for the party, but she would certainly see it later. (Which she did and "was deeply moved by it. So many people have said it was boring but I found every minute interesting. I didn't even mind Oedipus' pink beard which so many people found ridiculous.")

The only dancers she had invited to the party were Fracci, of course, and her own top five.

> All the rest were singers, directors, plus about 10 "society" folk. . . . We really had a mixture of all kinds of languages. I tried to spend as much

time as possible with Fournet, the conductor, and Eda Pierre, the Martinique singer, as they spoke nothing but French. The person I found most interesting was William Marshall, who was the narrator in "Oedipus." He comes from Gary, Indiana, and started life as a steel-worker. He is intelligent, handsome and talented. Carol Fox said she was sure the man who sang Oedipus and his boy friend would not come to the party, but they did and they were the last to leave at 3:30 a.m.

The next day was fortunately her day off. She had dinner with Tom that night. "That case has ruined our lives."

At the opening of Menegatti's production of *Don Pasquale* she sat with Carla Fracci, who

> wore her long (to the ground) mink coat and kept it on all evening. She told me she bought the coat just to make an impression at the opera. She must have smothered in it as it was a very warm night. She wore her hair loose down her back and looked very dramatic. . . .

> Thanksgiving dinner was very agreeable. Buz Paschen [the husband of Maria Tallchief] picked me up and took me to his mother's for a family dinner at 4 p.m. Marjorie [née Tallchief] and George Skibine and their 16-year-old twins and Elise Reiman Hotchkiss and Mrs. Tallchief were there, plus the Paschen family. We drank for an hour and then had a delicious feast. I sat between George Skibine Sr. and George Skibine Jr. The twins are interesting boys studying at the Lycée in New York but they still speak English with a very foreign accent—they do not want to be dancers! George Sr. has been working with regional ballet companies in Louisville and Flint, Mich. He says he does it just because Marjorie wants the twins brought up in America. He says choreography in Europe is 100% easier and that he doesn't understand why anyone wants to stay here. I agree!

December

By now she was, of course, deep in the *Nutcracker* rehearsals. She was also working on both *Romeo and Juliet* and *Dancer's Ritual*, apparently in the unquestioning belief that the tour would open, as scheduled, on January 13. Actually Tom was still standing on his notification of cancellation, and though Columbia Artists was far too involved to accept such a decision, nothing was settled.

Romeo was almost exactly the way she wanted it to be. "I think (fingers crossed) it will be deeply moving." *Ritual*, however, was not going so well.

> Such a wild dress rehearsal [of *Nutcracker*] this morning at 11 with the house full (completely) of underprivileged school children. The lights were not ready, 2 dancers were out and all in all it was a pretty wild morning. The truth of the matter is that when the opera does not close until December 15 there is not time to get "Nuts" ready for Dec. 20. . . .

A telegram from Columbia came yesterday saying they would give us *all* the proceeds of the tour and not make a penny themselves, but we have to do the "business" of the tour. Tom will not do this, which means we may not do the tour. Tom said we have to cancel it, so that I feel my whole world has now completely crumbled. What to do! I didn't answer the Columbia telegram (which was not sent to *me*) as I really don't know what to say and they have to know in 24 hours. Well, I guess everything is lost now. Anyway, we'll get the "Nutcracker" on somehow.

Whether she answered Columbia's desperate ultimatum herself or persuaded Tom to do so is not in the record, but Columbia's terms were accepted, the tour seemed, for the moment, secure and *Nutcracker* opened "somehow."

The Holmes got here Sunday and rehearsed three days with us. Dolin arrived today and came to supper after one of the rehearsals. The Holmes came over and we ate in the kitchen. Anyway, lots of excitement all the time, and trying to get Romeo and Ritual ready at the same time. And I never get to see Tom. Life is one awful mess! . . .

Delfau and I just sat around and talked most of Xmas and at 4:30 we went to Carol Fox for Xmas dinner. Just Larkin, Carol, Victoria [their daughter], Larkin's mother and brother. Carol has a very sumptuous swank new apartment—extremely comfortable and extremely conventional. We had a marvelous dinner and a most agreeable time. The only thing that spoiled it was Carol's saying (when I complained of the terrible conditions of work at the opera) that *"nothing would ever change at the opera and that it would always be the same."*—What a depressing thought!

January

All my "stars" apparently refuse to go on tour unless they get the $70 weekly [which the union had just won for the corps] on top of their own salary. If they insist on this then we just cancel the tour, and I hope we do. The preparation for a tour has become impossible and the expenses are so astronomical that only the government can afford to do it. I think I will be bankrupt completely after this tour, even though Columbia is giving us the entire proceeds and not making a cent on us. What is it all coming to! . . .

Henning and Kirsten missed a performance the other day—they just didn't read the schedule right. Fortunately the Holmes were there and had just done a barre, so they went on for them. Yesterday I saw the matinee and evening both and came home between. The Robert Marshes came to dinner. He is music critic on Sun-Times and was not given tickets to "Nuts," so here we've been giving it for 4 years and he has never seen it. So *I* had to get the tickets and I went with them in the evening. It is exhausting to watch that ballet twice a day! I did not see it at all today – just sat in my dressing room and attended to *business*. Horrible! . . .

Really reached the depths of despair last week with Tom getting worse all the time and Felisa saying she was going to die any minute. I really felt like tacking an overdose of sleeping pills myself.

All my star dancers refused to go on tour unless they got the $70 per week extra (like the corps gets), so we just finally said to everyone "the tour is canceled completely and definitely." I went to the theatre last Sunday and expected to rehearse "Carmina" from 10 to 12 before the matinee, and that was when I told them the tour was canceled. Dick Carter, our television director from Channel 11, was there to work on "Carmina" with us, and we just sat there for 2 hours—it was like a funeral. I really just felt the end had come.

Then we had a lovely matinee of "Nuts." The house was sold out and so enthusiastic. I had no intention of taking a bow from the stage with the dancers, but I did just because everything was so nice. My Lithuanian friends sent me a ravishing big basket of flowers with lots of lovely ornaments in it and everything was very gala.

Then Monday we started digging into the tour repertoire (the tour was not called off because all the dancers agreed to forgo the extra $70 per week). We rehearsed on the big stage and every day there was a problem. One day Lyon and Healy came to take away the piano and I said "oh, can't you leave it a few days longer?" and they insinuated that for a bribe they could. So I gave them $15 and they left the piano. How low have I fallen!

The tour, stamped with the prescience of mortality, could scarcely have been more difficult. In addition to the objective realities of the situation, such as the shortage of money and especially the unions' indifference to both the aspect of quality and the responsibilities of collaboration, there was the subjective element in Ruth's nightmare that provided a dimension of grotesquerie. She was actually embracing this ordeal as a kind of toxin-antitoxin against the prolonged inevitability of Tom's death. She could not stay away from him, yet she must have a justification for staying away from him; she could not run away from the artistic agony of the tour, yet she must rationalize the leaving of it.

They opened on January 13 (of all superstitious numbers) in Coldwater (of all inauspicious names), Michigan.

We saved money by not having the orchestra rehearse in Chicago, but the orchestra did sound terrible, and I felt pretty miserable about it. However, with the audience we had I don't think anyone knew the difference. A typical Community Concerts audience—old people and children. . . . Nothing but complaints from the dancers about *everything*. . . . God, they get to be a bore! Dancers complaining about the cold (for me it was not cold at all). I can't wait for this tour to be over and I will never never never do another. . . .

No scenery possible for us . . . only the black curtains for everything. . . . I asked to have the black drop half up for "Ritual" and let down for the pas de deux only, and Larry had for "Child's Play" a tiny plastic drop (about 5 ft. square), and for these two "nothing" effects we had to engage 3 extra stagehands. So of course we had to abandon them. . . .

The Holmes got into a big fight with the stagehands. I arrived just at the end so wasn't quite sure what it was all about. . . .

The new union rule is that the day off is 36 hours instead of 12. . . .

David Holmes got into a big argument with Neil Spiegel, our chief stage man. Neil said it was impossible to hang the black curtain, and also impossible to put up our booms for the side lights, and David told him how he could have done it. Then Neil and Howard [Duncan, one of the stage crew] just yelled and yelled and yelled and David yelled louder—terrible language and everything wildly disagreeable. And such nice people in the theatre, so I'm sure they must have been disgusted with us (and I don't blame them). However, everyone loved our show in spite of the bad lighting and the bad orchestra.

Larry Long also furious tonight because his "Amor" costume doesn't fit him right. Why he couldn't have attended to this before he left Chicago I will never know. The same with David Holmes and his Romeo costume. Klekovic and Anna Marie had fittings and fittings and kept after the wardrobe department till their costumes were just right. So Larry swore at the company. . . . I just can't wait to get out of this filthy business. . . .

Sunday we had a matinee at Elkhart. A dreary theatre and no space at all backstage. I had to spend the entire performance in the booth way up high in the balcony with the spotlight man. I was so busy telling him what to do with the spotlight that I couldn't look at the dancing. In the middle of "Carmina" he said he had to go to the toilet. I said "well just wait till the intermission." But he just left—I should have told him to do his business right there! Well, in my desperation, I ran the spotlight. I hadn't the remotest idea how to do it, but I discovered how immediately. I really had no idea it was so easy.

There was a single Sunday matinee performance booked for Chicago, actually at the opera house, late in January. By this time, Tom had managed to slip quietly into Passavent Hospital, where, with whatever medical assistance he could obtain, he would work to the end to bring the Atwood case to a satisfactory conclusion. To be sure, he was concerned with Ruth's security and well-being, knowing her innocence of the world of affairs, and he planned for it with tenderness and foresight; but he was also animated by that old zeal for winning in court which was as indestructible as Ruth's obsession with the making of ballets.

She left the company at Marquette, Michigan, a week before the Chicago performance.

I've really had about all of the company I can take. I need to get away and think about all my terrible troubles.

Her flight to Chicago was canceled because of bad weather, so she went by the public bus, which took her from 7:20 in the morning to 7 in the evening.

It was a horrible trip. I had no breakfast. We stopped 20 minutes for lunch in some bus depot and I had a ham sandwich which I could hardly eat and coffee I could hardly drink. What a dreadful diet the American public has to put up with. It was horribly cold in Chicago and I had to wait one hour in the cold to get a taxi. I wanted to go directly to the hospital to see Tom but was just too exhausted. So I came home, ate some canned soup and went to bed.

She went to the hospital to see Tom every day. "He is just a pale shadow of himself and much as I love to go see him, it makes me feel desperately sad." She spent the days at her desk "paying bills and going over accounts," and also trying to make the Chicago performance look its best. She went to the warehouse, way over on the west side, and "had a terrible time" getting the *Bolero* screens, which had not been taken along on this sceneryless tour, to the opera house, "and of course it cost a fortune." She also sent to New York for Don Judge, her former stage manager and "régisseur," to come to Chicago to take care of the lighting for *Bolero*.

At night she went to the Joffrey Ballet, sometimes alone and sometimes with the Holmeses, who arrived two days before the performance and stayed at her apartment. On their first night there the three of them went to a party for some of the Joffrey dancers at Ann Barzel's apartment. "Very late getting home but lots of fun and interesting talk. Margaret Fisher spent the night and I had breakfast with her and then went back to bed."

Not until she got to the theatre on Sunday morning for a 9:30 orchestra rehearsal did she learn that the company manager had fired the incontinent spotlight operator for drunkenness and that Howard Duncan had simply had it and left. Don Judge had ordered the stage lighting company to send the same lights that had been used before for *Bolero*.

But of course they sent the wrong ones so we didn't have the same light effects behind the screens. I really did everything possible to get things right for our Chicago performance, but fate was against me. I splurged and had two spotlights instead of one. I crawled up the ladder to the spotlight room so I could help with the lights for "Carmina." Just before "Carmina" started one of the spotlights broke and we couldn't use it. The "Death" special overhead light on the stage didn't go on for the finale so the whole end of "Carmina" was practically in the dark—it just made me sick. Also, we had to use the local man for the adjusting of the "Carmina" tape and he did it so badly—it always seemed either too loud or too soft. . . . However we had a 98% full house and the dancers (what I could see of them) all danced well. The audience liked the performance. . . . I was very surprised at our wonderful reviews—they were all by new young critics whose names I didn't even know. It is nice that the young ones like my work.

After the performance she went directly to the hospital to see Tom.

I went to see him every day, of course, and spent a lot of time with him. It just completely breaks my heart to have that marvelous man just slowly fading away. I can hardly stand it. What with the tours ending and falling apart financially and Tom so desperately sick, I really feel as though I had come to the end too.

In and out of Chicago, down rather than up in spirits, though with occasional punctuations of accidental triumphs or successfully sought evasions:

Had tea with the Holmes and we discussed the forming of a small (10 people) company to go to Japan, etc. I don't know if the idea will work, but I would do almost anything to get out of the U.S. and away from the horrible domination of the American unions. . . .

The second we got to Nashville there were troubles. We were at the Grand Ole Opry House (where we played before). At least the place has "character" but a crazy mad place to be giving a performance. Our stage manager phoned me in despair—there were no possible chairs [for *Bolero*], so it was I who had to scout around and get some. Which of course I did. . . .

Tom is in Passavent Hospital so I have spent most of my time there. I try to keep him cheered up but he is slowly dying. I would like to die with him. I can't sleep at night for thinking of him. I worry about the company, too, but they seem relatively unimportant in comparison to him. I went to class once. My apartment is a mess and my whole life seems completely a mess now. My only consolation is how beautiful my company looks and how much people enjoy them. This is a little compensation. . . .

I had dinner at the hospital as usual with Tom, and having to say goodbye to him (as I was leaving the next a.m. to join the company) just nearly broke my heart. I could hardly watch the ballet that night [a benefit performance by the Harkness Ballet at $15 a seat], the tears kept coming so fast. . . .

After a disastrous and depressing performance at Deer Park, Long Island:

I decided not to go to York [Pennsylvania] with the company, as Dolin asked me to go to Montreal with him to see Les Grands Ballets Canadiens [with which he was associated] over the weekend and I said yes. . . . Butler's "Catulli" looked a hundred percent better than it did at Caramoor. . . . There was a reception for Trudeau backstage after the performance. I went with Dolin and met him privately and he is quite something. After he shook hands with the dancers, he sat on the floor and talked to them. Apparently he studied ballet and yoga. . . .

She also saw Fernand Nault's *Carmina*:

It is interesting for me to see the different versions of Carmina by various choreographers and I have to admit I still like mine the best.

In New York to the Oak Room at the Plaza:

I had to check my pants before going into the dining-room. I guess the dear old Plaza will never change. . . . Talked to Tom Thompson last night and he said Columbia is definitely enthusiastic about my having a group of 10 stars to travel in 1970 and 1971. I wonder if it will ever happen. . . .

In Miami:

We danced at Union Beach (Municipal Auditorium). Since we were there they have built a huge apron for the Gleason show. If we had known it and if we could have called a rehearsal for both lights and dancers, I could have made a better performance. The auditorium is impossible, of course. The people from the sides couldn't see at all. . . . The theatre (or rather the stadium) was jammed and wonderfully enthusiastic. Every seat was taken and after the performance, our local manager, Silverman, said I was the greatest choreographer in the world! [His address and phone number were duly noted on the margin of the page.] *Everyone* was saying how wonderful it was, so naturally I was pleased, but very tired. We are having a perfectly terrible financial struggle. . . . Our leading electrician is leaving and God knows what we will do. The union permits any of them to leave whenever they want to. . . . The company left at 8 a.m. and I am leaving now to see my Tom. . . .

March

I feel very lonesome here without my dancers. I go to the hospital every day. I stay 4 or 5 hours with Tom and usually have dinner with him. Each day he seems to get a little weaker, but thank God his brain is still all there. We discuss our bleak future a lot. Life without Tom, without my ballet, what on earth will it be—why live at all? . . . I went to class at Stone-Camryn two times. I took Tom's secretary to lunch and went up to his office one day—what a wild mess. He says it will take me three years to clean it out. My apartment will take me 2 years to clean out. What a lovely future! . . .

Went to class Monday, then spent most of the rest of the day at the hospital with Tom. His mind is, thank God, still all there, but his body is just disappearing. I can hardly stand it. . . . Had lunch with Margaret Fisher and Bentley and Walter, and after lunch had a long session with Carol Fox. She still thinks she is giving the dancers a big raise by giving them $97 a week, and of course it is really impossible for me to get a company together with that salary. I really feel that I have to give the whole thing up—my financial situation is impossible. I sent a 150-word night letter to Lowry of the Ford Foundation, but I'm sure my plea will be ignored. Any conversation with Carol Fox about ballet is so discouraging that when I leave her I feel that nothing is worthwhile. She gives endless (and very extravagant) opportunities to her Italian friends but not even a crumb for us. My soloists should certainly not stay with her and now that I will not have a tour next year, I will advise them to leave. What to do? I feel absolutely sunk. . . .

A friend of Effie Beals (my dear old colored maid and friend of a lifetime) telephoned and said that she had had a stroke and was in the County Hospital. I dropped everything and dashed over to see her. I had a hard time finding the 38th ward and wandered through all kinds of strange places to find it. It seemed to me that Dante's Inferno could not have dreamed up horrors worse than what I saw—almost all decrepit old, old people. I finally found Effie and we cried and cried and cried. She can't walk but her head and brain seem to be all right and she could talk. She said she was comfortable and the food was good, and she was glad to be "with her own people" (they were all black).

After seeing Effie I went over to see Tom—had another cry there and came home exhausted. I have spent 4 to 5 hours with him every day. It was wonderful being with him and my only wish is that I die before he does. I can't bear to see him, once such a tower of strength and now all skin and bones. . . . He tries to educate me about all the terrible things that are going to happen to me when he is gone. He has me practically scared to death. . . .

April

Tuesday I took Tom to Hammond. He came from the hospital in a wheel chair—a male nurse got him into the rented car with difficulty and we arrived in Hammond at noon. His lawyer met us there and we signed papers for the Atwood case till 3:30 p.m. and then drove back and put Tom back in his bed at the hospital. It was an exhausting day. But anyway *we* signed the Atwood agreement and now we have to wait for the other side to sign. It was all supposed to be finished by today, but there were the usual legal difficulties. One lawyer and his wife were supposed to leave for Japan today. They had to cancel their trip. I really feel this case will *never* end! As it is we've given away practically all our rights. . . .

May

Wednesday we had 3 lawyers at the hospital and we worked on "business" from 2 p.m. to 6 p.m. It is difficult for me to understand all the King Ranch problems, but strangely enough, I found it very interesting and maybe there is something in the world besides dancing after all! . . . We had another session Thursday, and [after lunch with Carol Fox and Donati, which included discussion of the plans for next season] had till 6 p.m. with the lawyers again. My husband is certainly a brilliant man—more I see of him, more I think he is really a great man! . . . Spent afternoons with our two new lawyers. Listening to the lawyers' talk makes a long, hard afternoon for me! But I guess I am learning slowly a little something about the business I have to attend to. . . .

She was already gradually preparing to move out of 1100, though there was still no place settled upon to move into. She gave a great many of her Dior dresses to the Chicago Historical Society, and made plans to sell or give away the bulk of her large print collection, her Dali (*Physician Lifting with Extreme Precaution the Cuticle of a Grand Piano*) and other paintings.

There were also ballets, parties and house guests, for the Royal Ballet was in town, and she took care of them all with high enthusiasm. But she missed only one dinner with Tom during it all.

Each time I come away with a broken heart and the only way I can live my life now is to do a million things as feverishly as possible. . . .

Finally had a confrontation with Carol Fox—a long conversation in which she told me she would not pay over $97 for corps de ballet for first year, 100 for second year and 105 for third year. I told her that for out-of-town dancers this was starvation wages and she said "I don't care if the dancers have to live on hard boiled eggs."

June

Have had one hell of a week—nothing but business, business, business. Tom put an ad in the London Times to get me a secretary—"the right job for the right person"—a very original ad. Well, we got fascinating answers. One lady sounded so good for the job that I wrote her a letter today and told her to come. What a chance! Will she or won't she come?

Actually she did come eventually to St. Tropez, but not for very long. Tom had had the advertisement inserted in both the London *Times* and the *Christian Science Monitor*, and it ran, in full, as follows:

> The Perfect Job for the Right Person—Do you know the theatre, including ballet and opera? Are you musical? Can you play the piano? Have you ever had experience in handling press and public relations? Can you drive a car? Do you like travel and living in Europe as well as the USA? Can you cook, and are you willing to take a course at the Cordon Bleu? Do you speak French or Italian? Are you between 40 and 50? And without family or marital commitments? Do you have any health defects? Yearly salary $12,000 for life. Please reply in detail with photographs.

July

His situation has become almost farcical. The "court" finally found out that he is at Passavent Hospital and so have put 2 guards in front of his door and no one but the doctor and I can go see him. Here his case is all settled and the state's stupid attorney has demanded to open it all up again because the contempt of court was not dismissed. How crazy can you be? The newspapers as usual report everything wrong, and there is lots of publicity in the papers. Thank God I am Ruth Fisher and not Ruth Page for this case!

There were, inevitably, more meetings with Carol Fox about the opera. Carol now offered the dancers $100 the first year and $105 the second year, but limited the soloists to two. Ruth continued to maintain, however, that that was not enough and that they would not return for less than $135. Whereupon Carol said, "Sorry, I'll have to look elsewhere." And she proceeded to invite the Boston Ballet (one of the beneficiaries of the Ford Foundation award) "to send a few couples here and there for such ballets as 'Ballo' and 'Traviata,' etc." which required mostly folk and social dancing. But when the time came, Ruth, who loved the opera quite as much as she hated it, actually stepped in and got the new dancers started.

Since her company was disbanded, she suggested bringing in Ballet Theatre to take over *The Nutcracker*, but the *Tribune* decided that they wanted to skip a year entirely and save their own revival of *The Nutcracker* for the reopening of McCormick Place, which was supposed to be finished in 1970.

August

The police are still outside his door but at least the judge kicked the attorney out of the case and the settlement can't be changed, so at least we don't have to go through the trial again. "Contempt of Court"—God knows when that will be settled.

Tom gave his clothes to his nephew, Morgan, whom they fitted, and Ruth told Margaret to add those that were in the house in Hubbard Woods. She herself presented all her scenery and costumes in the storehouse to George Verdak, who headed the dance collection at Butler University in Indianapolis. To go through the storehouse and sort things out was not only physically difficult but emotionally taxing.

My life now is just a series of getting things cleaned up—how I do miss the dancing—this life now for me is nothing.

The guards were taken away from the hospital door about September 1, but the hospital itself was still indignant at having been brought into the episode.

I started rehearsals with the Boston Ballet at the Civic Theatre last Monday at 11 a.m.—worked about 5 hours with the corps and almost finished the ballet of the Persian slaves in "Khovanshtchina". . . . It is wonderful to be working again. . . .

November

We finally decided to move Tom from the Passavent to the Whitehall. Tom doesn't want to move but I can't wait to get him out of there. I should have thought that just living in that tiny room with the awful food would have made him feel like a prisoner, but I never heard him complain even once. Anyway, they told him yesterday that they would start a lawsuit against him if he didn't get out. He would just adore another lawsuit, sick as he is, but he says he is leaving for my sake! I can't wait to get him out of there. I find the doctor most unsympathetic and he literally hasn't done one thing to help Tom. Tom has a bill of $10,000, none of which the doctor will take off Medicare, so I suppose we have to have another lawsuit about that. In the meantime Tom has no use of his body at all. He can't get out of bed and is completely miserable.

Friday I took Tom to Whitehall and spent the evening with him. I gave him the "Time" article about Bobby Seale and his "contempt of court" problem, and wanted him to explain it to me the next day. I called Sat. a.m. and he was dead.

Tom didn't want any funeral or any ceremony whatsoever and I intended to do as he asked. But Carol Fox called and said I absolutely had to do something. So finally after a lot of deliberation I decided to have a "party" for Tom—just invite his friends here to the apartment from 5 to 8 on Friday. Carol called some of the people, Margaret some, and I some. And it was one of the most interesting parties I have ever attended. I thought I would be weeping all the time but instead all the friends with their love made me feel almost cheerful. Irvine Page arrived Friday about 1:30 p.m. and Margaret came and Chris Mahon, my dearest friend at the opera. Maria and Buz Paschen were wonderful. Buz got a bartender and a maid and I ordered lots of hors d'oeuvres. . . . It was all a deeply moving experience—and now of course the aftermath.

Some Beginnings
to Conclude With

The aftermath that she foresaw would have been a bitter one if she had allowed it to be, but she refused to accept it as a reliving of calamity; instead she made a rebellious peace with catastrophe and set out replanting the ravished fields and building a world without Tom.

There were agonizing sequences of clearing out, giving away, document-signing—all symbols of dispersal, termination, dissolution. If she traveled even more than usual, it was in part because she could not bear to stay in the apartment. She had been there many a time indeed without Tom, but now his absence seemed to take on a presence of its own, and often after a single night there she packed up and left for somewhere—almost anywhere—else. The apartment itself, which had already been sold, existed in a state of suspended animation awaiting demolition.

She had now no ballet company, no further connection with the much hated, much loved opera, no annually triumphant *Nutcracker*. Without these mutually contributory responsibilities—demanding, inspiring, distressing—even Herbe Folle and Les Trois Pastèques lost urgency, since there were no more productions to be created there. It was an empty scene that faced her, with no abatement of the forces that impelled her and no corresponding outlet for their pressure.

At the recommendation of her financial advisers, official and unofficial, she undertook to set up a foundation to deal to some extent with such urgencies. These advisers fell into two factions so totally at odds in orientation and method that they might have been designed by nature to produce a dialectical productiveness in her interest. Actually both factions lost money

315

for her, and when she sat in meetings with them, it is no wonder that however successfully she may have feigned a grasp of their proceedings, she had not the least understanding of what they were talking about and no idea of how to make the decisions they expected of her. On the other hand, in spite of their good will and concern, they might have been feigning equally a grasp of her requirements, which dealt with the processes of adjusting life to art.

She was not at all sure how she wanted to use the foundation, but she knew that her only concern was to make ballets with a company of her own and a school to go with it. Her attorney managed to sell the remaining 375 or so acres of the Sauz Ranch in Texas at a good price, but as far as she could see, virtually all of it would go for taxes and legal costs. She had always been more pragmatic than the "business" people around her.

The first opportunity for the relief of some of her pressures came not through anybody's planning but out of the blue, and it seemed so remote from what she was pursuing that she was loath to accept it. Just before Christmas, after suitable overtures, Nicolas Petrov came from Pittsburgh to spend two days looking at the films of all her ballets. He had just undertaken the establishment of a ballet company in connection with Point Park College in downtown Pittsburgh. He was delighted with what she showed him and proposed that she restage all of them for him. She was certainly surprised and probably flattered by his enthusiasm, but far from exhilarated by the prospect of doing as he proposed.

What she wrote in the diary about it was an explicit revelation of her attitude toward the world she was entering:

> The thought of having to go to Pittsburgh to get my ballets on is absolutely repulsive to me. *Why* can't I stay in Chicago and do them here? Well, I'm sure now I'll never get to do that so I'll have to adjust to new conditions.

When she finally went to Pittsburgh to look the place over, however, she was favorably impressed. It was decided, accordingly, that she was to do the Daydé *Carmen* in mid-April; later there would be *Merry Widow, Romeo and Juliet* and *Fledermaus*. But the restaging of old works was of far less importance to her than the production of the two new works that had long been on her agenda and were already in the process of creation—*Alice in Wonderland* and *Catulli Carmina*.

Alice was most on her mind. She had already created parts of it on Klekovic; not that Alice was the kind of role she expected her to dance, but simply that Kleck was her own product from the start of her career and Ruth enjoyed working with her. Kleck, indeed, was the dancer she was proudest of, and she was planning to take her to Europe in the summer to provide her with an overview of Europe that would widen her range and deepen her artistry. But in the spring Ruth suddenly learned of a new European production of *Alice in Wonderland* that was to have its final performances at the Theater an der Wien in Vienna practically at once, so she hastily remade her plans, and off the two of them sped forthwith. The production pleased her not at all, but at least she had satisfied the curious necessity she seemed to have for seeing what other people were doing with material she was working on.

There would be five months between their departure and their return, and the European tour as a whole was a productive adventure culturally, socially, and practically, teeming according to precedent with the unexpected. Early on, Ruth and Patricia landed in Rome in the middle of a general strike, and if they had not been fortunate enough previously during a delay at the Paris airport to "pick up" a young and attractive American on his way to Tunis to build an airport there, they "might still have been waiting" in the Rome airport surrounded by luggage with neither porters nor taxis available. He took a shine to Patricia right away and "beaued" her around Rome (even arranging for her to visit him in Tunis a bit later). This left Ruth free at the moment to be "beaued" around in turn by her devoted John Crane, who was living and working in Rome, which made a pleasant interlude for both of them.

Before the diversified European spree was over, with its castles and cathedrals, its fun and games, tangible as well as intangible ends had been achieved. For one thing, the secretary previously engaged by correspondence duly arrived in St. Tropez from England, only to return thereto before long, never to be replaced. For another thing, Delfau, Irène Karinska, Gromtseff and a Paris maskmaker combined to produce scads of costumes for *Alice*. One whole trunkful of them almost got left behind in the final hasty and encumbered departure for the airport.

They were en route this time to Boston, for Ruth had arranged with Ted Shawn to spend the summer (without Kleck, of course) as choreographer-in-residence at Jacob's Pillow in the Berkshires, in order to devote herself to preparations for the première of *Alice* in Pittsburgh during the coming season. She had discovered a young New York dancer named Joyce Cuoco, who was not only talented and well taught but well disciplined (through such standard treadmills as the Radio City Music Hall corps de ballet), and was her very ideal of what Alice should be. Indeed, not since she created *Camille* for Marjorie Tallchief, had she been so moved to design a ballet explicitly for a dancer not of her own company. The other members of the summer cast would be, of course, only guinea pigs for the ultimate Pittsburgh cast.

The Pillow, what with its shortage of both living accommodations and working space, its hordes of summer students and the weekly stream of visiting performing companies for its theatre, provided a mere choreographer-in-residence with neither time nor place for rehearsing. When Delfau arrived, his unhappiness with the atmosphere in general and, specifically, the lack of appreciation for his work by Shawn (who was the epitome of nonchic), did nothing to make the summer more easygoing. But, of course, there was the delectable Cuoco, which compensated for much.

Then unexpectedly a second inspiration in another area flashed into the creative picture. Among the visiting companies there came Arthur Mitchell's Dance Theatre of Harlem for a week of performances. Ruth was delighted with it as a whole, but in particular there was a stunning creature named Lydia Abarca who enthralled her. She saw before her at once the potential Carmen of all Carmens, and by this time she was something of an expert on Carmens. Before the week was over, she had discussed with Mitchell the production for his company of still another *Carmen* (her fourth), this one transplanted from Spain to the Caribbean, where there was not only a commingling of Hispanic and black cultures but also the traditional art of the bullring. (Mitchell would have preferred the "barrio" in Harlem, but, fortunately or unfortunately, there was no bullfighting in Harlem.) Thus a third compulsive production was added to the impending *Alice* and the still distant *Catulli*.

Alice continued to impend for the better part of a year, through the logical confusions of a large institution, postponements, crises for Delfau over the unsatisfactory execution of his costume designs and a final cliff-hanging struggle with disaster when, late in the action, Joyce Cuoco was unable to appear. After having joined the Stuttgart Ballet as a replacement during its New York engagement, she had signed a permanent contract with it and could not be spared for either rehearsals or performances. Though an understudy for Alice was already prepared to step in, she hurt her foot and had to be replaced in turn by an understudy's understudy. In spite of everything, the performance was rapturously received by the local audience. . "I learned a lot," Ruth wrote in her best Pollyanna mood. "For one thing, that the success of 'Alice' does not depend on having a great Alice."

Ann Barzel came from Chicago to review it. So did Robert Marsh of the *Sun-Times,* and the headline on his review may have been the most soul-satisfying (if bitter) event of the whole episode. It read: "Chicago Première in Pittsburgh." Those were exactly her sentiments.

Meanwhile, through the long, drawn-out process of *Alice's* nascence, certain not fully exorcised ghosts from the past arose to intrude on the future. In November, to her complete surprise, Carol Fox invited her to dinner at the Tower Club and in the friendliest fashion suggested that she should set up and direct a new ballet company in Chicago. More and more it became plain that she meant the Lyric Opera's ballet. In February, she actually came to dinner at 1100, and with two of Ruth's advisers, including her attorney, they spent most of the evening discussing what might be done about it.

Carol at last came forth with the suggestion that Ruth go to Germany to see what she could find in the way of ballets for Lyric, just as she herself went to Europe from time to time on scouting missions for the opera. She was especially interested in a report on John Neumeier, the young dancer from Milwaukee who in his late twenties was already the quite successful director of the ballet of the Frankfurt Opera.

Ruth was extremely skeptical, not only by nature but also because of the scars she bore from her previous efforts to create a ballet for Lyric. But her two advisers offered no objection, and within a week she was en route to Germany and nearly a month of opera-house hopping, back and forth between Frankfurt, Cologne, Bonn, West Berlin, Munich and Stuttgart. She found prospering ballet companies everywhere, overflowing with American and British dancers and choreographers who had been unable to find any opportunities at home. There was apparently unlimited time for making productions (one company had spent five months on a production of *Coppélia*), working conditions were excellent and the art itself was in full flower.

Neumeier's production of the Prokofieff *Romeo and Juliet* she thought would make an ideal work to import to Chicago for the inauguration of the new project under consideration for Lyric. She did not see Neumeier dance the role of Romeo, but in general, though he did not have a marvelous technique, she very much liked his personality.

Everywhere she was received graciously and entertained by old friends among the American dancers and new ones among the Germans. In Munich who should turn up but Fritz Wilckens, out of the past; he had come from Seefeld to spend two days with her. She found him unchanged except physically, and "we laughed and laughed just as we used to," though it seemed strange to be with him without Kreutzberg. He had "not been to a ballet for twenty years," but he trotted along with her unquestioningly. The last day, they spent hours at the Neue Pinakothek (she really thought the thing she enjoyed most in the world was looking at pictures), and finally "we kissed goodbye and Fritz went back to Seefeld and I went back to the hotel. We said we would meet in Paradise. What a real charmer Fritzie is and what a friend. I adore him and I feel very lonely without him."

As a last-minute indulgence, just before she took the plane for home from Frankfurt, she "talked to Neumeier on the phone and then went to see the zebra skin that I have been looking at in the window every time I come to Frankfurt. I finally couldn't resist it and they tied it up in a package for me and off I went with my prize. I took the bus to the airport. . . ."

> What a trip—2 days in every town—almost like our one-night stands with my ballet company. . . . How sad it is that our dancers have to come to Germany to get jobs. Here there are hundreds of splendid opportunities. . . .

> If I had to live my life over again I would like to have been a director in
> any of the German theatres. Will I ever be able to get anything of
> importance really going in Chicago? Well I strongly doubt it.

As far as this particular mission was concerned, it was a well-founded
doubt. Toward the end of March there was a dinner party at Carol's apartment at which a group of people from the opera management, plus an
advisory guest from New York, were assembled to talk the matter over. Her
recommendations for a plan of action, including Neumeier's *Romeo* and half a
dozen other more or less immediately workable projects, fell on unresponsive
ears, and "it was a horrible evening." It was clear to her that she had knocked
herself out for nothing. Yet it was not for nothing, for this was the final
blow to any latent hope that she might achieve her goal of a genuine ballet
for Chicago through the opera establishment.

Progress on other fronts, however, was undeniable. Before her departure
for Germany she had arranged with the somewhat absent-minded gentleman in
charge of rentals in the Stevens Building to give her a lease on a very special
studio there. It was one with which she was thoroughly familiar, for Edna
McRae had long occupied it before her retirement from teaching, and it had
been Keith Allison's headquarters ever since. A week after her return a new
school was opened there with Larry Long in charge and the name of the Ruth
Page Foundation on the door.

It was something of a job to get the foundation legally established, for
this was the time when the government was cracking down on the proliferation
of personal foundations, since many of them were being set up as tax dodges.
She even had to give another ghastly series of lecture-demonstrations in the
public schools to emphasize her purely eleemosynary intent, though from the
very first her own school provided so many free scholarships for under-
privileged children, mostly blacks, that its physical dimensions were already
too small. It was to serve, however, as the base of operations for three and a
half years of activity directed toward the specific goal that she was more than
ever bent on pursuing. To start a company you must first have a school.

The new studio became chiefly Larry's domain at once, for within two
weeks she was swallowed up by Pittsburgh and *Alice.* Then the new *Carmen*
enticed her away—not, as she expected, to Harlem but to Spoleto, of all
places. Arthur Mitchell and his company, who had already appeared there in
the annual festivals, were to do so again this summer, and he had suggested
accordingly that it would be the most practical place and time to start
rehearsing.

This, to put it mildly, proved not to be the case. During the month she
spent there she managed to get in a total of ten hours of rehearsing, and eight
of those during the four days when Arthur had flown back to New York for a
meeting with the Ford Foundation. When he returned, he put a stop to all

her rehearsals on the ground that the dancers were too tired. One weekend he went of necessity to Berlin to confer with Patricia Neary, formerly of the New York City Ballet and now with the Berlin Ballet, about certain passages he had forgotten in *Agon*, the Balanchine-Stravinsky ballet which he was to present on his second Spoleto program. Until that difficult work actually went on, the company "worked itself into a dither over it."

If it was not one thing, it was another, and when Delfau arrived and saw the situation, he hazarded the opinion that "psychologically Mitchell does not want any other choreographer but himself." But, she argued, "It would have been so easy for him to say so—he keeps saying he wants to do 'Carmen.' In any event, it has been the most frustrating experience of my life." Delfau may have had a point, for he had already proved, and was to continue to do so, that he was a far shrewder judge of people than she was, probably because he did not like them as much as she did.

She succeeded at least, however, in getting Arthur's approval of Delfau's costume designs ("he seemed very impressed"). As for the setting, however, the effect of the slides, which Delfau had designed to be projected on three screens simultaneously, could not be even approximated on the single screen that was available.

Some of her unwanted free time was spent profitably on necessary chores. She had the costume sketches photographed and mailed off to Paris for execution. Some music composed by Coleridge-Taylor Perkinson for one of Mitchell's present ballets struck her as being especially excellent, so she undertook the task of having Van Grove's arrangement of *Carmen*, containing all the cuts, Xeroxed and sent off to him in New York so that he could make a new orchestration more appropriate to the new milieu of the work.

But though little or nothing was accomplished, and both Delfau and Orrin Kayan (who had come along to assist in the rehearsing) were disgruntled by the working situation and found no compensation whatever in the quality of the festival's programs, Spoleto was not without its moments for Ruth.

John Crane had driven her up from Rome, and Orrin was already there when she arrived.

> Thank God he arrived before I did and he got us all fixed up in the most amusing house imaginable. We call it our "palazzo"—kitchen in a sort of basement—2 bedrooms on first floor (no bathtub)—a living room on the 2nd floor and another living room on the 3rd floor. [Delfau was to use this one as his studio when he arrived a little later.] No ice-box, no telephone, no place to hang anything (one tiny closet) but the house is so beautiful it doesn't matter *at all*. Exquisite things all over the place and all done in beautiful taste. You have to go outside to get to each room and we each have 5 keys. It is deliciously quiet. We make coffee in the morning and then go out for all our other meals. . . .
>
> Orrin is a very charming companion and very thoughtful. He goes to the basement every morning and makes our coffee and brings it up to my

room. We have been every day to class. I just do the barre but it is certainly better than no exercise at all. I am so frustrated about not being able to rehearse that I can't sleep at night. We go to bed very late and it seems to me we do nothing but eat. . . .

Yesterday we went to Gian-Carlo Menotti's palazzo up on the hill just above the Duomo to a cocktail party and today I went there to lunch (without Orrin). I sat at Menotti's right and found him just as fascinating as everyone says. All kinds of attractive people—all ladies except Menotti and Harvey Lichtenstein. Very chic charming ladies. Priscilla Morgan seems to rule the roost—she appears very dynamic and efficient. We had a delicious Italian lunch. . . .

Life in our little palazzo is very agreeable and quite uncomfortable. I went to the Harlem company again last night. Orrin didn't want to go so I went alone. I didn't know one soul in the audience except sitting in a box were Buckie Fuller and Isamu Noguchi. How strange to see the latter after all these years. My old love—the man who really fascinated me above all others. He looks quite different as his head is completely bald and he has lost his poetic soulful look, but he still looks powerful and I was thrilled to see him again. Buckie looks much the same. But when I saw Ezra Pound in the Duomo, he really looks like walking death. I was glad to have a look at him even in his dying days. . . .

I invited Priscilla Morgan, Isamu and Buckie to lunch yesterday. Priscilla said she couldn't come unless they brought their "entourage." I had no idea who any of them were, but I had Ezra Pound on my left and Buckie Fuller on my right and Isamu next to Buckie. I couldn't get a word out of Ezra but Buckie talked a blue streak—wild marvelous ideas as usual. Isamu was quite talkative too. After lunch we went to a little park where there is a red sculpture for children to play in. I got inside it and got very dirty but it was really fun. Then we went to see Buckie's dome across the road. It is a new kind of theatre but no one is using it. It is a pity it is used for nothing. Buckie did something there last year called "Ballet of the Mind" but I couldn't quite figure out what it was—it sounded mighty like a "happening." Isamu walked home with me and I showed him my strange house and then we kissed and said goodbye. He leaves Spoleto today. . . .

On her way back to Chicago in late August, after time in St. Tropez and Paris, she stopped off in New York for two days to keep an appointment with Arthur Mitchell, his codirector Karel Shook, Perkinson, the composer, and Tania Leon, the company's musical director, and "we had a very satisfactory meeting about music" in the old church in Harlem where the company still had its headquarters. But her satisfaction about the music proved to be as unjustified in terms of action as her hopes for Spoleto had been—indeed, as the whole maddening situation would continue to be for the better part of the year to come. The difficulty of trying to do something creative for somebody else's company, which naturally had other things on its mind, only served to intensify her longing to establish at any cost a company of her own.

To complicate the drive in that direction still further, more ghosts from the past were making diversionary demands upon the present. Those talks with Columbia Artists immediately after the dissolution of her company about touring with a small group in simple programs along the line of lecture-demonstrations to be called "Invitation to the Dance," had resulted in the signing of contracts for two such tours which now had to be fulfilled.

Then in the midst of it all Ed Lee called to say that the rebuilding of McCormick Place was completed and they wanted to resume the *Nutcracker* productions this coming Christmas. It is not surprising to find her huddling with Larry Long and some of the foundation directors to discuss the necessity of forming at least the nucleus of a company straightway with headquarters in the school. For the tours she was able to call back a few of her old soloists and to pick up elsewhere the remaining few people she needed. For *Nuts* Larry had to do most of the rehearsing, since Ruth's time had already been so largely committed elsewhere. But Simon Sadoff was again on hand as conductor; Violette Verdy and Helgi Tomasson were engaged as the featured soloists; and even after the lapse of two years the production emerged as a huge success once more. "Without Larry," she wrote, "I really don't think I could have done it. Bless him. I hope I can leave a company for him when I die."

What took so much of her time away from the *Nutcracker* was, of course, the still maddening business of the Harlem *Carmen*. She was virtually commuting between Chicago and New York, even though Ken and Kleck had agreed to come to New York from Pittsburgh, where they were now working, to help out with rehearsals. When Delfau arrived, he was even less able than she to stand up under the confusion, the lack of rapport, the inexplicable delays and irresponsibilities. Perkinson's orchestration simply did not materialize from day to day. At length, as time went on, she turned the job over to Sadoff in desperation, but Mitchell insisted that it be done within his own company.

When the costumes arrived from Paris, they were received by the cast with high disdain and pronounced "tacky" by Mitchell himself. Whereupon Delfau simply disappeared for three days from the Plaza, where he and Ruth were staying. Later at a costume rehearsal, Carmen was to discard the upper half of the costume Delfau had designed and Karinska had made, and substitute a little something that had been whipped up in the company's own wardrobe department. At this point Delfau withdrew both himself and his costumes from the enterprise and advised Ruth to give up and go back to her old production by Daydé. Which in despair she prepared to do. For days the company rehearsed, as it were, two overlapping versions, trying to forget the one and learn the other. Clearly the contemporary Caribbean orientation had brought with it new musical rhythms, new accents, new dramatic emphases, and even much new choreography for the ensemble, which could not now simply be cast off with the costumes. After whatever torments of the soul, Delfau eventually returned and Daydé was abandoned. When in the spring the work actually came to performance at last, an enthusiastic audience made plain that it adored the production, the whole thing suddenly gelled for the dancers, they decided they loved the costumes, and Arthur changed his mind.

This first performance, however, did not come about, in the sequence of events, as simply a new work in the repertory of the Dance Theatre of Harlem. Ruth had decided instead to make use of the occasion for certain purposes of her own, and *Carmen* became accordingly one part of a special program sponsored by the Ruth Page Foundation (the first production to be so sponsored) at the Civic Theatre in Chicago in mid-May. "Chicago and Harlem," the ads proclaimed, "Unite in Ballets of Love and Death." The rest of the program consisted of *Carmina Burana* and a new pas de deux called *Three Preludes* (Rachmaninoff) by Ben Stevenson as an opener.

These works were performed by a company of twenty-five especially assembled for the occasion, with Kleck and Ken and Orrin as guests, under the deceptively familiar title of Chicago Ballet. The genuinely familiar title was Chicago Ballet Company, but the deviation was too slight to be generally noticed. It was nevertheless significant of developments behind the scenes, for the foundation was here moving, however deliberately toward the establishment of a company of its own, under a new legal setup to replace the old organization under which Ruth and Tom had operated for so long.

It proved to be a costly way to inaugurate this still formative venture, for the foundation had neither manager nor publicity director. Ruth herself had succeeded in wangling the hiring of the Civic Theatre (the small theatre in the opera-house complex) for the series of four performances that was planned. In addition to other considerations, she wanted enough performances to make a point of alternating roles in both ballets between the black and the white companies. It was she who engaged a local impresario to manage the engagement and a press agent to promote it.

It was she also who produced the first real publicity, much to her own surprise, only a week before the opening, when the Mid-America Ballet (an organization with the goal of uniting various ballet activities in the area into a single ballet company serving them all) gave a tea party in honor of her project at the Arts Club. It was one of those things that she simply took in graceful stride, expecting nothing. She did not even know that she was expected to make a speech, but as it turned out, she managed to do very well. She had never been so indiscreet and the press responded gratifyingly.

In particular, in the weekend "Panorama" section of the *Daily News* Richard Christiansen caught her style and the spirit of what she said with delightful perspicacity. He was too young ever to have seen her dance, but he decided that "if the lady danced as swiftly as she talks, she must have been one hell of a little ballerina."

Before the tea itself, there was an informal meeting of the board of governors of Mid-America. When that was over, she was introduced wittily and admiringly to the assembled guests; whereupon, Christiansen reports, "she laughed modestly and said 'I hardly know what to say after all that.' In the next hour she proceeded to say it all."

Whether she was exacerbated by her current dilemma, or piqued by the procedural practices of boards of governors, or genuinely inspired, she apparently laid it on the line, and for the first time she enunciated right off the top of her head, her financial, organizational, sociological and aesthetic credo, for all to hear.

She had once thought, she said, that it would be ideal to have one big company that would serve several cities, but now, she felt, every city wanted its own ballet. Every city, that is, except Chicago, which seemed to prefer imported companies with big "names" and was dubious about its own creative capacities. But there were already big companies to do the *Swan Lakes* and such, and do them better than a whipped-up Chicago company could. How much more to the point, then, to have a small company with its own artistic values, its own personality and, of course, its own repertoire. A Chicago ballet should be a Chicago ballet. "Why bring in Margot Fonteyn and Rudolf Nureyev all the time? I mean, I really love them but. . . ."

At this point Ann Barzel (critic for *Chicago Today*, member of the Illinois Arts Council, longtime champion of Chicago's dancers and campaigner for Chicago dance activities) thought it was about time to get around to the main object of the afternoon, which was to promote the forthcoming performances at the Civic. So she asked Ruth to give some specific information about that project.

"Well," said Ruth, according to Christiansen, "this is an absolutely crazy thing I'm doing. I really don't like to talk—ha, ha—I like to do things." Which was not as humorous as it may have sounded. She did manage, however, at least to name the two companies, black and white, which she was bringing together deliberately because they were black and white, and describe the program in general terms. She was clearly not going to make any pitch, so Ann once again sought to help her along by giving what Christiansen calls "a brief lecture" on her long and productive career in Chicago and elsewhere, "supplemented by ebullient reminiscences by Miss Page."

At last, in an effort to bring the curtain down, the chairman thanked Ruth for her helpful hints and added confidently that Mid-America would certainly have a ballet and a successful one. Says Christiansen: "He paused just a second there, and, sure enough, in rushed Miss Page."

And this is where she really came into her own. She pooh-poohed the concentration on success and urged them instead to concentrate on getting going. When somebody in the audience suggested that first they had to get the money, she pooh-poohed that idea also and told them to go into debt if necessary. Some companies, she said, have nothing to go on except money, but money is not what makes a company. "Be adventuresome, be chic."

"By this time," says Christiansen, "members of the hapless Mid-America board were beginning to shift nervously, glance at their watches and sweat bullets," until some experienced hostess rose to suggest that it was time for the tea drinking to "get going" and the rest was all cups and saucers.

When Ann Barzel reviewed the first performance the next weekend, her opening paragraph read as follows: " 'Be adventuresome, be chic' was Ruth Page's advice last week to a group planning a ballet. She is all of that in the ballets she is presenting at the Civic Theatre." She may have been the only one who realized that Ruth had made an important statement, a vital declaration of principle.

Certainly Ruth herself realized nothing of the sort. She summed up the occasion in the diary quite characteristically:

> I am afraid I was a little indiscreet. I was too frank. I inadvertently said that I was tired of Margot and Rudy. What I meant of course was that I was tired of every company having to have one or the other of them (or Villella) to fill a house. Anyway, Eleanor Page printed it in her society column! Christiansen in Daily News had a big article about my speech and everyone agreed the article was just like me! Anyway, at last we got a little publicity but it was due to Mid-America Ballet rather than to our publicity man.

It is doubtful if the "absolutely crazy thing" she did produced any overwhelming increase in Chicago's eagerness to have a ballet of its own. It was not until the following March, indeed, that the Chicago Ballet next made any formal appearances in its hometown, when it gave two performances at the Goodman Theatre with a company of seventeen, of whom only a half dozen had been in the larger cast of the *Carmen-Carmina* series. Ann Barzel, who was always on the side of the angels, could not get too excited about it, through her review was sympathetic and informative. What did not appear from the front of the house, however, was the substantial fact that the chairman of the Committee on Goodman Theatre of the Art Institute, Stanley M. Freehling, known for his philanthropic good deeds, his artistic good taste and his practical patronage of the arts, was very much in Ruth's corner in the fight for a Chicago ballet, well aware of day-by-day developments and willing to meet the inevitable discouragements as they arose.

But if things appeared to be moving slowly in the visible area of performing, there were significant developments in other areas less patently related to the main purpose. For one thing, at the time of the Goodman performances Ruth had already found a new apartment to take the place of 1100 and by May had moved into it. It was just around the corner from 1100, twice as large, in need not only of redecoration and refurnishing but also of extensive alterations to suit her requirements. It entailed, indeed, such a substantial capital investment as to constitute a stubborn declaration of determination to "stay on" and keep at it.

She was also still looking for that adequate studio space without which no company could possibly function. After exploring even the least likely buildings in the most unpromising localities, she found a large, square, substantial building, once the lodge of the Loyal Order of Moose, situated a block away from the Newberry Library in a restricted zone. (Ruth described it as "Tudor outside, but lots of Moose still inside.") It was far too expensive, and not until late December were all the financing and zoning difficulties to be resolved and the contract signed.

Meanwhile there was still unfinished business in Pittsburgh, for at last she was to get *Catulli Carmina* into performance in the fall. Edward Villella was to do Catullus, for which she considered him ideal. However, he was not only busy with the New York City Ballet, but had signed up for a personal tour of Australia. So she had to rehearse with him where and when she could find him, and Kenneth Johnson stood in for him when he was away.

In Paris and St. Tropez she and Delfau worked on the costumes and décor, in addition to all the rest of the annual Tropezian schedule, and she came home in August to the still prevailing chaos of the apartment. The alterations were incomplete, the decorating process was slow and maddening, and the pursuit of the necessary furniture took her to New York and everywhere else, until she wished ("almost!") that she had never got the apartment at all.

She rehearsed with Villella in New York until the moment of his departure for Australia on October 7. He did not return to Pittsburgh until November 6, three days before the scheduled première. She was still delighted with him and regretted only that there was too little time to rehearse him properly with the company. Then almost at once he hurt his back and could not even walk. So he flew to New York to see his doctor and promised to return in time for the dress rehearsal, even if he had to charter a plane. But the doctor absolutely forbade him to dance, and at the last minute Kenneth had to take over for him. As if the situation were not complicated enough, the scenery, which had arrived in New York from Paris on schedule, did not clear the customs for days, and again at the last minute Delfau had to design a slide to provide the décor.

Nevertheless, the songs were sung by Carnegie-Mellon University's Cameron Choir and the orchestra was made up of Pittsburgh Symphony men.

and the review next morning in the *Pittsburgh Press* was headed "Ballet a Winner Here—Even without Villella." If Ruth was not happy, at least the work had finally gone on, and with live music, and if there should ever be another opportunity to produce it, there it was. In spite of her many nagging doubts throughout its long preparatory course about its inherent producibility as a ballet, it had come off well.

The program had also included *Bolero*, about which there had been some apprehensions in advance by the more jittery members of the management, but it apparently shocked no one.

It was high time for her to get back to Chicago, for a major scheme for the funding of the Chicago Ballet had been devised and was to be presented with appropriate panache on November 20. It was certainly not her idea, for she had no mind for ways and means, but it had been under discussion for some time with Stanley Freehling, Edward Gordon, executive director of Ravinia, and Jerold Solovy, her attorney, all of whom were among the directors of her foundation, and it could not fail to appeal, if not to her faint financial instincts, at least to her strong performing ones.

Invitations to a dinner at the Arts Club were sent to some two hundred of the city's leaders in the arts, and when they assembled in due course in considerable splendor, she made "A Proposal to the City of Chicago" in the name of the Ruth Page Foundation. The document, on Foundation stationery, which she read, stipulated, in essence, that in order to establish a resident professional Chicago ballet company, the Foundation would donate $750,000 ($250,000 per year for three years) toward the founding of a new Illinois not-for-profit corporation to be known as Chicago Ballet, with the proviso that a similar amount be contributed by the public. Part of the Foundation's contribution would consist of the maintenance of the Ruth Page Foundation School of Dance at the cost of approximately $30,000 per year, to be operated in conjunction with the new company. A public board of directors would be formed for the company, and Ruth would be employed as an artistic director without salary.

The speech she proceeded to make was typed on Chicago Ballet stationery and signed with her familiar bold and dramatic signature, indicating her awareness that it was also a "document." It had the flair and the personal warmth so characteristic of her, and said a great deal in little.

> I was hoping [she began] that some group or some budding young genius would come along and get a ballet going in Chicago so that I would have no executive or financial problems and could put on some of my ballets when and if I wanted to. But nothing seems to have happened, so I am making this offer to see if we can get some action. I think we all agree that it's important that Chicago have a ballet company of its own on a par with our Symphony, our Opera, our exciting Chicago theatre, and our Art Institute.

The start, she said, obviously had to be a school, but the one she had opened two years ago had already been outgrown. "I have been looking for thirty years for adequate space in Chicago, and I have finally found a proper place." But the contract had not been signed, so "keep your fingers crossed."

Her second major point was that "the policy of a Chicago ballet should be to establish an artistic entity of our own. Most of the new ballet companies in this country all have the same ballets in their repertoires." In establishing a repertory she would like to import new ballets from Europe, and she mentioned Ashton, Béjart, Flindt, Neumeier as immediate possibilities. She would also like to invite American choreographers—Sybil Shearer, Katherine Dunham, Larry Long, Richard Arve, for example—not to mention "a whole storehouseful of my ballets that have never been seen in Chicago with scenery and costumes by André Delfau, Georges Wakhevitch, Antoni Clavé, Leonore Fini, Bernard Daydé, Isamu Noguchi, Rolf Gérard, and so on. . . . I have a new full-evening version of 'Alice in Wonderland' and 'Alice Through the Looking Glass' burning to be produced with projections, costumes and music, all ready, waiting and paid for." The company should involve, as this work would, the many talented children in the area who "get so much joy" out of dancing in the "Nutcracker."

In conclusion:

> I think it's necessary for me to steer this ship for a while. I have great confidence in my associate, Larry Long, and we both will welcome new blood to help us. If we are to accomplish this ambitious program, we need support from the state, from the city, and from all the people of Illinois. And we need your ideas and your sympathy with our growing pains. I wish we could spring "fully armed and brandishing a sharp javelin" like Athene from the brow of Zeus, and just maybe with your help we can.

The press response next day was excellent, especially in its understanding of the Chicago "situation." This is how her diary recorded the event:

> I spent most of Monday getting ready for the money raising party on Thursday. I had to speak, so as I didn't want to make any mistakes, I wrote it out. It seemed to take forever as I wanted it to be very short. Finally it was very short and to the point. The party was at the Arts Club. We had cocktails, then Stanley Freehling spoke first (very well), then Richard Christiansen introduced me and then I came on dressed in my eggplant color jacket with the feathers around the neck and satin pants. I was very succinct and said what was necessary to say. . . . Then a delicious simple dinner that Gerry Freund had arranged. I tried to talk to everyone. We had, as one paper said, "everyone who is anyone." Well, we'll see what happens. Will we get any money?! . . . So now that evening is over, thank heavens, and now we have to get a board together.

Without even stopping for breath, since there were actually no boundaries between the multiple phases of such a single-minded life, she went right on:

> Delfau has just about finished the mural and it is very lovely and gay and
> fun. Delfau has helped so much on the apartment. He really gets things
> done and helps me so much. The apartment will be *so* lovely *if* it ever gets
> finished! I am *exhausted*!

She had found a most congenial and amusing friend in Maryland
McCormick, the widow of Colonel McCormick, who was the owner of the
apartment that shared with hers the thirteenth floor of their building, and
who had told her that she was the thirteenth widow to move into the building.

The two of them decided early on to give a New Year's Eve party
together, to which ultimately they invited two hundred guests. "Pat Collins
of the Racquet Club [which was to do the catering] came over and we
decided on the food."

It was a hectic day for her, what with press pictures of her in her new
home before her Delfau murals, a business conference there with her attorney,
the arrival of a professional guest from Europe, whom, in the confusion, she
did not even recognize at first. . . . "Finally I just dumped everything in the
closet and I was ready at the very last minute. . . . Everyone seemed to be
there [including the governors of three states] except those who go away for
the holidays. . . . It was a brilliant idea for Maryland and me to give the party
together, because I think it was really fun for our guests to see both our
apartments. As she says, hers 'has nothing in it less than 300 years old and
mine is day after tomorrow.' "

But things were not all fun by any means. There were endless meetings
to discuss who would be selected for the board of directors of Chicago Ballet,
and financial arrangements had to be settled about the purchase of the Moose
Lodge; there was the long and familiar routine of preparing, and living through,
the *Nutcracker* season, with another big party for sixty of the dancers after
the closing performance on January 2. The very next day, as soon as she was
free, she was off for a week in Copenhagen to pass judgment on Flindt's
Triumph of Death as a possible importation.

On January 24 "Stanley Freehling invited the committee he had chosen
to run Chicago Ballet to lunch at First National Bank. The party was given on
the 57th floor of the bank and it was a very swank party. I gave a little
speech. I don't know if it was good or not. We had a very distinguished
crowd—a lot of bankers and business men, so *maybe* we can get going! Who
knows."

Two days later the company began giving performances in the surrounding areas, as the result of a small grant from the Illinois Arts Council to
promote ballet performances in the state. The National Endowment for the
Arts had already made a $10,000 administrative grant.

There were more money-raising sessions, more speechmakings, more
subcommittees appointed, some of them apparently less concerned with raising

money than with overhauling, remaking, and back-seat driving. She was learning the hard way the price that had to be paid, in the coin of artistic and administrative freedom, for the "public's" participation in basic financing.

On April 24 they took possession of the Moose Lodge, and she set about getting estimates on the cost (which was considerable) of transforming the largest of the several potential studios into a well-equipped experimental theatre. That was really what she wanted most of all. In due course the Ruth Page Foundation's new home on North Dearborn Street, with its four large studios, was ready to house a summer school, with guest teachers in addition to the regular faculty, and something like 450 students. And Ruth went off to St. Tropez.

During the summer, advertisements in the professional dance publications announced auditions for dancers in both Chicago and New York in October, with offers of "extended AGMA contracts." Ruth was listed as "Founding Director" and Larry Long and Ben Stevenson as "Co-Artistic Directors." The announcement was scarcely in print, however, before Larry resigned on the basis of differences over personnel. The new company of sixteen, indeed, emerged with only three dancers who had been in the old one, and they in secondary capacities, while the leading figures consisted chiefly of former members of the recently disbanded National Ballet of Washington, of which the English-born Stevenson had been codirector with Frederic Franklin.

On November 26, however, one year and six days after the Arts Club "Proposal," Chicago Ballet gave a second money-raising dinner party for two hundred distinguished guests, this time in the foundation's new home, with a performance in the quasi-experimental theatre. The board of directors, with Stanley M. Freehling as chairman and Mrs. Leonard S. O'Connor as president, included forty-one other ladies and gentlemen known for their interest in the arts, who thoroughly justified Ruth's earlier characterization of them, when they first assembled at lunch on the fifty-seventh floor of the First National Bank building, as "very distinguished."

After dinner there was a ballet program consisting of three numbers: *Introducing the Company* (Britten) and *Courante* (Bach), both choreographed by Ben Stevenson, and the *Esmeralda Pas de Deux* (Gluzunov). The *Courante* was "made possible by a generous gift from Mrs. J. Dennis Freund," whom one of the critics was to praise in general for putting her money where her mouth was. He might well have included the less tangible but equally valuable contribution of her imaginative and efficient executive mind.

The leading dancers were Carmen Mathe, Deidre Grogan, Dorio Perez, Michelle Lees and Dennis Poole. The other members of the company were Bircute Barodicaite, Charlotte Gehm, Janis Harris, Jennifer Holmes, Suzanna Longley, Rosemary Miles, Cynthia Ann Roses, Michael Bjerknes, Tom Boyd, James Lewis and William Sterner.

The cost of the dinner and refreshments were "met by the generous contributions of Mr. and Mrs. Roger Bensinger [who were two of Ruth's favorite people] and Mr. and Mrs. Daggett Harvey," and paintings, from "an exhibition entitled 'Dance and Theatre in the Orient' by M. André Delfau" in the other studios, were for sale for the benefit of the organization.

The program also announced a series of some twenty-five performances in the studio during the early months of the new year and two others in an outside theatre at the end of May.

A few days later Eleanor Page, in a long and felicitous interview in the *Tribune* dealing with "a day in the life of Ruth Page," provided in her closing paragraphs further details of the eventful evening. After "some 200 festively clad future ballet supporters" had met for cocktails in one of the newly transformed studios, containing a grand piano, black candelabra and white chrysanthemums, they moved into a larger, mirror-lined studio to dine "at tables decorated with more of the mums-and-candles arrangement."

> Stanley Freehling arises to thank the ladies "who put the evening together" (Mrs. Len O'Connor, Mrs. Daggett Harvey, Mrs. J. Dennis Freund), then to toast "an 'in' lady, and by 'in' I mean incredible, incomparable, indomitable, incorrigible—Ruth Page." Like a flash, Ruth is standing on the seat of her chair, radiant, throwing her arms with those dramatic sleeves over her head.

> "I hope you like our new pad," she says as the applause subsides, then continues, "I want to start a restaurant in the basement. We have a company of 16. I want 30. I want to have experimental ballet here. Then I want to move to the Auditorium. That's all I want."

> Brief and to the point, that's Ruth.

What happens in the future with Chicago Ballet is, of course, for the future to say, but it is certainly a beginning—of both a new ballet for Chicago and a new Ruth. Not that she has changed one iota in character or quality, but that she has won a major battle, and a deeply personal one, in her relationship to the city she never wanted to live in and never wanted to leave. It is an attitude quite comparable to the love-hate she has borne toward opera, which she has found ridiculous, impossible, stupid, glorious, ecstatic and overwhelming.

Her basic conflict with Chicago has been the innate conflict between the centrifugal gesture and the centripetal, between the creator-distributor and the consumer-garnerer. Like everybody else, she will always have to face criticism of her work, some of it undoubtedly sound and some of it the kind of invidious bitchery that in a self-contained community frequently manages to contrive failure for a desirable project by the doctrine of divide and destroy. Chicago is not the only such community that has thus canceled itself out in this field.

Ruth threatened for years to go to France to live; that she did not do so was apparently due to the fact that her dearly beloved Tom was bound to Chicago by both professional establishment and inner necessity. Now that Tom was gone, why did she not leave? The answer is clear: she wanted to stay. The aura of warmly chosen permanence hangs over the new home she has created for herself, with everything about it geared to the future.

As for France, Clavé has long wanted to buy all her property in St. Tropez in order to build a new studio on her land on the shore adjacent to his own property. He even offered to supply her with a studio of her own within such a building for all the six weeks of her annual summer stay. He has also had his eye on the little Paris house in his own old neighborhood of Montparnasse. Now for the first time she has looked on the whole project with at least tempered approval, though at the last minute she could not bring herself to part with the little Herbe Folle, so rich in memories.

It is doubtful that with her creative voracity she will ever find in the semipublicly directed Chicago Ballet sufficient opportunity to produce as much as she must. Even with McCormick Place and the apparently everlasting success of her *Nutcracker* there, plus the hoped-for installation of *Alice in Wonderland* as a comparable Easter feature, she may still be under compulsions to go to the ends of the earth to produce works for other companies. But wherever she may have to travel to work out her new creations, it will always be Chicago that she is really making them for.

Certainly there is nobody else visible with comparable background and sufficient will to make Chicago create for itself, and just as certainly there is no other community that, in the utmost recesses of her heart, she wants to create for. She has met the enemy, and if, unlike Commodore Perry, she is in large measure theirs, yet by a curious but deeply fundamental quirk, they are also hers.

December 23, 1974

Index